Shifting the Color Line

Shifting the Color Line

Race and the American Welfare State

Robert C. Lieberman

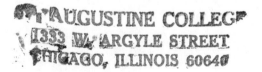
Harvard University Press

Cambridge, Massachusetts, and London, England

Copyright © 1998 by the President and Fellows of Harvard College
All rights reserved
Printed in the United States of America
Second printing, 2001

First Harvard University Press paperback edition, 2001

Library of Congress Cataloging-in-Publication Data

Lieberman, Robert C., 1964–
    Shifting the color line : race and the American welfare state /
Robert C. Lieberman.
        p.   cm.
    Includes bibliographical references and index.
    ISBN 0-674-74562-0 (cloth)
    ISBN 0-674-00711-5 (pbk.)
    1. Afro-Americans—Politics and government.
2. Afro-Americans—Economic conditions.
3. Public welfare—United States.
4. United States—Social policy—1993–
5. United States—Race relations.   I. Title.
E185.615.L4778 1998
305.896′073—dc21   97-42373

For Lauren

Contents

Preface

In the fall of 1974, I entered the fifth grade in the public schools of the Boston suburb where I grew up. At the same time, the Boston Public Schools embarked on a court-ordered school desegregation plan that involved sending both black and white children on buses to schools in neighborhoods dominated by the other race. Busing in Boston provoked intense political conflict and sometimes violent resistance, and it was impossible, even for a ten-year-old whose main preoccupations were music lessons and the ever-tragic fortunes of his beloved Red Sox, to avoid confronting the meaning of this crisis. I am told, although I do not remember the incident, that one day that fall I burst into tears at school because I was having trouble writing an assigned essay on the question, "What Does Busing in Boston Mean for Me?" I surely knew, although at ten I would not have expressed it in this way, that segregation was wrong and that it symbolized an American legacy of slavery and racism that was at odds with the liberal and egalitarian principles on which our politics and society profess themselves to be based. But even though all of New England, if not the whole country, was watching with rapt attention as events in Boston unfolded, I evidently found it hard to fathom how they would affect my life. It was all too easy for my family and our friends and neighbors, living in an almost exclusively white suburb, to express our approval or disapproval of this or that action, secure in the belief (due to the Supreme Court's rejection earlier that year of metropolitan desegregation) that our quiet neighborhoods, good schools, and sheltered lives were quite safe from the consequences of the struggle that went on not ten miles away. What could busing in Boston possibly have meant to me? Little surprise that this question presented me with a profound puzzle and something of an existential crisis.

This book is an attempt to answer that question, even though it is about neither the Boston busing crisis nor school desegregation. Nor is the question as narrow as it seems, for it really asks us to contemplate what it means for all Americans to live in a society that is divided along overlapping lines of race, class, and residence. It is tempting to observe that the civil rights revolution of this century has been a resounding success and to conclude that the significance of the color line in American political life has declined. African-Americans, who were once denied the most basic rights of citizenship, are now in most respects welcomed as full members of society. They have achieved not only the right to vote, finally, but also access to the ladder of success and achievement in American society—schools, jobs, professions, political offices, and (to some extent) neighborhoods that were once absolutely closed to them. Public expressions of out-and-out racism that were once commonplace are now, for the most part, frowned upon. The great moral dilemma of American politics—how to account for the presence of a racial caste in a society that espouses a creed of liberty and equality—has been largely resolved. If life circumstances and opportunities remain unequal, as they surely do, the problem is of an altogether different character and the barriers to the fulfillment of the American dream are no longer primarily racial. In this view, my answer to the question "What Does Busing in Boston Mean for Me?" would have to be "Not much." The racial problems of the neighborhoods and schools of an aging, industrial city are, perhaps, the residue of an older order of racial imbalance, but they do not reflect the current state of American politics. The events of the last generation have seemingly erased the color line that W. E. B. Du Bois prophesied would be "the problem of the twentieth century."

But there is an alternative view of our history, a bleaker one, to be sure, but one that is in many ways truer to the real contours of race, class, and politics in American life. Although racism is in retreat, white fear and rage live, from the snub in the street to the sinister rumblings of white supremacist militias. Although African-Americans can vote, the worth of their votes and their access to real political power remain in serious question. Although African-Americans now compete for access to schools and jobs, the terms of that competition are the subject of intense controversy. And although formal, legal racial barriers to opportunity are gone, that opportunity still passes by a substantial segment of the African-American population, the increasingly isolated ghetto poor, or "underclass." In an earlier era, the color line marked a clear boundary between black and white in multiple domains—political, economic, social, and geographic. Although these explicit barriers are gone, systematic racial inequalities remain embedded within a society that is, outwardly at least, increasingly integrated. In this alternative view, the color line has not so much faded as shifted, moving away from the surface of American politics—our everyday beliefs and practices—and burrowing deep into the core of American political institutions.

Approached from this point of view, the question "What Does Busing in Boston Mean for Me?" suggests a different answer: "Quite a lot." Many of the central issues in American politics still revolve around racial difference. Fundamental questions of voting rights and representation remain to be settled, exemplified in controversies over the drawing of congressional districts. Affirmative action, a set of policies designed to create equal opportunity, is under attack for allegedly stifling opportunity. And the welfare state, the very programs enacted to attack poverty and spread economic opportunity, is being scaled back, the victim of a politics that pits middle-class white suburbs against poor black cities (an exaggeration, perhaps, but only a slight one). Suddenly, the question about busing in Boston—and, more generally, the question about the consequences of racial politics for the larger society—takes on great urgency. These issues, among others, organize the partisan and ideological debates of our time, suggesting that race continues to be of momentous consequence in American politics.

Through the lens of the last of these issues—the welfare state—this book chronicles the shifting of the color line and attempts to answer the question that has nagged at me for more than twenty years: How does race change politics? The question is, of necessity, a historical one, because it involves a process that unfolds over time, often in surprising ways. Political institutions and public policies take distinctive shapes at particular moments that reflect racial imbalances (among others, of course) in political power. As I did research, however, I discovered that this question makes little sense without its converse: How does politics change race? Racial categories are themselves the product of politics, for it is political institutions and public policies that define racial boundaries by allocating power, resources, and status.

These two questions come together in the story of the American welfare state and the construction of the urban "underclass." Racial politics shaped the welfare state in important ways. The welfare state, in turn, helped to redraw lines of division within and between races by sorting both black and white Americans into categories defined by their relationship to programs of social provision. Thus to tell the story of race and the American welfare state is to reconsider the political origins of the predominantly African-American ghetto poor, the "underclass," a subject of intense dispute. This book, then, also tries to sort out some of the competing arguments about the existence and growth of an "underclass," especially claims that implicate welfare in expanding urban poverty. Finally, in the aftermath of legislation ending the federal government's guarantee of assistance to poor children, signed by President Clinton in 1996, it is essential that we seek to understand precisely what government can and cannot do to address the interlocking political crises of race and welfare in the United States now that one of the pillars of the New Deal welfare state has crumbled. Such understanding is essential if we are to reconstruct, on the ruins of the past, an edifice of social provision and inclusive citizenship worthy of such a prosperous nation. This book is my own small gesture toward this task and my own answer not only to the question that pierced my youth but to its even more compelling corollary: What can we do about the racial inequality that remains in our midst?

Acknowledgments

In writing this book, as in so much else, I have been blessed with extraordinary teachers, colleagues, friends, and family.

Although convention dictates that she come last, Lauren Osborne's contribution defies convention. She doubtless read more drafts of more chapters than she cares to remember, and, although she edits for a living, she unfailingly spent evenings and weekends with "just one more version." She wielded a ruthless and keen editorial pencil with grace and good humor, and she insisted on the highest standards of clarity and logic in the text. More than all of this, however, she offered perspective, comfort, companionship, and love. Our son, Benjamin, arrived as I was finishing the book, just in time to save me from tinkering too much.

Paul Peterson, Theda Skocpol, and Sidney Verba, my teachers at Harvard, guided me through the solitary journey of writing a doctoral dissertation with equal measures of artful cajoling and candid admonition. The late Judith Shklar, an inspiring and humane scholar and teacher, led me to the topic of this book. Her passionate conviction about the centrality of race to American politics is evident on every page.

Many friends and colleagues gave generous help and constructive advice. Jennifer Hochschild, Ira Katznelson, James Morone, Martin Shefter, and Richard Valelly all read the entire work in manuscript, and their comments forced me to sharpen, streamline, and clarify. Tony Marx, Bob Shapiro, John Skrentny, Rogers Smith, Tom Sugrue, and Margaret Weir each read excerpts and gave indispensable counsel. Michael Aronson of Harvard University Press was a deft and patient guide through the publication process.

In addition to the Department of Government at Harvard, several institutions—the Center of Domestic and Comparative Policy Studies at Princeton and the Department of Political Science and the School of International and Public Affairs at Columbia—offered supportive and stimulating environments for research and writing. I am especially grateful to John Ruggie and Lisa Anderson for relieving me of some of the burdens of faculty life so that I could finish the dissertation and the book in what passes for a reasonable amount of time. Financial support came from a National Science Foundation Graduate Fellowship, Mellon/Harvard Dissertation Fellowships, and a summer grant from the Columbia University Council for Research in the Social Sciences. An earlier version of Chapter 2 appeared as "Race and the Organization of Welfare Policy" in *Classifying by Race,* ed. Paul E. Peterson (Princeton University Press, 1995), and it is reprinted with the kind permission of Princeton University Press.

These debts and many unmentioned others I gladly acknowledge. I fear I can offer little in return for so much effort and concern but my true and honest thanks, a healthy share of the credit for this book's merits, and absolution from blame for its imperfections.

1

Race, Institutions, and Welfare in American Political Development

"I have no fear," Martin Luther King Jr. wrote in his famous letter from the Birmingham city jail in 1963, "about the outcome of our struggle in Birmingham, even if our motives are at present misunderstood. We will reach the goal of freedom in Birmingham and all over the nation, because the goal of America is freedom. Abused and scorned though we may be, our destiny is tied up with America's destiny."[1] In many ways—in the most obvious of ways—King's struggle, the African-American struggle for freedom and equality, was a resounding success, one of the noblest achievements in American history. Polls, schools, and workplaces, once bastions of white privilege and instruments of white supremacy, were forced open. Lunch counters, shops, drinking fountains, and bus seats, once the badges of inferiority (as the elder Justice Harlan put it), became sites of fierce battle and symbols of glorious victory. In the Smithsonian Institution in Washington stands a lunch counter from Greensboro, North Carolina, preserved as a memory piece, the nation's homage to the bravery and courage that were once in its midst. The white-sheeted Klan, the torch-bearing lynch mob, the Dixiecrat spellbinder, the angry governor in the schoolhouse door, the county registrar—these are the iconographic villains of yesterday, and they are all but gone, ground into the rich black topsoil of the cotton belt by moral force and political necessity.

As the civil rights movement unfolded in the middle of the twentieth century, the United States saw a revolution in racial attitudes. Between the 1940s and the 1960s, white Americans' core beliefs about African-Americans turned completely around. In 1942, for example, only thirty percent of the public expressed the belief that black and white children should attend the same schools; this percentage had doubled by 1963 and tripled by 1984. American beliefs about employment and housing opportunities for African-Americans and discrimination in public accommodations un-

1

derwent a similarly dramatic change.[2] By and large, American society now frowns upon outright expressions of old-fashioned racism.

But at the same time, from the remove of a generation, these victories ring hollow for many African-Americans as the liberal integrationist dream goes awry and with it King's optimistic vision of inexorable progress toward freedom and equality. The gap between black and white Americans, it seems, grows ever wider and deeper, and matters that divide Americans by race grow ever more prominent in American politics, culture, and society. Willie Horton and Sister Souljah have become household names, and campaigns for political office frequently feed on racial resentment and mistrust. The representation of African-Americans in electoral politics— the tension between black faces and black interests, as one analyst has aptly described it—is one of the most contentious issues of our time.[3] In judicial politics, too, with the nomination of Clarence Thomas to the Supreme Court, racial dividing lines took center stage, although Thomas's Eighteenth Brumaire united tragedy and farce in a single engrossing episode— from President Bush's cynical claim that Thomas was the "best qualified" person in the land for Thurgood Marshall's seat on the Court to Thomas's own whimper that he was the victim of a "high-tech lynching."[4] Even the cultural scene is awash with racial cleavages. In the latest in a numbing sequence of "trials of the century," a famous African-American athlete stood accused of murdering his white ex-wife and her friend. Before a juror was seated, a word of testimony heard, or a piece of evidence introduced, white Americans believed the man guilty, and African-Americans believed him innocent, possibly even the victim of a conspiracy by the very police force whose savage beating of a black man, caught on videotape, launched the worst urban unrest in decades. O.J. Simpson's acquittal set off waves of racial triumph and anguish that revealed more starkly than any episode in recent memory the deep political and emotional rifts between black and white Americans. We are divided more than ever over the meaning of equality of opportunity, and the precarious architecture of equality is teetering. Why is this happening? Why do we seem to be unravelling the tightly wound thread of the civil rights revolution and reopening points that so many of us thought and hoped were settled? Above all, if Martin Luther King won the civil rights revolution, why does race remain the most divisive and explosive fault line on the terrain of American politics and society?

Since the civil rights revolution reached its peak in the mid-1960s, the institutional grounds of racial politics have shifted dramatically. The 1960s saw, for the first time in American history, a governing coalition committed simultaneously to civil rights and broad social provision, although Southern Democrats continued to dissent from their party in both areas.[5] This coalition was backed by a Supreme Court that took an expansive view of the national government's constitutional commitments in these areas. The result of this configuration was an era of expanding political, social, and economic rights and opportunities for African-Americans. But in the 1970s, the tide of racial politics began to turn, a trend that has accelerated in recent years. Affirmative action has come under broad assault in Congress and the states. Structures of minority representation, too, are in retreat as the Supreme Court has repeatedly struck down legislative districts designed to elect African-Americans to public office. One can legitimately debate whether or not these and other developments constitute progress for African-Americans in American society and politics, but it is hard to deny that the institutional politics of race in the United States has entered a new era.

Nowhere is race more divisive and explosive than in the politics of welfare. Popular rhetoric and symbolism surrounding welfare are overwhelmingly negative, and they rely heavily on racial imagery that is sometimes quite explicit. At the same time, however, this rhetoric severely distorts the reality of Americans' relationship with their welfare state. Despite constant expressions of dissatisfaction with welfare policy, the public and policymakers support the basic principle of the welfare state—government assistance to those unable to help themselves.[6] More to the point, Americans continue to support the broad range of policies that constitute the welfare state—policies that include not just the ones we commonly call "welfare," such as Food Stamps, Medicaid, and, until recently, Aid to Families with Dependent Children (AFDC), but also other assistance programs such as Social Security, Medicare, and Unemployment Insurance. Even in the Republican era of the 1980s and 1990s, these policies have been more resilient than most observers would have predicted on the eve of Ronald Reagan's assumption of the presidency.[7]

But the fact remains that not all the components of the American welfare state enjoy the same depth or breadth of popular support. African-Americans, moreover, rarely have been widely included as honorable recipients of broad policies of social provision, and they are disproportionately segregated into the weakest, stingiest, and most politically vulnerable parts of the welfare state. Therein lies the source of much of the popular mistrust of welfare.[8]

Americans' understanding of, and sympathy for, the American welfare state has been severely compromised by the relentless and narrow focus on a small slice of the welfare state—AFDC—and a small slice of the poor—the urban "underclass."[9] So defined, welfare is frequently the object of racially focused antagonism and resentment, directed particularly at the apparent conditions of life in our decaying inner cities—idleness, immorality, family decay, and crime. Welfare, it seems to many, generates a whole set of undesirable and threatening consequences.[10] The popular image of welfare is of a program that pays young, unmarried black women in decrepit, violent, drug-infested neighborhoods to have many children by different men, none of whom they marry.

Despite being mostly false, this picture of an apparent urban "underclass" has a tremendous hold on the popular imagination and political sentiments of white Americans. African-Americans are increasingly isolated, geographically and economically, in inner cities that offer poor services, no jobs, and frightful settings in which to rear children.[11] The isolation of inner cities feeds the barricade mentality of white suburbanites, who resent their supposed subsidy of lives they deem pathological. To the working-class whites of suburban Macomb County, Michigan, "Detroit was just a big pit into which the state and federal government poured tax money, never to be heard from again: 'It's all just being funneled into the Detroit area, and it's not overflowing into the suburbs.'"[12] American cities themselves are increasingly isolated in the American and international political economies, and the African-Americans who live in them are being pushed even farther toward the margins of American life than their sharecropper grandparents and their slave great-great-grandparents ever were.[13]

Arguments over public policy and the roots of ghetto poverty have become bound up in the same questions of race and class that plague the larger society. One school of thought, represented most prominently by Charles Murray in *Losing Ground,* locates the source of the "underclass" in the cultural and behavioral characteristics of the predominantly black ghetto poor. Prodded by an overly generous and undemanding welfare state, Murray and others argue, the urban poor have chosen their own fate by preferring welfare to work and single parenthood to marriage. Welfare has, therefore, actually increased poverty and created a dependent and pathological "underclass." Another school of thought, led by William Julius Wilson, traces the conditions of urban life to broad structural changes in society and the economy that have systematically reduced the opportunities for inner-city blacks to work, marry, and rear children in a stable setting. To the arguments of the behavioral school, Wilson responds that the ghetto poor want desperately to work, marry, and have a chance at the American dream, but the circumstances of urban life have largely foreclosed those opportunities.[14] "Welfare as we knew it," to paraphrase Bill Clinton, was one of the few lifelines left for the ghetto poor, but by the 1990s it had become a political flashpoint, dividing cities from suburbs, poor Americans from the middle and working classes, and black from white. Roundly derided by both left and right, AFDC met its demise in 1996. But what should replace it? Should we let the welfare state wither away, as the behavioralists suggest, and let the urban poor work their way out of poverty and despair in the competitive economy? Or should we seek to rebuild a welfare state on grounds that can, perhaps, overcome the divisions of space, class, and race that fracture American politics? To answer these questions and to gain a better picture of how government can shape racial politics, we must understand clearly and precisely how the American welfare state has historically treated African-Americans and what role it played in the construction of the urban "underclass."

Whereas these segments of the American welfare state have become inextricably bound up with perceptions and constructions of racial difference, other social policies—especially the relatively generous and broadly inclusive network of social insurance—have included African-Americans fully and fairly, treating them equally as deserving beneficiaries. Americans tend to view these policies in entirely nonracial terms. The same questions, about simultaneous but apparently contradictory trends in American race politics, arise anew. Why, in an era of softening racial beliefs, did the politics of the American welfare state take such a racially divisive turn? And how did Social Security, the country's largest and most expensive social program, escape the racialized fate of other segments of the welfare state? The story grows ever more puzzling when we consider that many of the policies that comprise the American welfare state were born at the same moment, as part of the Social Security Act of 1935, the most important single act in the creation of the American welfare state.

The entwined histories of race and welfare and the peculiar uneven pattern of their development present a profound puzzle. The policies that the Social Security Act created sorted Americans by class, classifying their target populations by occupation and work status. In so doing, they also sorted Americans by race; in keeping with the prevailing racial norms of the 1930s and the institutional structure of American politics, welfare discriminated by design. Yet within a generation, some of these policies included some African-Americans fully and fairly, whereas others continued to make racial distinctions that kept most African-Americans in a subordinate economic position. Thus the character of social policy, which forged very different links with different segments of a population divided by race and class (as well as gender), played a role in recasting, over the course of a generation, the political meaning of race in American life and reshaping the political identities of African-Americans themselves. When, in the 1960s, issues of welfare, employment, and urban poverty began to emerge front and center in American politics, they collided with this reconstructed politics of race, precipitating a "welfare crisis" that has gripped American politics since the 1960s and shows no signs of abating.

This book confronts that puzzle with the argument that race inhibited the development of a strong, unitary, centralized welfare state in the United States, and that the fragmented American welfare state helped to reshape the politics of race and the place of racial minorities in American life. First, race influenced decisions about the institutional structure of New Deal social policy. By "race," I mean not simply biological or ascriptive differences among people—such differences, of course, have no intrinsic political meaning—but the ways in which these differences have been understood by Americans and inscribed in structures of political power. The racial structure of American society affected the politics of the mid-1930s in particular ways, shaping actions at the founding moment of the modern American welfare state. Specifically, the racial composition of the target populations of different policies affected the political possibilities for policymaking. But 1935 was no ordinary year; it was a critical moment when enduring welfare policy institutions were created, and the design of different policy institutions reflected racial distinctions among the populations the policies served.

Second, institutional structure influenced the way policies treated citizens of different races, creating new patterns of racial distinction in politics and society. Policies with different institutions operated differently and sorted Americans of various races into welfare categories differently. These institutional distinctions affected the results of welfare policy in two ways. Administratively, the treatment of African-Americans—the extent of their actual benefit from welfare programs—depended on institutional structure. Politically, the institutional structure also shaped future possibilities for African-Americans in the welfare state, either for continued exclusion, full and honorable inclusion, or inclusion accompanied by political and social degradation. These political changes wrought by the institutional structure of the welfare state played a central role in transforming the racial structure of American politics and society.

These two propositions come together in a comparative examination of three New Deal social policies, all created by the Social Security Act—Old-Age Insurance (OAI), Aid to Dependent Children (ADC), and Unemployment Insurance (UI).[15] Two of these policies remain in place today. The third, ADC (later AFDC), was a central pillar of the American welfare state before its repeal in 1996. The history of these policies presents two important puzzles that previous analyses of race and the American welfare state have not addressed. First, why did these policies, directed at different social and economic groups, all have similar racially relevant, or race-laden, exclusions? By "race-laden," I refer to the tendency of some policies to divide the population along racial lines without saying so in so many words. To illustrate, the Social Security Act did not state explicitly that the social programs it created should treat white and black Americans differently. But race-laden policies are not simply programs whose tendency to exclude by race is merely incidental or accidental. Race-laden policies, rather, reflect racially structured power arrangements—class conflicts, party coalitions, political institutions, and the like whose characters are shaped by racial distinction—that produce public policy. Moreover, they can be expected to affect blacks and whites differently in the normal course of their everyday operations, whether or not their framers or administrators intended that result. Racial bias in public policy, then, in a race-laden policy need not be the result of racism per se. It may instead result from institutions that mobilize and perpetuate racial bias in a society and its politics, even institutions that appear to be racially neutral.

The Social Security Act of 1935 was a mixture of policies, created in the same formative political impulse, that shared a common underlying goal—providing some measure of economic security for those who found themselves in need through circumstances beyond their control. However, they were aimed at target populations that differed sharply along many dimensions—employed persons (mostly men) on one hand and those deemed properly outside the labor force (mostly women and children) on the other. And yet each of the programs at its origin compromised the inclusion of African-Americans not only through race-laden eligibility requirements but also through administrative arrangements that restricted black access to benefits. Where African-Americans were potentially included among a policy's beneficiaries, Southerners demanded institutional structures that preserved a maximum of local control. Conversely, strong, national social policy institutions were politically possible only when African-Americans were excluded from the center.

The second puzzle is that despite similar racially relevant exclusions, the three policies have followed very different evolutionary paths, particularly in regard to their treatment of racial minorities. Each policy, like all public policies, included or excluded various groups at different points in its history, whether by statute—explicit definition in the law of who was eligible for benefits—or by administrative procedure, which can fill in gaps and ambiguities in the law. Old-Age Insurance progressed from statutory exclusion of African-Americans to administrative inclusion and finally to statutory inclusion. Aid to Dependent Children regressed, one might say, from statutory inclusion to administrative exclusion of African-Americans. Despite early patterns of administrative discrimination, however, later patterns of racial inclusion in ADC were accompanied by highly politicized racial polarization over welfare policy. The racial trajectories of the policies have been quite different; in particular, ADC has gone from discrimination to accusations of racial favoritism, whereas OAI has incorporated beneficiaries of all racial groups while staying mostly above the racial fray that surrounds the American welfare state. Unemployment Insurance began with the same statutory exclusion as OAI, but it did not grow toward greater racial inclusion as OAI did. Viewed retrospectively, these evolutionary paths acquire an air of inevitability. OAI is a popular middle-class entitlement whose African-American beneficiaries are honorably included as a matter of course. ADC, on the other hand, is an unpopular program whose disproportionately black beneficiaries are commonly vilified. But it is tautological to read inevitability into the results of parallel historical developments.[16] In 1935, these policies all contained racially relevant exclusions, yet they have evolved along very different paths.

The answer to these puzzles lies in the institutional structure of the three policies, which were both consequence and cause of patterns of racial politics. On one hand, Old-Age Insurance (which we now generically call "Social Security") explicitly excluded most African-Americans at its creation but was given a strong, unitary, *national* institutional structure. In the generation after 1935, it not only incorporated African-Americans fairly but also grew to encompass those African-American workers who were initially left out. Ironically, Old-Age Insurance has developed into not only the paradigm of a smoothly running national government bureaucracy but also the closest thing to a universal, color-blind social policy the United States has ever had. On the other hand, Aid to Dependent Children (the program most commonly called "welfare") had the potential to include many African-Americans among its beneficiaries. However, it was designed with a weak, decentralized, and *parochial* institutional structure. Its implementation discriminated against African-Americans, first denying them benefits and then making them the central focus of bitter political disputes over benefits, leading to crackdowns, retrenchment, and ever more race-laden welfare politics. Unemployment Insurance in many respects falls between the extremes mapped out by the other two programs—neither as dramatically exclusionary and national as OAI nor as potentially inclusionary and as parochial as ADC. But the institutional structure of Unemployment Insurance policy played an important role in keeping African-Americans at the margins of the political economy and inhibiting the development of a more comprehensive and racially inclusive employment policy.

Race, History, and Institutions

An argument linking race, institutions, and American political development also addresses a central social scientific question about the role of race in American society and politics. In the 1940s, Gunnar Myrdal identified a dilemma at the heart of American society and politics, between an American Creed of liberty and equality and the reality of racial domination.[17] Myrdal's powerful evocation of profound illiberalism in the midst of a putatively liberal society suggested that the key to resolving the dilemma was a transformation of racial attitudes and practices to bring American society into conformity with its own motivating ideals. "If America should follow its own deepest convictions," he wrote, "its well-being at home would be increased directly . . . *America is free to choose whether the Negro shall remain her liability or her opportunity.*"[18] Myrdal's optimistic perspective, looking forward to the postwar era, suggested that Americans both wanted to end the racial domination in their midst and had it in their power to do so through conventional politics and public policymaking. If Myrdal's faith in the power of the Creed to drown out racism and in liberal democratic politics to achieve this end were fully accurate, then the revolution in racial attitudes and the dissolution of the "outer" color line, the barrier to African-American participation in public life, should have had generally uniform effects on the incorporation of black Americans into the rights of social citizenship as embodied in the emerging welfare state.[19]

Myrdal's optimism was not entirely misplaced. Twenty years after he published *An American Dilemma,* Congress passed, and a Southern Democratic president signed, a Civil Rights Act and a Voting Rights Act that, together, assured full political citizenship for African-Americans. But the elements of New Deal social policy developed simultaneously but very differently, against the same background conditions of racial difference in American society. They posed a twofold challenge to a perspective that points to racism, understood as an ideology of racial exploitation, as the prime mover in shaping racial domination. First, the component pieces of the American welfare state have taken divergent racial paths from a common point of origin. Racism, if it was at work in shaping social policy and its effects, clearly operated differently on different policies. Second, by most measures, overt expressions of racism have declined since the 1930s, whereas racial conflict over the welfare state has intensified. The path toward the resolution of Myrdal's dilemma has been irregular at best. Our nobler ideals have prevailed in some cases, our baser instincts in others.

Jennifer Hochschild has outlined an alternative to the "anomaly" thesis that Myrdal advanced—a "symbiosis" thesis that holds that racism and American liberal democracy are mutually constitutive, that the American political order is built on a foundation of racial domination.[20] Hochschild's argument suggests that Americans face a different dilemma than Myrdal's, between the normal routines of democratic politics and policymaking and the liberal goal of ending racial domination. This perspective questions both whether Americans truly want to overcome the effects of racism and whether they have the capacity to do so without resorting to a more authoritative politics. Hochschild pinpoints the difficulty inherent in expecting a politically dominant racial majority to abandon the advantages that their dominance confers, and she demonstrates how even public policies that are aimed directly and explicitly at the system of racial domination can go awry. But once again, the heterogeneity of the racial configurations of New Deal social policy confound analysis. Some welfare policies mitigated racial division, whereas others exacerbated it.

To understand more precisely why the American welfare state has taken such divergent racial paths from a common point of origin, it is essential to consider how particular policies differ in the way they encode politically constructed racial distinctions.[21] The act of classifying persons or defining citizens by race is fundamentally a political one.[22] Distinctions among persons based on ancestry or skin color have no intrinsic political meaning but take on political significance when a nation's political order recognizes them to be meaningful. Such a moment can occur when a government imposes official policies of racial domination or, less formally, when elements of civil society revolve around racial distinctions in ways that impinge on politics. The characteristic texture of a nation's race relations, as Anthony Marx argues, depends critically on the ways in which national states "make race."[23] Thus the problem of race in American society—the very fact that we divide ourselves into racial groups and that assignment to one or another race plays such a large role in shaping the lives of citizens—is a consequence of political institutions. "As bundles of intersubjective, connected, and persistent norms," writes Ira Katznelson, "and as formal rules and organizations, institutions shape human interaction, limit and define the scope of choice, and confer social and political identities out of the welter of possibilities through language, incentives, and sanctions."[24] Institutions arrange the distribution and exercise of power in society. They create the conditions in which people can act on their beliefs and interests, but they also help to define those beliefs and interests. Even democratic institutions distribute power unevenly and confer greater capacity to some than to others to pursue their ends. Democratic government, as Grant McConnell has noted, can also mask the exercise of power by removing it from public institutions and placing it in private hands. Power masquerading as private interest can create and maintain social arrangements and political results that have a false air of authenticity and legitimacy. They seem "natural" because they appear to result not from government power but from a private sphere that is, in liberal theory, prior to government. But such arrangements are no more natural than the most artificial government program; they are created by people acting in institutional settings that allow them to define for themselves and others what society and politics will look like.[25] Decentralized and fragmented political institutions, for example, combined with illusory myths of organic localism or agrarian virtue, have profoundly influenced American political development in many ways, none more powerful than the endless definition and redefinition of what it means to be white or black in the United States.

When political institutions are embedded in a society that confers unequal status to different racial groups, the result may be a political order in which configurations of power reflect and reinforce racial differences even without explicitly codifying them.[26] Attention to the role of institutions in the construction of racial inequality suggests that the status of racial groups in society results not necessarily from the mobilization of racist ideology but from the normal workings of social and political arrangements.

In the late 1960s and 1970s, disillusioned social scientists and activists called this phenomenon "institutional racism," a phrase that persists in activist circles although it has fallen out of use in scholarship.[27] Although the claim of "institutional racism" often has a whiff of the polemic about it—and this is true in its contemporary usage more than ever[28]—it identifies a critical truth: that racial inequality can be "built into" the very structure of American politics, and that citizens need not have racist intentions for a society systematically to subjugate racial minorities.

But once again, the differences among the racial trajectories of New Deal social policies suggest that institutions differ in their susceptibility to institutional racism. Whereas some institutions may produce or perpetuate racially unequal social relations, others may remain racially neutral, or even compensate for racial inequality. Aid to Dependent Children and, to a lesser extent, Unemployment Insurance both reinforced certain kinds of racial disadvantage without making explicit racial distinctions. Old-Age Insurance, however, actually helped integrate African-American workers into the broad American middle class. Moreover, not all manifestations of institutional racism are alike. Whereas Aid to Dependent Children produced racially imbalanced administration, Unemployment Insurance did not; instead, Unemployment Insurance reinforced racial disadvantages in the labor market. What links these cases together is that they all demonstrate the work that institutions do in constructing and reconstructing the racial structure of American society and politics. What is at stake in a discussion of institutional racism is not simply whether it exists but the precise mechanisms by which particular institutions embody and make real socially and politically constructed racial differences.[29]

This study builds on the recent turn toward institutions in the study of the American welfare state to explore precisely these institutional mechanisms in the creation, implementation, and development of American social policy in the middle of the twentieth century.[30] The fragmentary nature of American political institutions produced a distinctive configuration of policies of social provision that differed not only in their content but also in their organizational form. The organization of policy, as much as its content, holds the key to an understanding of the divergent racial impact of different parts of the American welfare state. Translating policies into real effects on the lives of citizens involves the exercise of state power that is embodied in particular institutions—departments, agencies, boards, and so forth—that operate in particular ways. American social policymaking has produced not only a dizzying variety of policies but also a cacophony of institutions to administer them. The range of institutional forms has arisen from the characteristic circumstances of American political development—decentralized, patronage-based mass political parties linked to a state of weak bureaucratic capacity; a powerful Congress that privileges local and sectional representation; and federalism.[31] But these structural characteristics of American politics are deeply rooted in the racial divisions of American society, particularly of the South, whose political leaders could mobilize and manipulate them to protect the racial order.[32] As a result, the institutions of American social policy have reflected and transmitted the particular historical configurations of race relations embedded in the structures of political power that made social policy.

At the same time, as E. E. Schattschneider observed, "new policies create a new politics."[33] The institutions of social policy shape not only the concrete consequences of policy for citizens—who gets what, when, where, and how?—but also the politics of subsequent policymaking. Operating through institutions, social policies construct groups of citizens with new interests in welfare state activities, whether beneficiaries, taxpayers, or bureaucrats. These groups may develop stakes in particular policies or, under changing conditions, in particular kinds of reform. For these citizens and groups of citizens, policies can also alter their understanding of their relations not only with the government but also with their fellow citizens.[34] Through such processes of "policy feedback," social policies that reflect and encode racial division can reshape the links between African-Americans and the state by including or excluding them on particular terms. Social policies can also play a role in constructing divisions among races—defining a black middle class, for example, through honorable inclusion in social insurance programs. Finally, social policies can play a role in reconstructing the texture of relations among races through the patterns and terms of inclusion afforded to different racial groups. But this process of the political construction of race through social policy depends on the way welfare institutions treat African-Americans.

The Institutional Structure of Social Policy

All social policies involve the distribution (or redistribution) of goods by the state, and hence they impart power—the coercive authority to make binding decisions about who will receive and who will not. It is the institutional structure of social policy that allocates the power to make these distributive and redistributive decisions. Some social policy institutions allocate power relatively transparently and uniformly. In such policies, which I call national policies, decisions about allocations are clear, regular, and uniform throughout the country. The bureaucratic organizations that operate national policies are centralized (organizationally if not necessarily physically), streamlined, efficient, and effective. They respond to clear lines of authority exercised by regularly constituted public officials and are politically insulated from narrow, partial interests, whether exerted through the intercession of public officials or directly through lobbying. At the other end of the spectrum are parochial policies, policies that are fragmented both politically and administratively, so that the power to make allocative decisions is dispersed among many forces. Not only do administrators and officials of lower-level governments exercise substantial power over parochial policies, but such policies are also subject to political influence from partial, private interests that respond to narrow, local concerns.[35] Finally, policies can impose and reinforce disjunctions between groups and the political economy, disjunctions that can be ameliorated or made more severe by the nationalism or parochialism of institutional design.

These descriptions are ideal types that anchor a spectrum of possible structures along which actual policies might be located. No policy, of course, is either purely national or purely parochial, but these paradigms describe coherent and opposing models of institutional structure that can produce dramatically different real results. Some policies may have structures that are neither national nor parochial, assembling the elements of institutional structure in any variety of combinations. Table 1.1 summarizes the elements of institutional structure of the three policies that this study considers.

Institutional Structure: Law and Policy Design

The law that establishes and defines a policy gives the basic answer to two fundamental questions: Who pays, and who gets? Accordingly, the two elements of policy design that are components of the institutional structure of welfare policy are the structure of benefits and financing. All government policies make distinctions among citizens, conferring benefits or imposing costs on some and not on others according to certain criteria. But policies can differ according to the standards by which they identify and treat different categories of citizens. It is the law that spells out these

Table 1.1 Institutional Structure of Social Policy

	OAI (National)	ADC (Parochial)	UI (Hybrid)
Policy Design			
Benefits	Egalitarian	Discretionary	Partially discretionary
Financing	Contributory	Noncontributory	Mostly noncontributory; employer contributions into state fund; federal offset
Administrative Structure			
Level of government	National	State	State (benefits) National (financing)
Political influence	Insulated	Open	Open
Policy environment	Stable; unitary; autonomous; no appropriations	Unstable; decentralized; weak; annual appropriations	Less stable; unitary focus; cyclical; no appropriations
Public contact	Taxes: colonization of public and private capacity, automatic Benefits: direct, automatic	Client must apply; evaluative; punitive	Client must apply, but more automatic; narrowly evaluative

criteria, although it is precisely because laws are often vague and occasionally contradictory that the structure of policy institutions is so critically important in shaping the real impact of policies.[36]

A policy's benefit structure consists of the processes by which it is determined who does and does not actually receive benefits—who gets? Some policies establish carefully defined criteria and lay down clear and simple rules for administration. Such policies are procedurally *egalitarian* in that they treat individuals with the same relevant attributes equally.[37] Policies of this character are relatively self-regulating in that it is easy to tell whether an individual is receiving her due and whether in the aggregate the policy is being administered fairly and equitably. At the other extreme, policies can be *discretionary.* If clear benefit criteria are not written into the statute or if power is not clearly vested in a central authority, policies will grant wide discretion to subordinate administrators or governments. Discretionary policies need not be slanted on their face in order to discriminate against particular social groups; the very fact of discretion allows for the possibility that individuals in identical situations will not be treated identically.

The second component of policy design is the structure of financing— who pays? Many social policies in industrial countries are *contributory.* Contributory policies extract revenue exclusively from future or potential beneficiaries, and they may (although they need not) entail at least the illusion of a self-contained system in which contributions pay for benefits without recourse to other sources of revenue. Other policies are *noncontributory* and explicitly rely on general sources of revenue to fund benefits. These two elements of policy design, benefit structure and financing structure, together help to determine the size, social composition, and permanence of the program's constituency, both those who stand to benefit and those who assume the cost. Policies with egalitarian benefits and contributory financing will produce self-generating, perpetual, and unified constituencies, whereas discretionary, noncontributory policies will have constituencies that are more fragmented and separated politically from the general population. The structure of benefits and financing also influences the relationship of beneficiaries to other elements of the political system, particularly their status in the public mind as "deserving" or "undeserving," "honorable" or "dishonorable."[38]

As Table 1.1 indicates, Old-Age Insurance was egalitarian and contributory, whereas Aid to Dependent Children was discretionary and noncontributory. OAI, although it rather blatantly excluded most African-Americans from benefits through occupational exclusions, developed administrative practices that treated beneficiaries equally and fairly regardless of race. ADC, which granted most authority to state and local authorities, produced vast inequalities in the treatment of its target population. Unemployment Insurance, which was partly discretionary and partly contributory, was subject to many of the same parochial pressures as ADC and placed substantial power in the hands of local officials and administrators. However, the national criteria that were also part of UI's policy structure constrained the parochial forces, so that UI administration was notably more racially fair than ADC.

Institutional Structure: Organization and Administrative Structure

The law, however, does not by itself determine the outcomes of social policy. Even the most transparently drafted statute requires not only interpretation but translation from legal language into action, which, in turn, requires the mobilization of state capacity in the form of administrative organizations.[39] The second broad component of institutional structure, then, is bureaucratic or administrative structure, the organization of the governmental agency or agencies that administer the policy. Bureaucratic structure can have many attributes, ranging from aspects of an agency's internal organization and procedures and the character of its personnel and leadership to the political structures that link it to its superiors (such as the president and Congress), other agencies, interest groups, its clients, and the public at large.[40] The elements of bureaucratic structure identified here are those that relate particularly to the administrative capacity of welfare state institutions to operate the policies for which they are responsible and to affect policy development. There are four components of bureaucratic structure: the level of administration, national or state; the political permeability of an agency's operations; the agency's policy environment; and the nature of client and public relations that an agency conducts.

The first important aspect of administrative structure is the level of government at which administration is carried out. Is the program national or is it administered by state and local governments or at some combination of levels? The size of the political unit in which policy is made and carried out can have an important impact on the exercise of power. In smaller units, local majorities and private interests can much more easily capture public authority and bend it to their own uses.[41] The situation of state and local government in the federal structure also constrains their capacity to raise revenue and redistribute income, and the profusion of governments in the United States, as Martha Derthick puts its, "gives inequality a spatial form" because it allows communities to pursue varied policies in many areas.[42] The federal government, however, has fewer fiscal constraints and a more or less fixed constituency, which allow it to make and administer policy without fear of driving unhappy customers—either benefit recipients or taxpayers—elsewhere. The nature of the relationship between the federal government and lower levels of government is an important part of the question of centralization. Even parochial policies involve some federal control over state and local government, whether by statute or through administrative oversight. However, the extent and nature of this control can vary substantially.

The second aspect of bureaucratic structure is its political permeability. The political position a policy or agency occupies in the governmental structure depends, most generally, on the extent to which it is open to political influence, whether from political superiors, interest groups, or other sources.[43] Is it relatively autonomous in its ability to hire personnel and establish and execute rules and procedures? Do politicians and other concerned citizens have political interests at stake in its routine operations, or do they leave it free to do its work as long as it doesn't stir up too much discontent? Although patronage and other manifestations of political permeability are not inherently damaging to the smooth and equitable administration of welfare, they can expose public policies to intense cross pressures, pitting democratic accountability against the imperatives of effective policy in pursuit of collective benefits. Such conflict can be particularly intense where the individual burdens and benefits of policy are unevenly distributed among a population and where the pursuit of a policy's goals appears to some members of a political community to threaten their individual interests, even when the policy as a general principle has public support and has been duly adopted through democratically constituted institutions.[44] As Jennifer Hochschild has argued persuasively, this dilemma is especially and tragically acute when, as in the case of school desegregation, a policy seeks to overcome racial inequality. Not all policies are susceptible to this dilemma, however. In some cases, the pressures from politicians and the imperatives of smooth and effective policy administration may point an agency in the same direction. In such cases, the political levers on agency operations need not be overwhelming.[45] The coincidence between the motives and opportunities of an agency's political superiors is thus important in shaping policy implementation.

A third aspect of administrative structure is the agency's policy environment, or institutional context, the array of institutions that produce the policy the agency administers.[46] The policy environment encompasses the long-term outlook the agency faces for policy change, the possibility of fundamental redirection of its mission or structure, and the stability of its political environment. It shapes the level of control an agency wields over its own destiny as well as the prospects facing those who seek to reform its policy. All agencies face uncertainty in anticipating the demands that elected officials will make on them. How stable or unstable is the environment in which an agency operates? Can it be reasonably certain that it will be called upon to do next year basically what it does today? In five years? In twenty? How much control does the agency have over its own environment? Is it able to engage in planning and developing policy changes, or does it operate entirely at the beck and call of the political branches? Is the policy governing the agency's work made by a broad and diverse set of actors or by a more narrow and well-defined network? An agency's ability to influence the development of policy it administers can greatly enhance the stability of its operations and allow it more easily to accommodate new demands and an expanding and changing constituency.

Finally, what kind of relations does the agency have with private citizens, and on what scale, and how does it organize those relations?[47] Even though their activities have a large impact on our daily lives, many agencies of great moment (take the Federal Reserve Board) have essentially no direct contact with citizens. Others, such as the Consumer Product Safety Commission or the Food and Drug Administration, appear from time to time on the nightly news. Still others might have more direct contact with individual citizens either on paper, such as the Internal Revenue Service, or by human contact, such as the Postal Service. Among those agencies that have direct contact with citizens, contact can either be relatively automatic and thus invisible (such as having taxes deducted from a paycheck), or require citizen initiative (as in applying for a passport or a driver's license). It can be direct or it can occur with the assistance or through the agency of a private organization (such as the Farm Bureau for the Agricultural Extension Service).[48]

There are two parameters that define the kind of contact an agency has with its clients and the public. The first is the way the agency manages its public contact at the organizational level. This dimension considers whether an agency conducts its relations with the public by itself or whether it enlists other organizations to share in its work.[49] The ability to colonize the capacity of other organizations, in both the public and private sectors, can affect both an agency's competence at performing its own tasks and the goodwill the agency is able to generate both with the public and its political superiors. The second dimension of public contact is the nature of the direct interactions between agency operators and individual clients. These can be friendly, indifferent, or hostile; successful or endlessly frustrating; easy and automatic or distant and difficult. A strong public relations effort, aimed at both clients and the general public, can be of tremendous importance. The style and substance of client relations set a tone for the agency's political dealings with the public that can have a substantial impact on future policy developments.

The consequences of administrative structure for the political construction of racial differences can be profound indeed. As Table 1.1 summarizes, OAI was created with a strongly national institutional structure—centralized and uniform, politically independent and autonomous, stable, and popular. These attributes allowed it to translate its racially fair processes of administration into tremendous political strength that, in fact, overcame the racially divisive forces that were built into the policy at its founding moment. ADC, by contrast, was decentralized and fragmentary, volatile, and susceptible to a wide range of political pressure and influence—in short, decidedly parochial. On top of ADC's discretionary benefit structure, in which power over social policy decisions disappears from view in a tangled web of political and administrative structures, these institutional characteristics added to the program's political weakness and hardened its racial divisiveness into what has become since the 1960s one of the central dilemmas of American politics. Although UI left many policy and administrative decisions to state and local authorities, states remained more heavily constrained, both legislatively and administratively, in UI than in ADC. Although Unemployment Insurance was one of the political highlights of social policy in the New Deal, an era when American liberalism championed structural intervention in the capitalist economy as never before, the hybrid structure of UI has resulted in the curious stagnation of unemployment policy in American politics. The racial result has been the marginal incorporation of African-Americans in UI, but at a heavy price—shifting and hardening racial lines in the labor market and the political economy more generally.[50]

The institutions of social policy constituted a critical link in the developmental chain of racial politics in the United States. In the first instance, they were forged in what Joel Williamson has called "the crucible of race" —a politics fundamentally structured by racial division, especially the racial institutions, culture, and social structure of the South.[51] But more important, they themselves defined in critical ways the place of African-Americans in the welfare state and, by extension, in American politics and society. National institutions facilitated the full inclusion of African-Americans in the benefits of welfare, inviting a growing and increasingly stable black middle class into the full embrace of citizenship that the United States finally offered in the late twentieth century. At the same time, parochial institutions kept other African-Americans at arm's length, reinforcing weak ties to state and economy and fueling the calamitous political and economic isolation particularly of poor urban blacks.

The chapters that follow elaborate the story of race, institutions, and New Deal social policy. Chapter 2 explores the moment of creation of the new national welfare state, the Social Security Act of 1935. It examines the events and decisions that led to the creation of a widely diverse collection of institutions to administer the widely diverse collection of policies that made up the act, and it probes the role of race, class, and region in the development and adoption of these particular institutional forms. The result of the policy settlement of 1935 was a welfare state that classified by race, sorting African-Americans into parochially structured welfare policies and largely out of nationally structured social insurance.

The following three chapters trace the consequences of the institutional settlement of 1935 for the three policies respectively: Old-Age Insurance in Chapter 3, Aid to Dependent Children in Chapter 4, and Unemployment Insurance in Chapter 5. Each chapter has a similar structure. First, it describes in detail the essential and distinctive elements of the policy's institutional structure as created by the Social Security Act and established by the events of the late 1930s and early 1940s. Second, each examines the patterns of fairness or discrimination in the administration of the policy: Did institutions produce fair and equal treatment of African-Americans, or was their inclusion in welfare policy subject to discretion and discrimination? Third, each chapter then charts the effects of institutional structure on the subsequent evolution of the policies. In the generation after the New Deal, how did institutions structure policy development—toward expansion or retrenchment, racial inclusion, or isolation?

Finally, Chapter 6 offers some concluding reflections on the meaning of this historical-institutional expedition for the contemporary politics of race and welfare and especially for their convergence in debates about the urban "underclass." Popular narratives about the current state both of welfare politics and race politics embody a more or less implicit story about the connection between broad economic and political forces and the individual behavior of the poor, especially the African-American ghetto poor. But these narratives, whether on the left or the right, neglect the institutions that mediate between international economics and national politics, on the one hand, and people's everyday lives on the other. Attention to the historical role of institutions in constructing racial identities and shaping welfare politics adds sinew to these connections and suggests a new understanding not only of contemporary political dilemmas but also of American political development.

2

Race, Class, and the Organization of Social Policy: The Social Security Act

In the first two years of the New Deal, the Roosevelt administration's social policy was occupied with the relief effort, which addressed the immediate problems of joblessness and deprivation that the Depression had caused. But in 1934, prodded by the popular welfare programs of Dr. Francis Townsend and Senator Huey Long, the administration turned its sights toward the long-term problems of economic security. The desperate economic conditions of the Depression, the remarkable Democratic gain of congressional seats in the 1934 midterm elections, and Roosevelt's personal popularity combined to create the conditions for an extraordinary expansion of national authority in social welfare. In his campaign address to the Commonwealth Club of San Francisco, Roosevelt had laid out a vision of economic security protected by an engaged administrative state that would displace the dominance of party politics.[1] But the racial structure of American politics and society compromised Roosevelt's vision of an administrative state for economic security. The Social Security Act of 1935 produced a collection of social policies that was institutionally fragmented along lines constructed by class, race, and region.

All of the policies contained in the Social Security Act carried race-laden exclusions, features that inherently, whether by accident or design, excluded African-Americans from full participation in their benefits. Given the status of African-Americans in American society and politics in the 1930s, it is not surprising to find that the social policy innovations of that period largely excluded them, and scholars have often noted the racial disparities that resulted from the Social Security Act.[2] Several, especially Jill Quadagno, have stressed the racial structure of the South's distinctive political economy to account for the act's racial divisions. Others, most notably Gareth Davies and Martha Derthick, counter that race was at most incidental to the policy debates of 1935 that created the Social Security

Act. Instead, they stress the fiscal and administrative characteristics of Roosevelt's proposed policies as the principal factors shaping the act's ultimately exclusionary outcomes. Davies and Derthick are surely right to point out that racial exclusion was only one of many plausible and overlapping reasons for the act's final shape and that Southerners were not the only ones who supported its racially exclusionary features. But these policy arguments occurred within a broader context of race, class, region, and New Deal coalition politics that shaped both the views and the interests of policymakers, with the result that certain racially exclusionary policy instruments gained majority support, whereas others did not.[3]

Southern society combined labor-repressive agriculture with racial disenfranchisement and segregation to subdue African-Americans both economically and politically. Southern politics placed a tremendous premium on preserving the autonomy of local state structures from national interference, and these local political structures—built on the twin pillars of planter dominance and racial disenfranchisement—were constructed particularly to serve the elite white employers of African-American labor. Neither race nor class was primary in shaping the political and social structure of the South; both were deeply and simultaneously inscribed in the structures of Southern political power in the 1930s. As sociologist David James writes, "the same local political structure that stripped blacks of basic citizenship rights also denied them equal education and restricted their access to manufacturing jobs."[4] Just as race and class were inscribed in Southern politics, so Southern politics and its racial and class baggage were inscribed in national politics. The hegemony of the Democratic party in the South and the institutional structure of Congress combined to give white Southerners both a strong interest in directing new social benefits away from African-Americans and power beyond their numbers in national politics and policymaking. Southern Democrats, committed to preserving both racial segregation and the distinctive regional labor market, found themselves in a majority coalition during the New Deal with urban Northerners and organized labor, who were demanding a social democratic program of national social and employment policy.[5] This coalition—which Ira Katznelson, stressing its coexisting progressive and reactionary elements, has called "a marriage of Sweden and South Africa"[6]—created a national welfare state aimed at its constituent class groups, industrial workers and white Southern planters, and it did so by building new institutions on a foundation of racial inequality.

The Social Security Act constituted the most important and dramatic moment of expansion of national power in social welfare policy. This expansion of the American welfare state touched African-Americans little, if at all. But African-Americans were not simply excluded outright. The institutional terms on which the new welfare state grew reflected the capacities and opportunities of the forces of racial exclusion, and the shape of new institutions proved important for establishing the place of African-Americans in the welfare state. Built as it was on this racially structured class coalition, the act distinguished between programs for the working class and programs for the nonworking poor. In both categories, the act contained racially relevant exclusions. But the act realized these racial exclusions through different institutional means—in some cases by excluding the occupations in which most African-Americans worked, in others by drawing strict eligibility standards that many African-Americans could not meet, and in still others by preserving local autonomy and passing altogether on matters of inclusion and exclusion.

The principal institutional means by which the Social Security Act excluded African-Americans were the inclusive or exclusive scope of the target population and the institutional structure of policies. Racially, policies could be either inclusive or exclusive, and institutionally they could be either national or parochial. The framers of the Social Security Act, in the spirit of Roosevelt's pragmatic liberalism, hoped to create a national policy as far as possible. But in promoting strong centralized controls over the administration of welfare, they ran up against resilient parochial forces. On the inclusion dimension, the central issue was the status of agricultural and domestic workers, categories that included an enormous share of the African-Americans in the labor force. But providing social insurance coverage for these workers also challenged local traditions of racial segregation and dependence in the political economy. Along both dimensions, policies were designed to undermine the New Deal's more comprehensive aims in a racially biased way. In order to pass national old-age and unemployment insurance plans, the Roosevelt administration had to compromise inclusiveness and accept the exclusion of agricultural and domestic employees from the program, with notably imbalanced racial consequences. At the same time, Congress decentralized even further than the administration's proposal the public assistance programs on which poor African-Americans would be forced to rely, compromising national institutions to adopt a potentially inclusive policy. Finally, the policies differed in their relationship to the larger political economy—the ways in which they strengthened or weakened the ties of racially defined groups to the labor market and the opportunities created by economic growth. In particular, Unemployment Insurance reinforced racial segmentation in the economy, providing the benefits of stable employment and income support to white workers while denying them to African-Americans.

Race and class, of course, interact in this story, as they do in American political development more generally. African-Americans have always been disproportionately poor, so any policy that aims to attack poverty will affect them disproportionately. For similar reasons, any program that is directed at the middle class will bypass African-Americans disproportionately. Blacks, in short, are the particular victims of class bias in American social policy. It is my intention here to argue not that race trumps class as an explanation for the path of American political history, but that race and class were mutually constitutive in the making and growth of the American welfare state. It was not just any class divide that shaped American social policy, but a particular one that was deeply intertwined with racial and sectional politics. The racial structure of American society—embodied in a complex set of relationships among politically constructed racial categories, regional conflict, labor markets, and the characteristic fragmentation of American state institutions—rendered the enactment of racially inclusive, nationally administered social policies impossible in the 1930s.

In this chapter, I sketch the origins of these different institutional structures contained in the Social Security Act and trace them to the politics of class and race in the Democratic coalition and the structures of policymaking in the New Deal. Finally, I demonstrate the immediate racial consequences of these institutional arrangements. It is not my purpose to retell the story of the Social Security Act nor to replicate or replace others' analyses of the racial, regional, or class origins of welfare policy in the 1930s. Rather, my purpose is to stress the *institutional* consequences of New Deal welfare politics—the way the racial and class tensions of the New Deal coalition were "built into" welfare policy institutions in ways that would have serious consequences in the following generations.

Roosevelt and the Origins of the Social Security Act

When Franklin Roosevelt proposed what became the Social Security Act of 1935, he envisioned a comprehensive and coordinated program of economic security under the close direction of the federal government.[7] As Roosevelt conceived of social security, it would promote what T. H. Marshall would later call "the social rights of citizenship," access to public social provision for all of a society's members.[8] He wanted to build a program that would protect Americans against the "hazards and vicissitudes of life," encompassing assistance for the elderly, the unemployed, and dependent children. He told his secretary of labor, Frances Perkins, that, "There is no reason why everybody in the United States should not be covered. I see no reason why every child, from the day he is born, shouldn't be a member of the social security system . . . And there is no reason why just the industrial workers should get the benefit of this. Everybody ought to be in on it—the farmer and his wife and his family. I don't see why not . . . Cradle to the grave—from the cradle to the grave they ought to be in a social insurance system."[9] But, as Marshall suggested, social rights in a democracy must be built on civil rights—rights of speech, conscience, and property, and the right freely to pursue an occupation—and political rights—above all, the right to vote. In the 1930s, African-Americans were routinely and systematically denied both civil and political rights; consequently, social rights were largely out of their reach.[10] To the extent that a program such as Roosevelt sought provided universal social benefits, it threatened the political economy of the South, which was based on the utter economic dependence of mostly black agricultural labor. Any welfare policy that gave Southern farm workers sources of income independent of the planter elite and the political institutions that it dominated had the potential to undermine the rigid racial and class structures of the South.

The Roosevelt administration's social security plan, developed by the cabinet-level Committee on Economic Security (CES), proposed a dramatic expansion of the federal government's welfare responsibilities in order to extend the social rights of American citizenship. Although the members of the CES built on a foundation of state welfare programs, they anticipated that centralized policymaking and administration would "be an instrument for improving standards in backward States" and for improving the reach and adequacy of public assistance.[11] At the same time, Roosevelt did not call for an entirely national welfare system. In a special message to Congress in June 1934, he sketched the rough outlines of federal-state relations in an economic security policy:[12] "I believe there should be a maximum of cooperation between States and the Federal Government . . . Above all, I am convinced that States should meet at least a large portion of the cost of management, leaving to the Federal Government the responsibility of investing, maintaining, and safeguarding the funds constituting the necessary insurance resources."[13] Although he left it to the Committee on Economic Security, appointed three weeks later, to fill in these rather vague outlines, his preference for federal-state cooperation guided the committee's deliberations and helped shape the resulting legislation.[14]

Roosevelt had good reasons to believe that a purely national program would prove neither feasible nor desirable. Perhaps most important, Congress would never pass legislation creating such a program. The Congress was largely dominated by Southerners, some more conservative than others, but generally united in their skepticism of excessive federal domination of domestic policy to the exclusion of state and local governments. Although the image of Southern solidarity against the nation during the New Deal is somewhat exaggerated, Southern members did coalesce reliably on issues of perceived federal intervention, especially those affecting race and labor relations, matters that social security legislation profoundly touched.[15] Roosevelt could ill afford to alienate powerful Southern committee chairmen.[16] But his need to accommodate the South was emotional as well as political, due to his ties to Warm Springs, Georgia, where he had gone in the 1920s for treatment after his bout with polio in 1921; so convinced was he of the therapeutic value of the mineral springs that he bought the spa and established a nonprofit foundation to make the treatment more widely available.[17]

But congressional politics and emotional considerations aside, there were other reasons for the president to propose a cooperative federal-state economic security program. A former governor himself, and a particularly innovative one in his attempts to confront the despair of the Depression, Roosevelt was sympathetic to the appeal of state autonomy in welfare policy.[18] The federal government of the 1930s was poorly equipped to administer public assistance to individual citizens on anything like the scale he contemplated. Grants-in-aid to the states, however, were by then familiar, existing in areas such as highway construction, vocational education, and public health.[19] Many states had already adopted many of the essential pieces of the social security package, including old-age and mothers' pensions and unemployment insurance, and federal grants could enrich and extend these programs without requiring extensive new national capacity.[20] The Supreme Court, too, loomed as an apparent obstacle to the extension of federal policy. The challenge to the federal enactments of the First New Deal was mounting, and the constitutionality of the Social Security Act's expansion of federal responsibility was an important concern of its framers. At the time of Roosevelt's message, there was tremendous uncertainty about the path the Court would take, and the overturning of the National Industrial Recovery Act the following spring sent the administration into near panic.[21] Finally, the notion that states should tailor social policy to local conditions was congenial to the ideas of decentralization and policy experimentation that were gaining prominence within the Roosevelt administration in the early years of the New Deal.[22]

The major policies that made up the Roosevelt social security plan that was unveiled in January 1935 differed in many important respects—a national scheme of compulsory, contributory old-age insurance; federal grants for state-based assistance to the elderly and dependent children; and a cooperative federal-state unemployment insurance system. In the administration's original conception, these income-support policies were to be accompanied by "employment assurance," an active policy to provide jobs for the unemployed.[23] Despite their structural and substantive differences, these policies shared a number of critical characteristics. Taken together, they formed a comprehensive package of social policies of the kind that Roosevelt had anticipated in the Commonwealth Club address and would come to advocate even more strongly in the 1940s as his attention turned to the postwar world that he would not live to see.[24] They promised help to those who, for reasons beyond their control, were unable to support themselves. And within the limits imposed by political circumstances, they proposed generally racially inclusive, nationally structured policy institutions.

It was the last of these characteristics that attacked the racial and class divide in American society by proposing to move toward a broad-based scheme of social rights. Accordingly, it provoked the most serious opposition. Congress responded to this challenge by subtly but significantly defining more sharply the class divisions among the components of social security—social insurance for the industrial and commercial working class and public assistance for the poor. But this congressional redefinition also introduced racially relevant exclusions into the Social Security Act in the spring of 1935, so that by the time Roosevelt signed the legislation on 14 August, the package was both less inclusive and less national. But the racial boundaries around each program were not identical. Each element of Roosevelt's program challenged the racial structure of American society in a different way. Old-Age Insurance threatened to create a system of payments directly from the federal government to citizens, which held the potential to advance the social and economic status of working African-Americans, regardless of their place in the economic hierarchy, by providing them with an independent source of retirement income. Aid to Dependent Children potentially put Southern states in the position of paying benefits from their own treasuries to African-American women and children, many of whom otherwise worked in the fields or as servants in private homes on terms that differed little from the paternalistic social relations of slavery. Unemployment Insurance similarly created the prospect of states, under strong federal compulsion, paying benefits to unemployed black workers. By emphasizing the stabilization of employment as well as the payment of benefits, Unemployment Insurance also threatened to interfere with local manipulation of the South's agricultural labor market.

Not only was the challenge to the racial structure different in each case, but the political and institutional opportunities available were also different. Policymakers fashioned divergent institutional structures accordingly. The Roosevelt administration proposed social insurance programs that were as national and inclusive as political circumstances and historical legacies allowed. In some cases, Congress restricted inclusiveness in order to create national policies; in others, national structure was sacrificed for inclusiveness.[25] Given the way the racial structure was imprinted on the structure of power in American government, the national, racially inclusive policies that the president preferred were not possible; neither, however, was it possible in the depths of the Depression to continue the pattern of exclusive and parochial programs that had come to constitute the American welfare state in the first third of the twentieth century.

In the wake of his message to Congress, President Roosevelt created the Committee on Economic Security by executive order in late June 1934. With the secretary of labor as its chairman, the committee consisted as well of the secretaries of agriculture and the treasury, the attorney general, and the federal emergency relief administrator. In its deliberations, which stretched through the summer and fall and on into the winter of 1934–35, the CES considered the extent of coverage that was desirable. The committee members and staff accepted the president's stated preference for broad coverage of working Americans in the social insurance programs, and the question became one of feasibility—how difficult would it be to administer a program of economic security that included not just industrial workers but farmers, servants, the self-employed, and other categories that might pose particular problems? The committee's staff was divided on the possibility of including agricultural and domestic workers in the social insurance programs. Although many agreed with the president's goal of broad coverage, some influential staff members were pessimistic about the feasibility of adopting a European tax collection system that would have facilitated the administration of unemployment insurance to farmers and servants. Others worried that including farm and other seasonal workers might force their employers to pay taxes for employees who would never be eligible to collect benefits because they did not work enough weeks out of the year.[26]

In its initial draft of a report and proposed legislation, the staff recommended the exclusion of agricultural and domestic workers, but the committee itself, led by Perkins and Federal Emergency Relief Administrator Harry Hopkins, supported full inclusion.[27] "We are opposed," the committee stated in its final report, "to exclusions of any specified industries from the Federal act." And later, "we recommend that the contributory annuity system [OAI] include, on a compulsory basis, *all* manual workers and nonmanual workers earning less than $250 per month." The committee also addressed directly the problems of groups at the margin of the economy.

> Agricultural workers, domestic servants, home workers, and the many self-employed people constitute large groups in the population who have generally received little attention. In these groups are many who are at the very bottom of the economic scale. We believe that more attention will have to be given to these groups than they have received heretofore. We cannot be satisfied that we have a reasonably complete program for economic security unless some degree of protection is given these groups now generally neglected.[28]

The committee's report reflected the president's desire for broad coverage, and it paid particular attention to the occupations in which African-Americans were most likely to work. Even the administration's formulation of the proposal, however, did not include sharecroppers and tenant farmers, who were considered self-employed or independent contractors rather than wage employees.[29] Because the financing of Old-Age Insurance came from a tax on wages, this group of workers, which included many black and white farmers especially in the South, was excluded even from the broadest version of the OAI plan.

The institutional structure of the Social Security system received more attention in the committee's deliberations. In general, the committee's aim was to ensure adequate benefits nationwide, promote maximum uniformity from state to state, and encourage professional and competent administration of the various programs with a minimum of political interference, and it tried to square these aims with the president's preference for federal-state cooperation. As a rule, these goals called for national rather than parochial social security programs.

Despite these imperatives, the CES recommended an inclusive program that ranged in institutional structure from national Old-Age Insurance to fairly parochial public assistance. The principal barrier to an entirely national system of social insurance that the committee members foresaw was constitutional. Social policy advocates had severe doubts about how far the Supreme Court would be willing to go in allowing federal innovation, and this was an important consideration in the committee's decisions, affecting mostly Unemployment Insurance but also Old-Age Insurance. A second barrier to a federal system was politics. Perkins remarked that where "state jealousies and aspirations were involved," Congress would be unlikely to accept a system of social insurance that gave the federal government too much power.[30]

The major battleground on the issue of federal or state control was Unemployment Insurance.[31] The preliminary staff report on the issue favored an entirely national system, on the grounds that it would provide maximum uniformity and simplicity to the system, spread risk, and ensure adequate benefits throughout the country, but there was some disagreement among the staff and members of the technical board.[32] In November the CES's technical board reported to the committee on three possible unemployment insurance systems. The first was an exclusively national system, in keeping with the staff's preliminary recommendation. The other two were cooperative state-federal systems. The first of these, known as the "subsidy" plan, called for a federal tax whose revenues would be returned to the states to pay unemployment benefits. The second, based on the Wagner-Lewis unemployment bill of 1934, was called the "tax offset" plan. It called for a federal tax on employers, which could be "offset" by a credit for tax paid into a state unemployment fund. The purpose of the subsidy plan was to establish the nearest thing to a national unemployment insurance system and to allow for an easy transfer to a national system in the future. The Wagner-Lewis plan was designed to induce states to adopt their own unemployment plans by overcoming the competitive disadvantage that would result if one state adopted such a plan and its neighbors did not. At the committee's meeting on 9 November, the CES unanimously abandoned the federal system after considerable debate, apparently believing that an exclusively federal system was not attainable, no matter how desirable.[33]

The question was then between the two federal-state cooperative proposals. Proponents of the federal system, who included Harry Hopkins, Secretary of Agriculture Henry Wallace, and Assistant Secretary of the Treasury Josephine Roche, who represented Secretary Henry Morgenthau at most committee meetings, tended to favor the subsidy plan over the offset plan, because it was closer in spirit and substance to the national plan and because they believed it would allow for greater federal control of state activities. The offset plan, which the committee eventually adopted, allowed state governments greater autonomy.[34] The committee staff carefully considered the possibilities for federal supervision and administrative regulation of Unemployment Insurance under the offset plan.[35]

In contrast to Unemployment Insurance, the committee recommendations regarding Old-Age Insurance and the public assistance provisions of the economic security program required less debate. The staff spent some effort trying to devise a cooperative federal-state old-age insurance scheme without success. Thomas Eliot, the act's chief legal draftsman, recounts that he spent "an awful lot of time . . . trying to figure out how . . . state old age insurance schemes could be encouraged. As I recall it, the early part of the fall of '34 I was drafting a lot of plans and talking with a great many people and getting ideas. There wasn't anything that anybody could dream up that made much sense."[36] In the end, the staff was unanimous in advising the committee against a state-by-state program because of the tremendous difficulty involved in tracking millions of individual workers and their tax payments over their entire careers in a highly mobile population. The committee preferred to rely on the scope of the federal government's power to tax and spend by proposing a strictly national program in a constitutional manner.[37] For the public assistance programs—programs for the aged, the blind, and dependent children—the legacy of policies, such as mothers' pensions, that many states had already established (and for which advocates had fought long and hard) militated against national institutions, and the committee proposed grants-in-aid to the states. The administration also envisioned that these programs would help get the federal government out of the relief business. This part of the committee's recommendation was developed, according to Arthur J. Altmeyer, chairman of the CES technical board and later of the Social Security Board, "without the necessity for extended consideration."[38] However, the committee was intent on mitigating the parochialism of the public assistance programs as far as possible. It commissioned a staff study on the mechanisms available for federal direction of state expenditures under grant-in-aid programs, including the power to withhold federal contributions for noncompliance.[39] The committee's stringent provisions for federal over-sight of public assistance programs, designed to ensure adequacy and fair-ness, would be among the most contentious issues in the congressional debate on the bill.

African-American leaders wanted to go even farther toward creating national and inclusive policies.[40] "Negroes should fear the Wagner-Lewis Social Insurance Bill," said T. Arnold Hill of the National Urban League.[41] Charles H. Houston of the NAACP objected to the social security bill on the grounds that it was not sufficiently inclusive. First, it excluded tenant farmers and sharecroppers from the work-based programs—Old-Age In-surance as well as Unemployment Insurance—because these workers were not, technically speaking, employees.[42] Second, these two social insurance programs required a history of contributions from employers and employ-ees before individuals became eligible for benefits, meaning that those currently elderly or unemployed were not eligible for benefits, a burden that fell especially heavily on African-Americans. Finally, Houston pro-tested that agricultural wage laborers and domestic employees were to be excluded from these programs, a decision that had not even been made yet but that he treated as a foregone conclusion. These exclusions meant, Houston correctly estimated, that approximately three in five African-American workers would be left out of the national parts of the new social security apparatus.[43] The black elderly and unemployed would have to rely instead on public assistance programs for support, as would mothers and children.

The problem with the public assistance legs of the social security bill, according to Houston, was not that their terms excluded African-Ameri-cans but that they were institutionally biased. Houston testified that the NAACP favored strictly national public assistance programs that paid di-rect benefits from the federal government to their recipients. "From the point of view of the Negro," he told the Senate Finance Committee, "it would be much easier to get fair enforcement of a Federal law than to get a really effective old-age assistance law passed by southern legislatures. There are lots of decent, fair-minded people in the South; but in many States it would be political suicide for them to advocate a State old-age assistance law giving Negroes substantial benefits in large numbers." He also protested that "there is no Federal machinery for the payment of [un-employment] insurance."[44] Houston's objection in these statements was that the administration's bill placed too much power in the hands of state and local officials, and that doing so would prejudice the policy against fair and effective administration of assistance for African-Americans.

There was, in fact, a great deal of public support for national, inclusive social security schemes in the 1930s. Two such schemes were at the center of prominent social movements that threatened the New Deal from the left—Dr. Francis Townsend's Revolving Old-Age Pension plan and Senator Huey P. Long's Share Our Wealth plan.[45] These movements were important elements in the political atmosphere and applied critical pressure toward the expansion of the federal government's welfare role in a national, inclusive direction. Townsend was a Long Beach, California, physician who proposed that the federal government pay a monthly pension of $200 to every American over sixty, provided that they spend the entire sum each month. To fund these payments, he proposed a "transactions" tax, basically a sales tax, on the fairly fabulous principle that the pensions themselves would stimulate sufficient economic activity to cover their cost—that was what made them "revolving" pensions.[46] Townsend's great gift was neither as a legislative draftsman nor as an economic theorist—the Townsend plan was never in danger of passing—but as a political organizer. Townsend Clubs sprang up throughout the country to demand old-age pensions, creating a formidable political voice that caught the attention of legislators at all levels. Many Townsend Clubs remained active and influential through the 1940s.

A more serious political threat was the insurgent movement of Long, the domineering senator from Louisiana.[47] As governor, Long had built an imposing political machine in Louisiana as well as a prodigious political following among the poor and the working class, whose cause he championed against "trusts," corporations, and big oil companies. His vast program of public works—building roads, schools, and hospitals—probably prevented many Louisianans from suffering as much as they might have during the Depression and did much to modernize his state. A flamboyant and magnetic character, he entered the Senate in 1931 and began to rail against concentrations of wealth and power, trumpeting his "Share Our Wealth" plan of heavily confiscatory taxes on large fortunes and large family allowances that amounted to a guaranteed income. Like Townsend, Long developed a large national following, and Share Our Wealth Clubs sprouted nationwide. Significantly, Long's economic message was racially inclusive, although he was far from liberal on other racial issues. Roosevelt considered Long, whose presidential ambitions were ill concealed, a serious political rival and exerted considerable energy in an attempt to neutralize him before Long was assassinated in September 1935. In a 1934 White House meeting on the economic security proposal, Roosevelt even invoked Long as a further reason for decentralizing authority. "All the power shouldn't be in the hands of the federal government," he said. "Look— just think what would happen if all the power *was* concentrated here, and *Huey Long* became president!"[48]

Because of the desperate economic conditions of the Depression and the strength of the Townsend, Long, and other movements, very few members of Congress opposed the social security program outright. (The Social Security Act passed the House by a vote of 372 to 33 and the Senate by a vote of 77 to 6.)[49] For the most part, members of Congress—even Southerners—embraced the program's central aims. They accepted the new federal role and even pleaded for the expansion of federal funding levels for public assistance programs, for the South, more than the other regions of the country, desperately needed federal largesse to prevent widespread misery. But the near-unanimity of the congressional adoption of the Social Security Act masks considerable tension within Congress. In particular, Southern domination of Congress shaped the deliberations of 1935.

The pivotal structural position of the South in the Congress is, of course, a commonplace in analyses of the American political universe of the New Deal era.[50] Because of the South's one-party politics, based on its underlying racial structure, Southern congressional delegations were overwhelmingly Democratic, and individual Southern Democrats, once elected, were nearly assured of reelection.[51] Because of the strict seniority system by which members of Congress were promoted to positions of power, most notably committee chairs, Southern Democrats, because of their longevity in office, tended to rise disproportionately to these positions. Norms of committee autonomy and reciprocity had developed rapidly over the preceding quarter-century, and committee chairs were thus more powerful than ever.[52] And regardless of their general political outlook, Southerners tended to coalesce in opposition to racial liberalism and encroaching federal power.[53] As Roosevelt well understood, Southern cooperation was essential to the success of the administration's legislative agenda, and Southern votes were essential to the coalition that had nominated and elected him.

Specifically, Southerners played pivotal roles in the passage of the Social Security Act. Southern Democrats held a commanding position on the Senate Finance Committee. Chairman Pat Harrison of Mississippi was a key administration leader in the Senate. Out of fifteen Democrats on the committee, six were from the deep South and three more were from border states. On a committee of twenty-one members, this group held formidable power. House Ways and Means Committee chairman Robert "Muley" Doughton of North Carolina had somewhat weaker ties with the administration, but he too took an active role in promoting the legislation.[54] Only four of the eighteen Democrats (on a twenty-five-member committee) were Southerners and another four from border states; according to Thomas Eliot, Fred Vinson of Kentucky and Jere Cooper of Tennessee were the "dominant influences" on the committee.[55]

But Southerners were not, as they are often portrayed, monolithically conservative during the New Deal. It is true that many Southern Democrats were among the most vehement critics of the New Deal, but all Southerners were not conservative, nor were all conservative members of Congress from the South.[56] The South was of two minds in its relationship with the New Deal. Although always wary of expanding federal power, especially in areas like social policy that might undermine the South's racially stratified socioeconomic structure, the South desperately needed the New Deal's largesse. The Depression had worsened conditions in the already poor South, and the Southern states had neither the programs nor the fiscal capacity to respond.[57] It was not the case that the Southern states simply opposed welfare programs such as mothers' pensions. It was the case, however, that Southern states drastically scaled back the operation of such programs during the Depression, and that mothers' pensions and other programs did not operate in the counties where African-Americans were most heavily concentrated.[58] Hence, Southern members of Congress took a decidedly ambivalent stance toward the administration's social security proposal; they wanted to capture as much as they could of the new federal spending for relief and social insurance while at the same time resisting federal interference in their regional patterns of race and labor.[59] Southerners and Northerners alike recognized the New Deal's potential to undermine the traditional pattern of Southern race relations. Even the intermittent enforcement of crude racial equity in early New Deal relief efforts had shown that federal control of social policy was a challenge to state-sanctioned segregation and to the South's segregated labor market. African-Americans responded with increasing loyalty to Roosevelt and the Democratic Party, white Southerners with growing, if selective, fear of federal policy.[60] As a result, the Southern-dominated Congress balked not at the historic expansion of the welfare state but at the particular institutional configurations of inclusive, national policy that the administration proposal embodied.

There were two strategies available to soften the social security bill's national, inclusive character: Make it either less inclusive or less national. To do neither—that is, to accept either the Roosevelt proposal or one of the stronger alternatives—was clearly unacceptable to the committee barons of the House and Senate. To do both—essentially maintaining a status quo that left social welfare to the all but bankrupt states[61]—was also impossible, for that would amount to abdicating the federal government's responsibility for easing the country's immediate distress and providing some level of enduring economic security. These goals were the central theme of the Second New Deal, and Roosevelt was well poised to pursue them after the 1934 congressional elections produced a rare midterm gain in seats for the president's party.[62]

That left a choice between two alternative strategies. Congress could limit eligibility as far as possible to the mainstream of the working class— by and large the white, urban, industrial workers who formed the backbone of the Democratic coalition in the North. Or, Congress could denationalize programs, leaving states free to limit eligibility by their own legislative or administrative means. But because of the economic distress of the Depression and the imperative of Roosevelt's turn toward economic security as a political strategy, it was impossible to do both of these things simultaneously. Institutionally national policies were possible only when they could be restricted to a narrowly designed target population that was predominantly white. More inclusive programs with the potential to bridge the racial divide were possible only when they could be made less national. Both strategies accomplished the same end, but through different means, and both represented compromises between the two wings of the New Deal Democratic coalition.

In rewriting the Social Security Act through the winter and spring of 1935, Congress used both of these strategies in different ways to accommodate the racial structure. The national structure of Old-Age Insurance was not, as most accounts assume, set in stone. Thomas Eliot, the Labor Department lawyer who drafted the administration bill and became the first general counsel of the Social Security Board, spent much time in the fall of 1934 trying to devise a scheme that involved state-federal cooperation rather than a strictly national plan. His efforts were fruitless, however, and the Committee on Economic Security decided to proceed with a national OAI proposal despite worries about the constitutionality of a federal social insurance program.[63] The national structure of Old-Age Insurance was the Social Security Act's most important innovation and its greatest long-term success, despite the misgivings of its early opponents. It was the first general federal social welfare program, and it proposed to provide assistance directly from the federal government to individual citizens on a much larger scale than its predecessors such as the Freedmen's Bureau or military pensions.[64] But, like those earlier policies, it promised (or threatened) to provide assistance on equal terms to white and black citizens.[65]

Old-Age Insurance

The question of the inclusion or exclusion of agricultural and domestic workers was argued most strenuously in the debate on compulsory, contributory old-age insurance. Old-Age Insurance was proposed as a national program, and, although the administration had searched for alternatives, there was little suggestion that Congress should alter its institutional structure.[66] The reasons for exclusively federal administration, CES Executive Director Edwin E. Witte explained to the Finance Committee, were the long-term nature of the program and the tremendous mobility of the American workforce; Congress accepted this logic, although not entirely without question.[67] But the CES's decision that all workers should be covered came under immediate and persistent question in the hearings, and the Ways and Means and Finance Committees' decisions to eliminate them from coverage came under attack as well. In the end, an important step behind congressional acceptance of a national program of old-age insurance was the racial manipulation of the program's target population so that a national program was sure to be a segregated one.

As Charles Houston of the NAACP anticipated, the House Ways and Means Committee moved quickly to exclude agricultural and domestic workers from eligibility for the social insurance programs, Old-Age Insurance and Unemployment Insurance.[68] These exclusions removed about five million workers from old-age and unemployment coverage, and they meant that more than half of the black workers in the United States (more than three-fifths in the South) would not be eligible. "It is evident," said an editorial in the *Pittsburgh Courier,* one of the country's leading black newspapers, "that this has been done to satisfy reactionary elements in the South who cannot bear the thought of Negroes getting pensions and compensations."[69] This action surprised no one; agricultural and domestic workers were generally excluded from work-based social policies such as workmen's compensation. It was more significant that Roosevelt proposed their inclusion at all and continued to support it. Administration strategists were particularly worried about the political prospects of OAI. It was far from the most popular element of the bill and would very possibly have been defeated if it had not been part of a larger package. Members of Congress understood the program's intricacies poorly; what they did understand was that it represented a vast expansion of federal responsibility in social welfare, not to mention of federal tax receipts. Roosevelt and his lieutenants, however, recognized OAI's long-term political potential and were intent on establishing its national structure, even at the expense of broad inclusiveness.[70] The president, moreover, was neither able nor inclined to push Southern members of Congress too hard on matters that touched the racial structure of Southern society, which the Social Security Act most assuredly had the potential to do.[71] Instead, the racial structure affected the political possibilities for policymaking, forcing the administration to purchase a national policy at the cost of less than universal inclusion. When, at the end of floor debate and amendment in the House, the Republicans offered a final motion to strip Old-Age Insurance from the bill and increase Old-Age Assistance grants to the states, they were defeated by more than 100 votes and received little support from Southerners, who were satisfied that the new configuration—nationally structured but exclusionary by class and race—met their demands.[72]

The most prominent argument against inclusion was based on administrative feasibility. It would be too difficult, critics argued, to devise a system to collect payroll taxes from workers who worked not for large industrial or commercial firms but, generally, for private individuals or small farmers. This argument was raised most tellingly by supporters of the legislation, particularly by Treasury Secretary Morgenthau. Morgenthau told the Ways and Means Committee, apparently on the advice of the Bureau of Internal Revenue, that the Treasury Department already faced an "extremely formidable" task in devising a system to collect payroll taxes for social security. If agricultural, domestic, and casual workers were included, he said, "the task may well prove insuperable—certainly at the outset."[73] Morgenthau's testimony was something of a bombshell to his colleagues on the Committee on Economic Security, whom he had joined in unanimously taking the opposite position on precisely this question.[74]

Although advocating exclusion for administrative reasons, Morgenthau made it quite clear that he supported inclusion on philosophical and political grounds, and he agreed with a proposal for the delayed inclusion of farm and domestic workers. "I want to point out here," he told the committee, "that personally I hope these three groups can be included."

When Doughton and Vinson responded approvingly to Morgenthau's testimony, Representative John W. McCormack of Massachusetts answered that to exclude farmers and servants for administrative reasons would be to take "an attitude of defeatism." Recognizing that an affirmative act of Congress adding them to the program in the future would be difficult to achieve, McCormack suggested that they be included at the outset, but with a time lag of several years before coverage began, giving the Treasury Department ample time to devise a method of collection and reporting. To this proposal Morgenthau responded simply, "I would say that that would be ideal."[75]

Like Morgenthau, other social security advocates testified that they favored inclusion in principle but urged the committees not to include farm workers and servants for fear that the administrative burden would jeopardize the entire economic security program. Abraham Epstein, the executive secretary of the American Association for Social Security and a longtime crusader for social insurance, took this position, though he acknowledged that "this may sound strange coming from me."[76] Marion B. Folsom, assistant treasurer of Eastman Kodak and a member of the Advisory Council on Social Security, took a similar position, in that he accepted that farm workers and servants "might be brought in" eventually but felt that they should not be included at the outset. Folsom also indicated that the advisory council, which consisted of representatives of industry and labor as well as prominent social insurance advocates, had recommended exclusion by a narrow vote.[77] In the name of incrementalism, these and other supporters of inclusive old-age insurance recommended a course of action that they hoped would promote effective implementation and political staying power. These reformers, whose motives were certainly not racial, were operating in a state with historically weak administrative structures, which made them wary of taking on too much too fast. The administrative weakness of the American state thus made it even more difficult for the supporters of racial inclusion to press their case.

Nevertheless (and in contrast to Davies and Derthick's account), not all the administrative evidence was on the side of exclusion. Some advocates of inclusion made a strong case for a tax collection system that could potentially overcome the administrative burden posed by coverage of agricultural and domestic workers. J. Douglas Brown, a Princeton economist who served as a staff consultant to the CES on old-age security, gave detailed testimony to the Ways and Means Committee on the stamp-book system for collecting payroll taxes, which was then in use in several Euro-

pean social insurance systems.[78] Under the stamp system, each employee
would be issued a blank booklet into which employers would paste stamps
purchased from the post office or some other government agency indicating the amount of payroll tax paid. Brown even included in his testimony
an example of a stamp book from the British system of contributory health
insurance, which illustrated how a stamp system might work. Witte also
referred to the stamp system as the most efficacious way of collecting taxes
from groups such as domestic servants, and he suggested that there need
not be a single system for the collection of taxes but that different systems
might be used for different kinds of workers. The original administration
bill, although it left administrative discretion in the hands of the Treasury
Department, explicitly provided for a stamp-book system, a provision that
the Ways and Means Committee dropped.[79] These points, along with the
suggestion of deferred inclusion that Morgenthau supported, offered
Congress an array of options to make inclusion of agricultural and domestic workers feasible.

The proponents of inclusion also had a comparative argument on their
side. More than half of the countries that had compulsory, contributory
old-age insurance systems in the 1930s covered farm workers and domestics.[80] In other countries, the inclusion of agricultural workers in social
insurance hinged less on mundane questions of feasibility than on broader
political questions of class alliances, although administrative practicability
occasionally entered the equation as an argument against inclusion.[81] In
Germany, social insurance arose in the 1880s out of a coalition between a
landed aristocracy and an emerging industrial class—Bismarck's "marriage
of iron and rye"—against the increasing agitation of social democrats representing industrial workers. Industrial workers were the principal targets
of Bismarck's *Sozialpolitik;* agricultural workers, primarily peasants, did
not pose a similar political or social threat to the ruling order. However,
Germany moved very quickly to expand the scope of social insurance to
cover agricultural workers; feasibility was not an issue.[82] In Austria as well,
the initial exclusion of farm workers from social insurance was the result of
reform from above by an authoritarian bureaucracy interested in fore-
stalling the forces of socialism and democracy.[83] In general, the exclusion
of agricultural workers and other wage-earning groups characteristic of
pre-industrial society resulted from political coalitions in which landed
interests, often practicing labor-repressive agriculture, were allied either
with commercial interests or with urban workers. The United States was
no exception; the New Deal Democratic party was precisely such a coali-

tion, linking the urban workers of the North with the Bourbon planters of the South. Labor-repressive agriculture in the Southern United States, however, was built on the added element of racial distinction, and the Southern planter class used its strategic control of fragmented state institutions to shape the Social Security Act in order to preserve its position atop the racial structure.[84]

The committee members who brought up these occupational exclusions were invariably Southerners. Both chairmen, Harrison and Doughton, were relatively quiet during the hearings, preferring to let other members take the lead in questioning witnesses. But both dropped their usual silence to pursue the question of the inclusion of agricultural and domestic workers. Harrison, in fact, uttered barely a word beyond procedural formalities for more than a week after the Finance Committee began its hearings until he engaged Witte in a line of questioning searching for some evidence that there was opposition among the "experts" to the inclusion of farm workers.[85] Doughton similarly awoke from his general public silence to probe on this issue, and other Southern members also expressed interest. Ironically, one of the most vehement objections to exclusion came from an opponent of the bill. Republican Representative Daniel A. Reed of New York, arguing that the whole contributory system was unconstitutional, castigated the Ways and Means Committee for discriminating (his word) against farm workers and domestics.[86]

How accurate was Houston's claim that the old-age provisions of the bill advantaged white workers? To what extent would the exclusion of farm workers and servants have a disparate racial impact on the population that would benefit from Old-Age Insurance? How would this impact be geographically distributed? After all, the entire South was heavily agricultural, and exclusion would eliminate many whites from coverage as well.[87] An examination of census occupational data from 1930 shows that the exclusion of farm workers and servants contemplated by the bill did, in fact, have a racially imbalanced effect, and that this effect was national, touching the North as well as the South.

Census data are a rather blunt instrument for examining these occupational categories. First of all, the census is done only every ten years, so it offers only a snapshot of a single moment in a fast-changing labor force. This problem is especially acute for the 1930s, when the Great Depression caused greater than normal economic dislocation. The timing of the social security debate could not be worse for a comparison of its provisions with census data because it is equidistant from the 1930 and 1940 censuses. Second, the occupational categories reported in the census do not correspond precisely to the categories in the law, making the enumeration of potentially included or excluded workers difficult. However, no other source provides such a comprehensive picture of the national labor force during the 1930s. I have used 1930 census data here because its information would have been available to the actors in 1935, or at least it represents a demographic and political reality that they perceived and understood. The categories of agricultural workers counted in 1930 map easily onto the relevant social security categories. To approximate the number of domestic workers, I have used the 1930 census category "servants," which comes closest to approximating the sense that the act intends. If anything, this usage slightly undercounts the number of domestic workers actually excluded, because it does not capture household employees classified under other categories such as "launderers" or "cooks."[88]

Whereas only slightly more than one-fifth of white workers worked in agriculture and domestic service in 1930, these categories included fully half of the black workforce. Regionally, the disparity was greatest in the South, the most heavily agricultural area of the country. In the eleven former Confederate states, more than three-fifths of African-American workers were farmers or domestic servants, compared with slightly less than half of white workers. The racial disparity in these occupations, particularly in domestic service, existed well beyond the South. Still, there were far more African-Americans in the South than outside of the region, and two-thirds of the nearly 1.4 million black workers written out of OAI by these amendments were Southern. Within the South itself, a substantial majority (more than sixty percent) of the workers excluded were African-Americans, and in the cotton states of the Deep South (Mississippi, Alabama, Georgia, and South Carolina) more than three in four excluded workers were black.

Figure 2.1 shows the disparity between the share of black and white workers in agricultural and domestic work by state. These data include all workers occupied in agriculture—owners, tenants and sharecroppers, managers and foremen, wage laborers, and unpaid family workers—as well as servants. The figure for each state is simply the percentage of the white labor force in farm and domestic work subtracted from the percentage of the black labor force in these sectors. A positive difference means that black workers worked disproportionately in these occupations and hence were disproportionately excluded from OAI coverage—the higher the number, the greater the disproportion. Conversely, a negative difference indicates that African-Americans were underrepresented in farm and household occupations.[89]

Not surprisingly, the black-white disparity was generally greater in Southern states than elsewhere (represented by darker shadings in Figure 2.1). But many of the states in which blacks were most overrepresented in excluded occupations were not Southern but the industrial states of New England and the mid-Atlantic region. In the industrial heartland, the upper Midwestern states of Pennsylvania, Ohio, Illinois, and Michigan, the disparity was also positive, indicating the overrepresentation of black workers in excluded categories. With a few exceptions, only in the farm states of the plains and the mountain states was the disparity negative, meaning the disproportionate exclusion of whites from OAI coverage. But these were states with very small black populations, almost no blacks involved in

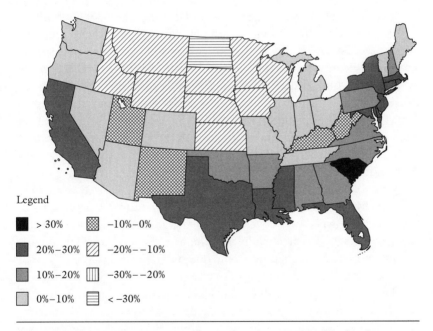

Legend

■ > 30%   ▨ −10%−0%

■ 20%−30%   ▨ −20%−−10%

■ 10%−20%   ▥ −30%−−20%

□ 0%−10%   ▤ < −30%

Figure 2.1. Racial disparity in percentage of workers in agricultural and domestic employment, 1930.

Source: U.S. Bureau of the Census, *Fifteenth Census of the United States: 1930, Population* (Washington, D.C.: Government Printing Office, 1933), vol. 4, tables 6, 11.

agriculture, and relatively low demand for household servants; only two of these states—Kentucky and West Virginia—had populations more than five percent black. The striking conclusion from these data is that the disproportionate presence of blacks in excluded occupations was nearly a nationwide phenomenon and, though heavy in the South, was just as heavy in the Northeast.

These data present only a partial picture of those excluded from Old-Age Insurance coverage under the Social Security Act. The self-employed were excluded by definition from the legislation because self-employment involves no employer-employee relationship, which forms the basis for the payroll tax. Employees of governments and nonprofit organizations were also excluded, the former because many already had pension plans, the latter because of their tax-exempt status. It is likely that in these categories most workers were white and that a tally of these groups would show that blacks were not disproportionately excluded from Old-Age Insurance on this account. But the data in Figure 2.1 do not precisely identify those workers who were the subject of the fight over agricultural and domestic workers. As Houston and Witte pointed out, neither farm owners nor tenants were considered employees for the purposes of the Social Security Act and were thus excluded from coverage as self-employed persons or independent contractors. Many farm workers were classified as unpaid family workers—the spouses and children of farmers—who received no wages and therefore would not participate in the system. The workers that the exclusion controversy affected were those who received wages for their work on farms, wage laborers and managers or foremen.

Figure 2.2 identifies more precisely the workers removed from OAI coverage by Congress. It replicates Figure 2.1 for this restricted class of workers, those who were covered under the administration bill but not under the congressional amendment. The new results show some important differences. First, there was only one state, North Dakota, in which blacks were underrepresented in farm labor and domestic service compared with whites (and North Dakota had a total black population in 1930 of only 377 people). In every other state, blacks were more likely to be found in these occupations than whites, although in many states the black population was quite small. This pattern indicates strongly that the Ways and Means amendment excluding these workers from the old-age insurance provisions of social security had a racially imbalanced impact throughout the country.

Second, the South was no longer distinctive compared with the rest of the country. Removing tenants and sharecroppers from the data removes many Southern farmers, both black and white. Whereas in Figure 2.1 the South and the Northeast both appeared as concentrated areas of racial disparity, here the South blends in with the rest of the country. If any region appears to be a pocket of racial exclusion, it is the eastern seaboard, both north and south. Southern states such as Mississippi and Arkansas, in which tenant farming was especially common, have shifted from heavy disparities to nearly even racial distribution in excluded categories (and hence from darker to lighter shadings in the maps).

In its initial form, OAI was consolidated as a national program that would reach the more privileged—and predominantly white—portions of the American working class. Built on the political power and the distinctive political economy of the South, the program nevertheless imprinted on the

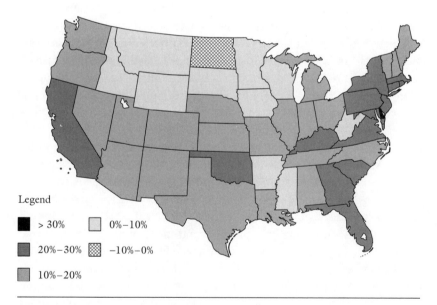

Figure 2.2. Racial disparity in percentage of workers in farm wage labor and domestic employment, 1930.

Source: U.S. Bureau of the Census, *Fifteenth Census of the United States: 1930, Population* (Washington, D.C.: Government Printing Office, 1933), vol. 4, tables 4, 6, 11.

emerging national welfare state the racial division that was a feature of the national labor market.

Aid to Dependent Children

A second major feature of the Social Security Act was public assistance—grants-in-aid to the states for purposes including pensions for the indigent elderly (Old-Age Assistance, or OAA) and Aid to Dependent Children (ADC). Under each, the federal government would grant funds to each state to defray part of the cost of its relief program, provided that the state program met certain minimum standards. The major difference between the two was that for OAA the federal government was to pay one-half of the state's cost up to a certain amount per recipient, whereas for ADC the federal share was one-third. But the administrative arrangements, which Southern congressmen fought to change, were the same for both.

It was not possible to tailor the target population of ADC by race. The exclusion of certain categories of workers was not a relevant issue in the public assistance debate as it was for Old-Age Insurance and Unemployment Insurance. In fact, several witnesses carefully reminded congressmen that farmers and farm workers, although ineligible for the contributory program, remained eligible for noncontributory public assistance.[90] Moreover, the federal adoption of subsidies for public assistance programs marked an important advance for African-Americans over mothers' pensions and other state programs because the Social Security Act required that the programs operate in all of a state's political subdivisions in order for the state to receive federal grants for that program. Once they took federal money for a public assistance program, Southern states could no longer run that program only in white counties.[91] The principle behind these public assistance programs was the relief of the "deserving poor," those who, due to life circumstances beyond their control such as old age or widowhood, could not support themselves. Furthermore, because these programs were to be funded out of general revenues and benefits did not depend on an individual's contributions or work history, they did not pose administrative problems such as tax collection and payroll reporting.

Precisely because eligibility for ADC was in principle open to all needy people in the relevant category, and blacks were not systematically excluded as they were from social insurance benefits, blacks throughout the country were more likely than whites to be among its beneficiaries. Blacks were substantially more likely to be poor than whites for a variety of reasons. Not only were black workers more likely to be unemployed, but their earnings were likely to be insufficient to bring them above the level of poverty, as Table 2.1 shows.

It is impossible to estimate with any precision the number of families, black or white, who would have been eligible for ADC in 1935. First, the federal act did not specify such eligibility requirements as residence and citizenship. Second, sufficiently detailed data that describe the income of black and white single-parent families do not exist for the period. But we can infer from a variety of aggregate data that blacks were more likely to be eligible to receive ADC benefits than whites. Table 2.1 presents the racial disparity in wage income by region in 1939. These data cover all wage or salary workers, excluding those on emergency work. It includes workers with nonwage income in addition to wages as well as those for whom wages were the only income. A drawback of these data is that farmers and tenants did not receive wages and are not included in these data, so that the table does not capture farm poverty. The data are also for individuals, and so do not give a picture of family need, the criterion for ADC eligibil-

Table 2.1 Percentage of Wage Earners Earning less than $1000 and $600, by Race, for the United States and Regions, 1939

| | < $1000 | | | < $600 | | |
Region	White	Nonwhite	Difference	White	Nonwhite	Difference
United States	**54.5**	**89.2**	**34.8**	**33.8**	**72.6**	**38.8**
New England	54.6	78.3	23.7	30.4	49.3	18.9
Mid-Atlantic	50.7	78.6	27.9	30.7	53.8	23.1
East North Central	50.0	75.1	25.1	30.7	50.0	19.3
West North Central	61.5	85.0	23.5	41.9	65.0	23.1
South Atlantic	59.8	92.5	32.7	35.8	78.8	43.0
East South Central	66.8	94.5	27.7	44.1	81.7	36.9
West South Central	64.1	95.4	27.7	44.8	83.2	38.4
Mountain	56.8	81.7	24.9	37.5	60.4	22.9
Pacific	48.3	80.7	32.4	29.8	50.2	20.4

Source: U.S. Bureau of the Census, *Sixteenth Census of the United States: 1940, Population, Wage or Salary Income in 1939* (Washington, D.C.: Government Printing Office, 1943), table 5, 75–86.

ity. But the table does give an indication of the large difference between the earnings of black and white workers. Because ADC benefits were not generally available to workers, even unemployed workers, these figures do not say anything directly about ADC eligibility, but they do provide a vivid picture of the racial gap in economic levels.

The table reports the percentage of wage workers in 1939 earning below two different wage levels: $600 and $1000 per year. The higher figure approximates the poverty threshold for a family of four in the mid-1930s. A 1935 Works Progress Administration study of the cost of living in fifty-nine cities reported that the average minimum annual income required to maintain a family of four was $1261, a level that Richard Sterner found to be "completely beyond the means of the general Negro population, particularly in the South." The study also found that an emergency budget, consisting of the merest subsistence, was possible at an average annual income of $903.[92] As a comparison, the average federal poverty threshold for a family of four in 1990, converted to 1939 dollars, was about $1420.[93] The lower figure considered in Table 2.1 approximates the annual level of support contemplated by the Social Security Act for a medium-sized family. The act provided for federal reimbursement for monthly payments of up to $18 for the first child and $12 for each subsequent child, although states were free to pay higher benefits at their own expense. Payments at these levels would translate to annual benefits of $504 for a family of three children and $648 for four children. Table 2.1 thus provides a glimpse at the extreme poverty of black wage earners.

Table 2.1 shows that blacks earned less than whites throughout the country. While one-half of all wage workers earned less than $1000, nine of ten nonwhite workers fell short of this threshold. One-third of white workers were below $600, compared with nearly three-fourths of non-whites. In every region, the racial differential appears at both levels. The disparity is greater in the South than elsewhere despite higher overall levels of poverty in the South. These figures suggest that black poverty was prevalent throughout the country and that any government program for the needy would find more blacks than whites among its clients.

Another aspect of ADC eligibility was the presence of only a single parent. ADC was a federal extension of state mothers' pension laws, which provided support for impoverished single mothers who could not otherwise care for their children at home.[94] Blacks in the 1930s were not only more likely to be poor, but black families were also more likely to be headed by a single parent. In 1930, thirty percent of all black families in the United States were single-parent families, and two-thirds of these were headed by women. By comparison, twenty percent of native white families had only a single parent, about three-fifths female-headed. Single black mothers also tended to have more children than single white mothers.[95] Each link in the chain, from the incidence of poverty to family structure and size, indicates that blacks were considerably overrepresented among potential beneficiaries of ADC.

Because African-Americans stood out as potential recipients of public assistance programs, particularly ADC, the question of institutional structure—the balance between national forces and parochial interests—became one of the most contentious issues of the congressional debate, and it certainly raised the ire of Southerners more than any other issue. The controversy focused on the nature of the requirements that the bill established for state plans. There were both general and specific objections. Specifically, members opposed the requirement that old-age and ADC payments be sufficient to provide "a reasonable subsistence compatible with decency and health" and to the requirement that state administrative operations, including the hiring of personnel, be acceptable to the federal government. More generally, they charged that the administration bill gave unelected federal officials arbitrary and unrestricted power to withhold funds from states that did not measure up to their standards of professionalism and liberality. Wilbur J. Cohen, Witte's assistant at the CES, later called the deletion of these standards, especially the "decency and health" mandate, "the bill's most significant long-range loss."[96] This significance was not lost on members who viewed these provisions as an unprecedented and dangerous intrusion into states' rights and particularly into the South's distinctive, racially structured political economy.

The most vociferous critic of the bill on the grounds that it gave the federal government too much power was Senator Harry F. Byrd of Virginia. On the third day of hearings, Byrd launched into a tirade against Witte, claiming that the bill gave the federal government "dictatorial power . . . over what the State is permitted to do . . . The administrator in Washington is to be the sole judge as to whether or not a State receives any of this appropriation from the Federal Government." A few moments later, Byrd turned up the rhetorical heat, invoking the classic phrases of states' rights:

Senator Byrd Do I understand, Doctor, that this Administrator has supreme power to deny a sovereign state of this Union any benefits of this pension system at all unless that State complies with the regulations that he makes and thinks are proper.

> Mr. Witte That is putting it in little stronger terms than I would.
> Senator Byrd Is that not the truth under this legislation if it is enacted as it is now?
> Mr. Witte Perhaps, theoretically, so.[97]

Witte's rather weak and disingenuous response was that although the Social Security Board technically could suspend payments to a state for noncompliance, the idea was that the board would simply review the state *law* establishing the program. Moreover, he pointed out, these provisions were no different from standards in other federal grant-in-aid laws, which had only rarely resulted in an outright suspension of payments to a state.[98] But as a more recent student of welfare policy has pointed out, "unlike the situation in highway policy . . . public assistance introduces problems of race, of sex, of religion, and of family relationships. It is hard to think of four areas most American politicians would rather avoid."[99]

Byrd was the loudest but not the only congressional critic of the federal control provisions of the bill. Harrison expressed concern about this question several times over the course of the hearings, but so did Hugo Black of Alabama, a New Deal supporter and one of the most perceptive members of the Finance Committee. Black referred to the bill as "federal coercion." The provisions for federal control also provoked opposition from Republicans Allen T. Treadway of Massachusetts, the ranking member of the Ways and Means Committee, and Senator Daniel O. Hastings of Delaware, who eventually supported the bill despite "the great damages which such action . . . will bring to the principles on which our Government was founded," namely state sovereignty.[100]

The race question lurked just beneath the surface of this debate, precipitated as it was largely by Southerners. When Representative Howard W. Smith of Virginia—who was to become famous when, as chairman of the House Rules Committee, he obstructed the passage of civil rights legislation—appeared before the Ways and Means Committee to oppose excessive federal controls, the race issue broke through. Smith proposed adding to the bill "a provision that would allow the States to differentiate between persons" in paying benefits. He went on to note that of Virginia's 116,000 people over age 65, "practically 25 percent are of one class that will probably qualify 100 percent." Thomas A. Jenkins of Ohio asked Smith what he meant, provoking an exchange that is worth quoting in full:

> Mr. Smith Of course, in the South we have a great many colored people, and they are largely of the laboring class.

Mr. Jenkins This is what I thought the gentleman had in mind. I should like to ask the gentleman, and also any member of this committee, whether in this law it is contemplated that there be any loophole by which any State could discriminate against any class of people? Mr. Smith No sir; I do not think so, and you will not find in my remarks any suggestion to that effect. It just so happens that that race is in our State very much of the laboring class and farm laboring class. But you will find no suggestion in my remarks of any suggested amendment that would be unconstitutional, if I may use that expression.[101]

This exchange demonstrates that Southern congressmen saw and understood the racial implications of creating a national welfare state that assigned the industrial working class to national policies and those at the margins of the industrial economy to parochial ones. Smith's attention to state control of welfare policy exposes for a brief but telling moment the deeply entwined logic of race, class, and power that shaped welfare policymaking. His invocation of the "constitutionality" of the South's concerns evokes the discourse of racial exclusion that white Southern elites constructed in the late nineteenth and early twentieth centuries as they sought to disenfranchise and segregate African-Americans while remaining within the bounds of the Civil War amendments, which seemed to prohibit these very moves.[102] When Captain Renault professes to be "shocked, shocked" to discover gambling at Rick's, we believe it is just a pretext to shut the place down; when the croupier hands him his winnings, which he happily pockets, we are sure. Smith's denial that he is interested in restricting black access to benefits rings just as false and is just as transparent.

To African-Americans, the implications of parochial administration was no secret, and African-American leaders vocally opposed the decentralization of ADC. The NAACP supported nationalizing public assistance and opposed the bill precisely because the standards, which Byrd and others so strenuously resisted, were too weak to prevent discriminatory administration at the state level. "From the point of view of the Negro," Houston told the Finance Committee, "it would be much easier to get fair enforcement of a Federal law than to get a really effective old-age assistance law passed by southern legislatures."[103] Representative Arthur W. Mitchell of Illinois, the first black Democrat ever to serve in Congress, made his maiden speech to the House on the bill criticizing state administration of public assistance and calling for greater federal financing and control. The

Amsterdam News, New York City's leading African-American newspaper, wrote that "most of us should be able to remember how state benefits are dispensed in the South." Inside the administration, Harry Hopkins echoed these worries.[104] Ever a thorn in the Roosevelt administration's side, Huey Long spoke bluntly of the racial consequences of parochialism: "Furthermore, who in the South is the most needful of pensions assistance? . . . Mr. President, it is the colored man. How many colored people do you think would get on one of these select lists? Let's be frank about this business. I am possibly the only Southern Senator here who can be frank about it."[105] The view that blacks were better served by federal than by state administration of government assistance was common among black leaders in the 1930s; the early history of the New Deal, during which federally sponsored relief and other programs actually reached blacks to a much greater extent than any government effort in generations, provided powerful evidence for this proposition. There were, of course, limits to the effectiveness of federal power to overcome local patterns of segregation—the federal government itself remained segregated, and even strong national authority often had to make its peace with local customs and institutions in order to accomplish anything. On balance, however, national welfare policy clearly offered African-Americans greater promise of fairness, progress, and opportunity.[106]

Nevertheless, the Ways and Means Committee, in closed session, relaxed the federal control provisions substantially. The committee eliminated the "decency and health" clause, giving states much more leeway in setting benefit levels. This move effectively removed any potential federal lever of *operational* control over state ADC administration, leaving the federal government with only the weaker and blunter power to approve or disapprove the *design* of state plans and thereby fulfilling Witte's rather artless response to Byrd's inquiry.[107] The committee also removed personnel matters from the administrative requirements, relaxed the minimum eligibility standards, and provided for a hearing before the federal government could cut off a state's funding. Witte, who attended many of the committee's executive sessions, had little doubt that these amendments resulted from Southern fears of federal interference. "The Southern members," he wrote, "did not want to give authority to anyone in Washington to deny aid to any state because it discriminated against Negroes in the administration" of public assistance.[108]

The Southern assault on the federal control potential of the bill continued in the floor debate, even after the Ways and Means amendments.

One member, Representative E. E. Cox of Georgia, gave the classic Jeffersonian argument in defense of states' rights. Lamenting the decline of the Democratic party's adherence to decentralized and limited government, he predicted the rise of a third party "to lead the people of this country who adhere to the belief that the Federal Government is a government of delegated powers, and is sovereign only to the extent of supreme and exclusive exercise of those powers."[109] This was perhaps the most overwrought attack on the bill, but it was not atypical. The contrasting rhetoric of two of the bill's most important Senate supporters perhaps best embodies the tension inherent in the creation of a national welfare state and the sectional—and hence racial and class—stresses that were already apparent in the governing coalition that produced it. Pat Harrison, whose legislative prowess helped shepherd the bill through the Senate, was almost apologetic in explaining to his colleagues that the public assistance titles of the bill contained "an absolute minimum of Federal participation." Robert Wagner, the preeminent legislative leader of the New Deal's Northern urban liberal arm, celebrated the "fundamental requirements" that the bill imposed on the states, which would help ensure generally uniform and adequate benefits.[110] That these two senators, approaching the matter from opposite perspectives, could agree at all seems astonishing; the grounds of their agreement suggests that the space available for compromise on these questions was narrow indeed.

These rhetorical attacks on the bill, however, masked deep ambiguity among Southerners about the federal role in social security and revealed the inconsistency in their invocation of states' rights. The use of states' rights as an argument against certain aspects of the public assistance requirements contrasts sharply with the striking absence of such arguments in the debate on Old-Age Insurance, surely a much greater assumption of national power. A consistent constitutional objection to centralization ought to have appeared there as well. If Southerners or others objected on principle to the expansion of the national government's powers and responsibilities in the Social Security Act, they would have been more inclined simply to oppose the bill altogether. However, almost no Southerners voted against the bill (nor did almost anyone else, for that matter). The South in particular, and the states in general, desperately needed expanded federal involvement both to meet the short-term need for relief and to establish long-term economic security programs. A few Southerners—most notably Harry Byrd—took a consistent position in support of states' rights and voted against the bill. But most railed against the encroachment of federal power at the same time that they supported the bill, accepting not only the federal benefits it created but also the federal power it represented, and in fact they used states' rights arguments selectively. The careful manipulation of the target populations and administrative structures meant that they could support the Social Security Act without believing that they had undermined the important right that they wished to preserve for their states—the right to maintain an economic and social system of segregation and white supremacy.

Although they attacked excessive federal power, many Southerners supported a series of amendments to provide federal public assistance funds to poor states that could not afford the matching funds required by the grant-in-aid programs. In support of one such amendment, Representative William M. Colmer of Mississippi raised the specter of "a new imaginary line . . . like a veritable Mason and Dixon's line that would divide this great country of ours into two sections," rich and poor. The imagery of his remarks left little doubt about where he thought that line would be drawn. All of these amendments were either withdrawn or defeated by voice vote, but of ten members who spoke in favor, five were from the South and three from border states. It took John McCormack to point out to these members the logical, not to mention political, inconsistencies of their position—in favor of entirely federal funding of public assistance but opposed to federal control.[111]

Unemployment Insurance

The question of federal control also shaped the debate on Unemployment Insurance, the third major component of the Social Security Act. During the first decades of the twentieth century, American reformers came to favor unemployment insurance schemes that focused principally on regulating employment and preventing unemployment rather than on providing income for the unemployed.[112] The Depression experience of Great Britain, whose unemployment insurance system began to resemble a permanent "dole," heightened this emphasis among American intellectuals and policymakers, including Franklin Roosevelt.[113] In 1932, Wisconsin adopted the country's first unemployment insurance scheme along these lines, funded by a payroll tax on employers with tax breaks for companies that laid off few employees. The Wisconsin approach to unemployment insurance quickly ran into two serious obstacles. The first was the problem of interstate competition. Firms in states that levied unemployment taxes on employers would be at a competitive disadvantage compared with firms not subject to such taxes. This problem had severely hindered the progress of unemployment compensation proposals in the United States and was the crucial impetus behind the drive for a federal role.[114] The Social Security Act of 1935 overcame the interstate competition problem by imposing a federal payroll tax against which employers could take a credit for state unemployment taxes. The inducement worked; by the middle of 1937 every state had passed an unemployment insurance law.[115]

The second obstacle to the preventive approach was the unemployment insurance plan developed in Ohio, which was concerned with maintaining an adequate fund to aid unemployed workers and their families rather than stabilizing the labor market. The Wisconsin approach lowered tax rates for employers that maintained stable levels of employment, providing an incentive against large fluctuations in employment but also possibly compromising the amount of money available for benefits. The Ohio plan, which promised more adequate benefits for the unemployed, had strong support, not least from organized labor. But the Committee on Economic Security, which wrote the legislation, was staffed prominently by Wisconsin economists who were veterans of that state's unemployment battles and had personal stakes in protecting the Wisconsin plan. The House Ways and Means Committee eliminated the Wisconsin option on the grounds that it would reintroduce the problem of interstate competition, but the Senate Finance Committee, at the urging of Senator Robert LaFollette of Wisconsin, restored the Wisconsin option. In the end, the Social Security Act was agnostic on the type of plan states could adopt, and Wisconsin-style variable tax rates that rewarded stable employers became the norm.[116]

The failure of the Ohio plan to gain widespread adoption had important consequences for Unemployment Insurance and its meaning for African-Americans. Merit rating, the system of variable tax rates aimed at stabilizing employment, meant lower revenues for state programs and, consequently, downward pressure on UI benefits, not to mention frequent fiscal crises for state UI funds. But the turn away from income support as a basis for Unemployment Insurance was also a turn away from the comprehensive employment policy component of Franklin Roosevelt's economic security program. In his message to Congress of January 1935 introducing the Social Security Act, the president advanced a vision of Unemployment Insurance as part of a larger program of employment security. He acknowledged the need to stabilize employment but added that "this can be helped by the intelligent planning of both public and private employment.

It can also be helped by correlating the system with public employment so that a person who has exhausted his benefits may be eligible for some form of public work."[117] Roosevelt recognized that stabilizing employment was only part of the game; as the experience of the Depression had already shown and as John Maynard Keynes would elaborate later in the decade, an economy could sustain stable employment at a frighteningly low level. In keeping with his idea of "cradle-to-grave" economic security, Roosevelt saw in 1935 an opportunity to create an interconnected system of unemployment insurance and public works that would not only stabilize private employment but also provide both adequate benefits during inevitable periods of unemployment and public employment as a last resort. But the Social Security Act sheared off the last two of these functions, leaving a narrow and rigid legacy for Unemployment Insurance in the American welfare state. In rejecting more comprehensive visions of unemployment insurance, the United States rejected the pieces of employment policy that had the most to offer African-Americans. As African-Americans left the land and traveled to the city in search of a living, coming under the protection of Unemployment Insurance, they discovered that the program ironically failed them, not because it excluded them either categorically or administratively but because its structural boundaries replicated those of the labor market.

For a number of reasons, however, the exclusion of agricultural and domestic workers produced considerably less comment in the debate on Unemployment Insurance than in the OAI debate. First, the explicit considerations were essentially the same, principally the administrative difficulty of collecting taxes from employers of farmers and servants. Abraham Epstein, for example, made a case for exclusion identical to his argument regarding Old-Age Insurance.[118] The suggestion that inclusion would prove excessively burdensome to farmers also appeared, as did the claim that exclusion was unfair and unjustifiable.[119] But beyond these brief recapitulations, these arguments were not prominent.

The second reason that the exclusion issue was dormant in the discussion of Unemployment Insurance is that there were two more fundamental questions that arose about the structure of the bill's unemployment program, both of which received more attention and also affected the potential racial imbalance of the program. First, the cooperative federal-state character of the program, which had been contentious in the Committee on Economic Security, also proved controversial in Congress. Second, a competing proposal for a more comprehensive, national program of unemployment relief had some support in Congress.

This alternative proposal, known as the Lundeen plan after its sponsor, Farmer-Labor Representative Ernest Lundeen of Minnesota, was for a national system of unemployment compensation paid by the federal government to all unemployed workers and financed from general revenues, not through a system of employer or employee contributions. It was attractive to many members of Congress because, unlike the social security bill, it would have provided immediate relief to the millions of Americans who were out of work at that moment. Lundeen stressed that it was an inclusive, national program that would place very little discretion in the hands of administrators.[120] The administration plan, in contrast, was a prospective measure that protected only workers whose employers had made contributions on their behalf to a compensation fund while they were working. Its purpose, its proponents stressed, was not only to compensate the unemployed but primarily to prevent unemployment by providing employers with an incentive to stabilize employment.[121] The Lundeen bill was approved by the House Labor Committee but was defeated when offered as an amendment to the social security bill.

The victory of the administration's plan over the Lundeen plan constituted a critical moment for African-Americans and their participation in employment and unemployment policy. In the short term, only employed workers would potentially benefit from unemployment compensation. In the long term, individuals or groups who tended to be chronically unemployed would be denied coverage. Both of these consequences had the effect of excluding blacks from coverage at a greater rate than whites, in addition to the effects of excluding agricultural and domestic workers outlined in Figures 2.1 and 2.2. The cumulative result was the definition of a boundary around unemployment insurance, a boundary demarcated by the racially segmented structure of the labor market. African-American workers were largely consigned not only to sectors that were excluded from coverage but also to casual and intermittent work that further detached them from the benefits—both remunerative and stabilizing—of unemployment insurance. Those benefits, the administration's plan made clear, were for the white workers of Northern industry.

African-American leaders understood very well what was at stake in the unemployment insurance debate, and they opposed the restrictive features of the administration's plan. Charles Houston of the NAACP argued against the unemployment insurance provisions of the social security bill on the grounds that it did not provide for already unemployed workers. In response to the administration's argument that it also hoped to expand its public works program in order to meet this problem, Houston pointed out that in many instances public works hiring was discriminatory. Finally, Houston pointed out that the bill included protections for organized labor, whereas blacks tended to be unorganized. The NAACP supported the Lundeen bill, as did other African-American organizations. T. Arnold Hill of the National Urban League spoke and wrote in favor of the Lundeen bill specifically because it was both national and racially inclusive. It also contained a nondiscrimination clause, for which African-American groups had unsuccessfully lobbied in the administration's bill.[122]

In immediate terms, Unemployment Insurance was doubly discriminatory against African-American workers. As with OAI, occupational exclusions worked to limit African-American participation in unemployment insurance. But a policy that required steady work *before* eligibility for benefits worked against even those African-Americans who worked in the industrial and commercial jobs covered by the plan because it did not provide relief for workers who were then unemployed. Figure 2.3 shows the

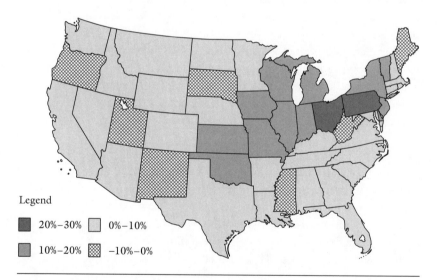

Figure 2.3. Racial disparity in unemployment rate for workers in covered occupations, 1937.

Sources: U.S. Census of Partial Employment, Unemployment, and Occupations, *Final Report on Total and Partial Unemployment, 1937* (Washington, D.C.: Government Printing Office, 1938), table 3; U.S. Bureau of the Census, *Sixteenth Census of the United States: 1940, Population* (Washington, D.C.: Government Printing Office, 1943), vol. 3, table 13.

racial disparity in the estimated unemployment rate for workers in occupations other than agriculture and domestic service—that is, for workers who were eligible for unemployment coverage.[123] Several comments are in order here about the data in Figure 2.3. First, the unemployment figures presented are from a special census of unemployment taken in 1937. This census counted only individuals who were unemployed and did not count the entire labor force, so it is impossible to calculate a precise unemployment rate. Instead, I have used as the base labor force for the unemployment rate population data from the 1940 census. I chose the 1940 census over 1930 for several reasons. First, 1937 is chronologically closer to 1940, so the estimate is likely to be more accurate. Second, the 1937 count, like the 1940 census, includes persons fourteen years or older in the labor force; until 1930 the count included persons ten years or older.[124] One drawback of the 1940 census is that it does not report occupations for new workers looking for work, presumably because the Depression greatly increased the number of Americans who had never held a job and thus could not report an occupation in the traditional sense. Thus the base for the percentages represented in Figure 2.3 is the total only of people working and experienced workers looking for work. It excludes those on emergency work, who presumably neither qualified for nor needed (as much) unemployment compensation. Because workers who had never had a job are included in the numerator but not in the denominator, the calculations probably slightly overestimate unemployment rates across the board. The concern here, however, is in racial *differences* in unemployment, so this slight error, as long as it is consistent, should not affect the conclusions.[125] Finally, because the special census did not report unemployment data for white workers, Figure 2.3 reports differences between the unemployment rate for black workers and the entire labor force, rather than the more telling black-white difference.

Black unemployment in UI-covered occupations was considerably higher than for the entire population. One in five black workers was out of work nationwide, compared with one in eight in the total labor force. As Figure 2.3 shows, the states with the highest disparity were northern-tier industrial states, in which black workers were generally shunned by labor unions and, with few skills and little seniority, were often the first workers to be let go in hard times.[126] The Southern states generally had lower rates of black unemployment and consequently smaller, but still mostly positive, disparities. Only seven states, including Mississippi, had black unemployment rates lower than the overall rate. In conjunction with the exclusion of farm workers and servants displayed in Figures 2.1 and 2.2, Figure 2.3 presents a picture of black exclusion from benefits at a consistently higher rate than the rest of the population.

Unemployment Insurance, like Old-Age Insurance, was designed to benefit mostly white, regularly employed industrial workers. In contrast to the development of OAI, however, the advocates of national Unemployment Insurance were unable to parlay these racially consequential restrictions of the program's target population into a truly national institutional structure. The data presented in Figure 2.3 suggest at least part of the reason for this result. In the short run, Unemployment Insurance offered protection only to currently employed workers, a predominantly white portion of an already predominantly white class of workers. But in the longer run—say, in future recessions—the disproportionate unemployment of African-Americans meant that black workers would be more likely to seek unemployment benefits. The institutional structure of the program was thus potentially consequential in defining the racial impact of Unemployment Insurance.

A thoroughly national program of unemployment insurance actually had substantial support in the administration, in Congress, and among interested groups.[127] African-American leaders in particular supported national unemployment insurance, and Charles Houston of the NAACP testified against the administration's proposal on the grounds that it was not sufficiently national and that parochial administration would work against black workers. Israel Amter, a leader of the American Communist Party and the secretary of the Communist-sponsored National Unemployed Councils, explicitly echoed this concern, warning that "the State governments may exercise discriminatory powers against certain sections of the population—for instance the Negro and the foreign-born."[128] Despite this support, entirely national unemployment insurance on the old-age insurance model was never really on the table. For one thing, its advocates feared that the Supreme Court would declare a national UI scheme unconstitutional—although the proponents of national Old-Age Insurance faced, and overcame, the same objection. For another, many members of Congress simply objected to the expansion of national power when state and local alternatives were available. Unlike contributory Old-Age Insurance, which was a novel proposition in American welfare politics, unemployment insurance had been on the drawing board in a number of states before 1935.[129]

Although the Committee on Economic Security had abandoned the idea of an entirely national unemployment insurance system in November 1934, there were continuing machinations, both within the administration and in Congress, and it was not until the defeat of the Lundeen plan that the idea of an inclusive, national program was finally put to rest.[130] So the question of institutional structure came down to a choice between levels of national control and mechanisms of parochial discretion. At stake in what appeared to be a narrow, technical decision were questions of national control and adequate benefits.[131] Those who preferred strong national control of UI policy and restricted state and local control of administration generally supported the subsidy plan, under which the federal government would collect taxes and distribute funds to the states.[132] William Green, president of the American Federation of Labor, for example, favored the subsidy plan because he felt that it would better allow the federal government to establish and enforce minimum standards for state legislation.[133]

At the same time, there was also support for the tax offset plan that the Committee on Economic Security had supported. Economist Alvin Hansen of the State Department, a member of the CES technical board, supported the tax offset plan for precisely the opposite reason, that it would give the federal government more control than the subsidy plan. Hansen argued that by keeping UI funds in the hands of the federal government, in the form of a trust fund in the Treasury, the tax offset plan would allow the federal government to control the administration of Unemployment Insurance more closely and thus avoid the decentralization and parochialism many feared.[134] Whether or not it was substantively preferable, the key administration insiders—Witte, Altmeyer, and Eliot—believed the tax offset plan to be politically the most practical, in Congress as well as the courts.

Even the tax offset plan, however, rankled some Southern representatives who did not like the federal standards that states would have to meet to qualify for a tax offset or for federal funding for administration. The Ways and Means Committee dropped some of these standards, most prominently the requirement that state unemployment insurance programs be staffed by civil service personnel. Southern opposition even to the tax offset plan, which granted the federal government only the mildest control of UI policy, alarmed administration officials and confirmed their belief that ceding control to the states was necessary to secure the passage of any unemployment insurance legislation. "I was glad," wrote Thomas Eliot, "that I'd so vehemently opposed the subsidy plan. I had done so in part because I thought the Court would strike it down; now I came to feel that its safe passage through Congress would have been problematical at best."[135] Southerners were not, however, the only members of Congress to voice worries about the assumption of national power in unemployment insurance. Senator Arthur Capper, a Kansas Republican, asked whether the administration's unemployment program sufficiently protected "the rights and privileges of the States to the extent that it should?".[136] Capper was a national board member of the NAACP, so his invocation of states' rights clearly carried no intent toward racial discrimination. Nevertheless, the potential racial consequences of even the partial parochialization of unemployment insurance were on full view.

The roots of the institutional structure of unemployment insurance were deep and complex, partaking not only of race-laden, class-based, and regional definitions of the program's target population but also of the policy legacy of state-level initiatives and partisan and institutional politics. The structure of the tax offset plan, neither entirely national nor parochial, did give the federal government a fair amount of control over the states, a danger for Southerners in a program with a potentially racially inclusive clientele. But the occupational exclusions and the link between benefits and work mitigated this concern and, as with Old-Age Insurance, made new federal administrative involvements palatable.

Conclusions

Despite differences in policy legacies and target populations, each of these three policies emerged in the Social Security Act with important racially relevant exclusions that were linked in significant ways to administrative structures. Old-Age Insurance and Unemployment Insurance excluded agricultural and domestic workers, eliminating most African-Americans from their benefits. Moreover, they relied on steady and long-term work, further restricting their applicability to African-Americans. Aid to Dependent Children, which had the potential to benefit many needy African-Americans, was stripped of even the modest mechanisms of federal supervision that the Roosevelt administration had tried to insert into an already parochial design. Each of these programs challenged the racial structure of American society in a distinctive way, creating new benefits or encouraging states to create or expand benefits that might have undermined the tight racial control that white Southerners maintained over their society and economy. In each case, Congress acted to expand the reach of national welfare policy, creating the template for a seemingly permanent national commitment to social provision. But in order to construct a legislative package that was broadly acceptable across regions and political parties, Roosevelt and his congressional interlocutors agreed to restrict the scope and reach of the new national capacity. The resulting compromise, though it created entirely new claims on the protection of the state for millions of citizens, still reinforced many existing structural divides in American society—divides of class (particularly occupation and status in the labor force), region, and gender. These divides were, perforce, also divides of race, and the institutional compromise of the Social Security Act effectively sorted Americans by race into different emerging welfare categories. In some cases, restricting the racial scope meant excluding heavily black occupations from national or quasi-national programs, whereas in other cases it meant restraining the breadth of federal supervisory powers over programs that threatened to aid a disproportionately black population.

The comparison of these three policies suggests that the racial structure of American society and politics, embedded as it was in class and regional conflict and reflected in structures of political power, shaped the institutional development of the American welfare state. Politically constructed differences in the target populations of the three policies produced not a unified national administrative welfare state, as Franklin Roosevelt envisioned, but a fragmented set of institutions. The Social Security Act represented an important advance for African-Americans. After the Civil War, the Freedmen's Bureau aided millions of freed slaves, and African-Americans who fought in the Civil War were included fairly and honorably in the system of Civil War pensions that flourished in the late nineteenth century.[137] For most African-Americans, however, social policy before the New Deal had done little. The New Deal dramatically expanded the national government's social policy commitments and capacities, providing to racial minorities at least the prospect of assistance in averting poverty. But the potential for racial inclusion severely constrained the state-building impulse of the New Deal. The only national social insurance program the Social Security Act produced was racially exclusionary in key ways because occupations heavily populated by African-Americans were excluded. At the same time, the public assistance programs that had the greatest potential to help some poor African-Americans immediately were parochially structured in ways that limited that potential.

What would be the consequences for African-Americans of this curious mixture of social policy institutions? The creation of these different social policy institutions in the New Deal set each policy on a unique path of political and institutional development. These divergent developments have reordered the racial structure of American society by selectively incorporating African-Americans into the welfare state in different ways. The irony, and the puzzle, of American welfare development is that the initial inclusion or exclusion of African-Americans in these policies in 1935 does not by itself predict how African-Americans would be treated by administrators or policymakers in the following generations. It is the race-laden administrative institutions of social policy that hold the key to the subsequent development of the American welfare state, as the next three chapters demonstrate.

3

Old-Age Insurance: From Exclusion to Inclusion

Old-Age Insurance was built on a shaky foundation in 1935. It was founded with occupational exclusions that left out most African-American workers, and any program of expansion would have to overcome these barriers. Linked to its race-laden exclusionary boundaries, however, was its centralized national administrative structure that would provide benefits to eligible workers as a matter of statutorily defined right. This link between racial exclusion and the national, rights-based structure of OAI appeared contradictory. But if de facto racial exclusion had made possible a strong institutional structure, this institutional structure pushed the program toward inclusion in what amounted to a process of policy feedback. The program's own institutional characteristics created political forces in both state and society that not only buttressed Social Security's fragile political support but also pushed it to expand. As millions of American workers acquired a stake in OAI, deep public support developed, and a network of group interests evolved to protect the program and its beneficiaries. As OAI's administrative apparatus grew in size and stature, its leaders grew in political and bureaucratic skill, creating an institutional platform on which to build an expanding social insurance regime. African-Americans, excluded at the outset by the class definition of the programs, gained entry into Social Security not simply through the bargaining of group politics but because the program itself created the political conditions that gave national politicians, program bureaucrats, and the program's original beneficiaries—white industrial workers—a common interest in an expanding target population. The impulse toward growth and inclusion overcame the imperatives of racial exclusion in the 1940s and 1950s, with the ironic result that the exclusionary Old-Age Insurance program of 1935 became, by the 1960s, perhaps the closest thing to a race-blind social program the United States has ever known.

The Social Security Act created the template of a strong, national institutional structure to administer Old-Age Insurance. But like any new enterprise, it was a risky proposition. And Social Security was not just any new enterprise, but a politically controversial new government program of historic scale and scope, not to mention dubious constitutionality, that propelled the American national government into social provision with a depth and permanence never before attempted. The early years of OAI were thus critical in filling out the institutional architecture that would support the program in the future and help to determine its treatment of African-Americans. The characteristics of the program laid out in the Social Security Act were important, but the establishment of an institutional pattern for Old-Age Insurance also depended on the political dynamics of the late 1930s, when party conflict, personal leadership, and historical contingency combined to anchor Social Security in the foundation of American politics.

Old-Age Insurance and the Politics of Institutional Structure

The institutional structure that the Social Security Act established for Old-Age Insurance was decidedly national. It was to be a straightforward, centralized program, administered by a single national bureaucracy that dealt directly with the program's clientele. It was also a fairly transparent policy; it was easy to grasp, at least in its broad outlines, and its implementation was easily observed, both by individuals and by the political system at large. The structure of the policy and its institutional characteristics amounted to a truly national program, which developed the capacity to deliver large amounts of assistance to millions of people effectively and efficiently, and thereby changed the landscape of American welfare politics.

The Policy Design of Old-Age Insurance

Old-Age Insurance began life in 1935 as a procedurally egalitarian policy, and it has remained so. The Social Security Act clearly stated rules to determine who was to pay taxes, how much they were to pay, who was eligible to receive benefits, and how much they were to receive. Most significantly, as many students of American welfare policy have noted, recipients of OAI benefits were not subject to a means test.[1] The only eligibility test was, in effect, procedural—whether an individual had spent the requisite number of years in covered employment, reached the appropriate age, and so forth. The amount of her benefit bore relation not to her need, but to her work and wage history, which had been duly recorded throughout her working life. The original 1935 formula linked benefits to the total amount of taxes a worker had paid throughout his working life. In 1939, before OAI benefit payments had even begun, the formula was changed so that benefit levels would be linked to a worker's wages toward the end of his career. This shift from "equity"—benefits as a return on taxes paid—toward "adequacy"—benefits based on some kind of need standard—did not alter the basic structure of the benefit, which could still be determined through the mechanical application of rules to individual cases, although it did signal a move toward a purer social insurance model of old-age benefits and away from a more redistributive welfare model.[2] Two people with identical work and wage histories could thus expect identical results when they retired, whereas someone who retired with a lower benefit than his neighbor could understand that this happened because he had a lower paying job than his neighbor, not because he was a victim of capriciously applied rules.

In addition to being procedurally egalitarian, OAI was, of course, a contributory program. Wage earners were to pay taxes into the program, and the only way to get benefits at the other end was to have paid taxes in the first place (or to be related to someone who had). The result of this combination of procedural equality and contributory financing was that OAI benefits acquired the status of rights that retired workers could claim against the government in return for having fulfilled their obligation to pay taxes while working. In fact, this was precisely how Social Security executives understood the program, and they deftly exploited this political view.[3] In 1953, the Republican-controlled House created a special Ways and Means subcommittee on Social Security, chaired by Carl T. Curtis of Nebraska, who was hostile to the idea of contributory social insurance. Arthur J. Altmeyer, who had retired as commissioner of social security at the end of the Truman administration, was summoned to appear before the subcommittee to defend the social insurance model of Social Security. Curtis objected to the characterization of OAI as "insurance," because it did not rest on explicit contracts between individuals and the insurer, in this case the federal government, and he insisted that the "right" to benefits was not secure because the federal government could erase it unilaterally simply by repealing the law. Altmeyer replied that he regarded OAI as a "statutory right" that is, he pointed out, enforceable in court, and that a statutory right is stronger than a contractual right "because you have a responsible legislative body, the Congress of the United States. You have at the present time about 90 million people who have accumulated wage credits. Now, it is inconceivable to me that the Congress of the United States would ever think of taking action to prejudice their rights that have developed under existing legislation."[4] Altmeyer, in essence, dared Curtis and the Republicans to repeal Old-Age Insurance. He understood that OAI created a strong expectation, approaching certainty, of future benefits in return for current obligations, an expectation (an "entitlement" in current lingo) that if anything has strengthened over time so that protecting Social Security benefits has become a necessary piety for both parties in presidential and congressional campaigns, even in the face of tremendous budget deficits.[5] In the 1990s, pundits dubbed Social Security the "third rail" of American politics—touch it and you die.

Most important, this combination of procedural equality and the linkage of benefits and contributions produced a pattern of policy feedback that gave the program an expansionary political logic.[6] In this feedback process, characteristics of the policy created political conditions not simply among elites but among a mass public that made the incorporation of new groups politically easy regardless of race or other characteristics. By linking benefits to contributions, OAI created a perpetual constituency for itself. As Roosevelt remarked in 1935, "with those taxes in there, no damn politician can ever scrap my social security program."[7] Those workers who began paying OAI taxes in 1937 (the first year taxes were collected) had an instant stake in the program and an interest in keeping the payroll tax as low as possible for as long as possible. This objective could be accomplished either by restricting benefits or by finding new sources of revenue, which meant, as long as there were uncovered workers, bringing new workers into the system. The constituency for OAI has always had a strong organizational presence in American politics, from the Townsend movement to the American Association of Retired Persons, which has effectively mobilized older Americans into one of the most powerful interest groups in Washington.[8] Although Jerry Cates argues that the early Social Security leaders promoted the expansion of OAI at the expense of public assistance for ideological reasons, it is clear that their behavior also conforms to this expansionary political logic.[9]

The Administrative Structure of Old-Age Insurance

National administration of OAI had important racial consequences for the program. National communities are clearly capable of strong, even violent, expressions of racism, as the tragic history of the twentieth century demonstrates all too well. At the same time, however, large, pluralist nations are also less susceptible to outright capture by majorities intent on suppressing the rights of minorities.[10] Throughout American history, the main beneficiaries of federalism have been Southern whites, "who have been given the freedom to oppress Negroes, first as slaves and later as a depressed caste," although social policy discrimination was by no means restricted to the South.[11] Administration at the national level meant a high level of professionalism in the Social Security Board and its successor, the Social Security Administration. Federal administration at least offered the possibility of protection against discrimination, as the experience of other New Deal policies demonstrated, and the national Democratic party's growing reliance on Northern black votes meant at least more uniform sensitivity at the national level to racial concerns.[12] It is a profound dilemma of American politics that policymaking and administration at some remove from direct popular scrutiny and control have often paved the most effective paths toward achieving the goals of an inclusive, liberal society.[13] The national setting of Old-Age Insurance, which deprived state and local majorities of any opportunity to discriminate in its administration, underscores this irony.

Within the federal government, Old-Age Insurance was also quite well insulated from political pressure. It had relatively little patronage to dispense, as most of the employees of the Social Security Board fell under federal civil service rules.[14] Until it started paying benefits in 1941, the work of OAI was almost entirely procedural—it produced very little in the way of concrete results, although it employed an awful lot of people doing an awful lot of work. As a procedural agency, it relied heavily on standard operating procedures and carefully defined routines to ensure smooth operations, and these administrative details generally provoked little political response.[15] By the time it did begin paying benefits and was thus potentially more subject to political scrutiny, its basic political stance of independent professionalism had already been established.[16] At the federal level, the operation of OAI was governed by the details of the Social Security Act. OAI required little in the way of rulemaking or adjudication, procedures that give interested parties access to policy implementation. And the Social Security Board, at least initially, was an independent agency, relatively immune even from presidential interference. Because OAI operated only at the federal level, it afforded no political access to actors at lower levels. The political independence of OAI has promoted both inclusive administration and expansion of the program.

Even at the national level there were relatively few points of access to the early operations of the Social Security Board, and it was not a contentious or controversial political battleground. The few areas where access and the interests of observers did coincide were relatively minor, and the stakes were small. Although the board was responsible for the other Social Security Act policies as well, the Bureau of Old-Age Insurance employed nearly two-thirds of its staff in 1937, reflecting OAI's status as the board's primary responsibility.[17] Because of the essentially procedural nature of the administration of OAI, the initial work of the board principally involved setting up the system to record the wage and tax data of the millions of workers who would enter the OAI system when it went into operation on 1 January 1937. As a result, the administrative decisions of the board and its staff principally concerned internal administrative details that were of little interest to outsiders. It was "grubby work, getting things set up," as one participant described it, not the sort of work that piqued the interest and attention of most political observers.[18]

There were incidents of controversy, one of which went to the heart of the prospects for black workers in the OAI system. The proposed application blank for establishing social security accounts included a line requesting the applicant's race. The ever-vigilant NAACP protested, fearing that such knowledge about individual applicants could be used for discriminatory purposes. The protest prompted a cordial but pointed exchange of letters between Walter White and Louis Resnick, the Social Security Board's chief public spokesman. Resnick claimed that the information was solely for the benign purpose of correctly identifying participating workers, as in communities where many people in the same community had the same name. "What has race to do with that?" White retorted. "Why did the blanks not make such further differentiation as blonde, brunette; Gentile, Protestant, Mohammedan, etc.; and other demarcation which would assist in identification?"[19] The NAACP's protest came to nothing, and the original Social Security application blanks requested racial information.

There were also, of course, fights with members of Congress, the most serious being a spat in 1937 with Senator Carter Glass of Virginia, chairman of the Appropriations Committee.[20] Senator Glass's feud with the board involved the two most common sources of conflict, personnel and the location of field offices. At Glass's behest, the board had reluctantly hired an undesirable and evidently unqualified employee as a highly paid "expert," although she complained to Glass that she was mistreated and underpaid. Further raising Glass's ire, the board initially slated a field office to be located in Lynchburg, his hometown, eliminated the office for budgetary reasons, and then reinstated it when the budget picture brightened. Glass responded by cutting the board's administrative appropriation by $1 million and reducing the salary of Frank Bane, the board's executive director, by $500.

Congressional interest in the board's activities was generally limited to matters of patronage and the odd distributional benefit. Ordinarily, civil service requirements limited congressional access to patronage. The "expert" clause of the Social Security Act, which allowed the board to evade civil service requirements for specialized employees, proved a double-edged sword for the board; it relied on the clause to find qualified professionals and pay them competitive salaries, but it complicated the board's relations with Congress, which saw the clause as a patronage opening, and the Civil Service Commission, which was reluctant to give clearance to many expert appointments. One of the original board members, Vincent Miles, was a Southerner and a member of the Democratic National Committee. He managed to smooth many political ruffles in the personnel process, and the board, always anxious about appropriations, paid particular attention to requests from members of the appropriations committees. Senator Joseph Guffey of Pennsylvania nearly opposed Thomas Eliot's confirmation as the Social Security Board's general counsel over a fairly petty patronage dispute. Patronage pressure often turned ugly, as when Congressman Fred Vinson nearly assaulted Altmeyer over an appointment, or when another member of the Ways and Means Committee worried that the board was hiring "too damned many New York Jews." On the whole, though, the board managed to make what it considered very few compromises in hiring, and it used its patronage opportunities skillfully to satisfy key members of Congress. Because of the nature of the board's work, it attracted little interest beyond these matters.[21]

The national nature of OAI and its relative insulation from political pressure produced a stable policymaking environment that allowed the program to weather formidable political turmoil and uncertainty in its early years. On the left, the Townsend movement persisted into the 1940s, pressing demands for expanded, noncontributory old-age pensions.[22] On the right, prompted by many in the business community, Republicans continued to oppose key elements of the program, particularly the payroll tax and the program's original financing scheme. The financing scheme of 1935 called for the accumulation of an enormous reserve fund in the

Treasury, which was projected to cover benefit payments until 1980. Surplus income in OAI's current accounts (that is, the excess of payroll tax collections over benefit payments) was to be invested in U.S. government securities. Conservatives worried about the deflationary impact of excessive taxation; in their more conspiratorial moments, they also feared that OAI was really a plot to produce revenue to finance other expansive government programs (much as liberals believed, in the 1980s, that the Reagan tax cut of 1981 was really the centerpiece of a plot—a "Trojan horse," Senator Daniel Patrick Moynihan called it—to squeeze federal expenditures and shrink popular programs).[23]

While OAI's opponents attacked, social security executives were able to train their sights on a long-term agenda and to use the organizational apparatus of the Social Security Board to advance the cause of social insurance.[24] In fact, the program's very characteristics required them to do so. Because of the policy's long-term orientation and the expectation of retirement benefits connected to workers' contributions, OAI program executives could be reasonably sure that the basic structure of the program, and hence their basic responsibilities, would remain intact in the long run. Moreover, the actuarial structure of social insurance, based on the long-term management of risk, required that Social Security executives look farther into the future than is common for public officials, even bureaucrats, whose time horizons rarely stretch beyond the next election or budget cycle. Second, OAI faced a unitary policymaking arena, the federal government, unlike parochial social programs for which policy decisions were made in multiple arenas. Because there was no state or local involvement, policymaking activity for OAI occurred only in the federal government. Third, OAI did not face an annual appropriations process for the funds that it was to pay to beneficiaries; whatever payments the statutory formulas required were automatically appropriated from the Social Security Trust Fund. As a result, OAI bureaucrats did not need to spend time and resources on a lengthy annual budget process, except for their own operating expenses.

As a result of its stability, unitary policymaking, and automatic funding, OAI developed strong capacity that allowed it to guide its own destiny. Social Security professionals in the federal government themselves became the most important source of proposals to expand OAI, and they have been at the center of a relatively closed, unitary policymaking system at the national level.[25] Social Security planning was planning in the broadest sense of the word—not merely the anticipation of the future but the attempt to pursue a rational, organized course of action by a government empowered to regulate the structure of economy and society. Just as the Social Security Board came into being, however, the planning impulse in American liberalism began to wane, to be superseded after the war by a liberalism of individual rights and market forces, leaving the management of aggregate consumer demand as a faint vestige of an earlier, more robust, Progressive liberalism.[26] Although planning has taken a backseat to budgeting in coordinating federal government activity since World War II, Social Security's isolation from the budgetary process has made it one of the few remaining bastions of planning in American politics.[27] The ability to plan and to anticipate with some confidence the course of future policy developments has undoubtedly helped the Social Security bureaucracy incorporate new groups quickly and effectively into the OAI system.

Finally, the administrators of OAI managed to deal effectively with the huge administrative problems of establishing direct contact with a vast client base largely by colonizing existing administrative capacity in both the public and private sectors. More than thirty million people registered for Social Security accounts between November 1936 and June 1937. These accounts required scrupulous record-keeping and constant updating, which were accomplished with the help of IBM mechanical punch-card readers and a central filing index that already occupied more than an acre at the Social Security Board's Baltimore headquarters by the end of the initial burst of registration.[28] This was a formidable task for a new agency that was simultaneously preoccupied with the mundane problems of personnel, office space, and organization. The board was also occupied with social provision to individuals on an unprecedented scale for the federal government. To compare its two most prominent predecessors in federally administered social policy, the Freedmen's Bureau had approximately four million potential clients, whereas the Bureau of Pensions at its peak had fewer than one million.[29]

The Social Security Board successfully colonized the capacity of other organizations, both public and private, to accomplish much of its most difficult and dirty work. First of all, the Social Security Act itself provided that the Bureau of Internal Revenue, a division of the Treasury Department, was to collect the payroll tax, and the board and the bureau quickly concluded an agreement over their division of duties.[30] Second, the board, in a rather ingenious maneuver, convinced the Post Office and the Treasury Department to undertake much of the work of registering employers and employees for OAI. The former would distribute and accept application forms, assist applicants with problems or questions, and type both the record cards that would be sent to the board and the identification cards that would be given to the applicants. The latter agreed to adopt regulations that would require all covered employers and employees to obtain accounts. Treasury also agreed to handle most of the paperwork involved in producing accurate employee wage records.[31] Finally, much of the burden of distributing and collecting employee registration forms fell on the private sector. The Post Office delivered the forms to businesses whose employees were covered by OAI, and those employers were principally responsible for having their employees fill them out, collecting them, and returning them to the Post Office for processing.[32]

Passing along the administrative burden of registration to other organizations had a number of advantages for the Social Security Board. First, the strategy made an almost impossible task possible. "Most of the credit" for the success of the initial registration effort, wrote Altmeyer, "belongs to the postmasters, postal clerks, and mail carriers throughout the nation who distributed the forms, helped applicants fill them out, and answered questions about the new law."[33] Second, farming out the immense short-run task of registration allowed the board to focus on its more important long-term problem, developing a record-keeping system to ensure accurate and dependable benefits in the future. Inducing the Post Office and Treasury Department to do much of the work of collecting information allowed the board to routinize much of its own work, which then consisted mostly of transcribing, preparing punch cards, and filing. Although several European consultants advised that the administration of taxes and benefits should be unified, as in European contributory systems, the division of functions actually benefited the board, which managed largely to avoid the appearance of direct responsibility for the more onerous aspects of Old-Age Insurance, notably taxes, and identify itself in the public mind with the program's more pleasant side, benefits.[34]

The colonization strategy also had political benefits for Old-Age Insurance. First, the Post Office was certainly a familiar and friendly presence in the life of every American as well as an organization with a strong service ethic and reputation. ("Neither snow, nor rain," reads the famous inscription over the columns of the main Post Office in New York, "nor heat, nor gloom of night stays these couriers from the swift completion of their appointed rounds.") Using the Post Office as its intermediary to employers and employees may have forestalled some of the fears that many might have felt had the unknown board itself come calling and asking for information. Roosevelt himself had envisioned the social insurance system operating through the Post Office. "The system ought to be operated," he told Frances Perkins,

> through the post office. Just simple and natural—nothing elaborate or alarming about it. The rural free delivery carrier ought to bring papers to the door and pick them up after they are filled out. The rural free delivery carrier ought to give each child his social insurance number and his policy or whatever takes the place of a policy. The rural free delivery carrier ought to be the one who picks up the claim of the man who is unemployed, or the old lady who wants old-age insurance benefits.[35]

Roosevelt's simple but powerful conception of a benevolent welfare state depended not only on the contributory tax and benefit structure but also on the development of a dense administrative network that could penetrate society without appearing to threaten it.[36]

The political stakes of the registration process increased in the middle of the 1936 presidential campaign. On 26 September in a campaign speech in Milwaukee, Alf Landon, the Republican nominee, denounced Social Security as a "fraud on the working man" and a "cruel hoax." The Social Security Act, he said, was "unjust, unworkable, stupidly drafted, and wastefully financed." He played particularly on the act as an expansion of national authority, raising fears of the "stern management of a paternal government," invoking American fears of the storm clouds of fascism that were gathering in Europe. "Imagine the field opened for federal snooping," Landon fulminated. "Are these 26 million going to be fingerprinted? Are their photographs going to be kept on file in a Washington office? Or are they going to have identification tags put around their necks?"[37] The speech launched an anti–Social Security campaign that featured posters in factories, leaflets in pay envelopes, and screaming headlines in Hearst newspapers the day before the election.[38] Within days of the speech, John Winant, the Republican chairman of the Social Security Board, resigned because he did not feel free, as the Republican "representative" on the board, to criticize Landon and defend the act. After his resignation, Winant and a small group of Social Security insiders met in New York to coordinate Roosevelt's response in defense of the program, an important foray into politics for the nominally nonpartisan Social Security Board.[39]

The anti-registration effort was pitched particularly at OAI's national institutional structure, which seemed politically vulnerable. But by side-stepping direct administrative responsibility for the public face of the registration process, the Social Security Board deflected the thrust of Landon's attacks. Moreover, by effectively detailing some of its expert staff to the Roosevelt campaign—and by shrewdly scheduling the actual registration to begin after the election, a decision for which Altmeyer took credit—the board took advantage of this potentially damaging episode to flex its political muscles and to build its own constituency both within the government and outside.

The strategy of colonization narrowed the direct responsibility of the Social Security Board and allowed it to develop competence. Moreover, the strategy also promoted goodwill among the public; the name "Social Security" eventually became nearly synonymous with popular and effective government. At the individual level, OAI's style of public contact reinforced this image of competence and friendliness. An individual's direct contact with the Social Security office was generally limited to one visit upon retirement. This one visit set in motion the procedures for the mailing of monthly benefit checks for the rest of the beneficiary's life. Because of the routine nature of the task and the successful management of the Social Security apparatus, Social Security employees who do the day-to-day administrative work of OAI have developed a strong service ethic that makes citizens' experiences with the agency reasonably pleasant and productive.

While the Social Security Board used the colonization strategy to its benefit, it also developed an in-house public relations operation that contributed to friendly public acceptance. After a few public relations gaffes in late 1935, the board hired as its director of informational service a former newspaperman with experience as a publicist for public and private social welfare organizations. Despite early organizational problems, the informational service played an important role in attacking negative images of OAI and fostering public goodwill. Most significant in this effort were the film trailers that the board produced beginning in 1936. These films, which were attached to newsreels and shown in theaters throughout the country, reached nearly 150 million people by March 1937. The first film, *We the People and Social Security,* was rushed through production to be ready in time for the 1936 election, and the film's producer himself drove from Washington to New York ten days before the election, distributing copies en route.[40] The board was also blessed with extraordinary political and administrative leaders who used these institutional tools with great skill to sell the expansion of social security to policymakers and the public.[41]

The cumulative result of this whole complex of structural factors was that in its earliest years, Old-Age Insurance developed into an efficient and effective program that Americans perceived as fair and that was poised to claim wide political support. The procedural fairness and national uniformity of the program, combined with a bureaucratic structure that also emphasized procedure, expertise, and a strong service ethic, contributed to the program's popularity and its political strength. For the workers who were initially included in OAI—first as contributors and then, gradually, as beneficiaries—the program became the lodestar of the welfare state, the symbol of a national state that was protective but not paternal, provident but not profligate.

But of course the initial target population of OAI was almost entirely white, not to mention male and urban. Despite the unprecedented development of strong state capacity for social provision, the prospects for African-Americans, women, and many others to achieve a modicum of economic security from the Social Security Act were not promising. The forces of racial exclusion in American politics and society were still strong and, on the eve of World War II, showed few signs of abating. Despite their increasing trust in the national government and the deepening identification of African-American voters with the New Deal and the Democratic Party, black organizations worried not only about the exclusion of African-Americans from the program but also about the treatment of those black workers who were included.

As a welfare policy, Old-Age Insurance seemed likely simply to reinforce and replicate existing, overlapping divisions of class and race in American society and politics. As an institution, however, it promised to be a countervailing force to the racially exclusionary impulse in American politics. More broadly, the creation of state capacity that established direct links between the national government and individual citizens held the potential to redefine the terms of American racial division simply by incorporating African-Americans fairly and honorably in a popular program of social provision. How did the institutional structure of Old-Age Insurance shape the inclusion of African-Americans? Were they treated fairly in the administration of the program as a matter of course, or were they the victims of discrimination even in a national institutional setting? How and why did the policy expand to incorporate initially excluded groups, broadening the program's racial base and obliterating the racial distinctions of 1935? The remainder of this chapter addresses these questions.

Racial Fairness in Old-Age Insurance

Ironically, one consequence of OAI's institutional structure was the smooth incorporation of black workers into the system, within the limits of their position in the economy, as early as the 1930s. The exclusion of occupational categories cut most African-Americans out of the program from the beginning. But defining the program's target population along class lines did not leave African-Americans out entirely, and there were still millions of black workers eligible for coverage. For them, the central question of OAI was whether they would be included on the same terms as their white counterparts, or whether the implementation of the program would create administrative barriers to their participation. "Relief practice is always more restrictive than relief law," Frances Fox Piven and Richard Cloward have observed. In the history of American welfare policy, they argue, statutes restrict eligibility for relief, whereas administrative practices impose restrictions even beyond statutory limits.[42] Did this pattern, common to the very definition of relief in the Anglo-American world, apply to social insurance as well?

Statutory discrimination in Old-Age Insurance operated only de facto, through occupational exclusions, and not de jure. Although, as I have argued, racial exclusion was not merely incidental to the definition of OAI's target population, it was not explicit. On one hand, the Social Security Act itself made no explicit distinction on the basis of race in any of its programs, as some other countries did.[43] On the other hand, it did not include the explicit anti-discrimination provisions that black organizations recommended.[44] The act was, on its face, entirely neutral with respect to race, although the appearance of race neutrality masked racial imbalances that emerged from inequalities in the political economy. Contemporary critics of the anti-black bias in Old-Age Insurance, in fact, attribute this bias to underlying political and economic structures and not to explicit racial restrictions.[45]

But even within its own boundaries, Old-Age Insurance might have discriminated against African-Americans even further, through administration. Laws do not execute themselves, and the administrative institutions and procedures that they establish to translate policy into action may not produce the same results for everyone. The administration of OAI, in fact, was a matter of concern to black leaders. The NAACP wanted to ensure that OAI administration was as race-blind as possible so that bureaucrats could not deny claims or reduce benefits to black retirees. In his protest to the Social Security Board over the inclusion of the race question on the proposed Social Security application blank, NAACP secretary Walter White expressed fear that knowledge of an applicant's race would "inevitably be used in various ways, both obvious and subtle, to practice discrimination based upon race."[46] The color-blind approach has long been centrally important in American civil rights law and discourse, and the NAACP's concern about bringing racial characteristics of individuals into the administration of OAI fits into a long tradition of similar objections, from required photographs on civil service applications to the Equal Employment Opportunity Commission's race and gender employment reports.[47] In this case, however, the worry was needless.

If administration was, in fact, discriminatory, data on OAI participation should show significant racial disparities that cannot be otherwise explained. Specifically, levels of black participation should be below their expected levels given black patterns of occupation and earnings. One indicator of black participation is the level of applications for Social Security account numbers. In the early years, the Social Security number was not the all-purpose identifier that it has since become, and having a number was not taken for granted. I assume, therefore, that applicants for numbers were those who worked or expected or desired to work in covered employment. Certainly there would have been no reason for someone regularly employed as a farm laborer or domestic servant to register for a number in the late 1930s. We would expect, then, that the ratio of white to black applicants would approximate the ratio of white to black workers in the covered labor force.

Estimating the extent of OAI coverage of the labor force is possible using detailed occupation data from the census.[48] Exclusions from OAI in the Social Security Act took two forms. The first was occupational, the exclusion of workers in particular occupations or industries—agriculture, domestic service, railroads (railroad workers had a separate pension system), shipping, nonprofit organizations, and government. The second source of exclusion was self-employment, regardless of industry.

The self-employment category in particular makes estimating total exclusions difficult. For example, a lawyer working in private practice would be considered self-employed and therefore not covered. A lawyer working in the legal department of a corporation would not be self-employed and would be covered. However, a lawyer working for the government or a nonprofit organization would not be self-employed, but would be excluded from coverage on occupational grounds.

Unfortunately, the census does not distinguish in most occupational categories between workers who are and are not self-employed, so to estimate the number of self-employed workers, the count of noncovered workers includes all categories in which workers are likely to be self-employed—mostly professions organized around private practice. Including all workers in these categories as self-employed probably has the effect of slightly overestimating the number of workers excluded from OAI, because not all workers in these ambiguous categories would have been self-employed (as the lawyer example shows). Moreover, this overestimation is probably larger for whites than for blacks, because black workers in these categories make up only a minuscule proportion of total black exclusions.

Table 3.1 lists the excluded categories in the 1930 Census and shows the total number of workers and the number of black workers in each. The totals at the bottom of Table 3.1 show that approximately 18.6 million workers were excluded from OAI coverage, of whom 3 million were black. In 1930 there were approximately 48.8 million gainfully employed workers in the United States, of whom 5.5 million (11.3 percent) were black.[49] Accordingly, 30.2 million workers (62 percent of all workers) and 2.5 million black workers (45 percent of black workers) were eligible for OAI coverage. Thus although black workers composed about 11 percent of the total labor force, they composed only approximately 8 percent of the covered labor force. Moreover, the possible overestimation of total exclusions corresponds with an underestimation of total covered workers, which implies that this estimate may be slightly high. If there were significant discrimination in the application process, then, black application figures should in the early years of OAI fall substantially below 8 percent.

In fact, the level of black applications began at approximately this level in 1936 and rose steadily through the first ten years of OAI. Figure 3.1 shows the annual and cumulative percentage of black applicants for Social Security numbers through 1960. In the initial year of registration (actually from mid-November 1936 through 1937), 37.2 million people applied for Social Security numbers, including 2.8 million blacks, or 7.6 percent. In subsequent years, blacks accounted for more than 10 percent of applications in almost every year, and the cumulative total of black applicants rose

Table 3.1 Workers Excluded from Old-Age Insurance Coverage, 1930

Category	Total	Black
Agriculture (total)	10,471,998	1,987,839
Domestic workers		
Cooks—other	321,722	220,538
Servants—other	1,240,086	494,092
Self-employed		
Fishermen & oystermen	73,280	7,162
Lumber-owners	5,650	61
Architects	22,000	63
Artists	57,265	430
Authors	12,449	49
Dentists	71,055	1,773
Insurance agents	256,927	6,286
Lawyers	160,605	1,247
Musicians	165,128	10,583
Osteopaths	6,117	114
Photographers	39,529	545
Physicians	153,803	3,805
Veterinarians	11,863	134
Cleaners—owners	16,775	1,464
Laundry—owners	15,440	247
Retail dealers	1,703,522	28,213
Seamen		
Boatmen, canal-men	5,643	282
Captains, masters, mates	24,485	203
Sailors, deck hands	64,700	6,659
Railroad (total)	1,171,056	119,499
Government and nonprofit		
Public service	856,927	50,203
Teachers	1,062,615	54,683
Nurses	294,189	5,728
Clergy	148,848	25,034
College professors	61,905	2,146
Total	**18,608,753**	**3,030,892**

Source: U.S. Bureau of the Census, *Fifteenth Census of the United States: 1930, Population* (Washington, D.C.: Government Printing Office, 1933), vol. 4, table 13, 25–34.

consistently, leveling off at around 11 percent in the 1950s. By sometime in the 1940s, the cumulative percentage of black applicants reached parity with the proportion of blacks in the entire labor force, although it is hard to tell precisely when this happened because cumulative application statistics include people who dropped out of the labor force for reasons such as disability, retirement, or death. These data show quite clearly that in soliciting or accepting applications for account numbers, the administration of Old-Age Insurance was not discriminatory.

The reason that so many black workers applied for Social Security numbers even though they were underrepresented in the covered population is undoubtedly that many blacks shifted back and forth between covered and noncovered employment. Farm labor, for many, was seasonal work, and it was typical for people whose principal labor was farm work (and whom the Census would have identified as agricultural laborers) to take other jobs between seasons.[50] In 1946 the Treasury Department reported that 26 percent of the country's hired farm workers had earnings that year from

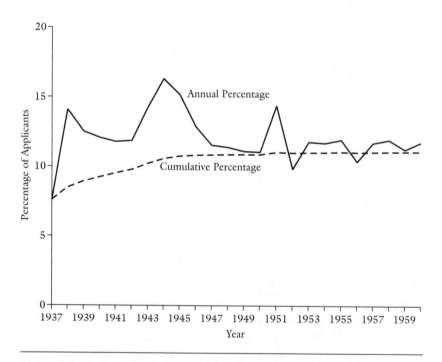

Figure 3.1. Black applicants for Social Security numbers, 1937–1960.
Source: Social Security Bulletin.

nonfarm work, and in 1950 Altmeyer testified that of 4.6 million hired farm workers, 45 percent had at one time or another made payroll contributions to OAI through covered employment.[51] Clearly this was a widespread phenomenon and helps account for the high level of black applications.

More important than applications as an indicator of administrative fairness in OAI is the tendency of African-Americans actually to receive benefits in numbers and amounts commensurate to their participation in the covered labor force. Once again, because of exclusion from coverage, we expect blacks to be represented among beneficiaries in approximate proportion to their share of the covered labor force. Such factors as chronically higher rates of black unemployment, movement in and out of covered jobs, and shorter life expectancy for blacks suggest that the black proportion of beneficiaries should lag slightly behind the black proportion of the labor force. Significantly smaller numbers of black beneficiaries would be an indication of administrative discrimination, although it is hard to define precisely how much of a lag would constitute "significantly smaller numbers." But we should also expect blacks to receive smaller amounts because benefits are related to wages, and black workers, even where covered, have generally been in lower-wage jobs. Benefit rates for blacks significantly below the wage differential would also indicate discriminatory administration. It is clearly impossible to measure precisely "expected" benefit levels under conditions of administrative fairness, so there is a certain amount of guesswork involved in trying to infer nondiscrimination. But widespread and systematic discrimination would certainly produce egregious and persistent disparities.

As the occupational definition of the program's target population changed during the 1940s and 1950s, so did its racial composition. Tables 3.2 and 3.3, like Table 3.1, list the categories of excluded workers from the 1950 and 1960 Censuses, respectively. In 1950, the labor force numbered about 60 million and the nonwhite labor force about 6.1 million (10.2 percent). Table 3.2 shows that 16 million workers, of whom 2.2 million were nonwhite, were in noncovered occupations. The total covered labor force, therefore, was approximately 44 million workers (73 percent of all workers), and the covered nonwhite labor force numbered 3.9 million (64 percent of nonwhite workers). Thus nonwhites made up nearly 9 percent of the covered labor force.[52] Table 3.3 reveals the dramatic impact of the amendments of the 1950s, which greatly expanded OAI coverage. By 1960, the number of excluded workers had been substantially reduced,

Table 3.2 Workers Excluded from Old-Age Insurance, 1950

Category	Total	Nonwhite
Agriculture		
Farmers/farm managers	4,306,253	523,550
Farm laborers/foremen	2,399,794	540,623
Domestic workers	1,407,466	818,337
Self-employed		
Accountants/auditors	376,459	1,766
Architects	23,823	229
Artists	77,473	1,357
Dentists	72,810	1,748
Insurance agents	324,310	8,812
Lawyers	180,461	1,587
Musicians	153,456	8,876
Physicians	191,947	4,841
Pharmacists	80,855	1,355
Real estate agents	120,325	2,199
Therapists and healers	12,077	516
Other professionals	623,428	20,848
Managers and proprietors	2,518,396	72,237
Fishermen	66,572	6,478
Government and nonprofit		
State and local officials	110,951	1,166
Mail carriers	161,702	12,437
Firefighters	109,416	1,478
Police officers	212,685	4,230
Clergy	160,694	18,584
College professors	124,686	4,503
Social workers	91,533	6,795
Social scientists	35,201	701
Teachers	1,120,605	87,799
Dietitians/nutritionists	21,059	1,798
Librarians	49,027	1,576
Nurses	463,495	16,137
Railroad employees	382,745	77,260
Total	**16,009,624**	**2,249,733**

Source: U.S. Bureau of the Census, *Census of Population: 1950* (Washington, D.C.: Government Printing Office, 1953), vol. 2, part 1, table 128, 276–278.

Table 3.3 Workers Excluded from Old-Age Insurance, 1960

Category	Total	Nonwhite
Self-employed		
Artists	107,705	3,138
Dentists	81,249	2,879
Lawyers	213,058	2,722
Musicians	197,529	11,017
Pharmacists	85,482	2,256
Physicians	229,590	10,070
Insurance agents	416,015	9,968
Real estate agents	148,957	3,095
Government and nonprofit		
College professors	178,676	7,824
Dietitians/nutritionists	24,757	3,951
Librarians	72,431	3,964
Nurses	633,783	39,875
Social scientists	57,155	1,519
Social/welfare workers	136,364	16,108
Mail carriers	197,402	21,678
Teachers	1,683,666	142,189
Railroad workers	133,295	39,279
Total	**4,594,114**	**321,262**

Source: U.S. Bureau of the Census, *Census of Population, 1960* (Washington, D.C.: Government Printing Office, 1964), vol. 1, pt. 1, table 205, I-554–I-546.

almost to zero in the case of nonwhites. Of 68 million people in the labor force, only 4.6 million were in occupations that remained uncovered by OAI. For nonwhites, fewer than 400,000 workers out of 7.2 million remained uncovered. Significantly, by 1960 nonwhite workers were covered at a slightly *higher* rate (96 percent) than all workers (93 percent), and the nonwhite percentage of the covered labor force matched the nonwhite percentage of the total labor force (both just under 11 percent). Sometime in the 1950s, African-Americans achieved proportional "parity" with whites in OAI coverage.

With these data in hand, it is easy to observe that the nonwhite share of beneficiaries does lag slightly, but only slightly, behind the nonwhite proportion of the labor force. Figure 3.2 shows that nonwhites comprised between 6 and 7 percent of total beneficiaries through the 1950s and reveals an accelerating upward trend. This trend suggests that OAI was moving toward greater racial inclusion even before legislative changes in the 1950s that brought excluded workers into the system. Benefit data, moreover, reflect prior rather than current employment conditions, because benefits were paid only after retirement or death, based on an individual's wage history. This was also true of newly covered categories of workers; rather than being "blanketed in" and becoming immediately eligible for benefits, they started at the beginning and had to build eligibility through contributions over time.[53] Changes in coverage, therefore, affected the number of beneficiaries only very slowly. Thus significant expansions of coverage that occurred in 1950 and 1954 produced only very small immediate increases in nonwhite beneficiaries. Over time, however, the proportion of nonwhite beneficiaries rose steadily, surpassing the nonwhite proportion of covered workers. An exception to the rule of delayed benefits was the addition of disability compensation in 1956 (with the first payments made in 1957). Black workers were overrepresented among disability recipients, but this accounts for only a small proportion of the increase beginning in

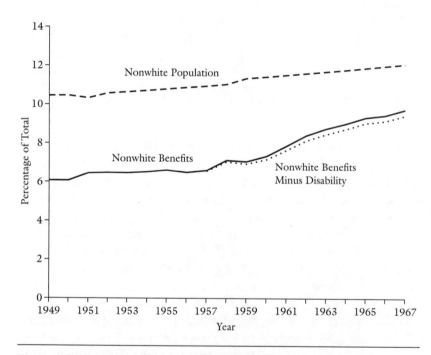

Figure 3.2. Nonwhite OAI recipients and population as percentage of total, 1949–1967.

Source: Social Security Bulletin.

the late 1950s. The bottom line of Figure 3.2 charts nonwhite benefits excluding disability payments and reveals that even without disability benefits, nonwhite payments rose at an accelerating rate beginning in the late 1950s.

Nonwhite beneficiaries also received smaller payments than their white counterparts, because nonwhite workers received, on average, lower wages and OAI benefits were tied to wages. But OAI benefits were also slightly progressive—redistributive toward lower-income workers—because the benefit formula set a floor and a ceiling on benefits. Because African-American workers tended to earn less, they were more likely to be bumped up to the minimum benefit, whereas higher earning whites were more likely to be restricted to the maximum. As a result, without discrimination, we should observe that the ratio of black to white benefit levels was at least as high as the ratio of black to white incomes, and this is precisely what Figure 3.3 reveals. The top line shows the average per capita payment to nonwhite beneficiaries as a percentage of the average per capita payment to

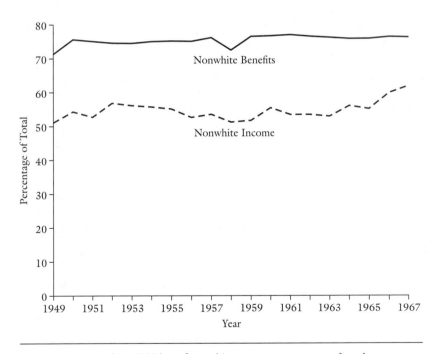

Figure 3.3. Nonwhite OAI benefits and income as percentage of total, 1949–1967.

Source: Social Security Bulletin.

all beneficiaries. Nonwhite benefits were consistently around 75 percent of overall benefits, a substantial lag. But compare that number with the lower line in Figure 3.3, which shows the median income for nonwhite families as a percentage of the median white family income.[54] Whereas nonwhite workers earned just a little more than half of what whites earned (climbing to 60 percent in the late 1960s), nonwhite OAI recipients were getting 75 percent. Nonwhite OAI recipients in fact did considerably better compared with their white counterparts than nonwhite earners did compared with theirs. In sum, these data suggest that there was no administrative discrimination in Old-Age Insurance, and reports of interested observers corroborate this conclusion. A 1937 NAACP memorandum that documented discrimination in public assistance found no equivalent discrimination in OAI. Twelve years later, Edgar G. Brown, director of the National Negro Council, testified that his organization had "had little or no evidence of discriminatory administration."[55]

The lack of administrative discrimination in OAI is quite remarkable and the trend toward inclusion even more so, especially given the subordinate place of African-Americans in the American political economy. Racial inclusion did not result from the traditional give and take of pluralist, interest-group politics. The political forces for inclusion were not sufficiently numerous, organized, or vocal to extract such a concession from policymakers, whereas the forces of racial exclusion remained strong. Black political leverage in national politics, although growing, was still weak, and because the program already excluded more than half the country's black workers, black voters did not form much of its natural constituency. Finally, the political status of OAI was precarious in the late 1930s and 1940s. It faced the ongoing Townsend movement for universal noncontributory old-age pensions on the left and Republican attacks on the financing system and on the very principles of social insurance on the right.[56] Being seen as a program that provided substantial benefits to African-Americans could have been politically dangerous to OAI. Politically, the early years of social security hardly seemed promising for fostering racial equality and inclusion in the American welfare state.

If group politics did not promote racial inclusion, there must have been something inherent in the program itself that made it happen. The Social Security Act transformed the American political landscape and, through a process of policy feedback, altered the political forces in state and society that shaped the subsequent development of Old-Age Insurance.[57] First, the act expanded the national government's capacity to administer social provision directly to citizens on a mass scale. The Social Security Board, later the Social Security Administration, effectively managed the intense administrative demands of the program and quickly became an important player in the welfare policy game, shaping and guiding debates over the next generation. Second, the program's own constituency, increasingly organized and mobilized, created a strong base of support for OAI and its expansion. Third, mass public opinion came increasingly to support the program as it was constituted, making possible the politics of OAI expansion. All of these developments grew out of the particular structure of the program itself and its distinctive institutional presence in national welfare politics. The new institutions and new politics created by the Social Security Act thus helped shape the redefinition of American racial boundaries by fostering racially inclusive Old-Age Insurance.

Institutional Structure and the Development of Old-Age Insurance

Not only did the institutional structure of Old-Age Insurance produce racially fair administration, it also generated political forces that overcame the program's racially exclusionary origins. One of the great ironies of the history of American social policy is that Old-Age Insurance, which was created in a racially exclusionary way, grew within a generation into a broad, popular, and inclusive program of social insurance covering almost all American workers regardless of race. Administrative fairness alone could not have achieved this result, because large groups of workers remained excluded from the program by law. But administrative fairness and the image of fairness that Social Security executives worked hard to create in the public mind surely contributed to the program's acceptance. More important, the same institutional structure that produced administrative fairness created both the political logic of expansion and the political capacity in both state and society to engineer expansion, promoting the incorporation of African-Americans into the structure of American social provision.

The Social Security Act created a new pattern of welfare politics. The linkage between taxes and benefits created a perpetual constituency for OAI, which had an interest in low taxes and high benefits. In the early years many contributed and few received benefits, but as soon as the checks started flowing out, fiscal pressures existed on the system to gather enough revenue to meet current obligations. As long as the constituency was "incomplete," as long as there were working Americans who did not contribute, those already in the system had a strong incentive to cover new workers—the alternative was raising payroll tax rates. A 1946 study by the National Planning Association made this logic explicit. Expanding OAI coverage to all workers, including farmers and farm employees, would more than double the program's revenue projection by 1950. However, the projected benefit payments by 1950 would increase by only sixty percent. Even extending these projections as far forward as 1980, the study still showed revenue increases outstripping benefit increases; the projections for 1980 under full coverage showed revenue still slightly more than doubling and benefit payments increasing by about ninety percent compared with the restricted coverage that prevailed in the 1940s.[58] This incentive created a powerful logic of expansion for OAI—including new groups proved to be the best strategy for fiscally-minded politicians. The act also created the Social Security Board (later the Social Security Administration), which administered Old-Age Insurance as well as the federal responsibilities for the other social security policies. The Social Security Board combined national administrative capacity with an extraordinary public relations apparatus and unusually strong planning capacities, all of which it used to pursue OAI's expansionary logic.[59]

The logic of expansion of Old-Age Insurance operated against a background of both continuity and change. Politically, the resistance of Southern Democrats to the inclusion of predominantly black occupational groups in OAI continued. The politics of Social Security, however, no longer revolved around the legitimacy of national administrative authority, and the rhetoric of states' rights that Southerners and others had mobilized in 1935 to voice their skepticism no longer provided a relevant context. Instead, the very existence of a national program of social security created interests in society, around which groups formed to press demands on the state.[60] Southerners and other opponents of expansion latched onto the demands of excluded groups, or, more pertinently, on the absence of such demands. On at least one occasion, the old racist rhetoric appeared. But with Congress and the presidency in Republican hands for the first time since before the New Deal, Southern power was momentarily broken. Only in the last brief moment of unified Republican control before forty years of Democratic dominance did Congress at last vote to grant OAI protection to farm workers and servants, ending the program's inherent racial imbalance.

The arguments over the administrative feasibility of covering agricultural and domestic workers also continued. Advocates of expansion both in and out of the government did extensive research on the techniques that other countries used for such coverage, and they presented their research in hearings and publications. Studies by a congressional panel and the Treasury Department in the 1940s that affirmed the feasibility of coverage added little of substance to the arguments and demonstrations of a dozen years earlier, although the latter signaled an important shift in the views of the Treasury Department, which had declared in 1935 that coverage would pose administrative problems. Finally, the very administrative success of the Social Security Board, along with its own careful and tireless efforts on behalf of expansion, helped overcome administrative qualms.

Finally, the place of African-Americans in the political economy began to change dramatically. Just as the introduction of the cotton gin in the early nineteenth century had made possible the large-scale cultivation of cotton with black labor—first as slaves, then as tenants, sharecroppers, and wage laborers—the introduction of the mechanical cotton picker beginning in the 1940s made possible the large-scale cultivation of cotton with very little black labor at all. The mechanization of cotton farming, which was itself accelerated by Southern labor shortages during and after World War II, made what was an already brutal economic system even worse for Southern farm workers, both black and white, and many of them found themselves replaced by more efficient and reliable machines. At the same time, Northern cities seemed to offer African-Americans greater opportunities for economic and social mobility. Just as the transformation of the cotton economy pushed many African-Americans off the land, the seductive lure of the "promised land" pulled them north.[61]

As Southern agriculture mechanized, five million black Southerners moved north between 1940 and 1970, "one of the largest and most rapid mass internal movements of people in history."[62] As African-Americans migrated, they entered industrial and commercial employment in ever larger numbers, increasingly gaining OAI coverage. Two factors sped the entry of African-American workers into OAI-covered employment. First, as the Depression ended, prosperity returned, and production increased, more jobs were available. Second, the defense production of World War II, which was itself largely responsible for ending the Depression, created unprecedented, if still small, opportunities for black entry into industries that had traditionally been closed to them. The Fair Employment Practices Commission, created by President Roosevelt in 1941, symbolized, and even weakly enforced, these new opportunities.[63]

In addition to modestly increasing employment opportunities for black Americans, the war heightened both the sense of injustice about their political, social, and economic place in American life and their expectations that the government should and would do something about their plight. The consequences of these shifting attitudes were sometimes destructive— as in race riots in Detroit, Los Angeles, and New York in 1943[64]—and sometimes constructive—as in the integration of the armed forces in 1948. Combined with the mass migration north, which nationalized racial questions more vividly than any event since the Civil War, the attitudes that the war unleashed created a backdrop of heightened awareness of racial issues against which all the issues of postwar politics, including the reform of Social Security, played themselves out.[65]

The New Deal also transformed the Democratic party, beginning the long process of driving apart the two halves of the unstable coalition that Roosevelt had assembled. The South no longer played nearly as prominent a role in the Democratic coalition as it had in the 1930s. Although the committee system and the seniority norm continued to allow Southern Democrats to dominate the leadership of Congress, the South was no longer the only reliable part of the Democrats' national coalition. While the Democrats gained strength among Northern urban ethnic and black voters, they began slowly to lose support in the traditionally unassailable South. In 1936, the party dropped its rule requiring a majority of two-thirds at its national convention to nominate a presidential candidate, ending the South's effective veto on the selection of national candidates.[66] Over time, the tension between Northern urban liberals and Southern segregationists within the New Deal coalition grew wider; the Northerners, who relied increasingly on black votes, grew bolder while the Southerners screamed louder. Republicans, who did not adopt a consistently conservative stance on racial issues until the 1960s, tended to form coalitions with Northern Democrats against Southerners on issues of race and labor relations.[67]

Amidst all of the social, economic, and political changes, the institutional structure of Social Security organized and contained the political struggles surrounding Old-Age Insurance. Through the turmoil and tumult of the war and its aftermath, OAI's program executives soldiered on, laying foundations of solid management, effective administration, and shrewd politics in the 1930s that would pay off in subsequent decades. Although opposition to the expansion of OAI—and, indeed, to its very existence—continued, the logic of expansion that flowed out of the policy's institutional structure took root and, in less than twenty years, bore fruit for millions of African-American workers.

Expanded Exclusion: The 1939 Amendments

In 1939, the Social Security Act underwent its first major amendment, and the exclusion of agricultural and domestic workers was again on the table. The amendments arose principally out of opposition to the system of financing Old-Age Insurance adopted in 1935, which called for substantial increases in payroll tax rates—from 2 percent (1 percent each on employers and employees) in 1937 to 6 percent in 1949—and a delay in paying benefits, in effect building up a large "reserve" of funds in the Treasury. In 1937, a group of Republican senators led by Arthur Vandenberg of Michigan engineered the appointment of an advisory council to examine this and other issues and to recommend amendments. Vandenberg's proposal covered not just the reform of the financing system for OAI but also the extension of coverage to farmers and domestic servants.[68]

Nevertheless, Arthur Altmeyer, by then chairman of the Social Security Board, had misgivings about the council, which Roosevelt shared. Altmeyer feared that it would be stacked against the New Dealers' vision of progressive and expansive social insurance and that it might undermine support for Social Security and buttress the claims of some Republicans that the program taxed working Americans simply to feed a bloated government. Altmeyer was also called on the carpet by the House Ways and Means Democrats, who had been bypassed in the creation of the council. In an astute and prescient memorandum to Roosevelt, Altmeyer expressed his concern and began to lay out an agenda for the advisory council that covered not only revision of the financing of old-age insurance but also other issues that Altmeyer considered important for the longer term.[69]

Because of the institutional capacity that the Social Security Board had already developed, and because of Altmeyer's shrewd foresight, the Advisory Council on Social Security was not a free agent. As it turned out, the council operated under the guidance and influence of the Social Security Board, and the council's recommendations were nearly identical to the points that Altmeyer had sketched out in his memo to the president. The close tandem operations of the advisory council and the Social Security Board, insulated from the hostile political pressures of congressional Republicans, reveal how quickly the Social Security establishment in the federal government developed both the institutional capacity and the authority of expertise to direct policymaking for OAI. Policy demands from Congress or from societal forces precipitated the episode; they did not, however, control the flow of events, propose alternatives, or ordain the result.[70] The advisory council was largely made up of friends of the program; at least ten of its twenty-five members had played some role in the creation of Social Security four years earlier, including Edwin Witte and council chairman J. Douglas Brown. More important was the advisory council's reliance on Social Security Board staff for technical advice and support and the board's vigilant attention to the council's work. Social Security Board staff members supplied the advisory council with almost all its information about the workings of the system, which they portrayed as extremely complicated, enabling them to interpret their own data to the council members. The board also supplied the advisory council with a steady stream of draft recommendations, designed to minimize conflict while furthering the board's policy goals. Wilbur Cohen, by then twenty-six and a seasoned veteran of Social Security politics, himself coordinated the board's staff work, served as conduit between the board and the advisory council, and then acted as the board's principal liaison to Congress, where he once again sat in on all the closed sessions of the House Ways and Means and Senate Finance Committees.[71] In fact, the council worked so well as a front for the Social Security Board, providing recommendations with a "nonpartisan" and "expert" imprimatur that they would have lacked coming directly from the board itself, that the "nonpartisan" or "bipartisan" council became a standard tool with which Social Security program executives promoted later amendments and program expansions.[72]

From the beginning of its deliberations in late 1937, the advisory council considered the extension of coverage to farm and domestic workers as an important part of its agenda, agreeing that coverage of these groups was "socially desirable," a phrase that appears in nearly every draft of the council's report.[73] Initially there was resistance to the idea of adding workers to the system because expansion would exacerbate the reserve financing problems that had precipitated the amendment in the first place. M. A. Linton, an actuary and a member of the council, estimated that including all workers would require a reserve of $85 billion, which, he said, "borders on the fantastic."[74] Others, by contrast, were concerned that the addition of new workers to the system would create a net drain on the reserve due to the more difficult and costly administrative methods associated with covering these workers.[75]

But once the council decided to recommend abandoning the reserve and moving to pay-as-you-go financing, the council members enthusiastically supported the principle of inclusion, provided the administrative difficulties could be solved. Administrative difficulty had, of course, been the ostensible objection in 1935 to covering agricultural and domestic workers, and as they had in the earlier debate, the advocates of extended coverage acknowledged this problem again in 1939.[76] But Altmeyer, along with his Social Security Board staff and his allies outside the government, had worked hard in the intervening years to answer these objections. Social Security insiders believed by 1939 that they could incorporate farm workers and servants into the old-age insurance system efficiently and effectively, and they saw benefits, both political and humane, in doing so.

Ewan Clague, the director of the board's Bureau of Research and Statistics, laid out for the advisory council as early as 1937 the principal objections that were frequently advanced to extending coverage. There were, he proposed, four basic problems, three administrative and one financial.[77] The first was the high proportion of employees to employers. Many farmers hired only a few workers, and many households as few as one, meaning that the Social Security Board would have to deal with a large number of employers relative to the number of covered employees. Many farm workers and domestic servants received a portion of their wages not in cash but in kind, such as room and board or a portion of the crop. Calculating the value of in-kind payments and the taxes due posed a second administrative burden. Third was simply the difficulty of collecting and recording payroll taxes. Small farms and households, it was argued, were not generally operated as businesses and were not equipped to compile payroll data and collect and remit taxes for their employees. Moreover, farm and domestic employees tended to shift frequently from job to job and employer to employer, further complicating the process of collecting and reporting taxes. Finally, the financial objection was that most farm and household workers were unlikely to pay taxes that would match the benefits they would ultimately receive, and they would constitute a fiscal drag on what was supposed to be a self-sufficient contributory system.

The principal response to the administrative objections was the stamp book, which had been a favorite topic of J. Douglas Brown in 1935 but which had received little attention from other quarters. In the interim, however, the stamp-book method had been the subject of extensive study, and the board's staff had begun to work out the details of how it might operate in the social security system. In 1938, in the midst of the advisory council's deliberations, Wilbur Cohen prepared a long memorandum about the intricacies of such a system. He reported, for example, that it would require fifteen denominations of stamps in order to ensure that every possible level of monthly tax payments could be entered with a maximum of three stamps. He also outlined criteria for judging a stamp-book system—simplicity for employers and the government, equity and clarity for workers—and argued that the board was prepared to meet these criteria. Cohen concluded that "it seems possible and practicable to include agricultural laborers and domestic servants," echoing Clague's argument that "there are no insurmountable difficulties involved in the extension of coverage to these groups."[78]

As Cohen outlined it, the stamp-book proposal met two of the three administrative problems that Clague raised. By collecting payments through the sale of stamps at the post office, for example, the Treasury Department would not have to add to its already formidable payroll collection and reporting system the millions of small farms and households who hired workers. The stamp books would provide simple physical records of contributions paid, which were easily transferrable into government records and, perhaps more important, enforceable by the employees themselves. J. Douglas Brown, the stamp book's greatest champion, cited the experience of other countries where the stamp system enabled social insurance systems to cover farmers and domestics, and he even argued that the very tangibility of the stamp book itself would contribute to a worker's feeling of economic security. "There is something in human nature," he said, perhaps rather hyperbolically, "that fits into the notion of putting stamps in a book . . . Stamp collecting is widespread. So it is a part of human instinct to use stamps as a method of indicating accomplishment."[79] As for the problem of in-kind payments, Clague argued that the problem was not the administrative mechanics of devising a formula for taxing payments in kind—some occupations already covered also received in-kind payments—but "the psychological reaction to the necessity of applying the formula in almost every instance."[80]

As for the financial problem—that these workers would not contribute enough in taxes to cover the cost of their benefits—it turned out that many workers moved back and forth between covered and noncovered occupations. As a result, many farm and household workers were making contributions anyway. Farm hands, for example, would take other work during the winter, and domestics would take work in hotels, laundries, or restaurants as well as private homes, suggesting that the line between excluded and included workers was largely artificial. One analyst estimated that in

1930 there were well over half a million people classified in the census as working in agriculture who also worked temporarily in nonagricultural employment, and many such workers might have acquired rights to benefits by virtue of their temporary covered employment.[81]

But the unexpectedly high level of migration of workers between covered and uncovered jobs also became an argument in favor of extending coverage, precisely because some workers could become eligible for old-age insurance benefits in this way. The institutional linkage between contributions and benefits was crucial to the development of the policy. Because these workers paid taxes into the system for only part of the year, presumably in very poorly paid jobs, their contributions to the system were extremely small. But because of the benefit structure, which provided for a minimum monthly benefit of $10 a month regardless of the recipient's income, their payments would not be likely to cover the benefits for which they would qualify. This was supposed to be the argument *against* adding farm and domestic labor to the old-age insurance system—that they would constitute a drag on the system's reserves. But if many of these workers were already in the system, then covering their employment on a farm or in a household as well as their other employment would both increase revenue and give them a chance to earn a higher benefit. In addition, as Witte pointed out, these workers were likely to be the neediest in old age, and would likely qualify for public assistance if they were shut out of the contributory system. Finally, the presence of so many of these workers in the system (see Figure 3.1) already helped overcome the administrative objection as well, because it meant that many had already received social security numbers and had wage records with the federal government.

In its initial consideration of the issue, the advisory council leaned toward a very weak recommendation about the inclusion of agricultural and domestic workers. Early discussions of excluded groups relied on racial images, such as the "colored woman" domestic worker "who goes from house to house for a day's work here and a day's work there," and who could not reliably remember all her employers.[82] In April 1938, the prevailing position in the council was that the lack of information about the possibility of coverage mandated that no immediate change should be made. A memorandum prepared for the council's October 1938 meeting suggested that coverage should be extended "as rapidly as feasible to include additional groups" but adds that "the coverage of farm laborers and domestic employees . . . is socially desirable but administrative difficulties involved in such coverage warrant postponement of action at this time."[83]

But at the climactic council meeting on 22 October, the council adopted a nearly unqualified recommendation of support for the extension of coverage to farm and domestic labor. The recommendation repeated the language about the social desirability of extending coverage, adding that it should take effect, if administratively possible, by 1 January 1940. What controversy there was came over the proposed date. Several council members were still skeptical of the feasibility of coverage, despite the work of Cohen and others on the stamp-book system. Alvin Hansen, the Harvard economist, suggested, correctly as it turned out, that Congress would never adopt such a proposal but might adopt a more modest one. "We would like to have them all covered," replied Marion Folsom of Eastman Kodak. J. Douglas Brown, the council chairman, ended the discussion by saying, "I think we should vote the way we feel and let Congress take it or leave it." The council adopted the strong language in favor of coverage by a 9 to 4 vote; all four dissenters indicated that they would have supported language that did not include a proposed date.[84]

Unlike 1935, when it was quiet on the issue, the farm lobby immediately flagged agricultural coverage as an undesirable amendment. The *New York Times* reported on the first day of the 1939 congressional session that "those from the Farm Belt said this would be fought to the bitter end."[85] Altmeyer relates that when he urged Ways and Means Chairman Doughton to include farmers and domestics, Doughton replied, "Doctor, when the first farmer with manure on his shoes comes to me and asks to be covered, I will be willing to consider it." (Whether "manure" is Doughton's word or Altmeyer's bowdlerization remains a mystery.) Doughton's quip was, in fact, quite disingenuous, because the recommendations did not encompass the coverage of farmers per se, who wielded substantial political clout in Congress, but wage laborers on farms, who wielded none at all. Nevertheless, Doughton maintained this attitude to the coverage of farm workers throughout his career, even expressing it publicly, with serious consequences.[86]

African-American leaders continued to advocate broadening OAI coverage. Although the NAACP itself did not send a representative to testify, support for expansion of OAI remained prominent on the association's agenda throughout the late 1930s.[87] The National Negro Congress, an umbrella association of black organizations that aspired to do on economic issues what the NAACP was doing on civil rights, did send a representative to Capitol Hill during the hearings on the amendment package.[88] John P. Davis, the congress's executive secretary, testified in favor of inclusion before the Ways and Means Committee. Interestingly, his testimony focused less on the disproportionate impact of these exclusions on black Americans, which the NAACP had emphasized in 1935, than on the desperately low wages, high unemployment, and poor working conditions of these workers, racially neutral appeals that any advocate of social insurance could have made.[89] By making a class-based appeal on behalf of a racial group, Davis was attempting to tie African-American interests into the broader liberal side of the New Deal coalition.

The other leg of that coalition, organized labor, also supported inclusion in 1939. Although William Green of the AFL had been lukewarm toward the inclusion of farm workers in 1935, both the AFL and the CIO supported inclusion in 1939. In particular, the United Cannery, Agricultural, Packing and Allied Workers of America, a CIO union that was seeking to organize farm laborers, strongly supported inclusion before the Ways and Means Committee, and Green's AFL deputy made a general statement of support.[90] The race-labor coalition that was beginning to form in the late 1930s allowed African-Americans to pursue a selective social welfare agenda. The structure of Social Security gave organized labor and American blacks a common interest in the program's expansion that did not require a deep attachment from either group to the other's core commitments. This alignment of forces within the Democratic assemblage, however, was doubly likely to provoke the conservative coalition of Southern Democrats and Republicans that limited the New Deal's reach.[91]

The extension of coverage to agricultural and domestic labor was almost the only significant recommendation of the advisory council that Congress did not adopt. There is little evidence that the congressional committees seriously entertained the thought of extending coverage to these groups; in fact, the House Ways and Means Committee voted unanimously not to do so before its hearings were even over.[92] Congress did not oppose all extensions of coverage to previously excluded groups—seamen, for example, were brought into the old-age and unemployment insurance system. Nor were all recommendations for extension dismissed as perfunctorily— the exclusion of employees of religious organizations was continued only after considerable debate. The basic status of farmers and servants in the social security system, however, was considered uniquely to be a settled question, unworthy of a serious place on the national agenda.

But the farm lobby won more than a simple continuation of the exclusion. It also won an expansion of the definition of "agricultural labor" to include not only farm hands but also workers engaged in the processing of agricultural products on the farm (but not in commercial operations, such as canneries, that were separate from farms). The chief impulse for this amendment came from fruit growers, who had a champion on the Ways and Means Committee, Representative Frank Buck of California, a fruit grower himself in private life. According to the NAACP, the amendment had substantial support from Southern members as well.[93] As Buck himself described the amendment, it would apply, for example, to the workers at a fruit orchard who wash, grade, and pack fruit after it is picked, not strictly farming operations but incidental to preparing produce for market.[94]

The effect of the Buck amendment was to remove from OAI coverage several hundred thousand employees who had originally been covered and at least to reinforce the racial disparity inherent in the initial exclusion.[95] Detailed data do not exist to determine precisely how many workers the Buck amendment pushed out of the OAI system, but there are some clues to suggest that black workers may have borne a disproportionate share of the brunt. For example, one of the newly exempt activities that the Ways and Means Committee report mentioned was the production of turpentine. In 1935, turpentine production was one of the industries in which African-Americans most predominated—more than eighty percent of the workers on turpentine farms and distilleries in 1930 were black.[96] Not all the occupations that the amendment touched affected black workers— there were probably very few blacks involved in maple syrup production, for example. Some, however, such as cotton gin operators, were probably heavily black, although it is impossible to know for sure.

As in 1935, Congress's decision to continue and expand these race-laden exclusions against the recommendation of the executive branch reflects the strategic position of Southerners in Congress, although these decisions required the assent of non-Southerners as well. In particular, Southerners continued to play key roles on the House Ways and Means and Senate Finance Committees, where they controlled the agenda and could modify legislation behind closed doors to render it palatable to their colleagues. In addition to holding the chairs of both committees from the New Deal era through the 1970s, Southerners consistently occupied the lion's share of the most senior seats on these powerful committees. Ways and Means and Finance chairmen were among the most influential Washington politicians of the middle of the century—from Robert Doughton and Pat Harrison to Russell Long and Wilbur Mills—and they often played the legislative game like virtuoso musicians, dazzling audiences with their command of detail and sheer political skill.[97] Among the committee baronies of the House, Ways and Means was a dukedom. Ways and Means bills customarily came to the House floor under closed rules, meaning that no amendments were allowed. Moreover, the Democrats on the Ways and Means Committee made committee assignments for the other Democratic members of the House. Consequently, the committee and its chairman received unusual deference from colleagues, from the lowliest freshman to the speaker of the House.

In the late 1930s, Southern ascendancy on these key committees, and hence apparent Southern influence over Social Security policy, was just beginning; it was to reach its peak in the 1940s and 1950s.[98] The South's institutional power was still sufficient to restrict the target population of OAI and maintain its racial boundaries. Southern power was dependent not only on the Democrats' continuing congressional majority but also on the weakness of countervailing political forces. In 1939, the South prevailed despite the growing political capacity of the Social Security Board and the program's evolving logic of expansion. But over the next decade, these forces gathered strength, leaving the powerful South unable to prevent the deracialization of social insurance.

The Move Toward Inclusion

World War II brought a period of apparent stagnation to the development of the Social Security program, but it was not without significance for the future of Old-Age Insurance. The most important event of the war period was the beginning of OAI benefit payments in 1940. This was the primary task for which the Social Security Board had been preparing itself for nearly five years, and it took considerable pride in processing 111,000 benefit claims in the first six months of the year.[99] This rather humble beginning was in fact the cornerstone event of the political logic of expansion that would shape the program for decades, as the public began to understand the link between their contributions and benefits.

Although the war crowded almost all domestic affairs off the national agenda, President Roosevelt consistently recommended expansion of Old-Age Insurance in his annual messages, and Altmeyer speculates that he was signalling his intention to push for legislation after the war.[100] When the war's end put Social Security back on the agenda as part of the reconversion program, largely due to the concerns of veterans whose war service jeopardized wage credits they had accumulated previously, President Truman followed his predecessor's lead and urged Congress to expand OAI coverage.

After the war, the Social Security Board continued to act as the central node in OAI's institutional network. In 1946, the Ways and Means Committee received a report that it had commissioned the previous year on the expansion of Social Security from an ostensibly independent advisory board, which actually got most of its information, as well as considerable coaching, from the Social Security Board.[101] The report argued, predictably, that there were no plausible obstacles to including farm and domestic workers in OAI, picking up right where the board had left off in 1939.

Coverage of agricultural workers was "particularly important," the report argued, because so many of them move in and out of covered employment, making contributions without ever qualifying for benefits. This situation "will continue to give rise to anomalous and inequitable situations and to interfere with the attainment of the fullest social good possible" under OAI. Furthermore, noncovered jobs became less attractive to workers than covered jobs, and employers were finding it difficult to attract workers for this reason. It pointed out that the standard administrative objection was exaggerated because of the concentration of most farm labor on a small number of large farms; whereas one-half of the hired farm workers worked on the 500,000 largest farms, two-thirds of the country's farms used no hired labor at all. Finally, the report argued, when weighed against the social and economic benefits of coverage, the additional administrative burden, even if it led to added cost and "operational imperfections," was quite small. The considerations for domestic labor were similar.[102]

In the hearings on the 1946 amendments, there was extensive testimony in favor of the inclusion of agricultural and domestic workers. The National Council of Negro Women, Mary McLeod Bethune's organization, testified, as did two national farm organizations, the Grange and the National Farmers Union, but not the American Farm Bureau Federation, the most powerful arm of the farm lobby and the only one with significant Southern roots.[103] A representative of the National Farm Labor Union, the successor to the Southern Tenant Farmers Union, which organized many black farm workers, also testified. Secretary of Commerce Henry Wallace, who had supported inclusion in 1935 as a member of the Committee on Economic Security, strongly supported coverage. In an attempt to undermine Wallace's position, Conservative Congressman A. Willis Robertson claimed incorrectly that even Arthur Altmeyer had been opposed to the stamp-book plan for collecting and recording OAI contributions. Wallace firmly corrected him. "We went into that in 1934," the secretary responded, "and I felt then it was a practical way. I still think it is a practical way." Although Wallace recognized that "in the first instance it would seem a nuisance to the farmers to do it," he did not find this a sufficient objection.[104] Although the 1946 amendments dealt primarily with the issue of reintegrating returning veterans (for whom the war meant a long interruption in their employment that could limit their benefit claims), it was clear that pressure for expansion of OAI was growing.

The next step toward inclusion came from the Treasury Department, which reported in 1947 that "administrative considerations no longer constitute a barrier to expanded coverage." The background economic and political conditions for the extension of the Social Security tax were in place, the department argued. During the war, more people had begun filing income tax returns due to lower personal exemptions as well as wartime inflation. This fact, along with the increase in farm aid and rationing programs, made the farm population more "record conscious" and hence more able to cope with the payroll tax. The Treasury report proposed three possible systems for collecting taxes from agricultural and domestic workers and outlined the advantages and disadvantages of each.[105] Significantly, the report represented the end of the Treasury Department's objection to the extension of coverage, which had been something of a bombshell to the administration in 1935, although the report offered little new evidence or argument to the claims proponents of extension had been making for twelve years.

The brief postwar Republican interregnum in Congress blunted whatever momentum OAI might have gathered toward expansion. President Truman advocated substantial additions to Social Security, including disability and health benefits as well as extended coverage, yet the opposition Congress took little action except to pass, over Truman's veto, two bills restricting coverage but not fundamentally altering the program. These years produced a stalemate between a president committed to the New Deal and inclined to expand its scope and a Congress hostile to most of the New Deal's legacy—a stalemate that Truman exploited to brilliant effect in his reelection campaign in 1948. Yet although Congress significantly rolled back one major New Deal advance—in labor law—Social Security did not face such a fundamental challenge, an indication, perhaps, of its growing legitimacy as an essential feature of the American political landscape.

The Beginnings of Inclusion: The 1950 Amendments

In 1949, after Truman was reelected and the Democrats recaptured control of Capitol Hill, Congress undertook a major revision of Social Security, which involved an extension of coverage as well as increases in taxes and benefits and changes in the public assistance programs.[106] Once again the president, the Social Security Administration, and an advisory council recommended expansion of OAI to include agricultural and domestic workers, as they had in 1935 and again in 1939. Once again, Wilbur Cohen seemed to be everywhere: drafting the administration bill with Altmeyer, lobbying Congress, orchestrating public relations, even helping to draft the Ways and Means Committee's report on the legislation.[107] This time, despite some resistance along traditional lines, Congress did not shut the door completely, and the result was a breakthrough, a bill that provided coverage for some, but not all, farm workers and servants.

The most striking feature of the debate over inclusion in 1949 and 1950, in contrast to earlier debates, is the prominent role of pressure groups and organized interests. Although the conventional wisdom is that public opinion and pressure groups have played little direct role in shaping Social Security policy, they certainly appeared in considerably greater force in 1950 than they had before.[108] Not only did the congressional hearings produce a parade of group representatives (unlike earlier hearings, which featured more elite "expert" testimony and less advocacy), but the politics of interests also figured much more heavily in the words and actions of policymakers.

This pattern reflects the position that Social Security had acquired in American political life and, more generally, the new political landscape that the New Deal had created, and it illustrates the process of policy feedback that governed the course of the policy's development. The policy enactment of 1935 fed back into the political process by affecting the political resources both of policymaking and administrative elites and of the program's public clientele. The institutional structure of Old-Age Insurance produced an impressive expansion of administrative capacity at the national level as well as a network of politically astute administrators who effectively promoted the expansion of the program from their position within the state. Old-Age Insurance created a constituency for itself, and policymakers now had to attend to the millions of clients OAI already had, who had developed a set of expectations about how they would be treated and had organized to see that those expectations were fulfilled. Moreover, that constituency included African-Americans without compromising OAI's popularity or political status. The pressure for expansion of the program to include farm workers and servants, among others, came from a variety of groups with different reasons behind their positions. What linked these diverse groups was not goodwill for the well-being of poor farm laborers, and certainly not the desire to extend government benefits to African-Americans, but their common desire for the protection and expansion of their own relationship to OAI. Without their own stake in OAI, they would have had no interest in anyone else's. In this sense, OAI created the conditions for its own expansion that overcame the same forces that had blocked expansion in the past. African-Americans thus benefited from being part of a broad, cross-class coalition. But the terms of the coalition, and the larger state-society relations that it bespoke, emerged from the institutional structure of the very policy to which African-Americans sought entry. Because Old-Age Insurance was a national program, with effective administration and strong, politically astute leadership, working African-Americans were able to transcend the tangle of race and class that led to their initial exclusion. Despite the severe racial disadvantages still abroad in American society and politics, Old-Age Insurance contributed centrally to the political construction of the black working class.

The principal argument in the debate on extended coverage was over the views of farmers about coverage for themselves and their employees. Debate over the desires and opinions of OAI's potential clients was itself a departure from the earlier episodes, although organized labor had played a role in defining the possibilities for the 1935 act.[109] As Marion Folsom told the Ways and Means Committee, "the people who were brought into the system originally were not consulted in any great detail about it. It was felt that it was a good plan. I feel that sooner or later you will find that the demand is going to be to come into the system."[110] This time around, members of Congress were especially interested in the views of farmers and their organizations. Ways and Means Chairman Robert Doughton, who was born during the Civil War and was 85 years old when the committee held hearings in 1949, took this view, as he had in 1939.

The three major farm organizations divided on the question of coverage for farmers themselves, and they broke down along regional lines. The Southern-dominated, conservative American Farm Bureau Federation (AFBF) opposed coverage; the National Grange and the National Farmers Union, based more in the Midwest and West, supported it, although hardly in ringing terms.[111] As Senator Robert Taft of Ohio noted, "the farm organizations which appeared before the committee favored the program, but . . . they have not been what we might call pressing hard."[112] At the same time, however, all three organizations supported coverage for hired farm workers. There were several reasons for their support. First, because farm workers were poorly paid, farm states had extremely high public assistance burdens for old-age support. Because noncontributory Old-Age Assistance (OAA) pensions (which, in contrast to OAI, provided assistance to the elderly poor) were funded from state as well as federal taxes, farmers felt that they were paying extra taxes to support their workers in old age. Second, they corroborated the point that the Ways and Means staff report had made in 1946, namely that farmers were finding it hard to find workers who had been working in covered employment and did not want to jeopardize their eligibility.[113] Third, the AFBF in particular saw coverage of farm workers as an opportunity to extend its reach into the farm community. "Much educational work will be necessary," its representative told the Finance Committee, "among both farmers and workers to keep the mechanical side of the collection of taxes from becoming overly burdensome."[114] Who was better positioned to do this education than the local farm bureau? Because of its links with the Agricultural Extension Service, the AFBF had a privileged position in the farm sector as a quasi-governmental organization. Extension of OAI coverage would give the AFBF a further opportunity not only to provide a service, OAI tax assistance, to farmers but also to use its organizational capacity on behalf of the government. The extension of coverage thus presented an institution-building opportunity to the AFBF.

In addition to the farm organizations, representatives of farm workers themselves appeared before the congressional committees to ask for coverage. Both the AFL and the CIO had affiliated farm workers' unions, each of which sent representatives to testify.[115] In fact, OAI coverage was one of the issues around which the AFL affiliate, the National Farm Labor Union, planned a major organizing drive in 1950.[116] Farm workers were not highly organized, however, and their appeals for coverage received little attention. Still, their presence represented a new factor. In the 1930s, Doughton had said that he would consider coverage for farmers when they asked for it. Now they were calling his bluff.

Other groups demanded OAI coverage for agricultural and domestic workers as well. Public assistance officials from a number of states, mostly agricultural and some Southern, testified in favor of extending coverage.[117] Like the farmers, they were concerned about the rising costs of state-funded public assistance programs, which were a particular burden in poorer farm states. Kentucky's director of public assistance reported, for example, that his state had more than three times as many OAA beneficiaries as OAI recipients.[118] This was the typical pattern; it was in the farm states, especially in the South, that the aged population relied most heavily on public assistance, topped by Louisiana, where nearly four in five people over age 65 received OAA in 1948.[119] A number of women's organizations, including the National Consumers' League, the National Women's Trade Union League, and the YWCA, testified in particular support of extending coverage to domestic workers, most of whom were women.[120] And several veterans' and religious organizations also advocated expanded coverage.

The 1950 debate also produced the strongest demand yet from black organizations for inclusion, as well as evidence of continuing Southern resistance. Clarence Mitchell of the NAACP reminded the Finance Committee of the predominance of blacks in these occupations, and he pointed out the pattern of agricultural exclusion from federal labor protection, such as the minimum wage and the National Labor Relations Act. Mitchell received unusually dismissive treatment from Doughton, who repeatedly challenged his testimony and told him flat out that his statement was "exactly contrary to the experience of most people."[121] That the chairman reacted this way to an NAACP official who, after all, offered testimony that was hardly new to the committee suggests Doughton's unease with the prospect. The employment director of the Harlem YWCA, an important African-American organization, wrote to Roosevelt in support of coverage for domestic workers, noting that sixty-four percent of the employed women in Harlem were household employees. Edgar G. Brown of the National Negro Council testified in favor of expansion, as did Elmer W. Henderson of the American Council on Human Rights, a federation of black fraternal organizations.[122]

By 1950, the institutional structure of Old-Age Insurance and the program's logic of expansion had created a new politics of Social Security that impelled the program toward growth. OAI enjoyed overwhelming popularity despite the skepticism that had greeted it in 1935.[123] The program's clients were increasingly organized to protect and enhance their stake, and what is more, they had an interest in expanding the program's target population to help ensure its long-term financial and political prospects. As a result, African-American potential clients were able to demand coverage on the program's own terms, terms that depended not on their racial identity but on their status as working, contributing citizens who deserved social rights as a matter of course.[124] But neither these structural imperatives nor the activities of the NAACP and other advocates of inclusion was sufficient to overcome the resilient forces of exclusion. The power of

Southern Democrats remained central to the workings of Congress, and the stubborn resistance of the aptly nicknamed "Muley" Doughton stood in the way.

Despite the overwhelming demand for the extension of coverage and the apparent lack of opposition, the forces of exclusion remained resilient. The resistance of the Ways and Means Committee to coverage for farm and domestic workers seems rather puzzling. The committee's reluctance seemed to stem from several factors. First, Doughton was skeptical of the idea and was unwilling to accept the testimony he heard that, for example, both farmers and farm workers wanted coverage for the latter. He and the committee seemed to be waiting for the kind of resounding and unequivocal voice that unorganized farm workers and household servants could, of course, not provide. By setting such a standard, far beyond the strength and clarity of the voice the committee had heard in 1935, Doughton essentially rigged the game so these groups could not win. Second, Doughton and the committee continued to express skepticism of the administrative feasibility of coverage for nonindustrial workers, even though this point had been resolved almost beyond question. Finally, Southern power on the Ways and Means Committee was near its peak, giving the cagey Doughton ample institutional resources to carry the day.

The institutional structure of the program contributed not only to the demand for expanded coverage but also to the argument that such coverage would be possible. Once again, the committees heard extensive testimony on the administrative question, including a detailed statement from the commissioner of internal revenue, who supported inclusion, echoing the conclusions of the Treasury Department's 1947 report.[125] Oscar Pogge, the director of the Bureau of Old-Age and Survivors Insurance, stressed the bureau's extensive field operation and its emphasis on direct personal service to its clients, arguing, in essence, that this aspect of the bureau's institutional structure made the administrative problems of expanded coverage particularly tractable. As a national program with a public image of friendly efficiency, fostered by a strong service ethic and a careful public relations operation, OAI made its own expansion both administratively feasible and politically palatable. Pogge also reminded the committee that the administrative burden of coverage for farm workers would fall almost exclusively on large-scale farmers; fifty percent of all hired farm labor in the country worked on only 100,000 large-scale farms, and less than thirty percent of all farmers hired ninety-six percent of the labor.[126]

Pogge's predecessor as OAI director, John Corson, argued that "in the recent past, American farmers and housewives proved their ability to cooperate under various stamp systems and programs that required record keeping and reports," such as commodity credit programs and wartime rationing. The Baltimore Urban League sent a group of women to testify that American housewives were willing and able to comply with expanded coverage. One of them, Mrs. Donald B. Van Hollen, remarked that if women could run an efficient home, including managing rationing stamps, they could certainly manage OAI coverage for their servants. "The 'little woman,'" she said, "is no longer a helpless, clinging vine. I am sure that no stamp system or any other reasonable and intelligent method of requiring the reporting of wages holds any terrors today. We have coped with more difficult problems than that. If you will just write your instructions so that we can understand them, you'll find us cooperative and willing to comply." Clarence Mitchell of the NAACP put the same point more condescendingly. "Anyone who knows how to keep a bridge score," he quipped, "should be able to learn how to operate under a stamp plan."[127]

There were some more colorful presentations to the committee on this point. W. A. Heller, a 74-year-old Texan, recounted his conversations with farmers around the wagon yard and with local housewives, who generally opposed coverage "on account of the bookkeeping." After he read an article about the stamp-book proposal "by a man named Snyder—I think he is Secretary of the Treasury" [he was], he asked around some more and found that his friends "would go for that." And the profit-seeking proprietors of the H. W. Nichols Sales Book Company of Cincinnati used their testimony to pitch their Nichols Simplified Record Book to the Ways and Means Committee as the way to make coverage feasible for everyone, not the only time a company used such a forum to advertise its own products.[128] Besides relieving the tedium of the hearings for congressmen, these items reinforced the conclusions of the more serious testimony that American farms and households were certainly able by 1950 to comply with OAI coverage for their employees.

The House passed a bill that extended OAI coverage potentially to more than 10 million people, including a small number of "regularly employed" domestics but not agricultural workers. Despite the nearly unanimous testimony in favor of coverage for farm workers, Doughton's committee maintained its resistance. In its report, the Ways and Means Committee put off the farm worker issue for "further study," a common death-knell for legislative proposals.[129] Even this limited inclusion of domestic workers, estimated at between one-third and one-half of the country's household workers, attracted the ire of racially conservative Southerners. "I do not want to see remain in this bill the provision about domestic servants," said William Colmer of Mississippi. "Every one of you is going to hear about this when you get home."[130] At the same time, many farm-state members and Northern liberals lamented the lack of coverage for farmers and farm workers.

Significantly, the largest new group that the House bill included was almost entirely white. This was the nonfarm self-employed, who numbered between four and five million people. As the data in Table 3.2 show, the categories most likely to include self-employed workers in the 1950 Census totaled nearly 4.9 million people, of whom only 133,000 were nonwhite, less than three percent. Extending coverage to the self-employed thus would have brought nearly one in three excluded workers, but almost no blacks, into the OAI system, increasing the racial imbalance in an already imbalanced program. The same objections applied to this group—that it would pose difficult administrative problems, that these workers did not want coverage, and so forth. In fact, the testimony about coverage of this group was much more ambiguous than the testimony about farm workers. But neither this fact nor the supposed administrative barriers stood in the way of coverage, suggesting that racial imbalance was once again at work in the case of farm workers and domestics.

The Senate Finance Committee took a small but significant step, adding certain regularly employed farm workers, probably about one-third of the total. In his remarks on the Senate floor presenting the bill, Chairman Walter George of Georgia stressed the imbalance between public assistance programs and OAI. More people received public assistance benefits than OAI. Total expenditures for public assistance were $2 billion, compared with only $700 million for OAI. This level of spending placed a great burden on state budgets, especially in agricultural states where more retirees relied on public assistance and fiscal pressures were generally tighter. George also contrasted the merits of OAI—procedural egalitarianism and the linkage of contributions and benefits—to the inequity of Old-Age Assistance.[131] Congress had to respond to political pressure for a more generous, flat-rate, noncontributory pension, pressure created by the Townsend movement and inflamed by a few states where Old-Age Assistance benefits were extremely generous. The basic thrust of the amendment, then, was to increase benefits substantially, which would require new revenue.[132] Both committees agreed to the first payroll tax increase in the program's history, but in order to minimize tax increases, new sources of revenue were required. Proffering the usual pieties about administrative feasibility, George, who would later resist further inclusion of farm workers tooth and nail, acceded to a small expansion in this direction, knowing it could be scaled down in conference with the House.

On the Senate floor, an amendment to relax the standards for coverage of farm workers to double the number included was defeated, but the sponsorship of the amendment gives some indication of the potential sources of support for inclusion: offering the amendment were a Northern liberal, Herbert Lehman of New York; a Westerner from an agricultural state, James Murray of Montana; and a Southern liberal, Claude Pepper of Florida.[133] The final bill that Truman signed contained a compromise that included farm workers who worked full-time on sixty days or more in a calendar quarter, provided that the quarter was preceded by a qualifying quarter.[134] The compromise slightly reduced the total number of farm workers included and, significantly, effectively eliminated seasonal workers from coverage. But farm workers at least became eligible for OAI for the first time, a small step, but one that pointed the way toward a truly race-blind old-age insurance program.

The debates over the 1950 Social Security amendments suggest that new forces were shaping policy but that the old forces of racial exclusion remained. The terms of debate, especially as the House Ways and Means Committee framed them, were reminiscent of the 1930s, when the exclusionary provisions first took hold, and the comparison between the committee's positions on farm and domestic workers on one hand and the self-employed on the other reinforce the impact of continued racial exclusion. At the same time, new forces, created by the structure of the OAI program itself, provided the impulse toward greater inclusion and the breaking of the racial imbalance that had held sway for fifteen years.

Full Inclusion: The 1954 Amendments

The amendments of 1954 finally brought agricultural and domestic workers, except those most irregularly employed, into the OAI system. The partial inclusion of the 1950 legislation undoubtedly paved the way for full inclusion four years later. The 1954 amendments extended OAI coverage to an additional two million farm workers and several hundred thousand domestic workers, among others. Significantly, the amendments also reversed the exclusion of cotton-gin, turpentine, and other agricultural processing workers who had been removed from the system in 1939.

The same forces were arrayed on both sides of the issue. The farm and farm labor organizations once again supported inclusion, except for the AFBF, which was resistant. Proponents once again promoted OAI as an alternative to public assistance. Although neither the NAACP nor other black organizations testified in favor of expansion in 1954, the black press, which had denounced the 1950 act as "inadequate," hailed the 1954 legislation's passage as an important step toward economic equality.[135] The only significant opposition came, once again, from conservative Southern Democrats in Congress, who had successfully blocked inclusion in the past.

But in 1954, Southern Democrats were no longer in charge. The 1952 election swept the Republicans, behind Dwight Eisenhower, into control of Congress, displacing a Georgian and a Tennessean from the chairs of the Finance and Ways and Means Committees and putting in their places Eugene Millikin of Colorado, a moderate senator, and Daniel Reed of New York, who had opposed OAI as unconstitutional as a junior member of the minority in 1935. Despite the uncertainty produced by two decades of Republican hostility to Social Security, President Eisenhower, along with yet another advisory council that was effectively a puppet of the Social Security professionals, supported expansion of the program. Although Altmeyer was no longer running Social Security, Wilbur Cohen was still around, however, and even from within a Republican administration he was the nerve center of the legislative operation.[136]

Republican support represents the true coming-of-age of the OAI program. By 1954, six million people were receiving benefits, more than twice the number in 1950. Annual payments totaled more than $3 billion, a fourfold real increase since 1950 and nearly one-seventh of the federal government's domestic spending. In that time, the average monthly benefit had risen nearly eighty-five percent.[137] As the program grew and more people received higher payments, Republicans risked incurring the wrath of a large constituency by opposing it. The institutional structure of OAI, its contributory nature and the illusion that it did not entail "government spending," allowed Republicans to support it while still generally opposing the governmental expansion of the New Deal, and both the 1948 and 1952 Republican platforms expressed support for the program.[138] Even Alf Landon, who had excoriated Social Security in the 1936 campaign against Roosevelt, was a strong supporter of the program by 1940.[139] As a Republican leader opposed to the resilient policy commitments of the New Deal regime, Eisenhower recognized the limitations of his position and accommodated those commitments where he had to.[140] "Should any political party attempt to abolish social security," Eisenhower wrote, "you would not hear of that party again in our political history." Ike added that only "a tiny splinter group" of right-wingers believed that the Republicans would take such a position, "but their number is negligible and they are stupid."[141]

The most serious challenges to OAI from within the Republican fold, mounted by the United States Chamber of Commerce and Representative Carl Curtis of Nebraska, did not oppose extension of the program. Instead, they proposed a universal minimum retirement benefit financed on a "pay-as-you-go" basis combined with the abolition of federal grants to the states for Old-Age Assistance. This proposal would have jettisoned the fundamental structure of OAI, the links among contributions, wages, and benefits, and made taxes and payments subject to annual congressional action, an arena in which the Chamber of Commerce believed it could better further its interest in low business taxes. The Chamber of Commerce proposal went down in flames when Federal Security Administrator Oveta Culp Hobby convened a closed-door advisory group on social security stacked with chamber representatives. News of the group leaked to the press, which dubbed it the "Hobby Lobby" and depicted it as a big-business and Republican plot to undermine old-age security. The administration—with the ubiquitous Wilbur Cohen as agent provocateur—was forced to expand the group into a traditional advisory council, which, of course, recommended retaining OAI's structure and extending coverage.[142]

Curtis was appointed by Ways and Means Chairman Daniel Reed to head a select subcommittee on social security. In appointing Curtis, Reed passed over the more senior but more moderate Robert W. Kean of New Jersey, a longtime supporter of OAI, suggesting that the subcommittee's outlook would be hostile. Indeed it was. Curtis had to resort to a subpoena to get Arthur Altmeyer, who had retired from the Social Security Administration, to testify. The purpose of the subcommittee's hearings seemed to be to bait Altmeyer into acknowledging that Old-Age Insurance was not "insurance" at all, because no contract existed between an individual and the government, which could lower benefits or eliminate the program at any time by legislation. Altmeyer freely admitted that this was so and calmly explained the principle of social insurance and reviewed the history of OAI. Curtis became increasingly irate, and his chief counsel actually began shouting at Altmeyer at the top of his lungs. The subcommittee hearings, intended to undermine public support for OAI by exposing its precariousness, backfired on both Curtis and Reed. Thanks not only to Altmeyer's unflappability but also to the structure of OAI itself, their attempt to undermine the program's political support failed, and they were both left with no choice but to support the contributory principle.[143] Hailing the 1954 amendments, the *New York Times* noted approvingly that "both political parties have fully accepted the premise that social security is a proper concern of the Federal Government."[144] As a result, the Republicans tried to out-Democrat the Democrats and proposed another sweeping expansion of OAI that Congress passed relatively unscathed, somewhat to the Democrats' embarrassment.[145] The newfound Republican support for OAI, combined with the newfound minority status of Southern Democrats, meant that full inclusion was all but inevitable.

The last gasp of Southern resistance, however, was heard in Congress. In the House, Howard Smith of Virginia, who had raised the race issue in 1935, tried to block the rule providing for consideration of the amendments on the House floor, a tactic he would use with great skill in later years to obstruct civil rights legislation. Judge Smith's objection was that, under the closed-rule tradition of the Ways and Means Committee, there was no opportunity for the House to strike the farm and farm-worker provisions of the bill. Of the eight representatives who voted against the bill, six were Southern Democrats. (Smith himself voted "present.")[146]

In the Senate, John Stennis of Mississippi dredged up, for the last time in the fight over this issue, the racist language and traditions of the Old South. He offered an amendment to drop the farm-workers provision of the bill, leaving the 1950 restrictions. "I oppose," he said, "the trend of adding people to the social security system, not by the thousands or hundreds of thousands, but by the millions," even though dropping farm workers alone would not address this particular objection. "The basic concept of the social security system," he continued, "is that it is supposed to be for industrial workers," which had never been true. Finally he addressed his central objection to the new provision: "Under the bill we are to bring in all the groups of migrant and reckless and irresponsible workers, who will pay virtually nothing, and the entire burden will fall on the employer, and those workers will get a vested right in the fund to which they will contribute very little."[147] Stennis's speech evoked the traditional racial imagery of American political and social discourse; he might as well have added "lazy and shiftless" to "reckless and irresponsible." In the midst of the uproar over *Brown* v. *Board of Education,* which had been decided three months earlier, his message could hardly have been clearer.

Stennis received some support from other Southerners, but he was opposed by Northerners from farm states and, significantly, by Democrat Spessard L. Holland of Florida. Although Florida's agricultural labor force was nearly half black in 1950 (compared with one-third for the South as a whole), it was beginning to attract retirees from around the country, many of whom would rely on OAI. Bringing new workers into the system, even at the cost of substantially integrating OAI coverage, would help safeguard these benefits.[148] Holland's vocal support for inclusion of agricultural workers captures the essence of OAI's political logic of inclusion and its challenge to the traditional forces of racial exclusion. Here was a Southern Democratic senator for whom the imperatives of expansion overcame Southern solidarity on a matter of race. The Senate quickly defeated Stennis's amendment, putting the issue of agricultural exclusion to rest almost for good.

The two Democratic Senators on the conference committee, Walter George of Georgia and Harry Byrd of Virginia, refused to sign the conference report to protect, as George explained to his colleagues, against "creeping socialism," and particularly to protect against the inclusion of farmers and their employees. It is fittingly ironic that almost nineteen years to the day from the signing of the Social Security Act, two of the architects of its racial exclusion now found themselves helpless to prevent the last racial barrier in Old-Age Insurance from coming down.

4

Aid to Dependent Children and the Political Construction of the "Underclass"

As Old-Age Insurance was developing toward full racial inclusion and promoting the political construction of a black middle class, Aid to Dependent Children was also changing into a more inclusive program. This transformation was not toward broad, generous inclusion, however, but toward an austere and restrictive welfare regime that, although originally designed precisely *not* to reach African-Americans, in the end perpetuated and deepened their political, economic, and social isolation by including them. Both the mechanisms of exclusion and the terms of inclusion were different from the beginning, as were the political consequences. Rather than categorical exclusion along occupational lines, African-American exclusion from ADC was administrative, the result of the program's severe institutional parochialism established in 1935. Parochial institutions not only enabled but also invited local policymakers and administrators to create widely varying ADC programs that, in different ways, shaped the access of poor black women and children to benefits.

In contrast to national Old-Age Insurance, Aid to Dependent Children under the Social Security Act was a thoroughly parochial program. ADC sought to expand and regularize the mothers' pensions that many states had already adopted by providing matching funds to states who agreed to meet certain minimum requirements. Because the ADC framework already assumed a large state and local role in administering the program, the focus of Southern attention in Congress was on removing what they considered to be onerous federal restrictions on state policy. Most significantly, Congress removed the requirements that benefits provide "a reasonable subsistence compatible with decency and health" and that states hire public assistance personnel on a merit system. The clear implication of these changes was to create the conditions for discrimination by state and local governments against African-Americans, who in fact stood to benefit

118

more than whites from the program due to the greater proportion of black children who lived in poor, single-parent families.

These race-laden institutional decisions set the stage for local politicians and bureaucrats, rather than their national counterparts, to set the terms not only of racial inclusion or exclusion but also of the development of the program. As a result, welfare policymaking and administration reflected local and regional political configurations. In the South, this meant that ADC simply did not reach blacks in any remote proportion to their need, or even their apparent ability to meet the basic definition of the program's target population. White Southern elites, jealous of their region's racially stratified social and economic structure, in effect captured ADC to protect their status. This result of the class and race origins of ADC's parochialism is thoroughly unsurprising. More startling, and in many ways more important, is the reproduction of this pattern in the North, but with a sinister twist. Although the badges of racial distinction in Chicago and Detroit were nowhere near as stark or obvious as in the Mississippi Delta and the Carolina lowlands, they existed nonetheless. Equally jealous of their own distinctive structures of political power, Northern white politicians captured ADC for their own purposes, ostensibly quite different from Southern purposes but in the end quite the same. As African-Americans streamed north in the middle of the century in search of the "promised land" of freedom and opportunity, they gained freer and wider access to public assistance. Without the protection of national institutions, however, black recipients of ADC were increasingly isolated from the political and economic mainstream, and their newfound claim to public social provision proved a Pyrrhic victory, undermined in the end by the increasingly "locked in" effects of parochial institutions.

Institutional Structure, Social Policy, and Race

Clearly it was not economic disadvantage that kept African-Americans out of ADC. On the contrary, it was precisely their disproportionate economic distress that gave ADC and other public assistance programs the potential to be of particular benefit to black Americans. Nor was there explicit legal discrimination at the federal level; the Social Security Act itself mentioned few restrictions on eligibility and anticipated that states would award benefits based principally on need.[1] At the same time, the act contained no protection against discrimination. In the 1935 debates, George Edmund Haynes, the executive secretary of the Race Relations Department of the

National Council of Churches (NCC), asked the Senate Finance Committee to include a clause in the Social Security Act prohibiting racial discrimination in the administration of federally funded public assistance programs. Haynes offered convincing testimony that explicit federal guidance could be effective in equalizing the distribution of government benefits.[2] Congress did not heed this plea, and the absence of the nondiscrimination clause that has since become standard issue for federal grant legislation opened the door, as the NCC feared, for administrative discrimination.

That there was substantial discrimination in the administration of ADC is beyond question; in many cases, particularly in the South, black families were less likely to be deemed eligible than white families, and those African-Americans that were eligible got smaller payments. But much of the evidence for discriminatory treatment is anecdotal. Previous studies do not demonstrate clearly that administrative discrimination in ADC was universal, or even common, especially outside the South, and some even suggest that black families in Northern cities faced little, if any, discrimination.[3] It is true that a systematic examination of this question faces several obstacles, including the lack of comprehensive data about the race of public assistance recipients over time and the tricky problem of assessing the adequacy of benefits against the level of need and deprivation that different segments of the population faced. Still, there is ample evidence that suggests that blacks were generally poorly treated in the administration of ADC, both in the South and elsewhere.

What made discrimination a possibility—a near certainty in the eyes of African-American observers and their allies—was the institutional structure of Aid to Dependent Children. In keeping with its roots in state mothers' pension policies, and even deeper roots in the Anglo-American tradition of local poor relief, ADC was essentially a local program. Under the Social Security Act, states established ADC programs with some federal funding and limited federal supervision. Unlike Old-Age Insurance, where national policymakers and bureaucrats had direct and exclusive control over the details of the policy's design and its implementation, ADC was subject to widely dispersed political and administrative authority. Institutional differences between the programs go a long way toward an explanation of their different developmental paths, the one toward race-blind inclusion and expansion and the other toward racial division, isolation, and retrenchment. Whereas OAI institutions promoted the growth of a politically constructed black middle class, ADC institutions have promoted the political construction of a different, far less benign political identity for a different part of the African-American population—the ghetto poor, or urban "underclass."

The Policy Design of ADC: Discretionary and Noncontributory

In contrast to OAI's procedural egalitarianism, ADC was a doubly discretionary program. First, the Social Security Act did not create a uniform policy for the entire country. Instead, it obliged the federal government to defray some of the costs that states incurred in administering their own ADC programs. In fact, not until 1955, when Nevada established one, did every state have an ADC program that met even the fairly minimal standards to receive federal grants. Second, the state programs did not establish self-executing rules that determined who received a benefit of what size. State laws set standards, but eligibility and benefits ultimately relied on subjective determinations of resources, need, and other criteria by individual caseworkers or administrators. A state could prescribe rules and procedures that on their face seemed reasonable and fair; the mere existence of rules, however, does not produce fair administration. In an Illinois investigation of Old-Age Assistance in 1939, for example, blacks charged that the requirement that applicants produce a birth certificate to prove their age was discriminatory. Although the rule itself seems innocuous, they pointed out that many blacks born in the South were never issued birth certificates, and many needy older blacks in Chicago were denied assistance as a result.[4]

ADC was also noncontributory, meaning that its beneficiaries were not drawing on funds to which they had acquired a claim by contributing. Unlike OAI, then, increasing ADC's constituency did not improve the program's financial health, and so there was no corresponding expansionary logic. Instead, increasing the caseload simply increased the fiscal burden on the state and federal governments, which had to rely on revenues collected from nonrecipients to pay benefits. Even if most people believed the program's beneficiaries to be "deserving" or "honorable," the structure of the program created a logic of constraint rather than the expansionary logic of OAI.[5] Moreover, these labels do not denote fixed moral categories but are themselves politically constructed, defined by laws and administrative practices that sort people into social policy categories. The "suitable home" policies that many states adopted, for example, fit this logic of constraint; they served to restrict eligibility for assistance by refining the target population even further according to some criteria of desert, while assuring the community that its money was not being squandered. But nonformulaic "suitable home" policies increased the administrative burden on caseworkers, making arbitrary shorthand judgments about the suitability of the home, as well as outright discrimination, considerably more likely.[6] Thus discretion created the opportunity for discriminatory administration of the program, and noncontribution created an incentive to keep the rolls as small as possible.

The combination of discretionary benefits, noncontributory financing, and state administration perpetuated racial subordination in the South and elsewhere as it was calculated to do. The Roosevelt administration had advocated stronger federal controls over state administration of ADC, which would have given the Social Security Board a considerable mandate to supervise state administration directly and to regulate the adequacy and fairness of state benefit programs rather than simply to approve state ADC laws in their broad outlines while leaving broad swaths of discretion to states. With this language removed by Southerners in Congress, the federal government was left with very little ability to exercise the kind of pressure that it had exerted on behalf of racial fairness in certain relief programs of the early New Deal.[7] By creating a program that combined weak fiscal capacity with weak national supervision, the framers of the welfare state in effect set in motion the institutionalization of ADC's logic of constraint. In the Depression, when economic despair was general all over the United States, the institutional constraints built into ADC may have meant little. But when prosperity and work returned, and women and children moved again toward the center of the social policy agenda, the scattered institutional legacy of the New Deal dealt a very poor hand to the federal government and a very good one to the states.

The Administrative Structure of ADC: Decentralized and Politicized

The most important feature of ADC's parochial institutional structure was its reliance on state and local administration. The federal government's role in ADC was to approve state plans and provide matching funds for the payment of benefits. To mollify the Southerners, administration witnesses had testified time and again in 1935 that the federal government's role would be restricted to approving the state's laws rather than interfering in administration. Without greater administrative control, the only sanction available to the board in a case of state noncompliance was to suspend all federal matching funds to the entire state, which it was understandably reluctant to do. As a result, the institutional structure of ADC left a great deal of room for racially discriminatory administration.

State control over ADC programs had several important effects. First, it produced wide variations in state policy, both benefit levels and eligibility criteria, as well as in the quality and competence of administration. As early as 1940, the Social Security Board documented bewildering variety among state plans, and a study nearly three decades later showed that rather than converging, state policies differed from one another more than ever.[8] Second, it left ADC policymaking and administration much more susceptible than national programs to the influence of local elites or majorities. One way to conceive of federal grant programs such as ADC is that the states are essentially agents of the federal government, paid to do the bidding of the higher authority. But even in such "principal-agent" relationships, it is costly at best (and impossible at worst) for the principal to monitor the agent's activities thoroughly. Moreover, in the case of ADC, the federal government did not have much leverage over the states. Short of cutting off all federal grants to a state, there was little the federal government could do to punish a rogue state or force it to behave. Social Security executives in the federal government worried about this problem a lot in 1935 and after, but the program's structure left them repeatedly powerless. But it is not clear that the "principal-agent" model is the right way to think about the federal-state relationship in ADC. Although federal money certainly carried with it certain responsibilities that would inevitably emanate from Washington, each individual ADC program was the creation of an independently constituted state government that chose, through its own political processes, to pursue welfare policy, with federal assistance and cooperation. In this model, the role of the federal government is not to control or even to supervise but to assist each state to attend to the welfare of its own citizens, sorting and treating them as it sees fit. State and local politicians, not surprisingly, adopted this view of the federal relationship in welfare policy, and it is not hard to see the potential consequences for African-Americans.

ADC was substantially more open than OAI to outside political influence. It was an important outlet for political patronage at the state and local levels, especially before, but even after, a statutory requirement for merit hiring was imposed in 1939. ADC was the most purely redistributive of policies, taking revenue from the haves and distributing it as benefits to the have-nots, and as such it generated intense and enduring political and ideological conflicts that broke largely along class lines.[9] In contrast to

OAI, the structure of ADC administration has invited political interest in management as well as results. Whereas OAI administration involved creating systems and procedures to ensure the correct collection and crediting of taxes and payment of benefits, the essential operations of ADC involved individual judgments about individual cases. Because the activities of state welfare administrators were, politically speaking, more visible than those of federal Social Security workers, they became a lightening rod for the program, attracting attention because they were the people who made the actual, operational decisions about who benefits. Not only could they attract criticism for making misjudgments about welfare, but they were responsible for the efficiency and economy of the program. If the "wrong" people were getting benefits, or if the program cost too much, politicians could blame bureaucratic executives; to forestall this eventuality, executives imposed careful procedural constraints on their subordinates to ensure efficiency and economy.[10] Local welfare agencies have not, typically, been highly professional enterprises; they have held little career appeal for professional social workers.[11] More important, however, were the incentives for local welfare offices built into the discretionary and decentralized political structure of ADC. Because the number of clients served and assisted was an easily measurable outcome, managers and workers had an incentive to maximize these indices of their activity, sacrificing not only kindness and civility but also the political goals of limiting the welfare rolls and curbing abuse.[12] Thus the technical requirements of welfare administration subverted the political goals of welfare policy, creating space for political investigations into welfare operations and legislative piling-on of additional restrictions and requirements.[13] ADC has been fertile ground for such investigations and amendments, as the long and repetitive history of welfare reform efforts testifies.

Whereas OAI operated in a stable policymaking environment characterized by unitary centralized administration and strong planning capacity, ADC's policymaking environment was from the beginning unstable and unpredictable. ADC had a short-term orientation; without the connection between current contributions and future benefits it contained no promise of future benefits to a discrete and potentially powerful group. Thus ADC was subject to constant political controversy, which increased uncertainty about the long-range demands that its administrators would face. Second, ADC faced multiple and decentralized policymaking venues. ADC policy was to be made in dozens, even hundreds or thousands, of jurisdictions at the federal, state, and local or county levels. Although the federal government, through its requirement for matching funds and the welfare "entitlement," set the basic requirements for ADC programs, central direction was sketchy at best. ADC administrators had to respond to a cacophony of policy direction from various sources, and welfare reformers have repeatedly faced tremendous obstacles due simply to the multilayered complexity of welfare policy and the multiple veto points available to opponents of reform. At each level of government, ADC had to rely on annual appropriations to fund benefit payments. Being thus subject to federal, state, and sometimes local budget processes required the expenditure of substantial bureaucratic and political resources on the part of ADC agencies and exposed them to continual controversy over their mission and performance.[14] In this complicated and volatile environment, ADC did not develop planning capacity comparable to that of OAI, where program executives were able to develop and effect a broad strategic vision. ADC policy, driven by diffuse short-term political forces such as budget cycles, was subject to intense ideological conflict, and ADC planning was reduced to tactical maneuvers in the interest of holding ground rather than advancing toward an objective. It is surprising neither that bureaucratic planning for welfare policy has not flourished, nor that, like the trench warfare of World War I, welfare reform battles have been fought for more than a generation over the same small patch of ground.[15]

ADC, finally, had none of OAI's advantages in its method and manner of citizen contact. It was not able to use outside organizational capacity to its own benefit. There were no easily separable tasks that ADC administrators could farm out to other agencies as Social Security executives managed to do. At the federal level, administrative responsibility for ADC was restricted to oversight of state plans and involved no public contact at all. At the state level, most states already had some kind of apparatus before 1935 that ostensibly administered mothers' pensions and other child welfare assistance.[16] ADC strengthened these organizations but for the most part did not fundamentally change the way they transacted their business with the public. Moreover, ADC's pattern of contact with individual clients has done nothing to enhance its reputation either with those clients or with the public at large. There was no automatic trigger, such as retirement, for an ADC application. Applicants were subject to intrusive and demeaning scrutiny of their homes and personal lives in order to satisfy the program's fiscal and political imperatives. Following the initial application, subsequent contact between clients and the agency tended to be punitive rather than helpful. Recipients were often subject to surprise visits from caseworkers and investigators to check up on the suitability of the home and search for evidence of other violations, and they could be summarily dropped from the program if they refused to let an investigator in.[17] ADC workers were often rude and unhelpful as a result of managerial constraints, and their decisions frequently appeared capricious. These characteristics have rendered ADC less than popular with clients and taxpayers alike.

What would happen when such a program—parochial and expressly political in the extreme—was administered to a target population that was poor, powerless, and disproportionately black? ADC's institutional structure certainly contained the seeds of discrimination, especially in the South. It contained none of the forces that led OAI to overcome quickly and completely the race-laden boundaries that demarcated the latter's target population. On the contrary, the institutional architecture of ADC threatened to reinforce the politically constructed position of African-Americans in American political life, placing further state sanction behind their position in a paternalistic social structure, at the discretionary mercy of white elites in almost every aspect of their lives. But the very dispersion of power in the institutional structure meant that these effects might not be uniform and that African-Americans in different parts of the country might be included more readily in ADC. What were the terms of African-American inclusion or exclusion in this pivotal welfare policy? How did they differ across states and regions? How did the parochial institutional structure of ADC affect the program's implementation? And, most important, how did a program designed to exclude African-Americans become so heavily identified with African-Americans that welfare dependency became central to a politically constructed definition of a black urban "underclass?"

Discrimination in ADC

Suggestive Evidence

The institutional structure of ADC as established in 1935 left ample room for discrimination against African-Americans by state and local officials. But "room for discrimination" and discrimination itself are not the same thing. It was not the mere possibility of discrimination but the actual patterns of discrimination laid down by actual administrators under the parochial institutional framework that would determine the boundaries of inclusion and exclusion in ADC. As with OAI, a first test for discriminatory administration of ADC is to compare the proportion of blacks in the recipient caseload with their proportion in the population. But because black families disproportionately met the basic eligibility criteria for ADC—poverty and the absence of one parent—racial proportions in the caseload that just match the proportions in the population are not sufficient evidence for nondiscrimination. If black and white families were treated equally in determinations of eligibility and benefit levels, we should observe, all other things being equal, *higher* proportions of black families receiving, on average, *higher* payments.[18]

In the South, we can easily observe the prevalence of discrimination in the program's very first years. As early as the late 1930s, every Southern state that had an ADC program awarded benefits to black children at a rate lower than their proportion in the population.[19] Moreover, as Table 4.1 reports, Southern states, with the exception of Tennessee, awarded smaller benefits to black children. The culture and society of the South undoubtedly discouraged African-Americans from approaching white public authorities even to apply for benefits to which they were legally entitled. For those black families who did apply for assistance, imbalanced application of "suitable home" regulations in the South to deny assistance to poor blacks is well documented and helps account for the underrepresentation of black families among ADC recipients, even in the face of greater need.[20] African-American women who received benefits for their children faced work requirements designed to keep them in the agricultural labor force.[21] Finally, even when black families were deemed eligible, they often received lower benefits than similarly situated white families, based on "the general belief in the South . . . that Negroes can get along with less than whites."[22]

Outside the South, the data are mixed. In a few Northern industrial states, black children were awarded relief at much higher rates than their proportion in the population, and in Pennsylvania, Ohio, and Indiana they received substantially higher average payments, suggesting that blacks may have received comparable treatment in those states. A 1941 study of public assistance in Philadelphia and St. Louis found that black families comprised about two-thirds of the ADC caseloads in those two cities.[23] But even in non-Southern states, there was substantial variation in the accessibility and generosity of benefits. New Jersey and the District of Columbia, for example, paid smaller benefits to black children than white. In 1939 the Illinois legislature opened an investigation into charges of unfair treatment of black applicants for Old-Age Assistance, suggesting that not all

Table 4.1 Racial Difference in ADC Payments, 1939–1940, in States with Black Populations over 100,000 in 1930[a]

| State | Average monthly $/child | | Difference | Percentage Difference |
	Black	White		
United States	**$13.09**	**$12.68**	**$0.41**	**3.2%**
Pennsylvania	18.13	14.42	3.71	25.7
Ohio	15.18	12.39	2.79	22.5
Indiana	15.03	12.50	2.53	20.2
Michigan	14.20	12.92	1.28	9.9
New York	24.15	22.08	2.07	9.4
Missouri	13.09	12.08	1.01	8.4
West Virginia	8.05	7.66	0.39	5.1
Tennessee	7.38	7.23	0.15	2.1
Maryland	11.34	11.65	−0.31	−2.7
Oklahoma	5.37	5.74	−0.37	−6.4
Washington, D.C.	12.24	13.20	−0.96	−7.3
New Jersey	12.45	13.44	−0.99	−7.4
Louisiana	8.55	9.58	−1.03	−10.8
Alabama	12.87	14.44	−1.57	−10.9
Virginia	5.78	6.56	−0.78	−11.9
North Carolina	5.93	7.03	−1.10	−15.6
Arkansas	3.52	4.24	−0.72	−17.0
Florida	7.30	10.61	−3.31	−31.2
South Carolina	4.03	6.46	−2.43	−37.6

Source: Adapted from Richard Sterner, *The Negro's Share: A study of Income, Consumption, Housing, and Public Assistance* (New York: Harper & Brothers, 1943), 285.

a. Sterner reports that in Georgia fewer than twenty-five black families were accepted for ADC payments during these years, too few to calculate reliable average payments.

Northern cities were immune from public assistance discrimination.[24] In his monumental study of African-American life in the 1940s, Gunnar Myrdal found that blacks were worst off in the rural South, where discrimination was rampant and benefit standards were very low. There was also, he found, discrimination in Southern cities, where the pressures of the farm labor market did not hold. There, although African-Americans were two or three times more likely than whites to receive ADC, they were even more disproportionately needy. On the contrary, Myrdal argued, there was very little welfare discrimination in the urban North.[25]

In the earliest years of ADC, the program thus appears to have been predominantly white; most blacks, after all, lived in the South, where local administration kept them off the rolls. However, during the 1940s and 1950s, the racial composition of the ADC caseload shifted dramatically, with black families making up considerably more of the caseload. Between 1942 and 1948, the number of black families on the ADC rolls in a sixteen-state study increased by 46 percent, and the proportion of non-white families rose from 21 to 30 percent.[26] In 1953 the black proportion of families receiving ADC was 36 percent, and by 1961 it reached 43 percent.[27] The growing proportion of black families on the ADC rolls was undoubtedly due largely to the mass migration of blacks from South to North that occurred in the decades after World War II. If Myrdal's conclusion about fairness in Northern cities is right, migration should have meant an increase not only in simple proportionality but also in the effectiveness of the program in improving the economic conditions of its beneficiaries. But as late as 1966, black families receiving public assistance were twice as likely to remain poor as white families, even though black families were also nearly twice as likely to be on public assistance in the first place.[28] Even in the South, the proportion of blacks on the ADC rolls rose during the 1940s and 1950s, although "suitable home" and work requirements still fostered discrimination.[29]

Despite the increasing presence of black families on the rolls, at the end of the first generation of ADC there was still evidence of discrimination. In 1969, a Department of Health, Education, and Welfare (HEW) study examined the characteristics of the welfare population. In a truly need-based program, the authors assumed, the neediest people would qualify for benefits; those deemed ineligible, therefore, should be, on average, less needy than recipients. The study, however, found the opposite: ADC recipients were, in fact, *better* off than ineligibles, suggesting that there remained in the late 1960s other factors impeding truly need-based distribution of ADC benefits. This was particularly true in states with very restrictive eligibility rules for benefits, suggesting that parochial administration promoted uneven standards for assistance. "The indication," the authors cautiously conclude, "is that noneconomic criteria bar some extremely deprived persons from public assistance in some states."[30]

The cumulative implication of these findings is that in the program's earliest years, restrictive local eligibility criteria prevented many needy people from receiving benefits. Thus, it seems that the parochial institutional structure of ADC had its intended and expected effect: It allowed Southern elites to keep African-Americans off the public welfare rolls at will, so that they could maintain both the paternalism of the low-wage agricultural labor market and the more general dependence of African-Americans on white power.

A Quantitative Study

But the question of discrimination in ADC deserves another, more systematic, visit. What, more precisely, were the terms of ADC discrimination in the South? If Myrdal and others were right that discrimination was much less prevalent, even nonexistent in Northern cities, why did it not disappear altogether as African-Americans left the rural South and moved to the urban North? In short, how did the parochial welfare institutions of the Social Security Act take root among widely different state and local political institutions in the generation after the New Deal and shape growing black inclusion in the program? Did the institutional structure of ADC inhibit or enable the incorporation of African-Americans?

All of this piecemeal evidence points to discrimination in the administration of ADC in both North and South, but without data identifying ADC recipients by race it is difficult to know the extent to which public assistance programs treated blacks and whites differently. An ecological approach to the problem, however, can overcome the lack of detailed information and suggest substantial and significant racial differences in the administration of ADC. This approach tests whether there was administrative discrimination in ADC by examining average levels of coverage and payments at the smallest administrative level for which data are available, in this case the county. Administrative differences could have led to demonstrably different coverage and payment outcomes, and if discrimination occurred systematically, counties with large black populations should have lower coverage rates and average payments, all other things being equal. A stronger version of the hypothesis is that discrimination was *more* likely in jurisdictions with greater black populations.[31] Where blacks made up a greater share of the population, politicians and administrators might have been more sensitive to the perception that ADC was simply a giveaway for blacks and to the possibility that high welfare expenditures might drive out revenue-producing citizens and businesses.[32] In either case, a significant negative relationship between black population and coverage rates or benefit levels would indicate discrimination. An empirical test of this hypothesis suggests that there were considerable disparities in the treatment of blacks and whites under ADC.

The county is the unit of analysis for two reasons. First, it was the basic administrative unit in the early decades of ADC. Whereas ADC policy was set by state governments and administration was under the control of statewide agencies, it was at the county level that caseworkers made operational decisions about eligibility and payment levels. Michael Harrington described the process in the 1950s:

> Standards were set for minimal payments required to give the people the basis of a subsistence existence. Then, as so often happens in the other America, each county would decide what percentage of the minimum it would provide. (Relief and welfare programs throughout the United States are completely uneven; it is much better to be poor in New York City than in Montgomery County [Ohio], and better to be poor in almost any place than Mississippi.)[33]

In many states, the county provided part of the funding for ADC benefits.[34] There was substantial variation among counties in the level of ADC benefits, even in the same state and within the parameters set by state law. In the generation after the Social Security Act, the centralization of public assistance programs—both federal authority over states and state authority over localities—increased. But even in 1967 there were still twenty-three states in which counties administered ADC.[35]

The second reason is that counties are the smallest units for which data are available, so they reduce the hazards of ecological inference, usually defined as inferring individual characteristics from relationships that appear in larger units.[36] This analysis is not, of course, immune from the ecological fallacy. In such an analysis, an estimate of a causal relationship is, in effect, the sum of two different causal relationships, an individual effect and an aggregate effect. A finding that counties with higher black populations had lower rates of ADC coverage may mean that black families were systematically denied benefits while white families were accepted—an individual effect. But without data about individual families, one cannot draw this conclusion definitively. It may be that all families, white and black, tended to be denied benefits in heavily black counties, just as many Southern whites in the Black Belt were denied the vote along with blacks—an aggregate effect.[37] Most likely, both were true, but without individual data we can observe only the cumulative impact of these two effects. But either interpretation is consistent with the existence of administrative discrimination. If it was harder to get benefits in areas where blacks tend to live, we can conclude that the system was administratively biased against blacks, even if some whites were affected in the process.

Each time a family applied for ADC benefits, the caseworker had to make two basic decisions: whether the family was eligible for benefits at all (based on poverty, the absence of a parent, and other criteria such as whether the home was "suitable" for rearing children) and if so, how much it should receive (based on need, the number of children, other sources of income, and state benefit policy).[38] Both of these determinations leave a great deal of discretion to individual street-level administrators, creating the possibility of discrimination.[39] Accordingly, we want to know two things about the administration of ADC: How likely were poor African-American families to get benefits, and how much did they get? The analysis, therefore, has two dependent variables: the percentage of poor families in the county that are on the ADC rolls, or ADC "coverage," and the average level of ADC payments per child. Coverage measures the extent to which ADC reaches its target population. It is calculated by expressing the average monthly number of families in the ADC caseload for each year as a percentage of the number of families with incomes below a threshold level.[40] Poverty was not, of course, the only criterion for ADC eligibility. The most important additional criterion is the absence of one parent, most likely the father, which simple poverty statistics cannot capture. Moreover, using a uniform poverty threshold through the country conceals differences from state to state and county to county in both the cost of living and the liberality of prevailing public welfare norms. As a result, this measure of coverage is a bit crude, but it captures at least some of the administrative variation in ADC. The payment variable is quite straightforward. It is simply the average monthly payment *per child* made to ADC recipients in the county. Payments were made to families, but the level of benefits varied with the number of children. Therefore, the per-child benefit amount not only controls for differences in family size but also more accurately reflects the consequences of local administrative decisions.

The principal explanatory variable in the analysis is the black percentage of the county's population, taken from the census. If there was administrative discrimination in ADC, the analysis should show a negative relationship between black population percentage and ADC benefits (both coverage and payments). It is possible, however, that an apparent effect of black population on benefits may be due entirely to regional differences between North and South. After all, most blacks lived in the South (still about sixty percent in 1960), Southern states were among the least generous, and many accounts of discrimination in public assistance contend that it was primarily a Southern phenomenon.[41] It is also possible, and quite plausible, that discrimination was more severe within the South than in the North—that is, even controlling for regional differences, the effect of black population on these measures of welfare benefits may be different in North and South. The analysis thus tests for the possibility that the effect of racial concentration was different in the South (defined simply as the former Confederate states).

Several other factors might also have affected the determination of welfare benefits. Most obvious is the relative wealth of the county.[42] Lower ADC benefits in counties with higher black population might be due not to racial discrimination but to the fact that blacks tended to be most concentrated in the poorest states and counties, which were least able to afford generous public assistance. The county median family income, although not a perfect measure of fiscal capacity to provide public assistance, controls for this effect. Wealthier counties would presumably have been able to afford more generous payments, so higher incomes should be associated with higher payments. However, higher income counties may also have had greater private charitable resources to alleviate poverty, and the shame of requesting welfare may be greater in wealthier areas, so higher income may also be associated with lower ADC coverage. Whatever the impact of county wealth, what is essential is that we can be confident that any observed effect of black population is independent, that even in equally poor counties, African-Americans seem to do worse (or better) than whites.[43]

Besides poverty, family structure was the other general criterion for ADC eligibility—specifically the presence of only a single parent. By 1960, African-American families were more than twice as likely as white families to be headed by single parents. Moreover, nonwhite female-headed families were more likely to have children to support, so that more than one in nine nonwhite families had a female head and children, compared with fewer than one in twenty-five white families.[44] Fair and uniform ADC administration should have produced higher rates of coverage in areas with more single-parent families, and it may be that the relationship between black population and ADC coverage reflected this sociological factor rather than racial bias. To control for this possibility, the analysis controls for the percentage of families headed by single parents in the county. If black population still alters ADC benefits significantly, the conclusion that there was administrative discrimination will be more certain. In fact, it seems likely that discriminatory administration should be *more* apparent when family structure is considered. There were substantial differences between whites and blacks in the causes of single-parent families. A 1948 study of ADC recipients showed that, on the one hand, more than two-thirds of white families receiving ADC were on the rolls due to divorce or the death or incapacitation of the father. On the other hand, parental absence without a legal decree and never-married parents accounted for more than three-fifths of the nonwhite ADC cases.[45] These latter situations raised red flags for local welfare workers, making discrimination against African-Americans more likely.

A third additional factor likely to affect ADC administration is the distinction between cities and the rest of the country. Northern blacks were concentrated in large cities, which have tended to contain concentrations of poverty and to have liberal Democratic political elites and hence to provide more liberal benefits. The analysis, then, also controls for these urban-rural differences. Finally, it is also possible that the effect of black population on ADC administration changed between the 1930s and the 1960s, becoming either more or less severe as both the economic situation of African-Americans and the racial attitudes of white Americans changed. The analysis tests this proposition as well.

The payment structure of ADC provided for larger payments for the first child in a family than for subsequent ones (presumably on the assumption that families benefit from economies of scale, that is, that rearing two children is less than twice as expensive as rearing one). This means that as family size grew, the average payment per child declined, although at a diminishing rate. Consequently, the average number of children per case is introduced as a control in the estimation of ADC payments. The analysis of ADC payments also controls for the statewide average payment per child, which is introduced to control for differences in the overall generosity of state policy. To control for systematic changes in ADC administration over time, such as rising benefit levels, the analysis contains dummy variables for the years 1950 (where appropriate) and 1960. Finally, the analysis also tests for changes between 1940 and 1960, in both the overall level of ADC coverage and benefits and the effect of black population.

A final critical factor that certainly affected ADC administration in counties was state policy. State policymakers, of course, played an important role in establishing the boundaries within which welfare administrators operated. State legislatures established upper and lower bounds on benefit levels, eligibility criteria, and rules and regulations for state administrators and caseworkers, and these legislative decisions were the product of many social, political, and economic factors.[46] What county welfare workers were able and inclined to do was shaped in large part by what their state governments did. Information from counties in different states may not, therefore, be strictly comparable—a stingy county in a generous state, for example, might still have been more generous than a generous county in a stingy state. The analysis, then, should take state policy differences into account, so that we can be sure that the effects we observe are administrative ones. To do this, the analysis contains a dummy variable for each state. For this analysis, state differences are not meaningful in and of themselves. But because they are included as controls, we can be confident that the effects that are reported are independent of policymaking at the state level and are, in fact, attributable to administrative decisions on the ground, so to speak.

The analysis uses county-level data on ADC payments as reported by state welfare authorities for 1940, 1950, and 1960 to test for the discriminatory administration of ADC between the 1930s and the 1960s. The years chosen are census years, so that census data can be integrated into the analysis. There are approximately 3100 counties (or equivalent administrative units) in the United States, so over the three years there are some 9300 possible observations. The sample used for the analysis consists of more than 6640 observations (nearly 70 percent of the total). It is not a random sample of the counties in the country; rather, it consists of data from readily available state reports. The limitation of a nonrandom sample, however, does not appear to have introduced any serious bias into the data (see the Appendix for a detailed comparison).[47] Finally, certain categories of census data—most notably income and family structure—were not available for 1940, so except where noted, the analysis actually covers only 1950 and 1960.

The results of the analysis show that there were significant racial and regional differences in the implementation of ADC. Figure 4.1 presents the clear difference between North and South in the level of ADC coverage. The graph displays the predicted level of coverage (again, the percentage of poor families in the county on the ADC rolls) across changes in the county's black population percentage, controlling for all other factors.[48] This figure presents results assuming that all the variables other than black population percentage are at their mean levels; in other words, the graph presents a picture of what ADC coverage would be in a mythical "average" county with different levels of black population. What is important is not the absolute levels of coverage (or payments, in later figures) shown, but the slopes of the lines, which indicate the nature and size of the relationship between the two attributes in which we are particularly interested—in this case, ADC coverage and black population percentage.

The regional difference is stark and immediately apparent. In the North, coverage rises sharply with the black population percentage of the county.

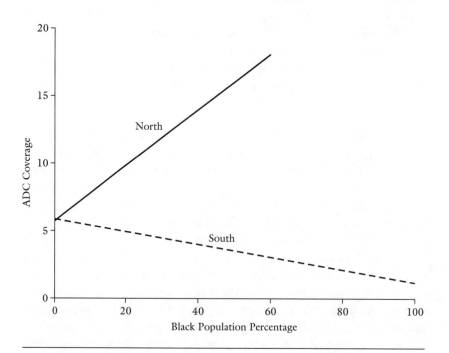

Figure 4.1. Race and ADC coverage.

The line for the North stops at the sixty percent black level simply because there were no Northern counties with African-American populations above that level. In the South, however, heavily black counties had slightly lower levels of coverage than all-white counties. ADC was clearly far from uniform nationally. Filtered through local institutions and reflecting local political, social, and economic practices, it took on dramatically different shapes in North and South. Northern blacks, it appears, were treated reasonably fairly by ADC administrators, at least in the first part of the two-stage decision, granting benefits. African-American families were more likely to fall into the eligible categories than whites, so it makes sense to find that ADC coverage rises along with black population density. In the South, however, areas with heavily concentrated African-American populations—especially the Black Belt counties of the deep South—had *lower* levels of coverage, despite the same conditions of higher eligibility among African-Americans. Southern black families, it seems, were *less* likely to receive ADC than similarly situated Southern whites. Without detailed knowledge of the racial mix of the ADC caseload and applicant pool, it is impossible to draw with certainty the conclusion that these racial differences resulted from discrimination by welfare workers against individual black applicants. It may simply be the case that everyone was less likely to be covered in heavily black counties, but this too indicates a structural bias against African-Americans in the ADC system.

One source of racial and regional differences in ADC coverage may have been the rate of applications for benefits from different groups, which depends in part on the social stigma attached to receiving welfare. In other words, it is possible that racial differences in ADC coverage resulted not from administrative discrimination against applicants for benefits or from some systematic bias in state and local ADC programs but from different views among black and white women about the propriety of public assistance and differences in their tendency to apply, or in a more general fear among Southern blacks of reprisal should they approach the state to request benefits. The stigma of welfare has been well documented by sociologists and economists, and it is possible that welfare stigma was weaker among blacks—particularly Northern blacks—than whites. The view that African-Americans feel less shame in collecting public assistance and would rather get ADC than work for a living certainly conforms to long-held popular conceptions (and misconceptions) of American welfare.[49] Gunnar Myrdal reported in the early 1940s that "public relief has become one of the major Negro occupations" in Northern cities, and Northern blacks may have been more willing than whites to apply for ADC.[50] But there is also evidence of strong welfare stigma among Northern urban blacks before the 1970s; a 1961 study in Chicago, for example, found that African-American families were more intent than white families on self-reliance and held out longer before seeking public assistance.[51] An economic analysis of welfare stigma in the 1970s found no significant difference between races.[52] And there is little evidence that Northern and Southern black women differed so much in their appraisal of welfare to account for the dramatic regional split in ADC coverage for African-Americans. It is extremely unlikely that racial and regional differences in ADC coverage are due to greater willingness among African-Americans to seek public assistance.

The more likely cause of the regional difference in ADC coverage in heavily black counties is that administrative rules were differently constituted and applied in North and South. Outright racial discrimination in the determination of ADC eligibility in the South is not hard to imagine. Many Southern blacks probably did not even get as far as the welfare office if Southern state and county welfare authorities were as punitive and discouraging as voting registrars. Because blacks were more likely to be poor, and poor black families were more likely to be headed by single parents, the flat relationship in the South probably indicates substantial discrimination. In the North, however, blacks were beginning to acquire political power in the 1940s and 1950s and were able to demand fairer access to their share of public benefits. The substantial positive relationship in the North means that blacks more nearly achieved parity with whites in ADC coverage, although this analysis cannot tell us for sure how close they came.

Although it was predominantly in the South that administrators restricted African-American access to ADC coverage, black families were at a disadvantage throughout the country in the level of benefits they were awarded. Figure 4.2 shows the strong, straightforward negative relationship between black population and the level of ADC payments. In all regions, counties with higher concentrations of African-Americans paid lower monthly benefits. The regional difference that appeared for ADC coverage was not significant, indicating that this negative relationship held equally in all parts of the country. A county with a black population of 20 percent paid, on average, only 60 cents per child less than an all-white county—a small amount, perhaps, but substantial when multiplied by several children for a family already living at the edge of subsistence. In the

South, where some counties were over 80 percent black, the difference between all-white and nearly all-black counties could be substantial. Compare two small, rural counties in Alabama in 1960. Lowndes County, in the heart of the Black Belt and more than 80 percent black, paid an average of $11.19 per child per month; Winston County, in the hill country of northern Alabama and about the same size but only one-half of one percent black, paid $14.25. Whether due to discrimination against individual African-American applicants or not, ADC was considerably stingier in areas where blacks tended to live.

The relationship shown in Figure 4.2 is a composite across time—an average, in a sense, of the relationship in the different years sampled—and so it does not reveal whether this negative slope was stable or subject to change. More detailed analysis (elaborated in the Appendix) reveals that in 1940 there was no significant relationship at all between black population percentage and ADC benefit levels. For 1940 alone, then, the line in Figure 4.2 would be horizontal. By 1950, however, the line had tilted to reach the downward slope that the graph displays, and in 1960 it was

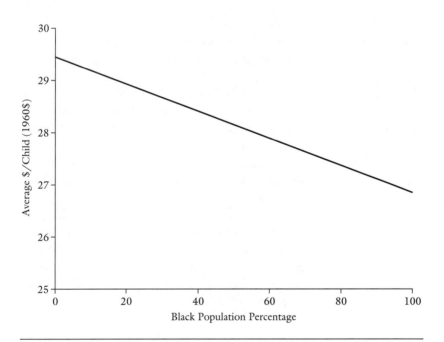

Figure 4.2. Race and ADC payments.

essentially the same. In the program's earliest years, in the late 1930s, the Depression remained; in the absence of work, it seems, welfare administrators were less likely to discriminate. But the pattern for African-American disadvantage in ADC administration was set during the 1940s, as local politicians and administrators, Northern and Southern alike, began to take advantage of the program's institutional structure and assumed control. By the end of the decade, if not earlier, the discriminatory die was cast.

Race, Welfare, and Urban Political Institutions

It takes no great leap of historical imagination to conjure up the conditions of ADC discrimination in the South, especially the rural, Black Belt South. There, where African-Americans constituted a subordinate caste, black families in need of assistance would likely have had to approach a county welfare board, located in the county seat, probably in the county courthouse. Like every other institution of consequence in the county, the welfare board was controlled by a local oligarchy of friends and neighbors, the local planters and the attendant merchants and professionals whose livelihoods derived from the cotton crop—and from the black labor that produced it. Moreover, these local political grandees, as well as the hangers-on who typically littered the courthouse square, were the heads of the very families whose houses were kept, meals cooked, clothes washed, children reared, and cotton chopped by the very African-American women who might come to them asking for benefits. If that scenario itself were not forbidding enough to prevent a woman from even making an application, the local authorities had ample latitude to find a reason not to grant her and her children assistance, or to give such a pittance that she would still have to work in their fields and houses. Without the impersonality and regularity of more modern, bureaucratic administration, it is easy to imagine that discrimination was common.

But in the cities of the North—vast, impersonal, and bureaucratic—the possibility of such discrimination seems more remote. In fact, we might expect the relationship between black population and ADC benefits to be reversed in major cities, that is, greater coverage and higher benefits in cities with higher African-American populations. Most Northern blacks, after all, have traditionally lived in the great industrial cities of the Northeast and Midwest, where they began to develop, in the years after the New Deal, a measure of political power that might have translated into more generous treatment by welfare authorities. Cities in general have been more generous providers of welfare benefits than rural areas or suburbs, but on top of their general relative liberality, city politicians have been particularly sensitive to the political demands of salient and discrete social groups. Or, as Steven Erie argues somewhat more pungently, city machines might have used ADC to "control the minority vote and siphon off discontent at minimal cost to the city treasury and to tax-conscious white homeowners." The Daley machine in Chicago, for example, both facilitated welfare applications for its black constituents and supported liberal benefits in the state legislature.[53] In his first campaign for mayor in 1955, Richard J. Daley relied heavily on support in the black wards controlled by African-American Congressman William Dawson, and he promised black voters a "Big, Generous, Liberal Chicago where Good Fellowship, and better Race relations are in keeping with the times."[54]

Erie's observation about the racial manipulation of ADC benefits suggests two hypotheses. The first is that more blacks in a city should uniformly have meant higher ADC coverage and payments, as white politicians tried to capture black votes. As black population grew, it would have become more costly for white politicians to "purchase" black allegiance through expanded welfare payments. The second, more sophisticated version of the hypothesis is that only in machine-controlled cities did a denser black population mean greater coverage or higher benefits; in nonmachine cities, without strong party organizations to coordinate benefits in the interest of mobilizing blocs of voters, discriminatory patterns would reappear. At first blush, these hypotheses do not seem entirely plausible. After some point, increasing welfare payments is probably not the best way to keep the white middle class happy.[55] A first test, however, suggests that the negative relationship between black population and welfare payments did exist in cities, just as it did elsewhere. Figure 4.3 shows a plot of the black population percentage in 1960 against the average ADC payment per person in October 1960 for twenty-one (mostly non-Southern) cities.[56] The negative relationship is quite clear to the eye, with most cities clustering in the upper left and lower right of the graph.

But the second of these hypotheses suggests that the administration of ADC may have been different in machine cities. To examine whether the presence of urban political organizations altered the fundamental relationship between race and ADC administration, I use David Mayhew's "traditional party organization" (TPO) score for each state, which assesses the prominence of such organizations in a state's politics in the late 1960s.[57] The TPO scale ranges from one (states with no traditional party organizations) to five (states where TPOs had continual, decisive influence over nominations and elections for a variety of offices). Although this measure is based on an assessment of the level of organization in a state and not in cities in particular, it is still a crude indicator of the extent to which we might expect the political manipulation of welfare benefits with the aim of influencing voting or other political behavior. Moreover, Mayhew's TPO scores generally reflect the presence (or absence) of city organizations, and he notes that "cities located in the same state almost always bear a family resemblance to each other in organizational forms."[58] If Erie is right and party machines manipulated welfare benefits for political reasons, this variable should have a significant impact on the outcomes of welfare administration.

The party proposition, however, is not simply that machine cities paid higher or lower benefits but that machine cities were more likely to give more generous benefits to African-Americans in return for political allegiance. If this was true, if welfare in cities was a form of group political currency rather than a more general attack on child poverty, then higher

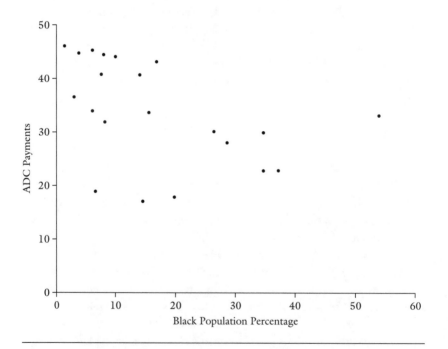

Figure 4.3. Black population and ADC payments in selected cities, 1961.

black populations in machine cities should have commanded better treatment, either because their votes were more valuable than a small minority's or because city fathers deemed their quiescence more necessary for public order. Statistically, therefore, the effect of black population percentage on ADC benefits should be greater—indicated by a steeper sloping line— where traditional party organization is stronger. In addition to the TPO score, then, the analysis contains an interactive term to test whether traditional party organizations alter the effect of black population.

The results provide strong support for the party hypotheses on the coverage side and none at all on the benefit side. Figures 4.4 and 4.5 reproduce the analysis for ADC coverage and benefits only in those counties containing cities of 100,000 or more. As Figure 4.4 shows, cities with higher black populations had higher rates of ADC coverage, suggesting that at some level urban ADC administration was associated with applicants' needs or with black political power in Northern cities. Although levels of coverage were generally lower in Southern cities than in the North, there was no strictly regional difference in the relationship between

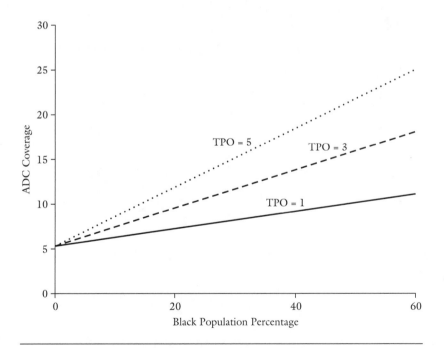

Figure 4.4. Race and ADC coverage, cities.

black population and ADC coverage. The effect of black population did not change significantly between 1950 and 1960, however, just as blacks were streaming into Northern cities from the South; if anything, African-Americans in cities fared *worse* in 1960 than they had in 1950 (see the Appendix for detailed analysis). If ADC benefits were used by urban party organizations as a political benefit, this result points to a curious decline in the political status of urban African-Americans in the 1950s, just as they were amassing numbers in Northern cities that gave them potential political clout. But with ADC still firmly in the hands of white local party politicians, it appears that the racialization of welfare was already underway.

Party organizations were, in fact, critically important in the administration of welfare. First, contrary to the arguments of revisionist scholars about urban party organizations, machine cities were generally stingier in doling out welfare benefits than non-organization cities.[59] ADC coverage in a "regular organization" city (with a TPO score of 5) was, on average, 3.5 percentage points lower than in a thoroughly non-organization city. But machines were not simply tighter with ADC eligibility; they were

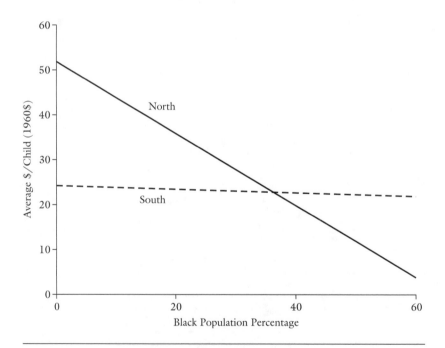

Figure 4.5. Race and ADC payments, cities.

politically selective. The level of party organization also increased the effect of black population substantially; the more heavily organized, the more the black population percentage mattered in raising the level of ADC coverage. The three lines in Figure 4.4 represent this effect. The solid line denotes non-organization cities. As we travel along this line from left to right, from all-white cities to predominantly black ones, the level of ADC coverage ambles slowly upward. It is impossible to say whether this represents fair treatment, but it is certainly a modest relationship. In highly organized cities—the top line—coverage increases much more sharply as we move toward higher levels of black population. In other words, even though they were generally stingier, highly organized urban parties paid more attention to discrete, visible political constituencies such as African-Americans. In cities, in fact, the racial impact of ADC administration depended almost entirely on the strength of party organizations.

Machine cities also paid higher benefits than nonmachine cities. Regular organization cities (or, more precisely, cities in organization states) provided over $6.00 more per child per month than non-organization cities. But what is striking about payment levels in cities is the regional difference in the treatment of African-Americans, shown in Figure 4.5. In Southern cities, the relationship between black population and benefit levels was almost identical to the relationship in the nation as a whole. A simple eyeball comparison between Figure 4.2 and the dashed line in Figure 4.5 is deceptive. The line in Figure 4.5 looks almost flat; in fact, its slope is slightly steeper than the one in Figure 4.2. The reason for this optical illusion is that the scale on the lefthand side of Figure 4.5 is much larger than in Figure 4.2. And the reason this scale is so much larger is also the most surprising result in Figure 4.5: the extremely strong negative relationship in Northern cities between black population and ADC payments.

Welfare pay scales in Northern cities were much more sensitive than in Southern cities to the presence of African-Americans. Although machine cities, which were mostly in the North, paid generally higher benefits than non-organization cities, party organization did not help African-Americans get higher ADC payments the same way it gave them access to the program. In contrast with ADC coverage, the level of party organization made no difference in the level of benefits paid to African-Americans. More African-Americans were granted benefits in machine cities than elsewhere but once granted benefits, they received no more than their fellow recipients, and they may have received less. Finally, this pattern, like others, was established sometime in the 1940s. The level of benefits paid in heavily black cities deteriorated during the 1940s but remained stable during the 1950s, mirroring the pattern in the rest of the country.

The structural position of African-Americans in city politics, along with the institutional structure of ADC, was crucial in determining the racial impact of welfare administration. The relationship of African-Americans to urban political organizations combined with the parochial structure of ADC, which gave these organizations control over the distribution of ADC funds, to make ADC a racial issue. Urban party organizations appear to have been a critical ingredient in the gradual shift in the racial makeup of ADC caseloads. As Southern blacks moved to Northern cities in the decades after World War II, they made up an increasing proportion of Northern ADC rolls, and this increase has contributed to the racially tinged air of crisis that has plagued the politics of welfare in the United States since the 1960s.[60]

Moreover, ADC in Northern cities appears to have been just as locally politicized, just as tied to local structures of political power, as in the archetypal Southern Black Belt county. A visit to the welfare office in Chicago or Philadelphia was no doubt less forbidding and threatening than a trip to the courthouse in a Black Belt county. Nonetheless, like the Southern courthouse gang, networks of party politicians and their apparatchiks surely dominated local welfare bureaus in party-controlled cities, where public benefits were the currency that bought the only political good that mattered, votes. Without the Southern structures of paternalism, welfare administration in the North did not work against African-Americans quite so automatically; the subordinate status of blacks was not yet so seamlessly woven into the structure of Northern urban society. But their treatment depended on their links, and on their racial community's links, to the organization.

Machine cities were thus not necessarily profligate welfare spenders; they did pay generous benefits, but to fewer people and in a politically targeted way. In doing so, they converted ADC from a redistributive benefit to a political, regime-building one and contributed to the patina of racial corruption that ADC began to acquire in the 1950s.[61] It is also significant that the distinctiveness of the South disappears in these city models as well. The finding that Southern cities resembled Northern cities in the racial impact of ADC administration supports V. O. Key's claim that the persistence of racial politics in the South in this period reflected the influence of the white grandees of the Black Belt to the exclusion of the more moderate urban South.[62]

The parochialism of ADC, which placed operational and political control largely in the hands of local politicians, established an institutional pattern that was bifurcated along racial and regional lines. Parochialism, an institutional response to the regional demands of Southern politicians in the 1930s, was now taken up by Northern politicians in a different vein, and the central-local tension inherent in the New Deal Democratic coalition seemed to reproduce itself on a different basis. In the South, where most African-Americans lived when the program was created, African-Americans were largely kept out of the program, probably by a combination of social stigma and discriminatory administration. In the North, where there were many fewer blacks in the 1930s, African-Americans were generally afforded access to ADC benefits, although they often received smaller payments than white families. However, Northern blacks were much more likely to live in cities, and Northern cities were much more likely to contain traditional party organizations that used ADC benefits as a distributive political tool, manipulating payments to achieve political rather than social or economic welfare goals. For urban politicians, ADC was convenient—it was often what one did for black constituents, just as one paved streets, fixed parking tickets, and gave one's neighbor's cousin a nice position in the city clerk's office. As long as black numbers in Northern cities and on Northern ADC rolls were fairly small, such traditional political manipulation of benefits seemed a harmless extension of business as usual, a small price to pay for the political cooperation and social quiescence of a discrete group. Institutional parochialism settled nicely in the structure of Northern welfare.

But African-Americans moved to these cities—to Chicago and Gary, to Cleveland and Pittsburgh, to Newark and New York—by the hundreds of thousands in the years after World War II, often suffering severely from the effects of social dislocation and economic discrimination. As they moved, they left behind the outright discrimination of Southern welfare institutions and entered political settings where the racial manipulation of ADC had been institutionalized through its links with local politics, made possible, and even necessary, by the program's parochial structure. African-Americans left the South to escape both racial and economic domination, and they moved north to find both freedom and economic opportunity. But in moving they entered a labor market that was itself already segregated—increasingly so in the decades after World War II—leaving them at the bitter edges of the soaring prosperity that the Cold War brought to American cities. For many African-Americans, then, ADC was necessary because of the conditions of their urban lives, and their numbers on urban welfare rolls began to grow, alarming the political leaders of Northern cities. What had begun as an easy and cheap way to manipulate votes grew during the 1940s and 1950s into an alarming and costly racialized give-away. The pattern of racial politicization laid down by Northern urban politicians in one era would return to haunt not only their own successors but advocates of welfare reform nationwide as well. Against a background of profound demographic and political changes, these institutions would play a crucial role in altering the racial structure of American politics.

The Development of ADC Policy: Toward Retrenchment

The institutions that were established to administer ADC did not integrate African-Americans smoothly as OAI did. Nor did ADC generate political pressure for expansion and greater inclusion that overcame the racial forces that shaped the program in the 1930s. Political and administrative forces gave control of the ADC program to state and local officials, who re-stricted and manipulated African-American access to the program. At the same time, dramatic socioeconomic and political changes transformed the racial structure of American society over the course of a generation. A mass migration of African-Americans from the rural South to the urban North combined with a frontal assault on legal segregation to change forever the place of African-Americans in American political life. Despite continuing discrimination, nearly half of the people receiving ADC benefits in the 1960s were black. The incorporation of African-Americans into OAI hap-pened along with, and because of, its development into a strong, adminis-tratively effective, and politically insulated part of the American state. But ADC, which had ambled along sleepily in its early years, suddenly awoke in the late 1950s to find that it was serving more and more African-Ameri-cans and attracting the nation's attention. ADC's parochial institutional apparatus, which had been designed precisely to prevent blacks from bene-fiting, ensured that their incorporation into the program occurred on unfavorable terms.

The institutional structure of Aid to Dependent Children and the politi-cal logic of constraint that it created not only kept African-Americans from benefiting administratively, but they also impeded and frustrated reform efforts that might have made ADC more inclusive and less racially and politically divisive. First, it became very difficult to enact systematic re-forms at all. The Social Security Act gave state and local governments great autonomy in devising and implementing ADC policy, and the costs of monitoring and disciplining recalcitrant states were high enough that Social Security program executives could not easily influence state activities. National officials have had to use administrative persuasion and diplomacy in the federal setting in their pursuit of greater uniformity, adequacy, and fairness in ADC administration. If they have failed to achieve these aims, their failure is a result of the institutional structure within which they operate and not of an ideological disposition against a stronger public assistance program.[63] Local discretion was not, of course, a new feature of federal-state grant-in-aid programs, but welfare grants raised issues that did not affect other federal grant programs. The norm of state and local control of welfare policy, which in fact evolved from centuries of English and American practice, stiffened resistance to federal action. National reform efforts had to contend, and usually compromise, with decentralizing forces. Second, even when the federal government did act to reform ADC, state administrative action could frustrate the intentions of national policymakers, producing results that were the opposite of lawmakers' aims.

Aid to Dependent Children's logic of constraint cast a long shadow over the growth of the American welfare state. The Social Security Act came at a critical juncture, a moment of decision about a new direction for the politics of American social provision. While the policy settlement of 1935 brought welfare enduringly to the center of the national political debate, in many ways it reinforced age-old local and parochial commitments. National welfare policymaking ever since has been held doubly hostage to the forces of parochialism. First, national policy is filtered through local institutions. The effects of national welfare policy changes have become clear only through local administration, and the logic of constraint is powerfully apparent in this decentralized setting. Second, this very fact has shaped the national politics of welfare policy. The commitment to parochial administration has itself become a powerful force in the politics of American social policy, imposing the logic of constraint on yet another level. Reformers who have sought to expand the national role in welfare policy or to restrict the autonomy of parochial institutions have run up against powerful resistance from the very forces of parochialism instituted by the Social Security Act itself.

The major theme of the history of ADC's development, even down to the present day, has been the struggle between national and parochial forces, specifically played out in the conflict between central and local authority. In some cases, the conflict was strictly administrative, as when states clashed with national authorities over the adoption and application of ADC rules and procedures. In other cases, the conflict was legislative, as parties and interests fought over the terms of reform. In still other instances, the conflict encompassed both legislation and administration and spilled over into the courts as welfare rights and civil rights became the common currency of social policy discourse.[64] Increasingly over the decades, the fate of African-Americans under ADC was bound up in these conflicts; as more African-American families entered the ADC system, the more they had at stake, and yet the more firmly entrenched ADC's institutional structure became. As ADC became more firmly associated in the public mind with race, and African-Americans in particular, the program's institutional logic led not to programmatic reforms that might have attacked poverty (and especially black poverty) more rigorously, but to further tightening that only heightened the program's inherent racial tensions. The intense politicization of ADC and the continued failure of reform in the face of intransigent institutions eventually drove many African-Americans toward protest as a mode of pursuing reform, perhaps the only strategy available to them but one that alienated them even further from American political life and its reforming possibilities.[65]

The Establishment of Parochialism

The 1939 Amendments to the Social Security Act made the first important change in ADC indirectly, by adding survivors' benefits to Old-Age Insurance. Originally, OAI provided for a small lump-sum payment to the estate of a covered worker who died. The 1939 amendment substituted monthly payments to the surviving spouses and children of covered workers regardless of the age at which they died. The effect of this change was to shift many "worthy widows" of working husbands out of ADC and into the social insurance system, where they could receive support directly from the federal government as a matter of right. Left eligible for ADC were abandoned or unmarried mothers, women whose husbands were in jail, or widows whose husbands had worked either in noncovered occupations or not at all. Shifting "worthy widows" into OAI contributed to the erosion of the "maternalist" foundations of ADC.[66] Rather than a program intended for needy single mothers generally and aimed specifically at "worthy widows," it became a residual program for those women and children who could not claim automatic benefits under the national OAI program.

Although this shift narrowed slightly the target population over which state and local authorities could exercise discretion, it changed the nature of this population from society's "worthy widows" to an increasingly suspect group of women who were defined not by their misfortune but by their behavior. The creation of national Survivors' Insurance within OAI did not, as one might suspect, decisively segregate the programs, directing "worthy" white widows to OAI and leaving an "undeserving" class of profligate black poor in the ADC category. In fact, data show that by the late 1940s, nonwhites received a disproportionate share of survivors' benefits. What the 1939 amendments did was to hone further the division between national and parochial social policy—the former for workers and their families and the latter for those cut off from the economic mainstream. By sharpening this class-based rule for sorting citizens, the 1939 changes reinforced the parochialism of welfare. Rather than capitalize on the presence of a "worthy" class of recipients in the ADC pool to strengthen public assistance by offering more robust national protection, the amendment expanded national social insurance at the political expense of parochial ADC. Ironically, the very existence of national OAI, instead of providing a model for the expansion of public assistance, made this move possible. As Theda Skocpol argues, the amendments helped to cement the apparent connection between ADC and behavior that was to become such an important racial, ideological, and political weapon.[67] But the divergent institutional structure of the two programs helped to ensure that the politics of welfare, race, and behavior would be parochial politics and would begin to play out in counties, cities, and states before entering the national political arena.

The narrowing of ADC's target population only intensified the national-parochial struggle in the politics of welfare. State and local governments found themselves responsible for a smaller but more culturally and politically suspect class of needy families. Locally financed and administered social provision for these people had always been a stingy and controversial venture, but now a structure existed for the national government to pick up part of the tab. The first move of state and local politicians, especially from the states with the neediest populations, was to increase the federal share of the ADC bill. Beginning with the debates on the Social Security Act in 1935, poorer states advocated a scheme of variable federal matching grants for public assistance so that the federal government would defray a higher percentage of the costs of public assistance grants in poorer states than in richer ones.

As it had in 1935, the issue of variable grants caused some shuffling of coalitions and some shifting of positions on federal-state relationships. The South, usually reluctant to support an increased federal role, took the lead in the 1930s and 1940s in supporting an increase in the federal share of ADC funding. In particular, Southerners from poor states generally favored variable grants even while resisting greater federal control over ADC administration. An unusual and tenuous alliance formed between these Southerners and the Social Security establishment, which favored more federal assistance to states that were less able to fund decent benefits. At the same time, even many supporters of more generous and less restrictive public assistance did not want to commit the federal government to an increasing share of public assistance expenditures. In 1939, the House-Senate conference on the Social Security Act Amendments deadlocked on precisely this issue, and Altmeyer was on the verge of brokering a compromise when President Roosevelt suddenly backed away from the idea, which Altmeyer thought he had endorsed. "Not one nickel more," Roosevelt said to Altmeyer, "not one solitary nickel. Once you get off the 50–50 matching basis, the sky's the limit and before you know it, we'll be paying the whole bill."[68]

The 1946 Social Security Amendments bill was also hung up in conference over variable grants, which the House rejected but the Senate approved. This time a compromise emerged under which the federal government matched two-thirds of the state's grant up to $9 a month, half of the amount thereafter up to $24 for the first child, and $15 for subsequent children. Under this scheme, poorer states that paid smaller benefits would effectively receive higher percentage grants, although the compromise did not achieve the Social Security Board's aim of inducing states to pay higher grants. In the House debate on the conference report, Republican Representative Thomas Jenkins of Ohio, who in 1935 had tweaked Howard Smith over Southern racial intentions in public assistance, asked "If the people of the Southern States are satisfied to pay small pensions, why should Congress be worried about it?"[69] Although Jenkins would no doubt have been distressed to discover the discrimination taking place in ADC administration, his comment summed up the prevailing indifference to the inadequacy of ADC.

However, the principle that Southern states should be "allowed" to pay low benefits rather than induced to increase their payments with additional federal money seemed quite "natural." But it was not natural; there was nothing in the nature of grants-in-aid, or of ADC in particular, that dictated such a position. An alternative formulation might have been that "allowing" Southern (and other) states to pay stingy ADC benefits subverted the program's primary aim by denying needy mothers the resources to rear their children in "decency and health," as the Roosevelt administration had initially sought. But the strongly decentralized structure of ADC, under which states had been making their own benefit decisions for a decade, impeded the latter interpretation and institutionalized the former. Many of the same politicians who had demanded parochialism in 1935 now sought to reverse it; many of the same politicians who had been skeptical of parochialism in 1935 now upheld it as in the nature of things, and their projection of parochialism's logic onto the normal politics of welfare made it very difficult to dislodge. Although it is doubtful that increased benefits would have found their way to many African-Americans in the South, this indifference and congressional acquiescence to the norms of state control virtually assured this result in the long run as well. When Congress finally adopted variable grants for ADC in 1958, they were severely restricted in scope and provided very little benefit to recipients even in the poorest states.[70] Jerry Cates argues that the slow progress of public assistance reforms is evidence of the Social Security establishment's opposition to liberalizing public assistance in favor of the conservative principles of social insurance. But the failure of variable grants, a liberalizing measure that could have tilted control of ADC toward the federal government, suggests rather that the impediment was resistance by politicians, either for reasons of principle (Eisenhower and other Republicans) or of fiscal constraint (Kennedy and Johnson). The Social Security Board consistently advocated variable grants in order to ensure decent assistance standards, only to be undercut by political disputes that arose out of the institutional logic of ADC itself.[71]

Congress was entirely willing, however, to impose demands on the states that neither compromised the fundamental parochialism of ADC nor cost the federal government money. In 1950, concerned particularly with the problem of fathers who abandoned their wives and children (foreshadowing today's "deadbeat dad" mantra), Congress adopted a provision calling for "Notification of Law Enforcement Officials," or "Noleo." Noleo required that in order to qualify for ADC, a woman claiming desertion had to identify the father of her children to a local law enforcement agency so that an effort could be made to find him and force him to support his family. As Wilbur Cohen explained the logic behind this step, "Congress . . . was responding to public opinion and at the same time attempting to work out something constructive without infringing on states' rights or broadening the area of Federal control over family matters or changing the basic principles of the ADC program."[72] Here the parochialism of ADC explicitly shaped a program amendment. This new requirement was particularly significant for two related reasons. First, it made an explicit connection between ADC eligibility and law enforcement, making "the welfare agency a vehicle of social compulsion," as one observer put it.[73] Second, the provision narrowed the autonomy of the state welfare agency, but not in favor of increased national control. Instead, Noleo gave local prosecutors a share of discretionary authority over ADC applicants and put many women in an exceedingly awkward position between turning down public assistance and subjecting their children's fathers to pursuit by the police. Clearly the introduction of law enforcement into the ADC process was unlikely to work to the benefit of African-Americans. Moreover, there is evidence that welfare workers invoked the Noleo provision more frequently with black applicants.[74] Thus, without appearing to alter the balance between state and federal control of the program, the Noleo amendment began to force the states into a punitive stance in ADC administration.

At the federal level, the 1950s were a period of stagnation in ADC policy, but because of the primacy of states and localities in making and administering welfare policy, ADC was substantially weakened. It was a decade of apparent affluence, and poverty was not highly visible in American society or politics.[75] The Eisenhower administration, which provided decisive support for the expansion of Old-Age Insurance in 1954, took a moderate and complacent position toward ADC. Eisenhower himself was privately quite conservative on social policy issues but recognized the political impossibility of rolling back the New Deal legacy entirely as some conservative Republicans wanted and expected him to do. Although he was alarmed at the growth of welfare spending, he was unwilling to take what might appear to be a socially irresponsible approach to welfare.[76] The Republicans, moreover, were still the more pro–civil rights party and were still credible competitors for black votes in the North; it was Eisenhower, after all, who sent federal troops to Little Rock, Arkansas, in 1957 to enforce the integration of Central High School.[77] Politically, Eisenhower could ill afford a harsh approach to welfare that might alienate the constituency for a more moderate approach, a coalition that included African-Americans. Unable politically to dismantle the national welfare role and disinclined to expand it, Eisenhower sought a middle path. His administration's policy, then, was to stress vocational rehabilitation over public support as a way of reversing the growth in ADC rolls. The focus on job training, however, amounted to a policy shift that might undermine the growing social welfare establishment, and so on this issue, as on other issues such as variable grants and federal participation, Eisenhower, the Social Security Administration, and the Democratic Congress (after 1954) fought to a stalemate.[78]

Parochialism Run Amok: From Louisiana to Newburgh

At the same time, however, state and local ADC policy was becoming more restrictive as caseloads were growing and as more African-Americans went onto the rolls. Despite hopes and predictions that welfare would, like the state in Marxian theory, "wither away," public assistance refused to disappear. ADC in particular grew, and after 1957 ADC claimed more recipients than any other public assistance program.[79] Because of the institutional structure of ADC and the stalemate over welfare policy in the national arena, it was left to states and local authorities to respond to changes in the ADC population. Without either direction or much in the way of additional funding from Washington, states responded by imposing increasingly severe administrative restrictions that had particularly dire effects for African-American beneficiaries. The most prominent of these were the "suitable home" policies that most states had written into their ADC laws early on.[80] These provisions, which generally restricted ADC eligibility to families whose households were deemed morally and physically "suitable" for rearing children, were originally intended to protect children from abuse and neglect by drawing public welfare workers' attention to the conditions of home life in evaluating cases.

But as public pressure and racial tension imposed limits on the growth of ADC, "suitable home" provisions increasingly became mechanisms for enforcing social and moral norms that had racially divisive consequences. Just as the Noleo amendment was an attack on deserting fathers, "suitable home" policies constituted a platform for an attack on illegitimacy, one of the principal circumstances of ADC eligibility. Under some state laws, sexual relations with anyone other than one's legal spouse were considered "promiscuous behavior," violating the "stable moral environment" necessary for a "suitable home" and potentially knocking the family off the rolls. Of course, this was a catch-22, as analysts such as Charles Murray have noted more recently: Marriage meant the end of eligibility by definition, whereas not being married threatened the end of eligibility by discretion.

Not only did such provisions potentially apply more often to African-Americans, among whom out-of-wedlock births were more common, but they also opened up vast new discretionary space for state welfare workers, who frequently used their discretion to discriminate.[81] Nine states, eight of them Southern, stiffened their "suitable home" requirements for ADC between 1952 and 1960, and by 1960 twenty-three states had such policies on the books.

Periodic purges of the welfare rolls by state and local government have been one of the most visible manifestations of ADC's parochialism and of parochialism's racial consequences. State and local policy changes, made possible by institutional parochialism, have rarely taken ADC in a liberalizing direction, and more often than not they have disproportionately swept African-Americans off the rolls. In the summer of 1960, "suitable home" policies burst controversially onto the national scene when Louisiana, in retaliation for court-ordered school desegregation, dropped over 6000 families including more than 23,000 children from its ADC rolls; in two months, the number of Louisianans receiving support from ADC fell by nearly thirty percent.[82] Ninety-five percent of those cut off were African-American, although African-Americans comprised only about two-thirds of the total ADC rolls in the state. The Louisiana crisis attracted the notice and the opprobrium of the national and international press. One interesting political reaction was that of the department of welfare in Richard Daley's Chicago, where the participants clearly and publicly acknowledged the racial element of Louisiana's move. The department's director raised nearly $4000 from his employees and donated it to the National Urban League in New York to aid Louisiana children who had been cut off from ADC, an unconventional but telling use of parochial welfare institutions by a political machine to curry favor with African-American constituents.[83]

The Louisiana affair also spurred the Social Security Administration, which had clung throughout the 1950s to its original view of "suitable home" policies as protective of children, into action. After a review of the policy, lame-duck Secretary of Health, Education, and Welfare Arthur F. Flemming ruled that states with "suitable home" policies could not cut off aid to any eligible family as long as the children remained in the home; if a home was deemed "unsuitable," the state should try to improve conditions or, failing that, remove the children from the home. "It is completely inconsistent," Flemming said, "to declare a home unsuitable for a child to receive assistance and at the same time permit him to remain in the same home exposed to the same environment."[84] Flemming thus graciously dumped a bitter feud between the states and the federal government on the incoming Democratic administration, which had no desire to take on such an explosive issue. The earnest efforts of a Republican administration to enforce the spirit of federal law changed little. The new Democratic president, who owed his election to Southern support, was unlikely to issue any further challenge to Louisiana's practices. "The last thing the new administration needs," said Wilbur Cohen, "is a conflict [over] the blacks and whites and states rights and federal rights."[85] The Kennedy administration discovered anew that the institutional structure of ADC gave the federal government only an extremely blunt instrument— the removal of all federal matching funds—to discipline a recalcitrant state. Moreover, the norm of state control of ADC was too strong for the administration to confront even if it wanted to, which it didn't. It was left with the powers of persuasion and negotiation, which did little to move Louisiana or the other states affected by the Flemming ruling—mostly, but not exclusively Southern—to soften their "suitable home" provisions more than absolutely necessary to comply with the ruling in the narrowest technical way. This dilemma, between the entrenched structure of state discretion and ADC's obvious inadequacies in improving children's lives, helped set the stage for the renewed prominence of anti-poverty policy and the first major attempt at expansion of ADC.

After the Louisiana controversy, the early 1960s saw a wave of highly publicized investigations and official crackdowns on ADC throughout the country. Politicians and administrators, especially at the state and local levels, developed an obsession with rooting out "fraud" and "abuse" from ADC around this time. Such concerns were inherent as *potential* side effects of a discretionary, noncontributory, decentralized policy, but they became particularly prominent in ADC just as the program became the largest of the public assistance programs and as African-Americans were becoming more prominent among its beneficiaries. In the 1950s, poverty in the United States was politically invisible; power, prosperity, and paranoia were the decade's themes. When Americans looked up in the 1960s, they discovered—thanks largely to the writings of Michael Harrington and Dwight Macdonald and a long-running investigation led by Senator John Sparkman—that poverty was still there.[86] But poverty had a very different face from the one it showed during the Depression, an increasingly black face. African-American poverty had moved out of the segmented, segregated South and into the bustling center of American life. Particularly in the great industrial cities of the Northeast and Midwest, poverty and growing public assistance rolls were increasingly concentrated among African-Americans, who appeared to many to be benefiting unworthily from the largesse of politicians who could manipulate benefits for political aims.[87] This newly racialized view of American poverty and ADC was far from accurate, but the institutional structure of ADC left it exposed to political attacks that raised the stock of such views. Although the "backlash" against social welfare and civil rights policies is usually attributed to the splintering of the civil rights movement, the explosion of racial hostility into violence, and the foundering of the Great Society in the middle of the decade, race-laden hostility to ADC was already building in the late 1950s and early 1960s—a "frontlash," as it were—as an outgrowth of ADC's structural weakness.[88]

The first and most famous of the ADC crackdowns came in Newburgh, New York, a small industrial city on the Hudson River.[89] In 1961, Joseph McD. Mitchell, Newburgh's new city manager, became alarmed at the city's growing welfare budget, and he instituted a set of draconian rules designed to uncover fraud and reduce the ADC rolls, beginning with a mandatory, military-style "muster" of ADC recipients at police precincts and following with a thirteen-point plan to reform the city's ADC and general assistance programs. Under Mitchell's plan, all able-bodied men would have to do public work or be refused aid; unwed mothers would lose benefits if they had another child; new ADC applicants would have to prove that they came to Newburgh with firm offers of employment; and all recipients would be limited to three months of benefits in a year.

The Newburgh crackdown was, in its rhetoric and intentions, partly an attack on the class and labor-market bases of ADC. Recipients of public assistance, Mitchell and his supporters asserted, were undeserving because they did not work, preferring to take advantage of the resources of a generous local government. But Mitchell's attack on ADC also embodied a strong racial animus. It zeroed in on the characteristics stereotypically associated with African-American ADC recipients—indolence, illegitimacy, and the tendency to migrate in order to get higher benefits. Mitchell charged that "migrant types from the South" were overburdening the city's welfare system. African-American migration was often associated with "shiftlessness," although it was more plausibly a rational response to the lack of economic opportunity in the South.[90] But other comparable cities in New York had smaller black populations and larger welfare rolls.[91] Black migration, then, was apparently not primarily responsible for boosting Northern welfare enrollments; if it had been, Newburgh's rolls would likely have been even larger. What was responsible, both for selectively enlarging welfare rolls and for encouraging purges such as Newburgh's, was ADC's parochial structure, which encouraged local politicians to be sensitive to the magnetic attraction of generous benefits and drew them into divisive political stances that pitted welfare recipients against both community standards and the community fisc.

In fact, many blacks had moved to Newburgh in the 1950s, and they constituted a disproportionate share of the city's ADC rolls, but the city by no means had a serious ADC crisis until Mitchell seemingly conjured one out of thin air. For example, the city's crackdown turned up only one able-bodied "welfare chiseler." Mitchell himself was a right-wing fanatic—a grotesque-comic character and an exemplar of the paranoid style—and he pandered to the ugliest strains of racism in a community that was just entering the decline that overtook so many Northern cities in the 1960s. After the welfare episode, his career took a series of rather bizarre and self-destructive turns. He was arrested in 1962 for trying to extort a bribe from two real estate developers, although he was acquitted. In 1963 he resigned his Newburgh position to accept a post as an organizer for the John Birch Society, although he announced several weeks later that he would not take the job after all. After his behavior prompted his expulsion from the International City Managers Association and made it impossible for him to get another government job, he became an organizer for the segregationist Citizens' Councils when they tried to branch out to the north in 1964.[92] Mitchell's ADC plan caused a deep rift in the city's government, and it was never implemented because the courts and the New York state Social Welfare Board deemed it illegal. The Newburgh welfare battle became a cause célèbre in the national press, which was alternately appalled at Mitchell's blather and enthusiastic at the prospect of rooting out the so-called fraud he had uncovered.[93] But Mitchell's escapade actually fit seamlessly into the structure of ADC. Newburgh tried to assert its local authority to contain its welfare expenditures by restricting access, particularly black access, to ADC. Although Mitchell may have lost the battle of Newburgh, the battle focused the country's attention not simply on the antics of a slightly deranged public administrator but on a spectacle that many Americans found scarier, a growing black welfare population.

The following year, the New Jersey legislature convened a special committee to investigate ADC expenditures. In the 1950s, New Jersey's benefits were among the most liberal in the country, its rules among the least restrictive. The committee noted that the ADC caseload had gone from 34 percent nonwhite in 1948 to 65 percent nonwhite in 1961. The committee's report cited "flagrant and wanton" and "revolting abuses shocking the public conscience." It condemned the "amoral existence of many ADC recipients," whom it portrayed largely as women who "maintain illicit relationships with men of shadowy existence" and "beget illegitimate child after child without apparent remorse or guilt."[94] The report went on to document many devious subterfuges used to evade the "man-in-the-house" rule. The report is not written in racial terms, nor does it identify the race of any of the cases it cites as examples, but its concerns reflect the traditional "pathological" view of African-American family life (three years before the Moynihan report) and are disturbingly similar to many popular contemporary views on race and poverty.

That same year, the Washington, D.C., Department of Public Welfare did a similar investigation of its ADC program at the behest of the District of Columbia appropriations subcommittees of the House and Senate and with the assistance and supervision of the General Accounting Office. This investigation involved careful audits of a random sample of the district's ADC caseload. Each family selected received an unannounced visit from a team of investigators armed with a detailed questionnaire that included items about the presence of televisions and telephones in the house and whether the recipient cashed her assistance check in a liquor store.[95] Of the 236 cases investigated, the study found that 141, or 60 percent, were ineligible for benefits, and these families were dropped from assistance. Twenty others required adjustments in their benefit levels (all but two of the adjustments were downward). Most of the cases ruled ineligible were violations of the "man-in-the-house" rule. Many had more than one violation, some of which were quite creative, such as one case dropped because of the presence of "coin-operated machines" (a telephone, two televisions, and a washing machine) in the home.[96] Investigations built on such premises, using such methods with such results, and coming at the moment they did in the life of the ADC program, could only have had racially imbalanced effects. Despite studies suggesting that such instances of fraud were greatly exaggerated and denials by federal officials that the D.C. results were typical, such race-laden accounts of fraud captured the national imagination and set the stage for the welfare proposals of the 1960s.[97]

Welfare Reform in the Parochial Mold: The 1962 Amendments

The expansion of social services to public assistance recipients was at the heart of the Public Welfare Amendments of 1962, the first comprehensive ADC reform attempted since the Social Security Act. In the wake of the Flemming ruling on the Louisiana affair, which drew attention to the lack of child welfare services in most states, the Kennedy administration proposed a package that would provide seventy-five percent federal matching grants to the states for social services to ADC families and vocational education and training programs for ADC parents. The guiding idea behind the proposal, the idea that has guided all American welfare reform efforts since, was to encourage, cajole, and ultimately pressure single women with children to enter the workforce rather than relying on public assistance to support themselves and their families. This conception of the function of ADC was far removed from the maternalist idea of mothers' pensions from which ADC was born in the 1930s.[98] Then the idea had been to honor motherhood and make it possible for women to rear their children in their own homes without having to go to work. Now the idea was to draw these women out of the home and into jobs. ADC had always been available only to families without work-based claims to social insurance and only in lieu of work. Now it was seen to breed dependency and possibly to bring out latent tendencies toward vice. The welfare reformers of the early 1960s wanted to stem these apparent trends and use the program to create and promote opportunities for self-support.

But because of the tightly defined target population of ADC, the racial impact of this transformation of vision was not neutral. African-Americans were disproportionately outside of the regular labor market, and so outside the ambit of social insurance programs such as unemployment insurance. They consequently made up a large but not overwhelming proportion of ADC beneficiaries—thirty percent in 1962.[99] Moreover, controversies such as Louisiana and Newburgh had heightened public awareness of ADC and focused national attention not only on the perceived defects of ADC but also on their connection with poverty, particularly black poverty. One study often cited by reform advocates in 1962 noted that the public has gained a false image of a mother who is shiftless and lazy, unwilling to work, promiscuous and neglectful of her children. She is seen as spending her time and her ADC check in the local bar while her children roam the streets and the cupboard stays bare. She is believed to be bearing child after child to get more ADC money, and complacently accepting the public largesse on which she lives.

This study found very few mothers, not more than 3 percent, who fit this image "in one or more ways."

It found no clear-cut cases of fraud.[100]

This image of ADC recipients as lazy, drunken, and promiscuous may have been mostly false, but it was quite clearly a sufficiently important element of the debate that even liberal reformers had to acknowledge it, if only to try and refute it. It was not, however, simply a change of mind en masse that constructed these images in the public mind. Rather, the image of ADC as fraudulent, and consequently of the urban black poor as clients of a corrupt and destructive system, were the fallout of an institutional structure that located these public beneficiaries in a parochial system. Whereas national social insurance absorbed working African-Americans quietly and routinely, public assistance increasingly isolated and exposed the visible minority of African-Americans who were unable to crack the mainstream of the political economy.

The centerpiece of the Kennedy proposal was the 75 percent matching grant to states for social services to ADC recipients. A social services grant had been established with 50 percent federal matching in 1956, but in 1958 only slightly more than half the counties in the country were served by full-time public child welfare workers. The shortage of trained professional welfare workers posed another acute problem even where social service programs existed; in 1960 only 4 percent of public assistance workers and 30 percent of child welfare workers had two years of graduate training in social work. With untrained caseworkers managing oversized caseloads, the Flemming ruling and other well-intentioned policies could have little practical effect.[101] The Kennedy administration's intent was to increase the availability and the level of social services available to public assistance clients by improving the incentives to states to create programs and by funding graduate training in social work. The administration package also proposed extending the temporary provision of ADC to children of unemployed parents (ADC-UP), providing ADC to parents as well as children (this was the act that renamed the program Aid to *Families* with

Dependent Children, the title it carried until its demise in 1996), and eliminating the residency requirements that many states had imposed for ADC eligibility.

Following the pattern for ADC reform proposals, the major controversies over the 1962 public welfare amendments concerned the balance of power between the federal government and the states. As usual, the states had the upper hand. One controversy centered on the residency requirement. This requirement, a remnant of the local relief tradition of the Poor Laws, was traditionally a tool used by Northern states to keep African-American migrants from the South off the rolls. In 1939, for example, Illinois lengthened the state residency requirement for recipients of public assistance from one to three years. "It is generally understood," wrote a columnist for the *Chicago Defender*, "that the residence requirement was lengthened in order to meet the problem supposedly created by race migrants."[102] Forty-three states had residency requirements of up to one year in 1961, and the administration proposed financial incentives to states without such requirements.[103] Opponents of the residency requirement cited a study of ADC recipients that found that "contrary to what most people believe, ADC mothers did not come to Illinois or to Cook County just to get on the ADC rolls . . . Most of the ADC mothers from other parts of the United States came from the deep South, particularly from Mississippi. Adjusting to urban living has been hard for them. Their most serious handicap is lack of education and training."[104] The Ways and Means Committee dropped this provision from the bill, maintaining broad state discretion in this arena.[105]

Another controversy centered on the federal-state balance of power in setting ADC benefit eligibility and payment levels. The Ways and Means Committee approved the extension of ADC-UP and added an increase in the federal matching of ADC grants, and Republicans opposed both on the grounds that they would lead to the "federalization" of public assistance, violating the basic decentralized structure of ADC. Two Republican members of the Ways and Means Committee, Bruce Alger of Texas and James B. Utt of California, protested against the "increasing Federal preeminence" in public assistance. "The rapidly emerging Federal direction and regimentation over public assistance," they charged, "has tended to be self-defeating in that it has lessened the initiative and activity of those public and private agencies that are closer to the scene of need and thereby better qualified to exercise administrative control in the interests of effectiveness and efficiency."[106] The specter of "federalization" was a powerful one, but the effect of the 1962 amendments was hardly as extreme as Alger and Utt feared. On balance, in fact, the legislation *increased* state and local discretion in ADC, both by giving state policymakers access to new social service programs and by vastly widening the discretion of individual ADC caseworkers, who now had an arsenal of services to which they could refer their clients.[107]

In a particularly important move, the Ways and Means Committee also inserted a paragraph into the bill that gave states broad new authority to assure that ADC grants were used "in the best interests of the child," allowing them to substitute protective services for direct payments without risking the loss of federal funds. Nelson Cruikshank, the director of the AFL-CIO's Social Security Department, objected to this vast increase in local discretion and called attention to its inherent discriminatory potential. "Under the guise of protecting the 'best interest of the child,'" he told the Finance Committee, "much harm could be done to people whose only offense was ignorance, membership in a minority group, or having more children than the critics deemed desirable." Marvin Larson of the American Public Welfare Association protested that if this determination of the "best interests of the child" occurred "simply in a welfare department, simply administratively, then there isn't any protection of the individual for a difference between his assistance from the public and somebody else's."[108] In other words, discrimination was more likely.

Many state and local governments supported this addition, as did the American Farm Bureau Federation, a frequent partner in parochial social policy coalitions. Rudolph P. Pohl, chairman of the Finance Committee of the Milwaukee County Board of Supervisors, perhaps inadvertently supported opponents' point about discrimination when he cited the dramatic increase (139 percent) in the number of nonwhite unmarried mothers in his city's ADC caseload between 1957 and 1961. "I do not believe," he said, "the unrestricted money payment, even when supplemented by adequate and skilled casework services, will by themselves reverse the continued increase in the number of unmarried mothers."[109] Pohl's testimony brought together many strands of ADC's policy development. As the chairman of a local government's finance committee, his primary concern was fiscal, and his primary obligation was to taxpayers and not to recipients of public assistance. Although he represented one of the most progressive cities and states in the nation with a long and proud legacy of generous social provision, he expressed alarm particularly at ADC's growing African-American clientele. In order to reduce expenditures and fight what he saw as a dangerous influx of black illegitimacy, he called not for a new national social policy regime that might have relieved local governments of the welfare burden but for new localized discretionary and punitive powers. Finally, Pohl's testimony illustrates the important link among race, decentralized ADC administration, and local political institutions, a link that was to play a critical role in shaping the War on Poverty and its impact.

In effect, the 1962 Kennedy proposal was an extension of the Eisenhower approach to ADC reform, a reversal from Old-Age Insurance. In the case of OAI, the Republican Eisenhower adopted the Democratic approach upon election, preventing the rolling back of the program. In the case of ADC, the new Democratic administration, rather than putting forward a more comprehensive reform that might have been more in keeping with the New Deal legacy, sent up a slightly enhanced version of a Republican proposal that envisioned the eventual demise of ADC itself (a precursor to President Clinton's promise to "end welfare as we know it").[110] This pattern suggests that the institutional logic of the programs, rather than ideology or party, has primarily directed the course of social policy development. There were partisan and ideological differences in each case, but partisan and ideological lines were drawn in a political space shaped and reshaped by earlier developments. The position of African-Americans in the social policy system—honorable beneficiaries of OAI and vilified victims of ADC—followed from these developments as well.

The effects of the 1962 amendments, when filtered through layers of politics and administration, were not quite what the administration intended. The amendments offered more money to increase the availability and improve the quality of social services for ADC recipients. But they did so at the cost of increasing state and local discretion in the application of ADC policy, and expanded discretion gave states the opportunity to twist the implementation of the new law to their own purposes. Providing more and better services meant hiring new caseworkers so that services would be available to more clients and each worker would have fewer cases. Even with the federal share increased to three-fourths, many states found that they had to increase their own contributions in order to comply. Some states, such as Mississippi, eventually dropped their ADC services because of rising costs.[111] In fact, after the 1962 amendments, total federal grants for welfare services grew more slowly in real terms than they had in the mid-1950s or the early 1960s, as Figure 4.6 shows, suggesting that the new federal funding did not translate into an increase in the level of services offered to ADC beneficiaries. The institutional structure of ADC thus frustrated the implementation of national welfare reform efforts, expanding state and local discretion and thwarting the aims of the legislation.

What Happened to Welfare?: The 1960s and the War on Poverty

The tumultuous 1960s were a watershed for the politics of welfare, as they were for American politics more generally. The "rediscovery" of poverty in America and John Kennedy's attention to it in the 1960 presidential campaign placed the issue squarely on the national political agenda for the decade. After Kennedy's assassination, President Johnson declared "war on poverty," committing his administration to a program of welfare state expansion on a scale that deliberately recalled the New Deal. But Johnson's war on poverty overlapped with another commitment, to racial

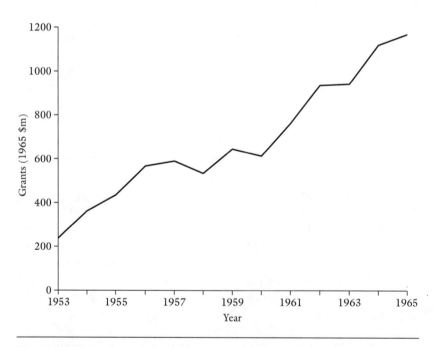

Figure 4.6. Federal grants for welfare services, 1953–1965.
Source: Sophie R. Dales, "Federal Grants," *Social Security Bulletin* 29 (June 1966), 14.

equality and equality of opportunity. Even before the passage of the Civil Rights and Voting Rights Acts, the civil rights movement was shifting its sights away from Jim Crow in the South and onto the deplorable economic conditions of African-Americans throughout the country. In such a context, the politics of race and the politics of welfare came together explicitly and explosively.

For many observers, particularly conservative opponents of the welfare state, the liberal excesses of the 1960s bear a great deal of the blame for the current state of welfare politics. The Great Society not only expanded existing welfare programs, but it created new ones that were explicitly aimed at particularly disadvantaged segments of the population—the rural poor and urban blacks, especially. In some accounts, such as that of Charles Murray, the new welfare regime failed because it encouraged behavior that wrecked the lives of precisely the people it was intended to help, increasing poverty in the end by promoting illegitimacy and idleness.[112] In other accounts more sympathetic to the Great Society impulse, the expansion of welfare failed politically precisely because it was targeted at the poor and the powerless and drove a wedge between the new welfare clients and the old working and middle classes.[113] But all of these accounts of the welfare crisis of the 1960s agree that the War on Poverty provoked fervent and spirited opposition that sapped its strength in short order.

The welfare state indeed grew in the 1960s. Not only was there a proliferation of new programs, but the established public assistance programs grew as well. By the time the 1962 Public Welfare Amendments were adopted, ADC had already entered a period of dramatic growth. Between 1960 and 1962, the number of families receiving ADC grew almost as much as during the entire decade of the 1950s; over the next five years the rolls would grow by nearly forty percent. Real spending on ADC benefits would double between 1960 and 1967.[114] But underlying the apparent explosion of welfare in the 1960s were trends that had begun in the outwardly stable 1950s and merely continued. Increasingly, ADC recipients lived in cities—from forty percent in 1950 to more than half in 1960 and nearly three-fifths by the end of the decade. In particular, they were increasingly found in Northern cities. And the racial composition of the ADC caseload was changing as well, but the African-American share of the recipient population grew much more dramatically in the 1950s than the 1960s.[115]

So what was it about the new politics of welfare in the 1960s that aroused such a vehement animus? The centerpiece of the War on Poverty—the Economic Opportunity Act of 1964—did not directly concern

ADC at all. But it amounted to an unprecedented attempt to reconfigure the institutional architecture of the American welfare state away from parochialism and toward a more national structure. In its substance, the War on Poverty addressed many of the same themes as the Public Welfare Amendments of 1962, dramatically expanding educational, vocational, and rehabilitative programs for the poor.[116] But it did so not by adding increments to the existing welfare structure but by attempting to recast altogether the institutional logic of the welfare state. First, it created the Office of Economic Opportunity, a vast new federal agency in the Executive Office of the President, outside the ambit of the traditional welfare bureaucracy, to oversee the new welfare regime. Second, through the Community Action Program and the doctrine of "maximum feasible participation" of a community's poor people in devising and administering the programs that were to help them, the act linked new federal capacity directly to citizens, bypassing the elaborate tangle of state and local officials that had controlled even federally funded public assistance under the New Deal. This new nexus of local participation and federal money and power (judicial as well as bureaucratic) helped many poor people—especially African-Americans in the rural South and the urban North—reduce both their reliance on ADC and their dependence on local political authorities. Although the Community Action Program and the other weapons in the War on Poverty's arsenal brought the federal government into direct action on social welfare, by their very nature they engaged entrenched local structures not only of economic status but of race and political authority as well.[117]

As with the 1962 ADC amendments, the central issues in the debate over the Economic Opportunity Act, both in 1964 and when it was amended the following year, revolved around the division of authority between the federal government and state and local agencies. Republicans and Southern Democrats were skeptical of the bill because of its potential to introduce the direct provision of welfare services by the federal government to the poor. Southern attacks on the mechanics of the programs successfully reduced the federal government's authority over the anti-poverty effort.[118] With the civil rights movement moving ahead at full throttle and the traditional racial structure of Southern society crumbling in its path, Southern members of Congress took the threat of "maximum feasible participation" very seriously. The reliable segregationist Howard Smith, who had opposed federal control of ADC in 1935 and later delayed the Civil Rights Act of 1957 by simply disappearing from Washington for two weeks and refusing to call a meeting of the Rules Committee, warned that the NAACP could receive anti-poverty money under the terms of the bill, as could the Ku Klux Klan or a "nudist colony."[119] In 1935, when the "party of Lincoln" still claimed the allegiance of African-Americans, it was an Ohio Republican, Thomas Jenkins, who sparred with Smith about his racial motives. But in 1964, the presidential nomination of Barry Goldwater marked the end of a century of Republican claims to be the party of civil rights, and another Ohio Republican, William H. Ayres, joined Smith's chorus, warning that "there won't be any white people" in the new anti-poverty programs.[120] Opponents managed to add a governor's veto over any anti-poverty grants to groups in his state, an important change considering that men such as George C. Wallace and Orval Faubus occupied Southern statehouses. Sure enough, of the five governor's vetoes exercised in 1965, four were by Southern governors, including one by Wallace, who rejected a community action grant to a biracial group in Birmingham, Alabama.[121] In 1965, when the Economic Opportunity Act was reauthorized, even the legendary 89th Congress could not repeal the governor's veto entirely, settling for a cumbersome procedure by which the Office of Economic Opportunity could override a governor's veto, a process almost guaranteed to increase tension between national and local politicians and administrators.

What finally brought the War on Poverty, and particularly the Community Action Program, to heel was a telling opposition coalition between parochial forces—segregationist Southern Democrats and Northern mayors—who were accustomed to exercising control over public assistance.[122] Provoked by the activities of the Child Development Group of Mississippi, Senators James Eastland and John Stennis denounced the War on Poverty as a thinly disguised, federally sponsored civil rights effort, and successfully reduced its funding in 1965. At the same time, mayors such as Richard Daley of Chicago, who had been able to use the parochial structure of ADC to manipulate the benefits of African-American constituents, found themselves confronted with federally backed, community-based welfare agencies that they could not control and that created sturdy political platforms for black political organization in opposition to local elites.[123] This coalition gained strength in the 1966 congressional elections, in which liberal Democrats lost seats in both the House and Senate, and in 1967 won passage of amendments sponsored by Representative Ethel Green of Oregon giving local mayors control of Community Action Agencies. It is one of the biting ironies of the 1960s that the great institutional innovation of the War on Poverty, an attempt to realize the New Deal ideal of national, inclusive social policy, was brought down by the same coalition—rural South and urban North—that created the American welfare state in the first place.

Although reform of ADC was not formally part of the War on Poverty, the conflict between national and parochial welfare visions spilled over into a new round of debate on ADC. In 1967, at the height of the War on Poverty fray, President Johnson proposed legislation to increase OAI benefits. The House Ways and Means Committee seized the opportunity to bring ADC into the controversy by adding to the bill several provisions building on both the Public Welfare Amendments of 1962 and the Economic Opportunity Act, but with a newly restrictive spin. There could be no better emblem of the divergent fortunes of Old-Age Insurance and Aid to Dependent Children than the Social Security Amendments of 1967, which simultaneously raised OAI benefits an average of thirteen percent and placed new and racially divisive restrictions on ADC benefits. Ways and Means added two major features to ADC. The first was *mandatory* state participation in work training for ADC recipients, with the reward to states of discretion to drop ADC recipients who refused to participate in work and training "without good cause." The other was a freeze on federal grants to states for ADC payments in cases of parental absence from the home, but not parental death or unemployment.[124] By contrast, the Johnson administration's welfare program called for federal ADC benefit standards and financial incentives for work training, among other liberalizations.

Like the battle over the War on Poverty, the contest between these alternatives was a fight between contending institutional visions of welfare. On one side, an administration committed to an expansive vision of racial equality in social citizenship sought to nationalize welfare and reduce local discretion in order to overcome the racial and behavioral divides that made ADC such a troubled and contentious program. On the other side, the parochial forces that ADC itself had spawned a generation earlier exerted further centrifugal influence on the program, pulling authority out of Washington and into the racially explosive politics of cities and states.

Liberals in the House denounced the Ways and Means provisions. Representative Hugh Carey of New York City objected that the ADC provisions would severely handicap large cities in the North that were still experiencing mostly African-American immigration and expecting increasing ADC burdens.[125] However, the bill came to the House under a rule that allowed no amendments and passed 416 to 3 because few members could afford to vote against an increase in OAI benefits.

When the Senate Finance Committee held hearings on the bill, opposition to the House ADC provisions was intense. The administration opposed them, as did organizations representing state public welfare workers and social workers. The bill's racial implications were poorly concealed. Mayor John V. Lindsay of New York explicitly linked the decentralization of ADC with racial conflict, warning that "the multiplication of areas of discretion in the delivery of public assistance and the added sanctions on individuals will most certainly aggravate tension in ghetto communities."[126] Clarence Mitchell of the NAACP contended that the freeze "denies assistance to those least responsible for their plight—the children who happen to be in the class covered by the cut-off formula." In his understated way, Mitchell acknowledged the fiscal pressure that legislators felt to limit welfare expenditures but then added, "I think it has a little of a racial overtone, too. You know, sometimes people drive through colored neighborhoods and they see a whole lot of colored people standing around on corners and assume they are all idlers and are just on relief and that kind of thing." Finally, in his most withering criticism, he suggested that the House bill promoted racially divided social experimentation that the nation would not tolerate if practiced on dogs:

> After I wrote that testimony this morning as I was leaving home, I happened to remember that I had better feed the dog and I opened one of those real pretty packages, I think they are called Gaines Burgers, or something like that. I don't know whether you have ever seen them, but they are real nice looking stuff. It looks like hamburger. Well, on this package there was the statement which said:
>
> This is processed under the continuous examination of the United States Department of Agriculture.
>
> I am sure that if somebody started experimenting with that dog food and saying that you don't give it to brown dogs or dogs of uncertain ancestry and that kind of thing, you would have a big hullabaloo in this country. I think that we ought to be just as concerned about experimenting with the lives of our children and the future of our children as we are about experimenting with the welfare of pets, and even more so.[127]

Mitchell's vivid testimony articulated clearly the heightened racial tension in the politics of ADC.

Even more vivid was a demonstration in the Finance Committee's hearing room staged by a group of African-American women, members of the National Welfare Rights Organization (NWRO).[128] The NWRO was a short-lived but influential movement that organized mostly black women to demand better access to ADC coverage through both protest and legal action. On 19 September, a group of women testified on behalf of the NWRO. The only senators in the room at the time were the committee's chairman, Russell Long of Louisiana, and Fred Harris of Oklahoma (typically only a few committee members are in the hearing room at any moment). The witnesses, upset at what they perceived to be a chilly reception from the committee, refused to leave the witness table until the entire committee was there to listen to them. They sat there for nearly three hours and remained even after Long recessed the hearing. The press was expelled from the room, and the women were reportedly threatened with arrest before they finally left. The next day Long—who quite deliberately cultivated a more courtly and conservative demeanor than his father, Huey—had them barred from the room, commenting that "if they can find the time to march the streets and if they can find the time to picket congressional committees, and if they can find the time to sit all day in committee hearings when they have been heard, and deny other people their right to be heard—people who have that much time available to them should have time to do some work." Long later derisively referred to them as a bunch of "brood mares."[129]

Despite Long's insult, the Finance Committee eliminated the freeze and softened the work requirement by allowing states to exempt mothers of preschool children. The full Senate further relaxed the work requirement, adopting an amendment offered by Senator Robert F. Kennedy to exempt women with school-age children as well. To this amendment, Long objected that a mother "would not have to do so much as swat a mosquito off her leg as a condition for getting aid from the government."[130] The Senate also adopted an amendment requiring states to offer ADC-UP, which only twenty-two states had adopted. In the conference committee, Long, who was not sympathetic to the liberal agenda of strong federal ADC requirements, agreed to the harsher House provisions on all the important details, accepting the welfare freeze and work training without exemptions and rejecting ADC benefit increases and the ADC-UP requirement. When the report of the conference committee returned to the Senate for final action in December, liberals, led by Harris and Robert Kennedy, attempted a filibuster. The liberal troops, though small in number, were confident that they could stall long enough to prevent any action by the Senate, whose members were anxious to get home for the Christmas holidays, and demand stronger welfare provisions. But on 15 December, Long noticed that Senator Joseph D. Tydings of Maryland, who was responsible for monitoring activity on the floor on behalf of the liberal group, was engrossed in conversation in the back of the chamber, while neither Harris nor Kennedy was present. Long, a master legislative tactician, seized his opportunity and quickly brought the bill to a vote, catching the liberals off guard. Tydings later contritely took full responsibility for falling down on the job, while Long gloated at his own skillful maneuver.[131] In the Senate's final vote, the only Southerner against the bill was the liberal Ralph Yarborough of Texas and one of only three Republicans against it was Edward W. Brooke of Massachusetts, the first black senator since Reconstruction.[132]

Despite the accelerated pace of attempts to reform ADC from the center in the 1960s, either directly through program amendments or indirectly through other anti-poverty policies, at decade's end ADC remained a highly discretionary program. ADC was administered on the ground by a complex bureaucracy staffed, ideally but by no means regularly, by trained professional social workers.[133] Despite a uniform trend toward the liberalization of state eligibility requirements between 1960 and 1970, the increasing bureaucratization of welfare has placed more discretion in the hands of individual caseworkers.[134] The steady accretion of rules and procedures from different levels of government, often contradictory and usually vague, made it impossible for local welfare workers to operate according to straightforward rules or procedures in determining eligibility. By the 1960s, the *Handbook of Public Assistance Administration,* in which the federal Bureau of Public Assistance compiled its policy statements and procedural directives, was five inches thick; on top of this workers had to contend with several other layers of rules and regulations.[135] Under these circumstances, welfare workers could hardly process applications without making frequent discretionary judgments in most cases. One study of ADC intake in New York City found that in nearly forty percent of new applications, workers could find reasons to justify at least two different outcomes (accept, reject, or defer). Nor did there seem to be any rule of thumb that determined the outcome in such discretionary cases.[136]

Administrative discretion in ADC could still work against African-Americans. In a study of welfare administration in Milwaukee, a recipient's race affected her relations with her caseworker in some respects but not in others. Workers were more likely to ask black women questions that went beyond the basic economic criteria—questions about marital status or marital plans, Noleo, and child care arrangements. The biggest racial difference in caseworker treatment was in the discussion of employment. Although more blacks than whites said they wanted jobs, caseworkers were less likely to discuss employment opportunities with black clients. As a result, African-Americans were much less successful at leaving the welfare rolls than whites.[137]

Conclusions

Over thirty years, Aid to Dependent Children evolved from a small program designed to discriminate against African-Americans to a large and ever-growing program that many Americans feared was directing too much money to African-Americans while imposing too few requirements on them. This transformation poses something of a historical paradox. How did a program that was structured to exclude African-Americans grow not just to include them but to serve them disproportionately? And why, once they had apparently overcome the initial barriers, did their inclusion prove so controversial and come to occupy the center of one of the enduring political conflicts of our time? This pattern is a puzzle if we assume that the motive force behind growing inclusion in the middle of the century was simply a softening of racial attitudes and a relaxation of discriminatory intent. Such a story would square nicely with a historical account that emphasizes the march toward racial equality in the 1940s and 1950s, from the Fair Employment Practices Commission to *Brown* v. *Board of Education* to the Civil Rights and Voting Rights Acts. These events certainly changed the face of American race relations and altered forever the racial structure of American politics and society. But if it were the case that the collapse of the color line and the decline of racial prejudice and segregation were primarily responsible for the growing availability of public social provision to African-Americans, we would then be hard-pressed to explain the simultaneously growing backlash against the racial profile of public assistance, and therein lies the central paradox of American welfare.

The answer to the paradox, the element that linked racial inclusion and racial retrenchment, was the institutional structure of ADC. By classifying the beneficiaries of public social provision by class characteristics and labor-market attachment, the Social Security Act effectively sorted Americans by race. By assigning the predominantly white working and middle classes to national social insurance, the structure of the welfare state ensured their protection. And by correspondingly assigning poor women and children, disproportionately African-American, to parochial public assistance, the same structural imperative operated in reverse. Subject to disparate local political imperatives and administrative norms, intense fiscal pressure, political uncertainty, and deep public skepticism, ADC never mobilized the political force that impelled Old-Age Insurance toward both inclusion *and* political support. In the early years, the result of these structural imperatives was, in fact, discrimination against African-Americans in ADC, especially in the South, whose congressmen had demanded ADC's extreme parochialism for precisely that reason. But as African-Americans spread out to the North, where the pressures for exclusion were not so central to political life, they entered the welfare system. But they did so on terms not of generosity but of political patronage, terms made possible precisely by the parochialism imposed by Southern influence. The expansion of ADC and African-American inclusion came about neither because racial antagonism declined nor because national policymakers willed it, but because local politicians capitalized on its parochial institutional structure to expand it for their own purposes. Once they had an entrenched interest in local control of welfare, parochialism was very difficult to dislodge, even as welfare became more of a burden than a boon to state and city governments. Decisions in 1935 about the structure of welfare institutions thus produced a configuration of interests and ideology that was effectively "locked in"; although the tight hold of the South on the Democratic party began to decline and the facade of states' rights became all but transparent, the pattern of parochialism laid down by the Southern politicians of the 1930s was recreated in the North, on only slightly different terms.

For African-Americans, this pattern has meant a continuing attachment to local political institutions, an attachment that has exposed many poor black Americans—particularly the urban black poor—not necessarily, or even predominantly, to direct discrimination, but more pervasively to political isolation. During the late 1950s and early 1960s, political opposition to ADC was increasingly bound up in racial conflict, and the Great Society, the largest assault on American poverty in a generation, actually managed to weaken ADC even further rather than building on it to create a more comprehensive welfare state.[138] The poor, disproportionately black clients of ADC have been, in effect, extruded from the mainstream of American life, not just economically and spatially but politically as well, and the structure of welfare institutions has played a large role as a motor of political isolation.[139] By so exposing African-Americans to such divisive political forces at the local level, without overarching national political forces able to offer even a whisper of protection, the institutional structure of ADC contributed mightily not only to the political degeneration of welfare but to the political construction of the urban "underclass" and the crisis that has for a generation surrounded it and engulfed the nation.

5

Unemployment Insurance: Inclusion, Exclusion, and Stagnation

Although it shares many characteristics with both Old-Age Insurance and Aid to Dependent Children, Unemployment Insurance presents a very different pattern of racial exclusion and development. The same occupational exclusions that restricted OAI coverage—agricultural and domestic labor most significantly—applied to Unemployment Insurance, excluding more than half the black workforce but only one-third of white workers. However, UI did not expand rapidly, as OAI did, to bring these excluded workers into the system. Nor has Unemployment Insurance been similarly transformed into a program of broad political favor and generous income support. Although it has become an accepted and essential part of the American economic and political landscape, it has generated neither the reverential support nor the expansionary drive that have blessed Old-Age Insurance. Like OAI, Unemployment Insurance was designed to reach a working population that was, by default if not by design, predominantly white. But like ADC, Unemployment Insurance had the potential to provide important benefits to eligible African-Americans, who have often been at the margins of the labor market and who have stood, as a result, in greater need of support while unemployed. Also like ADC, its provisions and procedures have allowed ample room for racial manipulation, both of laws and administrative practices. But despite these structural similarities to ADC, Unemployment Insurance programs have been designed and administered fairly and evenly across racial lines, and they have avoided the morass of racial politics that still infects welfare debates. Instead, the history of Unemployment Insurance has been remarkable principally because it has been so unremarkable, free of the political turbulence that has so often engulfed other parts of the American welfare state. Its development, in fact, has been quite stagnant, and it has undergone less significant reform than any other American welfare policy. These patterns of fair ad-

177

ministration, political quiescence, and static evolution all have their roots in the same institutional factors that have governed the development of Old-Age Insurance and Aid to Dependent Children.

But the true significance of Unemployment Insurance for African-Americans in the American political economy goes beyond this mixed administrative legacy. The essential barrier that Unemployment Insurance presents to African-Americans is not administrative but structural. Designed for a white industrial working population, Unemployment Insurance has important links to a broader set of macroeconomic policy aims—not only income support but also modest management of the labor market and job placement, as well as job training and expanded (if not full) employment in later years.[1] But these links have taken particular institutional forms with consequences that have had unfortunate effects for African-Americans, especially in the middle third of the twentieth century, when black Americans undertook one of the largest mass population movements in history, a shift that was not only geographical but economic and political as well. The institutional structure of Unemployment Insurance may not have fostered widespread racial discrimination within the policy's boundaries. However, the program's institutional structure drew those boundaries so tightly that, even absent the kind of racial manipulation that has affected ADC, the program has become less and less able to address the needs of African-Americans. Moreover, *unemployment* policy has become the American stand-in for *employment* policy, with distinct consequences not only for both branches of policy but for African-Americans as well.[2] The institutional structure of Unemployment Insurance has played a role in the political and economic isolation of black Americans.[3]

By its very design, Unemployment Insurance had a restricted purpose. It was not intended solely, or even primarily, to provide income support to the unemployed. Rather, it was designed to stabilize employment and to provide unemployment benefits of limited scope and amount as an adjunct to that aim. Thus the boundaries of exclusion and inclusion for UI were determined not only from within the program's own terms—by the definition of covered categories and administrative operations—but by the scope of the program itself. Even if all categories of workers were covered, and even if there were not one shred of discriminatory administration or policymaking in any state, county, or city anywhere in the country, Unemployment Insurance would *still* ignore the most serious problems of employment and unemployment for African-Americans. It is the terms of the program themselves that have failed to match the needs of African-Americans in the labor market, and not the particulars of the program within those terms.

Unemployment Insurance coverage was slow to expand, not bringing agricultural and domestic workers into the system until 1976. By then, only about fifteen percent of working African-Americans were in those occupations, and only one-third of the farm workers brought in under expanded coverage were black.[4] But Unemployment Insurance, unlike Old-Age Insurance, remained marginal to many African-Americans, not simply because its development was stagnant but primarily because it did not address the most pressing needs that African-Americans faced in the American political economy. Although Unemployment Insurance did not become a racial battleground, its institutional structure—partly national, partly parochial, and detached from the basic problems of a racially defined segment of the labor force—helped to divide the American working population along racial lines and restrict the possibilities for more far-reaching and racially inclusive approaches to employment and unemployment.

This chapter traces the career of Unemployment Insurance in the United States from 1935 to the 1960s. It begins with a discussion of the institutional structure of Unemployment Insurance as it was created by the Social Security Act and then proceeds to explore the consequences of institutional structure, first for the administrative treatment of African-Americans in the program and then for the policy's development in the generation after the New Deal. In its inclusiveness, institutional structure, and developmental path, UI represents, in many ways, an intermediate case between the poles marked out by Old-Age Insurance and Aid to Dependent Children. It demonstrates that racially fair administration is possible even where state and local officials retain a large measure of policy and operational control over social provision. But it also suggests that even where institutional development creates inclusive policy and fair administration, African-Americans can still be left behind.

The Institutional Structure of Unemployment Insurance

Unemployment Insurance as established by the Social Security Act of 1935 was neither entirely national nor entirely parochial. In some respects it approached the parochialism of Aid to Dependent Children. It left much autonomy in policymaking and administration to state and local authorities, and it was quite susceptible to narrow political influences. But in other respects it had national characteristics. It was considerably more uniform and procedural in its basic structure than ADC, although it contained some discretionary criteria that also distinguished it from Old-Age Insurance. Its institutional structure also allowed for much more centralized administrative control than ADC, although states still mediated between the federal government and individual citizens. The implications of UI's institutional structure for African-Americans similarly fell between the extremes of inclusionary expansion and racializing constraint. Although UI incorporated African-Americans administratively with some success, its growth was slow and halting at best.

The Policy Design of Unemployment Insurance

In its benefit and financing arrangements, Unemployment Insurance fell between the procedurally egalitarian and discretionary poles. It was procedurally egalitarian in the sense that there were straightforward rules, determined by state law, about eligibility and benefit levels that derived from an applicant's work and wage history; but it was also discretionary in the sense that executing the law required administrative decisions in individual cases.[5] Two basic questions about an applicant determined his eligibility for UI benefits, and these in effect separated UI eligibility into procedurally egalitarian and discretionary components.[6] The first was based on the verifiable facts of the applicant's employment history. As under OAI, in order to qualify for benefits, a worker had to have worked steadily in a covered job for a minimum amount of time, verifiable from state records based on employers' payroll tax returns. The applicant, of course, also had to have lost a covered job. Because African-Americans were more likely to be employed only intermittently, such qualifying requirements created another factor on top of occupational exclusions that could render them ineligible. However, once state policy was set it provided a clear guide for administration of UI in individual cases. This first question, whether a potential beneficiary met the procedural requirements of the law, closely resembled the procedurally egalitarian benefit provisions of Old-Age Insurance and left very little room for discriminatory administration.

But the second question was not one of procedural compliance but of personal conduct and prospective behavior, and here Unemployment Insurance began to resemble the discretionary aspects of Aid to Dependent Children. "Eligibility provisions" for UI, one early study noted, "must discriminate."[7] Unlike ADC, UI did not depend on a means test. But it generally required a "work test." In order to be eligible for UI benefits, an applicant had to show that his unemployment was beyond his own control and that he was committed to finding a new job. These criteria, designed to ensure that American Unemployment Insurance did not become a permanent substitute for work like the British "dole," put a great deal of discretion in the hands of the bureaucrats who made individual eligibility decisions. Unemployed workers could be disqualified from benefits if they left work voluntarily without "good cause"; if they were discharged for "misconduct"; if they refused an offer of "suitable work"; or if they received benefits through "fraudulent misrepresentation." Benefits could be reduced if they had other income from certain sources. And in some states, women who left work due to "marital obligations"—including pregnancy and childbirth—could be disqualified.[8]

Clearly these provisions, especially the phrases in quotation marks in the foregoing list, did not prescribe clear rules that could be uniformly applied without a fair amount of individual discretion. Especially in states where variable tax rates gave employers an interest in keeping the UI rolls low, such provisions created an opportunity for state administrators to discriminate in awarding benefits. The inherent problems of applying these kinds of qualifications have, over time, spawned increasingly complex and diverse laws and regulations that "have become so detailed and complex that it takes a great deal of training and much practice for unemployment insurance claims takers to properly apply the unemployment laws and rules to individual cases."[9] One participant-observer noted in the early 1950s that UI workers needed to know, among other things, "the character of the individual claimant. The claims-examiner inevitably becomes something of a psychologist. It is that kind of job. No matter how the area left to his discretion is narrowed, there will always be room for his personal judgment of the character of the claimant to influence his decision."[10] The proliferation of rules and regulations by no means eliminated discretion from the process; in fact, by mystifying eligibility criteria, it enhanced the importance of discretion, as caseworkers had to negotiate among complex and often contradictory rules and procedures.[11] In New Jersey, for example, certain rules gave claims workers license to evaluate applicants on a wide array of criteria of questionable relevance. Lack of promptness, for example, could be considered prima facie evidence that an applicant was not "available for work," and state law gave local unemployment offices the right to disqualify claimants who were deemed too "informally" dressed to be looking for a job.[12] Despite these complications, however, the discretionary opportunity for administrative discrimination in UI was comparatively small.

The financing of Unemployment Insurance was fundamentally contrib-

utory in that a worker would be eligible to receive benefits because, in return for his labor, his employer paid payroll taxes *on his individual behalf.*
Individuals could then claim UI benefits as a right of social citizenship that
derived from their status as workers, a status that went well beyond claims
to public assistance.[13] But Unemployment Insurance was only *quasi*-con-
tributory, because generally only employers and not employees contributed. Only ten states have ever required employee contributions, and by
1965, only three states did.[14] Unlike OAI, UI did not create the illusion of
a self-sustaining system of individual annuities; unemployed workers do
not believe themselves to be drawing "their own" money out of an "account" that the government keeps for them.[15]

The combination of quasi-egalitarian benefits and quasi-contributory
financing created a constituency divided, like that of ADC, between those
who contributed and those who received. The split, however, was of a
considerably different sort from that of ADC. Most important, both political and fiscal pressure on the UI system were most acute at the state and
not the national level. Policy decisions about eligibility and financing were
made by states. Within states, pressure was divided. Employers had an
interest in keeping their taxes low, and their principal outlet for this pressure was the experience rating system.[16] By stabilizing employment and
challenging individual claims, employers could keep their own tax liabili-
ties low and, consequently, maintain pressure on states to keep their UI
program small. On the other side, the pressure for higher benefits did
not come only from a weak and marginalized group of beneficiaries but
principally from organized labor, whose members constituted the bulk of
the potential beneficiaries of UI. Thus unlike ADC, the constituency for
higher UI benefits had substantial political weight. But in contrast to OAI,
it was locked in a perpetual fight with a countervailing and often more
powerful constituency for restricted taxation.[17]

The divided constituency of Unemployment Insurance also created a
heightened adversarial politics at the level of individual claims. In states
with experience rating plans, each employer's tax rate depended on his
record of creating or preventing unemployment. Employers with stable
employment over a long period pay lower rates, because they cost the
system less in benefit payments. When a worker became unemployed and
collected UI benefits, her benefits were "charged" against her former employer, and employers who were responsible for more unemployed workers pay higher tax rates.[18] In these states, it was in the interest of employers
to challenge the UI claims of their former employees, setting up an adver-

sarial relationship between employers and workers.[19] This adversarial relationship put the state UI agency into a judicial role in which it had to adjudicate impartially between competing claims in individual cases rather than simply making administrative decisions.[20] This common-law approach to the evolution of UI claims, which was characteristic of American labor law until the New Deal, has shaped the politics of Unemployment Insurance.[21] As in any common-law system, the Social Security Board began compiling a compendium of UI claims decisions, building up a written record of case law as a guide for state claims adjudicators and policymakers.[22] In addition to placing a substantial burden on state agencies, this judicial role has meant that any change in UI claims determinations would have to confront an increasingly dense background of cases, precedents, and usage that would be difficult to supplant.

The Administrative Structure of Unemployment Insurance

Unemployment Insurance as established in 1935 was most obviously a hybrid in its unique status as a joint federal-state program.[23] Benefits were financed by state taxes, and state laws set basic policies such as tax levels, eligibility requirements, benefit levels, and administrative procedures. State policies such as the levels and duration of benefits, the waiting period required after becoming unemployed, and the amount of work required for benefit eligibility varied significantly across states and provided state policymakers with substantial opportunities to manipulate UI policy in ways that might limit its reach across lines of class, gender, race, or any other social division inscribed in the state's political economy.[24] For example, by restricting eligibility to those who have worked a certain length of time (or earned a certain amount), states could limit the flow of UI benefits to workers with particularly stable employment, which would generally eliminate more nonunion workers than union members and more black than white workers. States could also restrict the conditions under which workers might leave their jobs and still qualify for benefits by imposing penalties on workers who fail the work test—by leaving a job voluntarily, for example, or by not seeking a new job. Such freedom gave states substantial leeway in setting the terms of UI.

At the same time, however, the level of federal participation in UI went well beyond the ADC model. First, the federal government set the baseline level of unemployment taxation through the federal payroll tax. Thus, even though states technically could levy unemployment taxes at any rate they liked, federal policy provided strong incentives for states to set their tax rates at the federal level. Second, the states were required to deposit the proceeds of their unemployment taxes into a federal trust fund, from which the Treasury Department returned it to the states only to pay unemployment benefits. Thus the states could not use the federal unemployment tax offset as a way of increasing general revenues to fund other expenditures. Third, the federal credit amounted to only ninety percent of the state tax, leaving the rest of the payroll tax collections in federal hands.

This residual federal revenue provided the means for the most important element of federal control in Unemployment Insurance, federal financing of state administration. Each year, the federal government granted funds to each state to cover the *total* cost of administering Unemployment Insurance, in contrast to ADC and other grant-in-aid programs. In those programs, administrative costs were split between the state and federal governments, and federal authorities had almost no useful administrative leverage. Federal administrative financing fundamentally shaped the federal-state relationship in the administration of UI, giving the federal government substantial control over the operation of state UI programs.[25] State employment agency budgets came principally from the federal government, rather than the state legislature, and so had to conform to a federal agency's standards of "proper administration," as the Social Security Act stated. In the early years of the program, the Social Security Board required the submission of highly detailed state budgets, justifying the number and pay of employees, the purchase or rental of equipment or office space, and other expenditures.[26] Federal financing of administration allowed federal bureaucrats to keep a close watch on state UI operations and placed a high premium on conformity with both formal and informal federal requirements. Recall that the "principal-agent" model did not capture altogether accurately the federal-state relationship in ADC; states were essentially "free agents" as long as they met some minimal requirements. In the case of UI, the states did, in effect, become agents of the federal government, taking direction about policy goals and administrative operations from Washington, and state officials saw their own roles in this light. Still, like any agents, state officials were not immune from the temptation to subvert and shirk, especially as the federal government began to rely more heavily on rules of thumb and other shortcuts in evaluating state activity.[27] The federal-state relationship has been fraught with conflict and resentment over renegade states, on the federal side, and federal intrusion, on the state side. Despite full federal financing, the state-federal relationship has been one of bargaining and cooperation between state and federal officials rather than direct federal command.[28]

To smooth over some of the rough spots in the federal-state relationship, both sides have often turned to the Interstate Conference of Employment Security Agencies (ICESA), an organization of state officials funded and partly staffed by the federal government.[29] The ICESA has been a vehicle both for state officials to share information with each other and convey their collective interests to the federal government and for federal authorities to coordinate state activities. It has met many of the administrative needs of the federal-state system, fostering communication among states on technical matters and improving the integration of a diffuse set of agencies. At the same time, it has filled an important political role, both as a common forum for state and federal officials and as the lobbying arm of the state agencies. In this latter role, the ICESA has drawn some criticism on the grounds that it uses federal money to lobby the federal government in violation of federal law and that it has, at various times, essentially captured the federal Bureau of Employment Security, pulling it in a generally conservative, pro-employer direction. Most important, despite its federal backing the ICESA has been a strong political force in resisting attempts to centralize and federalize Unemployment Insurance.[30]

In its susceptibility to outside political influence, Unemployment Insurance once again fell between two extremes defined by OAI and ADC. Because state legislatures determined taxation levels, benefits, and eligibility criteria, it was, like ADC, inherently subject to state political control. The overall level of state UI spending and taxation, as well as the distribution of benefits, flowed directly from the discretionary decisions of state and local functionaries. As a consequence, the staffing of state employment services agencies was an important point of contention. Many state politicians wanted control of personnel, not only for simple political patronage but also for potential influence over UI operations. Although the Social Security Act explicitly forbade the federal government from interfering in state personnel practices, national Social Security executives were dismayed at the apparent lack of professionalism in many states, and some analysts pointed to patronage pressures as the most important impediment to the smooth functioning of the system in its earliest years.[31]

Recall that political permeability creates a potential dilemma between the motives of democratically accountable politicians and the imperatives of effective policy. For OAI, political pressures and policy imperatives coincided. In the case of UI, however, the dilemma appeared. The susceptibility of operational decisionmaking to democratic political control threatened potentially to undermine one of the primary goals of UI policy, fair and adequate benefits to the unemployed. And because the racial distribution of benefits was, to some extent, traceable to the decisions of administrators, democratic accountability also threatened the program's racial fairness, even though racial equality was not an explicit goal of the program.

UI's relative permeability to contentious political influence, mostly at the state level, in fact affected both the operation and growth of the program. At the state level, the quality of UI administration was highly dependent on the state's personnel system but at the same time came under careful federal scrutiny. State agencies were constrained by their reliance on federal administrative grants, and federal administrators were constrained in turn by their reliance on Congress to fund those grants. These forces reinforced effective and nondiscriminatory administration of UI benefits by subjecting state operations to some federal supervision. At the same time, the political openness of UI administration shaped the politics of UI reform, to the detriment of African-American workers. At the state level, policymakers have had little political incentive to focus their efforts and attention on program expansion or reform in the absence of national policy changes. At the federal level, UI's relative permeability to political influence has made reform more difficult to achieve. The program created political openings not only for Congress but also for labor and business organizations as well as the ICESA to take careful interest in policy, leading to competing pressures on federal policymakers. The result of these political pressures that arise from the structural details of the Unemployment Insurance movement has been a piecemeal, ad hoc approach to reform that relies heavily on policy entrepreneurs outside state institutions. UI does not hold the same promise as OAI of an independent political force for reform that can potentially overcome the program's racially exclusionary origins.

Unemployment Insurance's policy environment was neither as stable as OAI's nor as unstable as ADC's. Like OAI, UI had a long-term orientation in that it sought to insure normally employed workers against short spells of unemployment, building a perpetual trust fund so that benefit funding was not subject to the appropriations process. Moreover, because the federal government paid all of the states' administrative costs for UI, state agencies were not even subject to state budget processes for funding. Most state agencies, in fact, worked out their administrative budgets in consultation with federal officials, bypassing state budget officers entirely.[32]

Unemployment Insurance executives thus did not need to spend time and resources maintaining support and building coalitions each year to ensure basic support for their program.

But Unemployment Insurance was also subject to fiscal uncertainty, particularly on the revenue side of the ledger. State UI funds have frequently approached insolvency, due to the political and structural constraints on tax rates that arise from federal law, merit rating, and other factors. Adequate financing has been a constant concern for state officials as well as federal officials, who must often act to fill the breach if a state fund begins to crumble.[33]

UI was also subject to the vagaries of the business cycle and was more liable to experience fiscal and administrative strain, especially in periods of high unemployment precisely when the most people would rely on it.[34] Policymaking for UI has tended to swing between calm periods of routine maintenance and episodes of feverish activity; policymakers have often had to take quick action to shore up the UI system in difficult economic times. This sort of oscillation between long- and short-term considerations has introduced substantial instability into UI's environment. UI executives were neither as free as their OAI counterparts to pursue long-term programmatic goals nor as constrained as ADC administrators by the yearly scramble for scarce dollars.

Like ADC, Unemployment Insurance policy was made in multiple venues, because each state set its own policy. Political authority over UI policy was widely dispersed, and state agencies were given a variety of avenues of access and influence. But because of the strong federal element in its federal-state structure, UI policymaking was more unitary than ADC. Although there were many differences in state policies, the strong sway of national policy has tended to focus attention on the national policymaking arena and mitigated somewhat the dispersion of policy influences. Moreover, the development of a strong network of state administrators, the ICESA, further mitigated a potentially atomistic approach toward UI policymaking and helped to create "an overall, regularized, continuing environment."[35] Although the national focus of UI policy and the network of officials tended to narrow the policy arena somewhat, comprehensive reform would still require action in multiple jurisdictions and, as with ADC, could be seen by state officials as an intrusion on their turf.

Hampered by fiscal uncertainty, cyclical variation, and multiple policymaking arenas, Unemployment Insurance did not develop the kind of planning capacity that OAI did. In the Social Security Board (later the

Social Security Administration), long-range planning goals focused on promoting and strengthening Old-Age Insurance to the exclusion of the board's other major responsibilities, Unemployment Insurance and public assistance (including Aid to Dependent Children). Expanding the national scope of UI would certainly have been congruent with a commitment to expanding OAI; both programs shared fundamental social insurance principles.[36] But the institutional setting of Unemployment Insurance militated against planning for UI in the federal government. When program executives are constantly putting out fiscal fires, reviewing state budgets, responding to business cycle troughs, managing relations with another federal agency, and monitoring legislative developments in fifty state legislatures, planning becomes a luxury they can ill afford. National UI executives indeed had ideological preferences for expansion and improvement of the Unemployment Insurance system, and it was certainly in their interest to pursue such objectives vigorously. But the policy environment was not conducive to the kind of planning—developing comprehensive policy proposals and devising political strategies—that could bring about those kinds of reforms, reforms that might have overcome race-laden imbalances in the program's structure by making it more universal and less susceptible to political manipulation.

Like OAI, UI benefited from colonizing the capacity of existing organizations, particularly state governments and the private sector. States collected taxes and paid benefits, but employers did most of the work of creating and keeping the employee records that would determine a claimant's eligibility for benefits. In some states, the UI office kept no employee records at all and required employers to report on workers' eligibility when they were laid off. This practice obviously rid the UI agencies of a great deal of work but potentially compromised their ability to pay benefits accurately and promptly.[37]

UI's most important organizational link was its connection with the United States Employment Service and the state employment services. This alliance proved, however, to be a double-edged sword. On one hand, UI was able to tap into the USES's organization and its network of field offices throughout the country that already had established relations with local businesses and labor organizations. On the other hand, the USES and state employment offices have not generally enjoyed the best of public reputations. First, public employment offices have often been swallowed up by other programs with which they have been associated: relief before 1935 and Unemployment Insurance since. Second, when the employment services have been most active and visible—principally during the Depression and after World War II—they have focused their efforts on particular groups of disadvantaged workers that have flooded the labor market at these moments, such as unskilled, inexperienced, handicapped, and older workers. Thus the employment services have acquired an image of catering to such groups to the exclusion of more "mainstream" workers.[38] Finally, and most important, through its association with public employment offices, Unemployment Insurance tapped into the most important source of racial disparities in the political economy, job discrimination—in this case, public-sanctioned and reinforced job discrimination. In Southern states, public employment services maintained separate offices for white and black workers at least through the 1960s; elsewhere employment service offices regularly accommodated "whites only" job orders.[39] Even in New York, a pioneer in anti-discrimination law, accusations of discriminatory practices in the state employment agency arose in 1959, leading to an investigation by the state Advisory Council on Employment and Unemployment Insurance. The agency was accused of failing to refer African-Americans and other nonwhites to private sector jobs, illegally recording the race of applicants with a system of dots on file cards, and discriminating against nonwhites in its own hiring and promotion. Taking the lead in pursuing the investigation was council member Constance Baker Motley, a protégée of Thurgood Marshall at the NAACP Legal Defense Fund, Inc.[40] UI's colonization of the USES certainly enhanced its capacity to undertake its primary mission but may have constrained its possibilities for promoting racial fairness in the labor market.

UI's dual constituency structured its patterns of public contact. Contact with unemployed workers was fairly routine and generally positive, usually involving little more than regular visits to a local office.[41] In most cases, benefit checks were mailed from a central office rather than distributed in person at local offices, perhaps a lost opportunity for UI agencies to develop goodwill among their clientele, but still essentially a service and not a burden.[42] UI was not, of course, without annoyances, ranging from the trivial—weekly visits to the employment office, for example—to the more intrusive, such as investigations of an applicant's circumstances to certify his eligibility. At the same time, employers were subject to elaborate rules and procedures regarding payroll taxes, record-keeping, and reporting. These two sets of client relations could come into conflict when one side or the other decided to appeal claims decisions. Thus even generally smooth operations and friendly client relations were subject to friction inherent in UI's dual constituency.

This friction spilled over into UI's public relations. Unemployment Insurance enjoyed a somewhat tarnished public image, unlike OAI, which was the subject of a concerted public relations campaign by the Social Security Board. UI's public relations efforts devolved on state governments, who mounted educational and advertising campaigns of varying intensity and competence, undoubtedly contributing to an uneven public reception.[43] UI's eligibility criteria also raised concerns about fraud and abuse that could be exploited by opponents and became important components of the public perception of the program. Investigations of UI fraud, which frequently targeted African-American workers, often made a splash in the newspapers, as in Massachusetts in the fall of 1941, when the successful prosecution of 180 fraud cases made front-page news throughout the state.[44] Public attitudes regarding UI abuse were often racially divided; in one 1965 Gallup poll, whites were significantly more likely than nonwhites to believe that "many people collect unemployment benefits even though they could find work."[45]

Unemployment Insurance was, in the end, unable to conceal or contain its deep structural ambiguities—universalism compromised by boundaries of class and race, egalitarianism compromised by decentralization and discretion, stability compromised by institutional fragmentation. These antinomies left African-Americans in a correspondingly ambiguous position. As a broad program for working people, UI attracted basic support and even allowed for the absorption of most eligible black workers on reasonably fair terms. It did not create the political conditions for expansion that could overcome the forces of racial exclusion. Even without fostering overt discrimination, however, Unemployment Insurance failed increasingly to address the most pressing needs of African-American workers in the economy, and its failure contributed to the reconstruction of the racial structure of the American political economy and of the politics of race, welfare, and urban poverty in the United States.

Old-Age Insurance, by virtue of a national institutional structure, incorporated African-Americans smoothly and grew in short order to encompass nearly the entire working population. By contrast, the parochial institutions of Aid to Dependent Children enabled local patterns of racial exclusion and inclusion to develop in patchwork fashion, perpetuating the dependence of African-Americans on local political and economic structures and fueling the fires of retrenchment. What did the hybrid structure of Unemployment Insurance, neither fully national nor parochial, portend for African-Americans? Would it encourage discrimination against African-American workers, or would it extend the right to benefits freely and fairly?

And would it create, in the generation after the New Deal, the impulse for growth and racial inclusion that could begin to erase the race-laden divide between participants and outsiders that were inherent in its origins?

Racial Fairness in the Administration of Unemployment Insurance

What evidence there is indicates that the administration of Unemployment Insurance was, for the most part, racially fair: African-Americans who worked in covered jobs generally got the benefits to which they were entitled. Evidence regarding past administrative outcomes of Unemployment Insurance is even scarcer than for Aid to Dependent Children. The institutional structure of public policies affected not only the broad patterns of policy implementation and development but also the mundane, supposedly neutral and scientific task of collecting program statistics.[46] The word "statistics," after all, comes from the word "state," and the practice of collecting and reporting information about public matters necessarily reflects political purposes. Public officials do not seek transparency or comprehensiveness in compiling public statistics; rather, they look at what they need to know to evaluate their own work or advance an agenda. The historical pattern of UI data collection is thus itself a consequence, a political construct, of the American approach to unemployment insurance, which has traditionally emphasized the industrial over the social consequences of the program.

As a result, the available historical data on UI do not tell us much about the characteristics of the recipients, racial or otherwise. As with ADC, there are very few UI data broken down by race from the period before the late 1960s, so the simple and direct racial comparisons like those for Old-Age Insurance in Chapter 3 are not possible. Neither is the rich ecological analysis that uncovered ADC discrimination in Chapter 4, because state agencies did not compile UI statistics by county, as they did with ADC data. Instead, state documents more commonly reported UI data—taxes collected, claims paid, and so forth—by industry. One proposed system of merit rating would actually have calculated tax rates by comparing the records of individual firms with others in the same industry, necessitating the compilation of statistics by industry but not by any other social category.[47] The Unemployment Insurance data that are available are a patchwork of statistics compiled by states and the federal government, special studies conducted by governments or private researchers, and scholarly works. Despite these limitations, the historical record shows quite clearly that there was little discrimination against African-Americans in the first generation of Unemployment Insurance.

The labor market doubly disadvantaged African-Americans with respect to Unemployment Insurance, excluding the neediest workers. First, they were more likely to be unemployed or intermittently employed than whites, increasing their need for benefits but decreasing the likelihood that they would receive benefits (whether because of ineligibility or exhaustion). It has simply been more difficult for African-Americans to get and keep jobs than for white Americans. There are numerous reasons for this handicap, ranging from lack of education and skills to social barriers to discrimination in hiring and firing. As a result, the unemployment rate for African-Americans has always been higher than for whites.[48]

Not only have African-Americans been more commonly unemployed, but they have also stayed unemployed for longer. Figure 5.1 shows, for whites and nonwhites, the annual average percentage of those unemployed who have been out of work for more than fifteen consecutive weeks.

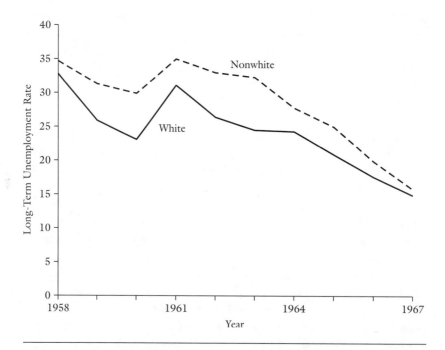

Figure 5.1. Long-term unemployment by race, 1958–1967.

Although the racial gap narrowed considerably by the late 1960s, African-Americans consistently experienced longer spells of unemployment than whites. In the early 1960s, approximately one person in ten in the labor force was nonwhite, one in five unemployed workers was nonwhite, and one in four workers unemployed twenty-seven weeks or more was nonwhite. These percentages were impervious to the business cycle; in fact, the nonwhite share of both the unemployed and the long-term unemployed was slightly *higher* in a boom year (1964) than in a recession year (1961), suggesting that whites benefited more than nonwhites from expanded employment opportunities in periods of economic growth.[49] One study of Unemployment Insurance in five states in the 1970s found that nonwhites were likely to remain unemployed for up to four months longer than whites.[50]

Longer spells of unemployment meant that African-Americans were likely to stay on the UI rolls longer, but they also meant a greater risk of "exhausting" benefits, remaining without a job beyond the maximum duration of benefits. Initially, some states set maximum durations as low as twelve weeks, although by the mid-1960s most states provided up to twenty-six weeks of benefits (with frequent extensions during periods of high unemployment).[51] Such limits on benefit duration posed no threat to workers who experienced brief periods of unemployment—a few weeks or even a couple of months. But to workers who found it harder to return to work, the maximum duration imposed a daunting limit on the amount of assistance that UI could provide, often leaving African-Americans with neither a job nor a claim on UI benefits and pushing them toward stigmatizing and stingy public assistance.

Unemployed African-Americans have, in fact, long been more likely to exhaust their benefits than whites. In Ohio, for example, in 1946, thirty-five percent of black male UI recipients and sixty-three percent of black female recipients exhausted their benefits.[52] A national study in the mid-1970s showed that in almost every state nonwhites were still more prone to exhaust their benefits than whites.[53] Regionally, nonwhites fared worst in the South, where only one-fourth of UI beneficiaries, but one-third of the benefit exhaustees, were nonwhite. Not only have nonwhites been more likely to exhaust their benefits, they have, some evidence suggests not surprisingly, tended to fare worse after exhaustion, remaining unemployed even longer after UI has run out.[54] Unemployment and limited Unemployment Insurance were riskier propositions for African-Americans than for whites. Because of their precarious position in the labor market,

African-Americans and other minorities had more to gain from Unemployment Insurance but more reason to consider it inadequate as well.

The second source of labor market disadvantage for African-Americans has been occupational exclusions. Those black workers who found employment were concentrated in industries not covered by Unemployment Insurance, less heavily over time to be sure but still disproportionately into the 1960s and beyond. Well after agricultural and domestic workers gained OAI coverage, they were still denied UI coverage. Unemployment rates in these noncovered industries in which African-Americans were concentrated were consistently higher than in covered sectors of the economy.[55] The structure of American Unemployment Insurance left many workers at the very margins of the program, particularly those who most needed assistance, whether because they had few resources on which to fall back during hard times, because they would have trouble finding a new job, or because they were swept up in the dramatic geographic and sectoral shift of midcentury. These burdens fell especially heavily on African-Americans.

At the same time, those African-Americans who did work in covered industries stood to benefit more than others precisely because of their greater probability of being unemployed and suffering long spells of unemployment. Their potentially disproportionate presence in the beneficiary population combined with the decentralization of UI administration suggests that, like Aid to Dependent Children, UI might have been fertile ground for administrative discrimination, resulting in black workers being shut out of benefits. Did African-American workers in the UI system receive what they deserved under the terms of the program?

By all accounts, the answer is yes. For those African-Americans who made it into the Unemployment Insurance system, the program treated them, for the most part, fairly. Although there is some evidence of intermittent racial discrimination in UI administration, there is no evidence of systematic racial manipulation of UI benefits comparable to that in ADC. Severe limits on the availability of relevant data hamper any analysis of racial discrimination in the administration of UI. There are simply no reports on the racial composition of UI beneficiaries before the late 1960s. Historically, one common sort of information that states reported was the distribution of UI claims by industry, and so a fruitful approach is to see whether industry groups where black workers were concentrated received proportionate shares of unemployment benefits. The structure of this analysis is similar to the ecological analysis of discrimination in ADC, except that the "local" units are economic sectors rather than geographical units.[56] Some states report the number of Unemployment Insurance beneficiaries by industrial category—that is, the number of UI claims paid to textile workers, construction workers, autoworkers, and so forth. If there was no discrimination in the determination of UI claims, the distribution of claims across sectors should match reasonably well the distribution of African-American unemployment. If, however, state policy or administrators systematically denied benefits to African-Americans, then industries in which many African-Americans were unemployed should have proportionally fewer claims, whereas claims should be clustered in industries where African-American unemployment was lower. By disaggregating unemployment and UI claims within states, this approach allows us to examine whether state administrators have systematically directed UI benefits away from certain groups and toward others. At the same time, this approach is a fairly blunt instrument. It provides only a very indirect glimpse of the racial consequences of UI administration, but its results further confirm the prediction of the institutional structure argument that discrimination in UI has been quite modest.

Once again, a warning against the ecological fallacy is in order. It is not possible, from these data, to infer that individual African-American applicants were the victims of discrimination. There are a variety of other possible reasons for such racial mismatching. For example, employers in some industries might have been more assiduous in challenging UI claims than others, resulting in fewer payments. Some industries might have been located in remote parts of the state, where local unemployment offices were hard to reach, resulting in lower claims. But whether or not individual discrimination actually occurred with any regularity, a finding of a racial mismatch would indicate a serious structural gap between white and African-American access to Unemployment Insurance.

The data for this analysis come from four states, in three different census years: South Carolina in 1940, New Jersey and Virginia in 1960, and West Virginia in 1970.[57] For each case, the distribution of UI claims is matched against the distribution of total unemployment and nonwhite unemployment. If the distributions are highly correlated—that is, if the distribution of unemployment among industries and between races closely predicts the distribution of UI claims—the conclusion is that there is no mismatch, and hence no discrimination. If the distributions are mismatched—not closely and significantly correlated—then there is possible evidence of discrimination in paying UI claims. Table 5.1 summarizes the results.

There is some evidence of discrimination against African-Americans in

Table 5.1 Racial Distribution of Unemployment Claims

State	Year	Mismatch?	Comments
South Carolina	1940	Yes	Textile disparity
New Jersey	1960	No	
Virginia	1960	No	
West Virginia	1970	Slight	Slight mining disparity

the earliest years of Unemployment Insurance. In South Carolina in 1940, there is a reasonably clear case of disproportionality, suggesting some administrative discrimination. Like the pattern of administration under more extreme parochialism in ADC, the administration of UI in the Deep South appears to have been tilted against African-Americans. In particular, the skewed distribution of UI claims in South Carolina in 1940 was strikingly evident in textile manufacturing.[58] One in four UI-eligible unemployed workers in the state were textile workers; they received one-half of all of the UI claims paid in South Carolina that year. But fewer than five percent of the nonwhite insured unemployed were textile workers. Thus half of the UI claims were going to a group from which African-Americans were almost entirely absent. Conversely, the industries in which the black unemployed were most heavily concentrated—construction and lumber and furniture, for example—received proportionately few UI benefits. These results suggest that there may have been some discrimination in the administration of UI in South Carolina, directing benefits away from African-Americans.

By 1960, however, evidence of such a mismatch between black unemployment and the distribution of Unemployment Insurance benefits had disappeared. The results in New Jersey and Virginia for that year suggest that UI claims were distributed fairly, even in a Southern state such as Virginia. To be fair, Virginia is not part of the Deep South, and it was one of the most urban and industrial of the Southern states in 1960, suggesting that race might have played a smaller role in its politics than in the realm of King Cotton.[59] Still, the finding that there was no racial mismatch in the payment of UI claims is striking, and it strongly suggests that there was no serious discrimination against African-Americans in the administration of UI benefits.

The West Virginia case merits particular attention, because in the early

1970s, the state conducted a five-year study of UI claims and published a detailed breakdown of UI claims data by race and industry.[60] With the data from the study, it is possible to chart more precisely any disparities between African-American eligibility for and receipt of Unemployment Insurance benefits, eliminating the need for the ecological inferences that the earlier data required.[61] First, African-Americans account for 3.4 percent of the insured unemployed in the categories covered by the study, whereas they make up 2.5 percent of the UI claims, a considerable difference. The lag of black claims behind black insured unemployment suggests that there may, typically, have been a small amount of administrative discrimination in UI administration. However, both for the total workforce and for African-Americans, the distribution of claims maps fairly well onto the distribution of unemployment. The only serious disparity occurs in the mining industry, where African-Americans are substantially underrepresented among UI claimants. Once again, the comparison of UI claims across sectors suggests marginal, but not widespread or systematic, discrimination against African-Americans in the provision of Unemployment Insurance benefits.

Although the sectoral approach is suggestive, the clearest and most direct approach to the question of discrimination in UI would be simply to compare the number of African-Americans who received UI benefits with the number unemployed in covered industries. Unfortunately, not until 1969 did the federal government begin compiling and reporting the race of UI claimants.[62] Thus the earliest year for which a detailed comparison of this sort is possible is 1970, when census data allow detailed calculations of unemployment rates by race. The data for this comparison are the nonwhite percentage of UI claims by state for 1970, from the Department of Labor's monthly report, and the estimated nonwhite percentage of the insured unemployed—those actually eligible to collect UI benefits—calculated from the 1970 Census. A few points are in order about the data. The nonwhite percentage of claims is simply the average of the monthly figures reported by the Department of Labor.[63] The annual average is weighted by the total number of claims in each month. The unemployment data are calculated from the 1970 Census.[64] The "insured unemployed" are those workers who, having worked most recently in a covered job, are currently unemployed, meaning that they are eligible to receive UI benefits as long as they pass the applicable work test. I estimated the insured unemployed rather crudely by subtracting from the entire labor force those workers in occupations that remained uncovered: farmers and farm workers, household employees, and professional and technical workers (who are mostly either self-employed or work for the government).[65] This comparison is the closest analogue to the direct proportionality test used in Chapter 4 to establish the fair administration of Old-Age Insurance. If there was no administrative discrimination in the payment of UI claims, then the non-white proportion of claims should be about the same as the nonwhite proportion of eligible workers. Larger negative differences would be more certain indicators of discrimination.

The results of this comparison, which appear in Figure 5.2, indicate that discrimination was rare indeed.[66] Nationally, nonwhites made up around sixteen percent of the insured unemployed but only thirteen percent of UI claims, a small gap, indicating that eligible nonwhites were slightly less likely than eligible whites to receive UI benefits. In general, there were slight regional differences; in the North, nonwhites were close to parity with whites, whereas in the South, the gap between eligibility and claims was nearly twice as large. The map shows that in most states, nonwhite UI

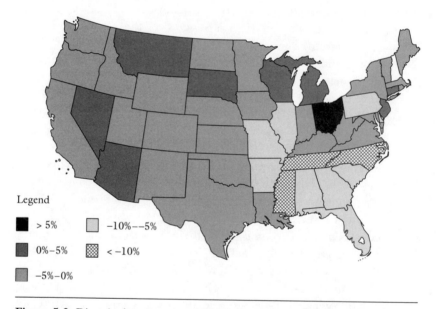

Legend

■ > 5%   □ −10%--5%

■ 0%–5%   ▨ < −10%

■ −5%–0%

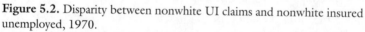

Figure 5.2. Disparity between nonwhite UI claims and nonwhite insured unemployed, 1970.

Sources: U.S. Department of Labor, Manpower Administration, *Unemployment Statistics* (monthly), 1970–71, table 1; U.S. Bureau of the Census, *1970 Census of Population* (Washington, D.C.: Government Printing Office, 1973), vol. 1, tables 172–173.

claims were close to parity with the nonwhite proportion of the insured unemployed, but in four-fifths of them nonwhites were less likely to be among claimants than they were to be eligible. The pattern of state results, in fact, presents a picture of essentially random variation from the national average, suggesting that a slight disadvantage for nonwhites in the UI claims process was the norm in 1970. The pattern in the South, however, is decisively not random. The Southern states show a particular concentration of racial disparities, indicated by lighter shading. These data suggest that UI administration was essentially fair, with the possibility of very slight discrimination against nonwhites in the payment of claims, although discrimination appears to have been more serious in the South.

At the same time that UI administration was slightly biased against them, nonwhites in covered occupations were considerably more likely to be unemployed than white workers. Figure 5.3 displays the difference between the nonwhite share of the UI-eligible labor force and the non-

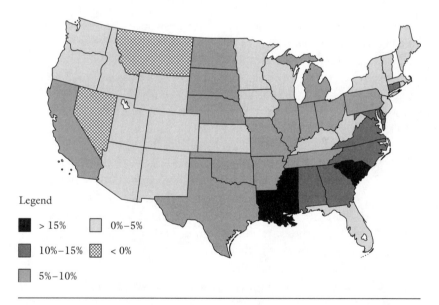

Figure 5.3. Disparity between nonwhite insured unemployed and nonwhite covered labor force, 1970.

Sources: U.S. Department of Labor, Manpower Administration, *Unemployment Statistics* (monthly), 1970–71, table 1; U.S. Bureau of the Census, *1970 Census of Population* (Washington, D.C.: Government Printing Office, 1973), vol. 1, tables 172–173.

white share of the insured unemployed. This comparison simply measures whether eligible nonwhites were more likely to become unemployed and thus potentially to file a claim for UI benefits. The clear answer is yes, particularly in the South. Whereas only one in ten members of the UI-eligible labor force was nonwhite nationally, one in six insured unemployed workers was nonwhite. In the South, the disparity was particularly pronounced, indicated by darker shading, although in every state but two nonwhite covered workers were more likely to be unemployed.

The principal mechanism for administrative discrimination in Unemployment Insurance was the work test, under which claimants could be disqualified if they had left work for the "wrong" reasons or were not seeking new work with sufficient vigor. There is scant evidence about disqualification rates for different races, but studies in the 1970s found significant differences between patterns of disqualification for whites and nonwhites.[67] In four of five states included in one study (the exception being New York), nonwhite claimants were significantly more likely than whites to be disqualified. Nonwhite workers were much more likely to have been discharged for misconduct, whereas whites were more likely to have been disqualified for quitting voluntarily or refusing a suitable offer of work. This pattern is entirely consistent with a combination of a closed labor market and discriminatory application of UI rules and discretion. A white worker might have been more likely to quit a job because she knew it would be easier for her to find a new one than for an African-American in the same position. Similarly, white workers would simply have had more opportunities to refuse offers of work because they got more offers. On one hand, racial differences in misconduct disqualifications may have reflected an actually greater likelihood of nonwhites' being discharged (whether the result of discrimination by employers or not). On the other hand, agencies may have applied disqualification rules more stringently to nonwhites than to whites, resulting in more findings of misconduct, although one study's author rightly cautions that agency discrimination was only one of several possible factors.[68]

These results suggest two conclusions. First, although there were some racial disparities in UI, there was not general, systematic, widespread discrimination against nonwhite applicants in the administration of Unemployment Insurance as there was in Aid to Dependent Children. Eligible nonwhites were only slightly, if at all, less likely to receive UI, except in the South. This finding is entirely consistent with the institutional structure argument's prediction of only marginal discrimination. The extremely pro-

nounced regional split reflects the hybrid federal-state nature of UI's structure. Like Old-Age Insurance, UI presents very little opportunity for local
authorities to discriminate, and there is substantial uniformity in the performance of UI administrators along racial lines. But the national structure
that constrains administrative discrimination, although stronger than in
ADC, is not absolute, allowing racial disparities in UI outcomes to appear
where pressure for them is strongest.

The second conclusion concerns UI's relationship to the labor market.
UI set up a dual system with particularly pronounced racial consequences.
African-Americans were particularly likely to remain outside the Unemployment Insurance system altogether as a result of occupational exclusions and chronic, intermittent, or part-time unemployment. For those
African-Americans who made it into the system, however, UI provided an
economic cushion of heightened importance. Because they were more
precariously employed, they could expect to need UI more than their
white counterparts. What is more, they could largely expect to get it.

Compared with other Social Security programs, contemporary observers seemed least concerned with the possibility of discrimination in the
administration of Unemployment Insurance. The NAACP received numerous complaints during the 1940s and 1950s from African-Americans
throughout the country about discriminatory treatment by UI officials.
One letter from Nagodoches, Texas, stated that African-Americans there
were "having a hard time getting [UI] paid to us," and requested that the
NAACP "make some investment for us and see that we get some considerations to our claims."[69] The NAACP's standard response was that differential treatment of UI claims does not amount to discrimination because
of the program's requirements. An early NAACP memorandum on discrimination in Social Security programs, which alludes to heavy discrimination in public assistance, does not mention discriminatory treatment of
African-Americans in UI as a problem (or even a potential problem).
Rather, the memorandum laments the narrow scope of Unemployment
Insurance under the Social Security Act and is concerned with the exclusion of occupational categories and discrimination in the labor market, not
with the discriminatory behavior of state and local agencies.[70]

Despite evidence of some administrative discrimination, observers have
repeatedly pointed to these two factors—occupational exclusions and labor market disadvantage—as the principal forces that exclude African-
Americans from the full benefits of Unemployment Insurance. From Alabama in the 1930s to California in the 1950s, studies of the UI program

have found that African-Americans were shut out of the program not because of biased implementation but because of their concentration in uncovered jobs. In 1937, for instance, nearly forty percent of Alabama's white workers worked in covered occupations, compared with only twenty-one percent of black workers. In California in 1950, African-Americans made up four percent of workers with UI wage credits, but six percent of workers without UI credits.[71] And in the mid-1960s, African-Americans remained at a substantial disadvantage in the labor market. Moreover, during the late 1950s and early 1960s, the prospects for African-American workers seemed to be getting worse, not better: Nonwhites went from twenty-five percent of the long-term unemployed in 1957 to thirty percent in 1963.[72] These forces, and not discrimination in the administrative apparatus of Unemployment Insurance, kept most African-Americans outside of the program, even as their political and economic circumstances began to change in the decades after the New Deal.

Race, Institutional Structure, and the Development of Unemployment Insurance

Administratively, Unemployment Insurance was a racially fair program. Its modestly parochial institutional structure managed to contain the centrifugal forces that provided openings for discrimination. At the same time, however, this structure was unable to set the program on a historical path toward expansion and greater inclusion. For OAI, the same institutional forces that produced color-blind administration paved the way for rapid expansion toward generous benefits and full inclusion of working Americans and their families regardless of race. But UI's scope grew slowly at best and benefits declined. More important than the lack of expanded coverage, however, were the institutional boundaries of Unemployment Insurance that isolated many African-Americans from the program's mainstream—the work test and other qualifying requirements, the decentralized policymaking apparatus, and the separation from more interventionist labor market policies that might have helped African-Americans and other minorities enter the industrial labor force on more equal terms. These institutional features rendered Unemployment Insurance, like Aid to Dependent Children, susceptible to parochial manipulation; they handed to state and local officials a repertoire of tools and techniques with which to restrict the reach of UI. When millions of African-Americans migrated North after the New Deal, they came into a world of scarce jobs, segregated neighborhoods, and restricted opportunity. Public assistance was available to them, but on racially and politically manipulated terms. Unemployment Insurance, however, was less readily available, partly because its terms were manipulated to narrow its scope even further, but mostly because the boundaries of the program did not encompass the new structures of inequality that arrived with the Great Migration. The institutional structure of the program, however, thwarted attempts at national reform, leaving African-Americans increasingly at the program's margins. The racially bounded structure of UI not only thwarted the program's development, it also contributed further to the political construction of the new, racially defined structures of urban poverty that arose in the United States after World War II.

To call the course of Unemployment Insurance policy "development" is perhaps misleading, for it was nearly stagnant in the generation after its founding. In one important respect it went backward—benefit levels declined compared with wages because there was not sufficient political pressure to maintain and increase benefit levels as there was in OAI. Figure 5.4

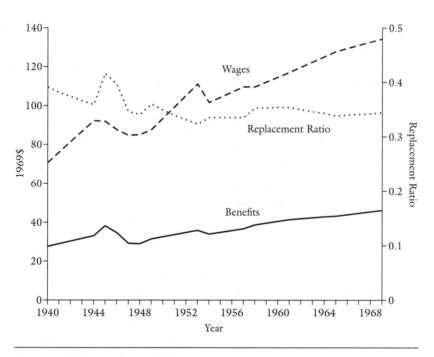

Figure 5.4. UI benefits, 1940–1969.
Source: Saul J. Blaustein, *Unemployment Insurance in the United States: The First Half Century* (Kalamazoo, Mich.: W. E. Upjohn Institute for Employment Research, 1993), 178, 190–191.

displays the trend in UI benefits between 1940 and 1969. The average weekly benefit, represented by the solid line, actually grew slightly in real terms, but average weekly wages in covered industries (the dashed line) grew faster. As a result, the "replacement ratio," the average share of wages replaced by UI benefits, declined. Benefits have often been barely adequate for subsistence and have never approached the target of fifty percent of wages that the Committee on Economic Security had lifted from Wisconsin's UI plan. Meanwhile, state tax rates declined steadily as industries took advantage of merit rating. In 1940, the average UI tax rate on employers was 2.7 percent; by 1969 it was 1.4 percent. The only significant change in national UI policy before 1970—a modest increase in coverage and the creation of a mechanism to shore up states in financial difficulty—came in 1954, just as OAI grew to nearly universal coverage.[73]

In 1935, the Committee on Economic Security had hoped that the tax offset plan would allow not only for the greatest federal control over UI short of a national program but also for the greatest possibility of nationalizing the program in the future. The federal-state structure did allow for substantial federal influence over UI policy, but it proved extremely resistant to fundamental change. Unlike Old-Age Insurance, Unemployment Insurance did not have an institutional logic of expansion. UI did not have a unified national constituency in favor of ever-growing benefits. Instead, it pitted tax-sensitive employers against workers in perpetual political competition over the terms of benefits. Moreover, interstate economic competition over tax rates and benefits levels placed further downward pressure on both sides of the equation.

It was hardly certain, however, given the administrative and policy levers that the federal government had over Unemployment Insurance policy, that the states would become the central players in the story of UI's policy development. Federal Social Security executives, along with Presidents Roosevelt and Truman, urged an expanded federal role in the UI system through the war and into the postwar years (although Truman, unlike Roosevelt, stopped short of proposing an outright national takeover of the program).[74] But federal action to change the balance of power in the system became increasingly difficult to pursue, and any window of opportunity that may have been opened, particularly by the war and the attendant problems of reconversion to a civilian economy, soon closed and states consolidated their control over UI policy. UI administration took on a common-law character as state-level administrative practice and procedure accrued and developed into established norms. Through the supervision of the federal government and the cooperative work of the ICESA, the states compared and clarified their administrative operations. The compilation and publication of the quasi-judicial claims decisions of state UI agencies generated a body of case law that governed administrative procedure across state lines, reflecting the persistence of the feudal form of master-servant relations in American labor.[75] In 1948, Congress even passed (over President Truman's veto) a law that explicitly adopted the traditional master-servant relationship as the definition of "employee" for the purpose of defining UI coverage.[76] As if to stretch the medieval metaphor, one analyst refers to the ICESA as a "professional guild."[77] Over the early years of UI, contours of state autonomy in Unemployment Insurance developed, with important consequences for African-Americans.

In some areas, the states had very little freedom at all. In the beginning, the federal tax was the most important instrument of racial exclusion from Unemployment Insurance. All industrial and commercial employers paid the three percent federal payroll tax whether their states had unemployment plans or not; this fact induced all states to establish UI programs for these workers. But the federal tax did not cover agricultural or household employers, so there was little incentive for any state to impose a tax on these employers to cover their workers unless all other states did as well.[78] As a result, few states covered these categories of workers before they were brought under the federal tax in 1976.[79]

Beyond these occupational exclusions, there were other provisions over which states exercised considerably more control that affected the availability of benefits to African-Americans. These provisions included not only benefit levels but also the criteria for eligibility that constituted the work test—things such as employment thresholds for benefits, length of benefit eligibility, and other factors designed to determine whether unemployment was truly involuntary.

State laws varied quite a bit on such requirements from the beginning, and they became significantly more restrictive over time. The most important eligibility provisions affecting African-Americans were base employment requirements, which specified how long an individual must have worked or how much he must have earned before becoming unemployed in order to qualify for benefits. These qualifying requirements constituted the retrospective part of the work test, intended to ensure that only workers with a substantial "attachment to the labor force" were entitled to benefits. A second important set of eligibility provisions affected not access to UI benefits but their adequacy. For example, states set the formula for calculating benefits and the maximum duration of benefit payments a recipient can receive in a given spell of unemployment. Because federal law contained no minimum standards for state UI programs, states were free to set these requirements at whatever level they chose.

In the face of racial disadvantages in the labor market, these kinds of provisions had the potential to restrict African-American access to UI benefits. Employment for African-American workers has always been more precarious, so they have been less likely than whites to meet any given qualifying requirements. Because African-Americans have always suffered from higher levels of unemployment and longer spells of unemployment, low limits on benefit duration have harmed African-Americans more. When African-Americans lived and worked primarily in the South and mostly in occupations outside of the UI system, such eligibility criteria meant little to them. But as they moved North and increasingly entered the industrial workforce, the terms of UI became an important factor in defining their attachment to the state and the economy and in the political construction of a stable urban black working class.

Did states, in fact, manipulate their eligibility requirements to the disadvantage of African-Americans? State Unemployment Insurance programs varied widely in the generation after the New Deal, but there were several important trends for the coverage of African-Americans. First, between the 1930s and the 1960s, states generally raised their qualifying thresholds for UI benefits, either by increasing the time-worked or wages-earned requirements. Thus for many African-Americans, Unemployment Insurance was a moving target; as they moved increasingly into industrial employment during and after World War II, states raised their eligibility standards to eliminate the intermittently employed. At the same time, however, states tended to liberalize their benefit duration provisions, so that states increasingly met the suggested federal standard of a minimum of twenty-six weeks of eligibility.[80] Unemployment Insurance benefits thus became more generous—providing higher payments for a longer time—but for an increasingly restricted group of workers that was likely to exclude African-Americans at the margins of the labor force.

Another set of eligibility requirements defined opportunities for discrimination through bureaucratic discretion, particularly by setting the terms of the work test. All states disqualified workers from benefits for leaving their jobs under certain conditions—quitting voluntarily, being fired for misconduct, and so forth. Most state laws also disallowed UI claims of workers who refused to accept "suitable work" or who were not "available for work" or "actively seeking work." These laws perforce required administrative rulings that could be applied differently by race or other characteristics, as was the case with ADC. States could also stiffen the penalties for these offenses by lengthening the disqualification period or by adopting sliding scales of disqualification depending on the seriousness of the violation.

After 1935, states stiffened these requirements as well, both imposing more demanding conditions and increasing penalties. For example, in 1948, only fifteen states had "actively seeking work" provisions on the books; by 1968, thirty states did.[81] Administrative applications of these elements of the work test undoubtedly worked against many African-Americans, denying them access to benefits, imposing stiff penalties, or forcing them into a Hobson's choice—either accept an undesirable job or lose your benefits—a dilemma that was only exacerbated by weakness and segregationism of state employment services.[82]

Although state eligibility requirements grew tougher during the generation after the New Deal, this development was not a direct response to the increasing presence of African-Americans in the covered workforce. States did not tailor their UI policies particularly to match the racial composition of their populations. Southern states, in fact, which originally imposed stiffer eligibility requirements than Northern states, liberalized their UI programs in the 1940s to match national norms more closely. But most Southern blacks worked in occupations that remained outside the UI system; it was in the North, where African-Americans were more likely to work in covered jobs, that racial manipulation of state policy might have occurred. It did not. States with higher black populations from the 1940s through the 1960s did not adopt more stringent policies, nor were the states with the greatest influx of African-Americans due to the Great Migration during and after World War II more likely than others to stiffen their UI statutes.[83]

So despite the quasi-parochial institutional structure of Unemployment Insurance, which gave states substantial freedom in setting the terms on which workers received coverage and qualified for benefits, states did not use this opportunity to restrict African-American access to UI benefits. Nor did the massive shift of black population from South to North, and from farm to factory, cause a similar shift in UI policy in Northern industrial states, where the problem of black unemployment, especially in the great cities of the Northeast and Midwest, was growing rapidly and becoming a chronic feature of the urban industrial landscape.[84] Why not? Why did UI not devolve, like ADC, into a quagmire of state and local racial politics in which state policymaking effectively limited or otherwise controlled the benefits available to African-Americans? It would not have been difficult for state policymakers to follow such a course, to redesign their Unemployment Insurance programs, whether subtly or openly, around the shifting racial balance of the Northern industrial labor force.

The structure of Unemployment Insurance militated against this policymaking path. Although states had considerable freedom in setting the terms of their UI programs, their freedom was not complete. Federal law and interstate competition did exert pressure on states to conform, more than in ADC, and in fact UI benefits varied less across states than ADC benefits. Since the end of World War II, the closest Unemployment Insurance came to basic structural change was in 1959, when a proposal to impose national benefit standards failed by two votes in the House Ways and Means Committee; even had Congress passed the bill, President Eisenhower was opposed and probably would have vetoed it.[85] Moreover, as the federal-state system was institutionalized, the shifts in the configuration of state policy slowed; change was commoner and faster before 1950 than after. By the 1950s, the program reached something of a steady state, albeit with some underlying change, but the state programs did not respond easily even to important demographic, social, and economic changes.[86] The system of merit rating and the adversarial system of benefit administration meant that within the states, the politics of Unemployment Insurance revolved around tax rates, finances, and the administration of benefits, and not the details of program policy.[87] Business-labor political competition dominated, especially in the Northern industrial states where African-Americans moved in large numbers after the war. This competition effectively separated the politics of class from the politics of race in UI.[88] In Old-Age Insurance, structural class imperatives and economic demands embraced without expressing claims of racial equality. In Aid to Dependent Children, the politics of class and race also coincided to exclude and ultimately isolate African-Americans. But in Unemployment Insurance, the class politics within the program had little to offer to a politics that could cross the program's race-laden boundary.

State UI policies proved resistant to substantial reform, and the dominance of state policymaking in the UI system has also impeded movements for reform at the national level. The imagery of state control over UI policy became an important element of UI policy debates at the national level as a tool deployed against reform in the name of "states' rights." However, "states' rights" was little more than a convenient argument for opponents of particular federal interventions rather than a position of deep moral or constitutional principle—very much like the definition of "interstate commerce" in late-nineteenth-century jurisprudence, twisted almost beyond recognition by a Supreme Court bent on overturning economic regulation.[89] In 1954, for example, the Eisenhower administration proposed extending coverage to workers in certain agricultural processing occupations and to federal government employees. Opponents argued that a federal extension to agricultural workers represented federal coercion and an infringement of state prerogatives to determine the limits of coverage, even though the near-universal exclusion of agricultural workers resulted from a logic established by the policy settlement of 1935. At the same time, many of the same people approved the federal extension of coverage to government workers, even though such a provision equally "infringed" on the latitude of state governments. The 1954 bill also sought to extend the federal UI tax to smaller firms, a provision that the business community vehemently opposed. One lobbyist for the United States Chamber of Commerce, Frank Cliffe of the H. J. Heinz Co., even acknowledged that setting the minimum firm size for federal taxation at eight in the Social Security Act had been arbitrary, but he defended it as if it were an important philosophical principle.[90] More often than not, these arguments impeded national reform, and thus the quasi-national structure of Unemployment Insurance meant that reform was nearly impossible at both state and federal levels.

Finally, any pressure for reform of Unemployment Insurance has come from outside the government. The planning capacity of the UI establishment in the government has been comparatively weak. During World War II, both Roosevelt, the Social Security Board, and the National Resources Planning Board advocated nationalizing the Unemployment Insurance System. The comprehensive national social security program of Senators Robert Wagner of New York and James Murray of Montana and Congressman John Dingell of Michigan included national and universal unemployment compensation.[91] But Harry Truman, while continuing his predecessor's call for the expansion of OAI, did not support nationalizing UI, and the Social Security Board quietly dropped the idea.[92] In his 1949 reorganization of the executive branch, Truman shifted responsibility for UI to the Department of Labor, a move that reinforced the pattern of pluralistic, interest-group politics that UI had developed. From the beginning, the politics of UI pitted countervailing constituencies against each other—organized labor, which supported strengthening and expanding the system, and business, which wanted to keep tax rates low.[93] The American labor movement, moreover, had a strong tradition of segregation and hostility to the full participation of African-Americans in the labor market, so that labor support has not always pushed UI reform in the most favorable direction for black workers.[94] The Department of Labor is one of the classic sites of clientelistic, interest-group politics in the American state, institutionally a place for incremental politics and bargaining over resources, not a launching ground for serious, structural policy reform. Moreover, its role in social policy has focused on labor standards rather than income support.[95]

Although it has not promoted pressure for the program's expansion, neither has the institutional structure of Unemployment Insurance promoted the kind of pressure for retrenchment that has afflicted Aid to Dependent Children. Public support for Unemployment Insurance has always been strong; at the same time, the public has expressed concern about abuse of UI that has frequently had racial overtones.[96] Even when imputations and investigations of fraud and abuse in Unemployment Insurance have been racially tinged, creating the potential for the racialization of the program in the political arena, support for the program has remained solid. But the problem for ADC has been the particular terms on which African-Americans gained inclusion into the program—through their extrusion from the mainstream urban economy and the political manipulation of welfare. The ironic contrast is that the ongoing exclusion of African-Americans from UI coverage, which has kept the most virulent strains of racial politics out of the UI system, has precluded the racialization of UI politics.

Still, the lack of policy development in Unemployment Insurance represented a particular failure for African-Americans. The policy largely excluded them at the outset, although the national control purchased by that exclusion managed to treat fairly those who did qualify for coverage. The stagnation of unemployment policy, combined with the failure of full employment policies and persistent labor market discrimination, meant that UI remained closed to many black workers and potential workers, relegating them to the public assistance rolls and exacerbating the racialization of ADC. Had the supporters of stronger national UI—Dingell, Murray, Wagner, and their allies—been able to take advantage of their opportunity in the 1940s to adopt comprehensive, national, and inclusive Unemployment Insurance, the welfare crisis that began in the 1960s might have been substantially mitigated. Instead, the incorporation of new, largely black groups of workers into the UI system moved at a glacial pace.

Although Unemployment Insurance and Old-Age Insurance were created in 1935 with the same racially relevant occupational exclusions, OAI quickly expanded to cover agricultural and domestic workers, bringing almost all African-American workers under its protective umbrella. Unemployment Insurance, however, expanded its coverage much more slowly, leaving African-Americans outside the system for much longer. Not until 1976 did Congress extend the federal UI tax to agricultural and domestic workers. Even after the federal act, however, not all states responded immediately to cover farm workers and domestic servants under their UI laws; Texas, for example, waited until 1985, and then the legislature acted only under pressure from the courts.[97]

The attempt to extend Unemployment Insurance coverage to new categories of workers began very soon after the passage of the Social Security Act, but unlike the movement for extended coverage under Old-Age Insurance, it progressed very slowly. The principal stated objection to the inclusion of agricultural and domestic workers in Unemployment Insurance, as was the case in OAI, was administrative difficulty, and the same arguments appeared on both sides—opponents claimed that coverage for farm workers and servants would impose too high a burden on employers, whereas supporters tried to show that coverage was feasible for these groups. New York covered some domestic workers without difficulty. Overseas, Britain extended unemployment coverage to farm workers in 1936, bringing in about 600,000 such workers by the end of that year, with no administrative problems.[98] Proponents argued once again for a stamp-book system to ease tax collection and record-keeping; the Pitney-Bowes Postage Meter Company produced an extensive memorandum on the virtues of the stamp system that was in fact an elaborate advertisement for its own products.[99] And after World War II, the argument that housewives who had managed wartime rationing could also manage UI taxation also made an appearance.[100] After OAI coverage was extended in 1954, administrative objections made no sense at all, yet they persisted.[101] And the continued exclusion of farm workers created problems for state politicians. Not only did unemployed farm workers often need public assistance to support themselves, increasing demands on state treasuries, the continued exclusion of agricultural labor discouraged unemployed workers from other sectors from accepting work on farms because they would not receive credit toward UI benefits, a problem that had plagued OAI as well.[102]

Through the 1950s and 1960s, a series of proposals to extend coverage to agricultural and domestic workers was defeated in Congress, beginning in 1954, the same year OAI coverage was extended to the same groups. In

1958, a proposal to extend coverage was linked to an emergency measure to extend UI benefits temporarily during the recession of that year. Led by Senator John F. Kennedy of Massachusetts and Representative Eugene McCarthy of Minnesota and supported by the AFL-CIO, the proposal was defeated in the House by the coalition of Republicans and Southern Democrats that reliably appeared on issues of race and labor, issues that converged powerfully on the question of extending the reach of Unemployment Insurance.[103] The fear of federalization was one important element in opposition to expansion of UI. Whereas business worried that increased federal control would lead to higher benefits and hence higher payroll taxes, Southerners worried that it would promote the extension of coverage, forcing states to pay benefits to African-Americans in larger numbers. Georgia's UI statute, in fact, instructed the commissioner of the state Employment Security Agency to "make every proper effort within his means to oppose and prevent any further action which would in his judgment tend to effect complete or substantial federalization" of UI responsibilities.[104]

The Southern opponents of extended coverage also relied on the same race-laden imagery—willful idleness and lassitude supported by the state—that was invoked in debates over OAI and ADC in the 1950s. Making these previously uncovered workers eligible for benefits, one Southern state official said, would "inject into unemployment insurance relief factors directly opposed to the insurance principles on which our State programs are based . . . [UI] was never intended as an indefinite sustenance nor as a general relief program. From the very beginning unemployment compensation has shunned the stigma of welfare and has fought the misnomer of 'rocking-chair money.'"[105] Another Southerner added that the beneficiaries of extended coverage would tend to be "unskilled females who follow a regular pattern of seasonal employment tied to farm harvest and domestic service work," a pattern that was already in steep decline.[106] Before the war, nearly two-thirds of African-American workers had worked in agriculture or domestic service; in 1960 fewer than one-third did, and by 1970 only one in six.

But to say simply that African-Americans moved off the land and into the factory is too facile, and therein lies the most fundamental problem that Unemployment Insurance posed for African-Americans—not that it failed to include them categorically, but that even when they moved into included categories they still did not receive adequate coverage because of the structural limitations inherent in the program itself. African-Americans in the Northern urban industrial political economy had a harder time finding and keeping jobs than white workers. Even though opportunity was greater for them in the North than in the South, they spent less time at work and more time out of work than whites. They were largely shut out of labor unions, social networks, and kinship groups that fed into stable industrial and commercial employment.[107]

As a result of the shifting racial structure of the Northern political economy, Unemployment Insurance was becoming more relevant for African-Americans despite continued occupational exclusions. But the unemployment that African-Americans faced in the North after World War II was not simply the kind of frictional unemployment that UI was equipped to ameliorate—short-term spells while on lay-off for retooling or model-year changeovers, for example, or other similar low-grade sources of temporary joblessness. Instead, the unemployment problem of the African-American community was one of chronic joblessness, frequent and long periods without work. Unemployment Insurance provided neither a solution to this problem—stabilizing employment accomplished nothing for those without jobs—nor a satisfactory source of assistance—many African-Americans either failed to qualify for benefits or exhausted their benefits without finding another job.

Even the more benign and potentially helpful aspect of the UI work test, the linkage of UI with the employment services and the emphasis on finding new work, worked against African-Americans. Often segregated and discriminatory, state employment services themselves were inhospitable places for their black clients and did little to help African-Americans find jobs.[108] But still, UI and the employment services did give their African-American clients at least a tenuous connection with the labor market—to get your benefit check you had at least to go down to the local employment office each week. Severe time limits on UI benefits meant that even this weak link with the labor market, this perfunctory public effort to match workers and jobs, was abruptly severed after twenty-six weeks, give or take a few. Often the only jobs available to African-American men— as day laborers working construction jobs or shoveling snow on public streets—paid less even than meager UI benefits. Many African-Americans either never saw a public employment office or ceased to see them and began to drop out of the labor market altogether. "The man-job relationship," wrote Elliot Liebow of the black men who passed their days on the Carry-out street corner in the mid-1960s, "is a tenuous one."[109] Thus the Unemployment Insurance system, a set of political institutions created to address the employment problems of a white industrial economy, not only proved inadequate to the new, multi-racial political economy that developed in the North in the generation after the New Deal, it also contributed to those problems by reinforcing the segregation that already infected the American workplace.

Another reform effort in the 1950s sought to address precisely these inadequacies of the UI system, but like the effort to expand coverage, it also ran up against the program's decentralized structure. This was an attempt, led by Senators Herbert H. Lehman of New York and John O. Pastore of Rhode Island and others to alter fundamentally the purpose of Unemployment Insurance away from employment stabilization and toward income support and countercyclical government spending.[110] The proposal would have imposed national benefit standards and ended merit rating of employer tax rates as well as expanding coverage, shifting the emphasis toward universality and generosity. It was based on a Keynesian understanding of the economy and the role of government, and particularly of employment policy, in the economy; but it reflected interventionist "social Keynesian" ideas that were on the defensive in the 1950s, soon to be replaced by more laissez-faire "commercial Keynesianism."[111] Higher UI benefits would generate greater government spending to stimulate the economy during recessions, and greater federal involvement in UI policy would signal government responsibility for restoring national economic growth and, presumably, job creation rather than simply inducing stable employment state by state.

The Lehman-Pastore proposal was defeated, as were other reform proposals, because it challenged too strongly the entrenched institutional decentralization of Unemployment Insurance. Even in the 1960s, during Democratic administrations that embraced Keynesian economic policy as well as the expansion of work-based policies of social provision and economic opportunity, UI proved impervious to reform.[112] The institutional structure of Unemployment Insurance, created in 1935 and entrenched over a generation, imposed strong and abiding limits on the trajectory of policy. The defeat of a Keynesian approach not only maintained UI's separation from the fundamental problems of African-Americans in the labor force, but it diminished UI's force as a potential platform for an expanded government role in employment policy in the future. Unemployment Insurance, by the 1960s, served neither as a stabilizing countercyclical stimulus, nor as a structural intervention in the labor market, nor even as a substantial source of income support for most of the unemployed.

To the extent that the political institutions of Unemployment Insurance defined a boundary in the labor force between the worthy and the unworthy, the deserving and the undeserving, the mainstream and the marginal, it was increasingly a racial boundary, one that relegated African-Americans to the edges of the political economy. But this result was not simply the replication in the North of the racial structure of the South. The structure of Unemployment Insurance, like the other pieces of the American welfare state, contributed to the reorganization and reconstruction of the racial structure of American society and to the political construction of the deepening divide between an African-American middle class and an urban "underclass." For a growing and increasingly stable black middle class, Unemployment Insurance provided, along with Old-Age Insurance, an honorable link to a welfare state that promoted an expansive view of social citizenship. For those African-Americans who found themselves increasingly cut off from the labor force, however, Unemployment Insurance offered nothing except detachment from the promise of social citizenship. Already limited in scope, the policy was fatally unequipped to address the new unemployment of the postwar African-American community, and it proved a poor platform for the kind of social, economic, and political intervention that might have softened or prevented the urban crisis that arose in the 1960s and continues to this day. Even after the triumph of the civil rights revolution and its message of hope and opportunity, the American political economy, structured by a welfare state in which was inscribed the legacy of a racially divided past, still could not redeem the promises of liberation and prosperity that seemed, for a brief moment, to offer redemption.

6

Race, Welfare, and the Future of American Politics

The New Deal embodied an intricate compromise between the national and inclusive impulses of Northern progressivism and the hierarchical and parochial imperatives of the South. This compromise—a compromise of section, ideology, class, and race—found expression in the public policy of the 1930s, policy that was shaped in a matrix of power that was itself a reflection of the particular configuration of racial division in American society. Franklin Roosevelt's social policy initiatives, and the political context in which they were forged, constituted an opportunity to redirect both the American welfare state and the politics of race in the United States toward greater inclusion and equality. In the depths of the Depression, with consecutive Democratic landslides behind it, and with the demands of the aged, the unemployed, and the dependent pressing in on Washington, the New Deal was a moment of possibility for a national, racially inclusive regime of social welfare policy that might have offered African-Americans some protection against the structures of dependence under which they lived.

It was, perhaps, inevitable that such a vision of an expansive and inclusive welfare state was not to be. But the precise terms of the compromise and the particular place it assigned to African-Americans in the new welfare state were not inevitable. As it was reached, the specifics of the New Deal compromise arose out of the politics of the Social Security Act in the administration and Congress, and they were sealed in the social policy institutions the act created. Any possibilities for broader racial inclusion in social policy evaporated before the ink from the president's pen was dry on 14 August 1935; the moment Franklin Roosevelt affixed his signature to the Social Security Act, a particular racial compromise became law—a compromise not of generalities but of specifics. A new set of rules was in place that would define for a generation and more who was in and who was

216

out of American social provision. African-Americans were decidedly out, but the terms on which they were excluded, the institutions designed to keep them out, differed in their racial porousness. In the generation following, African-Americans managed to enter selectively into the welfare state. The very selectivity of their shifting attachment to—and detachment from—the welfare state has been an ingredient in creating a fundamentally new politics of race in the United States; it was in the New Deal that the seeds of this new politics were sown.

The divergent paths of these three programs suggest that this link between race and social policy institutions has been a critical factor in shaping the development of the American welfare state. The demands of political actors to promote overlapping class and racial divisions in society find concrete expression not just in the content of policy but in particular institutional forms. Although different policies affect race relations in different ways—by challenging or buttressing particular legal, political, economic, or social relations—American social policies share a legacy of race-laden institutional structures. The ability to exclude African-Americans from benefits has been a central factor in the adoption of national policies, and the parochialism of other policies has often effectively restricted African-American participation. These administrative institutions then became important independent factors in either promoting or restricting the availability of social policy benefits to African-Americans by determining the extent to which benefits are actually available to eligible blacks. Moreover, administrative institutions fed back into the political process and affected the evolution of policy. By establishing fair and inclusive systems of administration, national institutions helped promote the expansion of social policies to encompass excluded racial groups without deepening racial conflict. Parochial institutions, however, did not incorporate racial minorities so easily. Because they were prone to discriminatory or selective administration of benefits, parochial policies perpetuated the exclusion and political manipulation of African-Americans. The incorporation of African-American beneficiaries into such policies produced not a smooth and steady process of expansion but a challenge to the legitimacy of the policies themselves. Finally, the very parochialism of these policies contributed to the frustration of attempts to promote fairer and more adequate social policies that would better serve all their beneficiaries, black or white.

Three major policies—Old-Age Insurance, Aid to Dependent Children, and Unemployment Insurance—made up the core of the Social Security Act. For each, policymakers responded differently to the structural pressures posed by the class and racial composition of the population that stood to benefit from the policy, manipulating either the target population to exclude African-Americans or the institutional structure toward more parochial arrangements. Given the position of African-Americans in American society and the political economy in 1935, national, racially inclusive social policy institutions were impossible. National policy was possible only for the protection of a set of beneficiaries restricted by class and, hence, by race. Racially inclusive policies were also possible, but only on condition that parochial administrative structures remain. Consequently, the Social Security Act produced the three policies considered here: a national but exclusionary system of Old-Age Insurance, an inclusive but parochial Aid to Dependent Children program, and a hybrid strain of Unemployment Insurance.

Decisions about institutional structure had important consequences for the administration and subsequent development of social policy, but they were not always consequences that the policymakers of 1935 intended or foresaw. The initial status of African-Americans under the various parts of the Social Security Act cannot alone account for subsequent developments in the racial character of the programs. Racially exclusionary programs, that is, did not necessarily continue to exclude African-Americans, while more potentially inclusive policies excluded them in a variety of ways. What persisted in both kinds of cases was not the short-lived patterns of inclusion and exclusion that were the immediate product of the policy settlement of 1935 but the more enduring institutions that that settlement created. These institutions, created in reaction to the racial structure of the 1930s, independently influenced the future politics of social policymaking that led either to national racial expansion or to continued parochialism. National policies, on one hand, were not only able to incorporate racial minorities through effective administration but were also more likely to develop into politically popular and expansionary programs. The national structure of Old-Age Insurance generated political forces that, when skillfully exploited by Social Security professionals in the federal government, promoted the program's own expansion, overcoming in the span of a generation the forces of racial exclusion that had shaped the program in the first place.

Parochial policies, on the other hand, mitigated the inclusive potential of public assistance by institutionalizing multiple and decentralized structures of power. The architecture of public assistance frustrated national reform, either by blocking reform attempts or, more subtly, by blunting the force even of successful national reforms. The parochial structure of Aid to Dependent Children followed this pattern, keeping policymaking power and administrative discretion in the hands of state and local officials and leaving African-Americans largely at their mercy. Not only did discrimination persist, but the racialized politicization of ADC that occurred through the manipulation of ADC by urban party organizations made even those African-Americans who did participate increasingly vulnerable to attack. Moreover, the changes in the American political economy that the New Deal wrought not only limited the possibilities for national reform of social policy, they restricted the possibilities of state-level reform as well by dividing potential cross-class, cross-race alliances at the state level and drawing their loyalties to different sets of federal and state policies.[1]

Unemployment Insurance, falling between these two institutional extremes, has moved much more slowly to incorporate new racial groups. At the same time, however, it has not inspired the racial and political conflict that have plagued ADC. Although UI is sufficiently national that reform efforts focused on the federal government, it has never had the expansionary push that has propelled OAI. By the same token, it is not so parochial that African-Americans have been entirely at the mercy of the racially manipulative local forces. Unemployment Insurance has thus had a fairly stable history, expanding toward greater adequacy and exclusion only very slowly but avoiding the pitfalls of racial politics. As a result, it has offered African-Americans neither expansive social benefits nor a platform for improving their status in the labor market.

Race, Institutions, and the Political Construction of the "Underclass"

The consequences of these institutional configurations, however, were not limited to establishing the status of African-Americans as clients or non-clients of the welfare state. The shape of welfare state institutions also played a central role in the construction and reconstruction of African-American political identities. American racial politics dwells less than it did a generation ago on racist attitudes and legal structures of racial segregation that rendered African-Americans less than citizens; these things are not altogether gone, but they no longer prevail. The basic fact of African-American citizenship is no longer in doubt. Instead, the central racial conflicts of our time involve questions about the texture and character of their citizenship: the legitimacy of their access to economic and educational opportunity (in arguments over affirmative action), to political power (in the struggle over minority representation in Congress), and to the welfare state (in the conflict over welfare reform and the urban "underclass").[2] The paradox of contemporary American racial politics is that even as the old conflicts over Jim Crow have been resolved, new racial fault lines have opened up, revealing wide political gaps between the races.

The era between the New Deal and the 1960s was a tumultuous and formative one for the politics of race and welfare, and for American politics more generally. The civil rights movement forced a revolution for African-Americans in American politics and society, toppling formal segregation. The Civil Rights Act of 1964 promised to open up new educational and economic opportunities, and the Voting Rights Act of 1965 offered millions of African-Americans the right to vote. Meanwhile, the migration of millions of African-Americans from the South to the North meant that racial politics was no longer predominantly a regional phenomenon. If black migrants found greater freedom and opportunity in the North than in the South, they still found themselves entering a racially segmented political economy that relegated them to the lowest rungs of the economic ladder and to increasingly segregated urban neighborhoods.[3] In cities such as Los Angeles, Detroit, and Newark, race riots in the 1960s exposed the increasing tension and rising stakes of racial conflict. In 1966, Martin Luther King, Jr., came to Chicago to fire the opening salvo of the civil rights movement in the North, a series of protests against residential segregation and the conditions of the black ghetto poor. King's Chicago sojourn, although it came to very little when it ran up against Mayor Daley, signaled a shift in the movement's focus away from Jim Crow, which was already in full retreat, and toward a broader set of economic and social concerns. Not the least of these was welfare.

During the same period, the American welfare state developed according to the template laid down in the New Deal: national social insurance, which grew to include African-Americans on fair and equal terms, and parochial public assistance, which did not. Consequently, those African-Americans who had stable jobs were connected politically to an increasingly dense network of public provision that helped to solidify a black middle class and differentiate it from the rest of the African-American community. This segment of the African-American population grew beginning in the 1960s, when policies such as affirmative action opened up new educational and professional opportunities for those African-Americans who were equipped to take advantage of them.[4] At the same time, parochial public assistance policies perpetuated the links of dependence between African-American welfare clients and local political authorities. In the 1960s, the War on Poverty mounted an assault on the parochialism of welfare by trying to reorient social policy institutions to sever these local links and replace them with direct links between national political authorities and local groups of welfare clients, particularly minorities, newly organized and mobilized into political activity by the civil rights movement.

The politicization of ADC profoundly affected the place of African-Americans in the Democratic party of Northern cities, shaping not only their own political interests and demands but the actions of white ethnic politicians who had so cozily assimilated the system of parochial public assistance into their modus operandi. As African-American numbers increased, and as greater demands were placed on the welfare system, Northern politicians found that ADC was no longer such a useful political tool. The perception that ADC was simply a corrupt giveaway to lazy migrants who refused to work gained increasing currency even among loyal Democratic voters, and it was fueled ironically by the very political uses to which ADC had been put by urban politicians since the beginning of the program. Meanwhile, African-American political leaders as well as grassroots organizations such as the NWRO began to focus demands on the adequacy of the welfare system among other economic issues, further fueling the perception that ADC was a "black" program.[5]

Thus conflicts over race and the welfare state, and particularly over the institutional form of welfare, came in the 1960s substantially to overlap. In the short run, the fallout from these overlapping conflicts was the demise of much of the national architecture of the War on Poverty; ten years after it was created, the Office of Economic Opportunity was quietly dismantled, and some of its individual programs (such as Head Start and Legal Services) reverted to the parochial institutional pattern typical of American welfare. In the longer run, the fallout of the institutional clash of the 1960s has been even more serious: a deep antipathy in American politics to national solutions to the perceived welfare "crisis" and the growing isolation of an urban, African-American population commonly styled the "underclass."

As it is commonly told, the story of the "underclass" that haunts American cities resembles nothing so much as a conventional mystery. The story opens with the discovery of the despair of urban America, particularly of African-Americans isolated in inner-city ghettos—poverty, unemployment, crime, drugs, family instability. How could these things be possible in our affluent society? To compound the mystery, why have they gotten worse since the 1960s, during a period (at least through the 1970s) that saw an increase in welfare spending, much of it targeted precisely at such urban ills, along with decline in racism and racial segregation and steady economic growth? There are many possible culprits in this story, and nearly as many detectives, but in the popular discourse of American politics in the 1990s, there seems to be one lead suspect: government itself.

The chief teller of this tale, which we might call "The Failure of Welfare," is Charles Murray, whose book, *Losing Ground,* quickly became the emblem of a new conservative paradigm in the analysis of welfare in the mid-1980s.[6] In the "failure of welfare" view, it is social welfare policies themselves, and especially the welfare policies of the War on Poverty, that are responsible for the rise of the "underclass." Not only does welfare fail to reduce poverty, it actually increases poverty by discouraging work. Moreover, it is also responsible for the apparent explosion of what Daniel Patrick Moynihan called the "tangle of pathologies" that afflict African-Americans in the city.[7] Murray and his colleagues argue, essentially, that the overly generous and ill-conceived welfare policies of the 1960s reward socially pernicious behavior—nonwork, out-of-wedlock childbearing, family breakup—and punish more socially acceptable alternatives. In this version of the story, the crime that the "underclass" embodies is behavioral and cultural, the sad litany of conditions of urban life. The criminal is the welfare state, which encourages and subsidizes this culture. And in the denouement of any self-respecting version of "The Failure of Welfare," the culprit is carted away and assigned to the dustbin of history; the welfare state, that is, is dismantled and the poor are left with no choice but to work their way out of poverty.

As a mystery, "The Failure of Welfare" makes a nice story. As social science, however, it has a small flaw: It is false. The historian Michael Katz has noted that "critics have subjected the evidence and methods of few books to such withering and authoritative criticism as they meted out to *Losing Ground.*"[8] And yet, despite the decisive empirical refutation of all of its causal propositions, the "failure of welfare" view retains its hold on the public imagination, fueled particularly by the racial imagery of the "underclass."[9] Its persistence and popularity—finding expression even in President Bill Clinton's promise (or threat, depending on your point of view) to "end welfare as we know it"—places a heavy burden on liberal analysts who do not share the conservative view that government policies are responsible for the deterioration of ghetto life.

The most vigorous and convincing response to the "failure of welfare" story has come from William Julius Wilson, who argues in *The Truly Disadvantaged* that the conditions of inner-city life are a consequence neither of government social policies nor of depraved cultural and behavioral norms but of larger economic and social forces.[10] The globalizing economy; the decline of American industry and the rise of the service economy; the flight of industrial firms from central cities to the suburbs and the concomitant flight of the skilled middle class; and, most controversially, the race-specific policies such as affirmative action that allowed some African-Americans to join this fleeing middle class—these are the forces that have led to mass black male joblessness in the inner city, the proximate causal root of the "underclass." For Wilson, the "underclass" (a term he first advocated and now disavows)[11] cannot legitimately be defined by any unifying behavioral or cultural attributes. Patterns of behavior in the ghetto—encompassing work, family structure, and childbearing—are strategic adaptations to desperate social and economic conditions; they do not emanate from a subculture that disdains the American dream. If anything, as Wilson and Jennifer Hochschild have shown, poor blacks—even those living in the ghetto—believe in the American dream of opportunity and success through work as much as, if not more than, anyone else in the country.[12] The "underclass," rather, is a "heterogeneous grouping of families and individuals who are outside the mainstream of the American occupational system."[13] The title of Wilson's most recent book neatly sums up his position: *When Work Disappears*. In this work, Wilson documents the new contours of urban poverty. Residents of the ghetto, he shows, want desperately to work, to live in clean and safe neighborhoods, and to build stable lives for themselves and their families. But the decimation of urban industry and racial segregation combine to frustrate these aims, cutting the ghetto poor off from opportunity and from hope.

The clash of these two perspectives blurs the clean plot lines of the mystery. First, it is no longer so clear that government is the culprit. The distress of the cities, in Wilson's picture, is the result of a broad and complicated array of social, economic, and political forces that cannot be usefully reduced to a single cause. Wilson, in fact, advocates substantial government involvement in transforming urban America, through programs for education, job training, social services, and economic growth. But second, and more important, it is not even clear what the nature of the crime is that government is accused of committing. What, to put it bluntly, is the "underclass"? Is it simply the behaviorally and culturally challenged remnant of a declining civilization, a population either unable or disinclined to seek conventional economic success? The "failure of welfare" view urges us to define the "underclass" in this way, as a group of people, either dangerous or pitiable, whose willful behavior both separates them from the rest of us and unites them in their undeservingness.[14] On the contrary, is the "underclass" the creation of large, impersonal forces? Or is it, perhaps, a mere rubric that we use to make moral and political judgments about a larger social transformation—encompassing the changing economy, the rise of the suburbs, shifting family norms, and persistent segregation—that has forever altered the face of American poverty?[15] Wilson's perspective, though hardly ignoring the unattractiveness of ghetto life, encourages us to situate the lives of the urban poor in a context defined by social and economic structures that are beyond the means of individuals to control.

Wilson brilliantly draws connections between social and economic structures, on the one hand, and the conditions of urban poverty on the other, and he shows how certain public policies have successfully addressed those conditions while others have failed. He distinguishes between "universal" programs, policies "designed to protect all citizens against sudden impoverishment," and "targeted" programs, policies intended to assist particular groups.[16] New Deal policies, he argues, were universal and have consequently enjoyed wide popularity and political success, whereas Great Society policies were targeted, particularly at the urban poor. As a result, these latter policies have inflamed popular discontent and have left urban African-Americans economically and geographically isolated and exposed to the unsparing forces of the social and economic transformation of the last generation

Convincing as it is, however, Wilson's attempt to shift the debate toward the structural transformations that define an "underclass" has not dislodged from the public mind either the government-as-culprit view or the animosity toward urban blacks that it frequently provokes. Wilson is entirely right to cast the problem as one of structure, but his analysis elides the critical political structures that shape both the making of public policies and their impact. The large forces that Wilson fingers might not have had the same impact on the fortunes of black urban communities without the presence of the particular social policy institutions that emerged from the New Deal. The parochialism of ADC institutionalized multiple and decentralized structures of power, leaving welfare recipients at the political and economic mercy of local officials. As jobs fled the inner cities and the middle class followed, those who remained—especially African-Americans —were left with little political recourse to national leadership or resources precisely because of the parochial structure of welfare that the New Deal created. The failure of the Great Society to overturn this institutional structure merely deepened their plight by furthering their political isolation. Similarly, Unemployment Insurance offered little to jobless African-Americans in the inner city. Although it incorporated black workers who were regularly employed, it gave no help to the most desperate of the unemployed, those who were left behind by a changing economy. At the same time, both Unemployment Insurance and Old-Age Insurance, because of their smooth inclusion of African-American workers alongside whites, helped forge a black middle class by linking these workers to a stable and popular regime of government social provision. The institutions of public policy, in short, affect the way policies treat different social groups, whether defined by race, class, gender, or any other characteristics—shaping not only the degree of a policy's universalism but also its ability to mediate between global patterns of social and economic change and the everyday lives of citizens. Attention to the institutional setting of social policy constitutes an essential addition to Wilson's structural perspective if it is successfully to challenge the simplistic behavioral and cultural narrative of "The Failure of Welfare."

The failure of "The Failure of Welfare" is precisely that it constructs this narrative without taking account of these real historical and political processes that shape public policy and its impact—that is, it takes neither politics nor history seriously. The fallacy of this view is the assumption that public policies execute themselves mechanistically, applying rigid rules with predictable results. Emblematic of this approach is Murray's pronouncement of supposed "laws" of social programs, derived through his famous "thought experiments" involving Harold and Phyllis, a hypothetical couple who decide to have a child, remain unmarried, and collect welfare rather than get married and work. But history teaches that social policies do not follow such rigid "laws." Public policies are not merely self-executing collections of laws and regulations, sanctions and incentives, that regulate citizens' behavior through economic stimuli and cultural cues. They are, rather, particular institutions that penetrate society, conferring benefits and burdens in specific ways.

From the beginning, welfare policy has not treated white and black Americans equally; some policies have treated some African-Americans fairly, fusing them to the great American middle class, whereas others have not, adding a measure of political isolation to the economic and geographic isolation that have shaped the new politics of race and poverty. Because it shaped these processes, the American welfare state is implicated in the political construction of the urban "underclass" as a designation for the black poor of the inner city—but not for the simplistic reasons that the "failure of welfare" view adopts. Social policies have uneven outcomes because policy is a complicated and difficult enterprise that works in various ways through different institutional forms that both reflect and transmit patterns of political power and racial subordination.

Reforming Welfare

This historical-institutional perspective suggests limits to the promise of the universal, race-neutral approach to social policy that Wilson, Theda Skocpol, and others champion as a way to renew the attack on poverty, especially the poverty of the African-American ghetto poor. They promote a program of broad, universal policies that would address the general social and economic needs of working and nonworking Americans alike, encompassing education and job training, employment, child care, health care, and the like. Because of the concentration of these needs among poor African-Americans in ghetto neighborhoods, such policies would, they argue, disproportionately benefit them. At the same time, because they address needs and anxieties that cut across the American middle class, they could garner widespread political support without being labeled as programs that give preferences to African-Americans at the expense of others. Skocpol suggests that African-Americans have historically fared best under social policies when they have been part of broad, cross-class and cross-race coalitions.[17] Certainly many of the universal programs that they champion as models of politically successful social provision—Social Security and Medicare, to name the most notable—have included African-Americans as honorable beneficiaries while appealing to a broad, predominantly white public. Robert Greenstein responds, however, that targeting can be a fruitful approach under certain conditions and especially under budget constraints that make the adoption of universal social initiatives extremely difficult.[18] Skocpol herself has lately chronicled how Bill Clinton's drive to create a new universal social benefit, health insurance, not only failed but became a platform for a successful anti-government campaign that broke a forty-year run of Democratic dominance in Congress.[19] Certainly not all universal, cross-class programs have been equally successful. Even some of the successes that Skocpol points to—Civil War pensions, for example, or the Sheppard-Towner maternity and infant health program of the 1920s— were short-lived and failed to develop into more general and comprehensive anti-poverty programs.[20]

But the history of New Deal welfare policy suggests that even apparently universal social policies may be less than universal and that the institutional structure of even broadly conceived policies can lead such policies to favor the dominant racial group. The promise of "targeting within universalism" in a policy's content can be subverted if policy institutions are not equipped to aim benefits at the right targets. Social Security and Unemployment Insurance, for example, the New Deal policies that champions of universalism hold up as models for contemporary reform, were originally far from universal. In their initial design, both policies effectively divided the workforce by class, race, and gender, constructing exclusive categories of social citizenship. The nonworking poor, increasingly African-American and female, were segregated into a very different set of programs that acquired the pejorative designation, "welfare." Whereas Social Security developed into a broadly universal and popular program, ADC and other "welfare" policies devolved into racial division, controversy, and decline. The divergent development of these New Deal policies, toward different patterns of racial inclusion and political support, are by no means implicit or immanent in a simple rendering of a program's universalism—the scope of its coverage and the reach of its benefits into the tax-paying middle class. The extent of a program's universalism, its effectiveness in attacking poverty, and its ability to claim widespread public support are not functions merely of the breadth of its target population but also of the political institutions that govern its operation and set the terms for its future politics. Because apparently universal policies differ in their institutional forms, the meaning and impact of their universalism differs. The appearance of universalism is easily compromised by politics and by history.

Also easily compromised is the appearance of race neutrality. For much of American history, two approaches to racial politics have contended for dominance: the color-blind, which purports to treat persons equally without reference to race, and the race-conscious, which treats people of different races differently, either to discriminate or to compensate for the effects of discrimination.[21] While color blindness evokes the deeply held American ideal of individual liberty, the history of American social policy demonstrates that apparently color-blind, race-neutral policies can have seriously imbalanced racial consequences. Policies and other political arrangements that appeared to be neutral with respect to race, it turns out, have often had racial divisions "built in," whether through imbalances in the position of African-Americans in politics and society or through institutions that translate color-blind laws into race-conscious effects. Deracialization, the sidestepping of direct confrontation of difficult racial issues, as Paul Peterson has advocated, can have grim political consequences.[22] Some commentators point to the value of deracialization in American political life as a contrast to the ugliness that can ensue when candidates for public office use racially loaded campaign appeals—such as George Bush's Willie Horton advertisement in the 1988 presidential campaign or Senator Jesse Helms's none-too-subtle 1990 commercial that preyed on white resentment of affirmative action—to say nothing of the flagrant racism of politicians such as David Duke in Louisiana. But for the same reasons that policies that appear race-neutral may not always turn out to be so, deracialization may mask hidden racialization. The institutions of American political life carry within them the legacy of racial division, and only frank and open discussion and consideration of this legacy and of the possible racial consequences of political action can hope to overcome them. Bill Clinton, who won the presidency in a fairly deracialized campaign, has taken a few small steps in this direction—his comments in the 1993 New York City mayoral campaign, his advocacy of a "racial justice" clause for death-penalty cases in 1994 crime legislation, his powerful Memphis speech to black ministers in November of 1993, his candid approach to affirmative action, and his initiative on race, launched in June 1997.[23] Race neutrality and deracialization need not, of course, always conceal sinister racial consequences; the history of Social Security proves otherwise. But the comparative history of Old-Age Insurance and Aid to Dependent Children suggests strongly that it is the institutional bases of public policies that fill the racial void left by neutrality, and that institutions can have consequences that are far from racially neutral.

The implication of this analysis for public policy is that broad, universal policies stand a better chance of succeeding if we pay careful and forthright attention to both institutional structure and racial consequences. The key to successful social policy for African-Americans has historically been national policies that have been able to overcome the native parochialism of American state institutions—a rare achievement in American political history. Moreover, the entrenched parochialism of the American welfare state has continually frustrated the kind of constructive institutional reform—most tragically in the 1960s—that could have incorporated African-Americans more centrally into the American political economy and the benefits of social citizenship. In particular, the distinction between national and local control and the extent of decentralized bureaucratic discretion are crucial in determining how social policy treats African-Americans. The broad policies that Wilson advocates to enhance economic opportunity for all are absolutely necessary if the United States is to maintain its promise as the land of opportunity. And Wilson is right that these policies must be race-neutral to succeed, both because they will need wide political support across racial lines and because they will fail if they do not address the crisis of the ghetto. But the irony of history is that for social policies to be truly race-neutral, they must be constructed taking careful account of their racial consequences, which means designing social policy institutions that have the best chance of treating African-Americans and other minorities fairly and equally. Concretely, this approach means the nationalization of welfare policy. Paul Peterson argues that national welfare standards would eliminate the problem of interstate economic competition that restricts the adequacy of welfare benefits. Without national welfare policy, we risk a "race to the bottom," as states try to outdo each other in attracting residents and businesses with low tax rates and correspondingly low welfare benefits.[24] But the nationalization of social policy—not just welfare, but any policy aimed at addressing the problems of the poor—should go beyond the setting of national benefits standards to encompass administrative design as well. If welfare policy were truly a national concern, located at a single level of government, with clear guidelines determining eligibility and benefits, we could be more confident that it would be administered fairly and effectively, treating all citizens equally regardless of race. Moreover, it would be less susceptible to the kind of polarization that has so bedeviled social policy since the New Deal, and its beneficiaries would perhaps shed some of the racialized stigma that currently attaches to many social benefits.

It may seem churlish to observe that in the American political universe of the late twentieth century it is unlikely that major new social initiatives will be forthcoming from the national government. Bill Clinton's major social initiative—which he called health security, consciously echoing Social Security—went down to rather ignominious defeat, and what began as a move toward serious national welfare reform ended in cuts and devolution rather than expansion into a comprehensive, national opportunity policy. But the fact remains that broad, universal social reform is unlikely in the near term, and until political conditions change, we will be left groping and inching our way toward reform. But we need not despair of the possibility of achieving any reform. Even smaller, "targeted" policies may succeed in incorporating African-Americans and achieving long-lasting political success if they come close to national institutional characteristics—nondiscretionary, federally administered, politically autonomous. Such policies might be less ambitious programs that do not, perhaps, seek to create broad new social benefits but instead address social problems of race and poverty on a more modest scale—child-support enforcement, for example, or programs that target jobs, education, and the school-to-work transition in the inner city. At the very least, national institutions can mitigate the political weakness of targeted programs, whereas institutional parochialism can threaten the most universal. African-Americans have suffered most when the institutions of American social policy have been parochial, and they have benefited most when those institutions have been national. Given current political conditions, it may be more important to attack public cynicism about government and to demonstrate that, under the right institutional conditions, government can work to address the most serious problems facing our society.

The history of the American welfare state is one of success as well as failure. It has indeed become a fulcrum of racial conflict in American politics, conflict that threatens to do away with the good as well as the bad. But for millions of Americans, both black and white, it has meant the difference between destitution and subsistence. For those who believe that a free and affluent society has an obligation to attack poverty and racial strife in its midst, the lessons of this history should be that government can, through wise and humane public policies executed through carefully designed institutions, allow all its citizens to live lives of dignity and security.[25] Until we understand how the institutions of social policy work, either to fan the flames of racial tension or douse them, we will be ill equipped to improve them and ill advised to throw them on the scrap heap.

Race in Politics and History

The history of race, institutions, and American social policy offers lessons not only for welfare and its reform but also for a deeper understanding of race and its place in American politics. Race is important in American politics not simply as an ascriptive characteristic that divides the polity into discrete groups but also as a motive force in the construction of political life. Racial division in any society is not a simple fact; it is a complex condition, deeply contextual and situated in a set of particular social relations. It is the product not merely of shades of skin pigmentation distributed among the population but of the belief that such differences matter and above all of structures that constitute regular patterns of social, economic, and political understanding and behavior according to these shadings. Political institutions, one form that such structures can take, can thus reflect the racial basis of social distinctions in the society's power structure. The state, in short, may stand on a racial foundation.

In societies with a history of racial slavery or colonialism or both, such politically constructed racial divisions may be encoded in the nation-state through formal legal structures of segregation or apartheid. But slavery and colonialism may not, either together or separately, wholly determine the racial structure of the state.[26] Moreover, race can infect the shape of political institutions even without being legally encoded in the state—as in social policy institutions, the party structure, or working-class development.[27] How, then, can we investigate and interpret the legacy of African slavery in shaping American political development? What does it mean, for example, when advocates trot out such a legacy as justification for policies such as affirmative action or civil rights protection? In the Haggadah, the Jewish text of the Passover ritual, the recounting of the Exodus begins "We were slaves to Pharaoh in Egypt." Later, the Haggadah cites the biblical commandment to explain to one's children that we celebrate Passover "because of what the Lord did for *me* when *I* went free from Egypt."[28] This is not, of course, literally accurate; no Jew today was actually enslaved in Egypt millennia ago. But in Jewish tradition, the trope of our own slavery plays a powerful role in defining a historical, political, and theological tradition. Through contemporary rituals, beliefs, and intellectual practices, modern Jews of widely varying schools and sects find their identity in a powerful connection to an ancient but always present legacy of slavery. In other traditions as well, the Exodus resonates as a narrative of political and spiritual liberation.[29]

Similarly, the legacy of African slavery in American political development is not one of literal enslavement. Surely no African-Americans alive today were themselves slaves; for the individual, perhaps, to talk of a legacy of slavery verges on the absurd. By the same token, however, the abolition of slavery did not by itself create fair and equal political, economic, or social conditions for the freed slaves or their descendants; Jim Crow and a host of other mechanisms of discrimination have kept African-Americans at a severe disadvantage ever since. And yet African-American identity remains powerfully bound up in a connection between present and past. The legacy of slavery lies somewhere between the small particularities of individual lives and the grand themes of racism and segregation.

The connection between race and social policy in the twentieth century suggests that political institutions constitute such a middle ground. African-American identity was forged in more than two and a half centuries of slavery. American political institutions—the three-fifths, fugitive-slave, and slave-trade clauses of the Constitution, of course, but also the party system and the electoral college—were created to accommodate slavery and contain the political conflict that it provoked. Even the fundamental political ideals of liberty and equality owe their peculiar American modes to the distinction between black slavery and white freedom that developed in the colonies in the seventeenth century.[30] These and other institutions, configurations of political power shaped by a particular form of racial oppression, outlived slavery and helped shape the identities and political fortunes of African-Americans long after abolition by affecting the legitimacy of racial groups' claims to a full share in civic life. This historical-institutional process of racial development does not depend particularly on explicit racism, although such antipathy has often played an important role in American political history. Rather, racial identity, constructed in and by politics, reshapes politics through institutions, which in turn reconstruct race. Through institutions, our racial past is present even in the silences of our politics.

The particular mechanisms by which this pattern has occurred and recurred in American political development remain an open question. As the history of race and social policy shows, the role of race in creating constraints and possibilities for American politics depends not only on timeless and universal principles but also on the often messy accidents of history and the active and creative agency of the people who make it. Recognizing the role of race in shaping the conditions in which this history occurs in no way diminishes the central role of individuals, many of them brave and visionary people, in charting the course of racial progress through American history (nor, by the same token, does it excuse those who have often stood on the other side of the struggle). The task for students of American political development is to explore further this interplay between stability and change in the racial development of American politics. How, at various times and in various spheres, have politically constructed racial differences affected the path of American political development? How much power do

African-Americans hold in their own hands to confront their own pre-
dicaments and challenge structures of power that prevent them to this
day from achieving the full portion of progress that American ideals promise? Is their fate in the hands of others? Or do the enduring regularities
of American politics militate altogether against any hope of racial progress, suggesting the need for either a thoroughgoing spiritual renewal or
a more substantial social and political revolution? These questions and
debates have recurred often in the history of the struggle for African-
American progress—from debates between Booker T. Washington and
W. E. B. DuBois to the tensions between Martin Luther King, Jr., and
Malcolm X and all they have come to symbolize. These are questions that
have no answers except in history and its lessons, in the patterns of the
construction and reconstruction of the meaning of race through political
institutions.

Race commonly appears in accounts of American politics as a feature of
American "exceptionalism," something that makes our politics unique and
therefore susceptible of analysis and interpretation in splendid isolation.
But the doctrine of American exceptionalism can easily become a self-
fulfilling prophecy; the more we study American politics by itself, the
deeper our ignorance of what makes it unique, of what specific patterns
and properties distinguish it from other possible or actual political realities.
By purporting to explain everything, "exceptionalism" as an idea explains
nothing. When we put names to the exceptional characteristics of American politics, they cease to be ontologically "exceptional." Rather, they are
revealed as only more or less different from characteristics of politics elsewhere.[31] If the United States were the only country in which racial distinctions ever corresponded in some way with social relations and political
power, then exceptionalism might be an appropriate starting point for
analysis. But surely it is not, and exceptionalism, therefore, begs all but the
most trivial questions about what race means in American political life. The
racial history of American politics is unique, but it is not *sui generis,* alone
in the evolutionary taxonomy of political conflict. Only comparative analysis can ultimately resolve the questions of similarity and difference that
American racial politics raises.

The United States shares with other societies legacies of slavery and
colonialism that have resulted in race-laden processes of state-building and
institutional development. But even in countries without such legacies,
political divisions based on racial differences are becoming increasingly
important. In France, for example, conflict between whites and Africans,

particularly in the south, has produced strong electoral showings for Jean-Marie Le Pen and his followers on a platform of race-based nativism. In Britain and Canada, racial tension is increasing, and conflicts over welfare, residential segregation, and affirmative action seem to echo American problems. Even post-apartheid South Africa, now governed by its black majority, is struggling with many of the same issues as change creeps over institutions long controlled by white Afrikaners. What will be the result in these countries of superimposing racial conflict onto long-standing matrices of political and social power? How will the political institutions of established nation-states respond to the insertion of racial conflict into existing political alignments? In the United States, racial conflict was present at the creation; American institutions are so bound up in this racial conflict that it is nearly impossible to isolate the role of race in political development. How do political institutions construct and reconstruct racial identities when national development has created an established institutional order before racial conflict arrives on the scene? Situating the stories of race and American political development in a wider comparative context might not only throw light on these questions but also illuminate what is distinctive about race in the American context.

As the nineteenth century turned, W. E. B. Du Bois admonished that "the problem of the twentieth century is the problem of the color line," and he was right.[32] Although this century has seen the shattering of the hard and brutal structures of segregation and the withering, if not the disappearance, of flagrantly racist attitudes, the color line remains. Sadly, were Du Bois to revisit American society in the twilight of the twentieth century, he would find that his thoughts apply equally well to the twenty-first; only he might add that the new color line is more subtle, more elusive, harder to crack. Unless we acknowledge, as Martin Luther King, Jr., reminded us from his Birmingham cell, that the destiny of African-Americans is inexorably bound to the fate of the nation, and until we discover the ways in which this is so, we can do little to prevent Du Bois's prescience about our own century from haunting the next as well.

Appendix: Quantitative Study of ADC

Most of the variables in the analysis are quite straightforward. At the end of the Appendix is the list of sources from which the ADC data set used in the quantitative analysis in this chapter was compiled. For each state and year, the entry lists the title and pertinent publication information about the printed sources. Following the bibliographic entry are any notes about unusual characteristics of the data taken from that source. Table A.1 summarizes the states included in the data set.

For the most part, data on average monthly number of recipients and average monthly payment were either taken directly from tables reporting that information or estimated by averaging monthly figures reported in the state sources. In many cases, the average monthly payment was calculated by dividing total annual expenditures by 12 and then by the average monthly number of families or children receiving ADC. Only exceptions to these procedures are noted here. Unless otherwise noted, data are for the calendar years 1940, 1950, and 1960.

The population and income variables are taken directly from census data. A few of the census variables require a little more explanation, however. The percentage of families with single parents was calculated by subtracting the number of married couples from the number of families as reported by the census. This is an imperfect estimate of the prevalence of single-parent families, but, according to census definitions, it comes reasonably close. Moreover, it is the only measure available in the census before 1960. The analysis defines as urban counties containing cities of 100,000 or more, designated with a dummy variable.

To test for regional differences between North and South, a dummy variable designates counties in the South, defined as the eleven former Confederate states.[1] An interactive term that multiplies the South dummy variable by the black population percentage allows a test for the possibility

235

that the effect of black population was different in the South than else-where. A significant negative coefficient for this variable would indicate more severe racial discrimination in the South; a positive coefficient, less severe discrimination.

Finally, dummy variables designate 1950 and 1960 to test for systematic changes over time in the levels of ADC coverage and benefits. Interactive terms that multiply these dummy variables by black population percentage test for changes in the effect of black population. Significant positive co-efficients for these interactive variables would indicate improving treat-ment, or less severe discrimination. Because some of the key data—par-ticularly income and family structure—were not available in the census before 1950, most of the analysis takes 1950 as the baseline and tests only for change between 1950 and 1960. In the case of ADC payments, sepa-rate regressions test for change between 1940 and 1950 by simply drop-ping the variables that were unavailable in 1940 and taking that year as the baseline. Such tests were not possible for ADC coverage because the cover-age variable itself is calculated using income data.

Table A.2 compares the sample data with national averages for a few key variables and shows that the counties in the sample are quite representative of the entire country. The table lists the mean values of the most important variables in the data set, weighted by the size of the county to make them comparable to national means for the same variables. The comparison shows that the counties in the sample have a slightly higher black popula-tion percentage and slightly lower income levels than the country as a whole. Similarly, the level of poverty and the percentage of poor families receiving ADC differ slightly. All of the differences that the table reports are statistically significant (at $p \le .01$). The sample is clearly imperfect, but, given the severe limitations of the availability of data on ADC administra-tion, it comes reasonably close to approximating the nation as a whole.

Table A.3 contains the results of the basic model of ADC coverage, which show the clear regional difference in the effect of African-American population. The effective coefficient for black population percentage is the sum of the reported coefficients for black population percentage (BPP) and the interactive term (South × BPP). In the North, the South dummy variable equals zero, so the interactive term is also zero, and this sum is simply the coefficient reported for BPP. Thus the effect of BPP on cover-age is significant and positive in the North and significant and slightly negative in the South, indicating that Southern counties with denser Afri-can-American populations had slightly lower levels of ADC coverage. The model reported in Table A.3 also controls, using dummy variables, for each state represented in the data. The other results in this analysis conform to expectations. ADC coverage was slightly higher in 1960 than in 1950, reflecting the slow growth of the program in the 1950s. The positive effect of black population percentage appears to have grown slightly between 1950 and 1960—suggesting that discrimination may have diminished somewhat—although this relationship disappeared in other versions of the analysis. Counties with more single-parent families had higher levels of coverage, as did cities. In order to facilitate the calculation of the predicted values displayed in Figure 4.2, separate regressions were performed on regional subsamples; these results, which are the same in all relevant respects, are reported in Table A.4.

Table A.5 contains the regression results for the basic model of ADC payments, once again controlling for each individual state in the data. The key result is the negative effect of black population percentage on benefit levels, an effect that was uniform throughout the country; neither regional variable produced significant results in this analysis. The other results in this model again conform to expectations. In particular, payments were higher in wealthier counties and in cities.

The second column of Table A.5 presents the test for changes before 1950, omitting the income and family structure variables that are not available for 1940. The results suggest that the effect of black population on ADC payments changed dramatically between 1940 and 1950, but not at all in the next decade. The baseline year for this analysis is 1940. For that year, the multiplicative terms combining black population percentage with 1950 and 1960 equal zero, so those terms drop out of the equation. Accordingly, in 1940 black population percentage had no effect on ADC payments levels; a county with many black residents paid just as much as a county with none. By 1950, however, the negative relationship had appeared; for that year, the effective impact of black population percentage is expressed by the sum of the baseline black population percentage (which is not statistically distinguishable from zero) and the interactive term for 1950. This operation reveals that by the end of the decade, the racial division in the level of ADC payments had appeared. Repeating the operation for 1960 suggests that little changed during the 1950s. The test is imperfect; because income and family structure data are not available for 1940, they do not appear in this analysis, but their absence does not change the basic pattern of declining benefits in predominantly black areas.

Tables A.6 and A.7 repeat the models of ADC coverage and payments, respectively, for the subsample of the data containing cities, with the addition of traditional party organization (TPO) variables. The TPO variable is simply the state's score on Mayhew's TPO scale, which runs from one to five. This variable tests whether coverage or payments were generally higher or lower in machine cities than in nonmachine cities. In order to test the Erie hypothesis, that black population had a stronger effect on ADC administration in machine cities, an interactive term is necessary. The interactive term consists of the county's black population multiplied by TPO (which has been rescaled from 1–5 to 0–4 so that the term will drop out in non-organization states). Interpreting this interactive term requires some care, because its magnitude varies with TPO score. In effect, it creates a sliding scale—if it is significant, it indicates that black population mattered more in cities where traditional party organizations were stronger. These reanalyses of welfare administration in the cities do not contain the state-by-state controls that the previous analysis did, for two reasons. First, there were too few cities in the analysis and too many states to control for to get reliable estimates of the relationships. Second, the state differences subsumed the differences across cities in party organization, making it impossible to observe the independent influence of traditional party organizations.

Table A.6 reports that cities with strong party organizations had generally lower levels of ADC coverage (indicated by the negative coefficient for TPO). But the most important result in Table A.6 is the significant positive coefficient for the TPO interactive term, which indicates that the stronger a city's party organization, the greater the positive effect of BPP on coverage. The first column of Table A.7 reports the strong negative effect of BPP on benefits levels in Northern cities and the much smaller effect in Southern cities. And the second column of Table A.7, like the second column of Table A.5, shows the significant change in the impact of BPP in the 1940s. The other results in these tables are similar to their nationwide counterparts.

Table A.1 States Included in the ADC Data Set

State	1940	1950	1960	State	1940	1950	1960
Alabama	x	x	x	New Hampshire	x		
Arizona		x	x	New Jersey			x
Arkansas	x			New York	x	x	x
California	x	x	x	North Carolina	x	x	x
Colorado	x	x	x	North Dakota	x	x	
D.C.	x		x	Ohio	x	x	x
Florida	x	x	x	Oklahoma	x	x	x
Georgia	x	x	x	Oregon	x	x	x
Idaho	x	x		Pennsylvania	x	x	
Indiana	x			South Carolina	x	x	x
Iowa		x		South Dakota		x	x
Louisiana		x	x	Tennessee		x	x
Maryland	x			Texas		x	x
Michigan	x	x	x	Utah	x	x	x
Minnesota	x	x		Virginia	x	x	x
Mississippi	x	x	x	Washington		x	x
Missouri	x	x	x	West Virginia	x	x	x
Montana	x	x		Wisconsin	x	x	x
Nebraska	x		x	Wyoming	x		
Nevada			x				

Table A.2 ADC Data Set: Comparison with U.S. Averages
(Data set means are weighted by county population.)

Black population percentage

Year	Data set mean	U.S. average
1940	10.3***	9.8
1950	11.0***	10.0
1960	12.3***	10.6

Median family income

Year	Data set mean	U.S. average
1950	$2976***	$3319
1960	5573***	5620

Percentage of families with income below $3000

Year	Data set mean	U.S. average
1960	22.3***	21.7

Average ADC payment

Year	Data set mean		U.S. average	
	Child	*Family*	*Child*	*Family*
1940	$14.42***	$33.17***	$13.45	$32.40
1950	28.87***	72.69***	28.03	71.45
1960	40.03***	110.52***	36.09	108.35

Percentage of poor families receiving ADC

Year	Data set mean	U.S. average
1960	7.8***	8.1

Note: Statistical significance of difference between means
(two-tailed test): *** $p \leq .01$.

Source for U.S. Average data: U.S. Census Bureau, *Historical Statistics of the United States, Colonial Times to 1970* (Washington, D.C.: Government Printing Office, 1975), 14, 289, 297, 356.

Table A.3 ADC Coverage

Dependent variable: Percentage of poor families receiving ADC	
Independent variable	Coefficient
Constant	2.04***
	(6.8)
1960	0.956***
	(5.7)
Black population percentage	0.302***
	(12.1)
Black population percentage × 1960	0.017***
	(3.0)
Median family income (1960; $1,000)	−0.425***
	(−6.4)
Percentage families with single parents	0.179***
	(9.3)
South × black population percentage	−0.350***
	(−13.9)
City	1.60***
	(5.2)
N	4223
Adjusted R^2	0.42

Notes: t-statistics in parentheses. Dummy variables for each state were included in the model but not reported here.

*** $p \leq .01$.

Table A.4 ADC Coverage, by Region

Dependent variable: Percentage of poor families receiving ADC

Independent variable	North	South
Constant	4.60***	1.44***
	(9.7)	(4.8)
1960	1.22***	0.407**
	(4.4)	(2.1)
Black population percentage	0.206***	−0.047***
	(5.0)	(−10.6)
Black population percentage × 1960	0.196***	0.021***
	(3.7)	(3.9)
Median family income	−0.672***	−0.207***
(1960; $1000)	(−5.8)	(−3.0)
Percentage families with single parents	0.159***	0.195***
	(5.1)	(9.0)
City	2.22***	0.808**
	(4.5)	(2.4)
N	2133	2090
Adjusted R^2	0.34	0.52

Notes: t-statistics in parentheses. Dummy variables for each state were included in the model but not reported here.

**p ≤ .05. ***p ≤ .01.

Table A.5 ADC Payments

Dependent variable: Monthly average ADC payment per child (1960 $)		
Independent variable	1	2
Constant	22.50***	23.90***
	(23.8)	(49.2)
1950	—	−1.46***
		(−3.7)
1960	−1.27***	−2.69***
	(−2.8)	(−4.5)
State average ADC payment	0.68***	0.71***
	(16.9)	(34.1)
Black population percentage	−0.03***	−0.01
	(−4.0)	(−1.1)
Black population percentage × 1950	—	−0.04***
		(−4.7)
Black population percentage × 1960	—	0.00
		(0.0)
Median family income (1960; $1000)	0.73***	—
	(7.7)	
Percentage families with single parents	0.12***	—
	(4.0)	
City	2.11***	4.68***
	(5.1)	(14.4)
Average children per ADC family	−5.47***	−4.50***
	(−28.0)	(−30.2)
N	3563	5411
Adjusted R^2	0.88	0.87

Notes: t-statistics in parentheses. Dummy variables for each state were included in the model but not reported here.

*** $p \leq .01$.

Table A.6 ADC Coverage, Cities

Dependent variable: Percentage of poor families receiving ADC	
Independent variable	Coefficient
Constant	6.96^{***}
	(6.3)
1960	2.76^{***}
	(3.5)
Black population percentage	0.097^{**}
	(2.1)
Black population percentage $\times$ 1960	-0.079^{*}
	(-1.8)
Percentage families with single parents	0.168^{*}
	(1.7)
South	-5.12^{***}
	(-6.7)
TPO	-0.883^{***}
	(-3.4)
(TPO $-$ 1) $\times$ black population	0.058^{***}
	(2.7)
N	141
Adjusted R^2	0.35

Note: t-statistics in parentheses.
$^{*}p \le .10.\ ^{**}p \le .05.\ ^{***}p \le .01.$

Table A.7 ADC Payments, Cities

Dependent variable: Average monthly ADC payment per child (1960 $)		
Independent variable	1	2
Constant	45.08***	69.90***
	(4.6)	(13.2)
1950	—	11.57***
		(5.5)
1960	−2.46	22.36***
	(−0.7)	(9.1)
Black population percentage	−0.80***	−0.88***
	(−4.9)	(−4.1)
Black population percentage × 1950	—	−0.43***
		(−2.9)
Black population percentage × 1960	−0.05	−0.42***
	(−0.5)	(−2.8)
Median family income (1960; $1000)	6.87***	—
	(4.8)	
Percentage families with single parents	0.78	—
	(3.3)	
South	−16.45***	−26.05***
	(−6.0)	(−9.7)
South × Black population percentage	0.76***	1.19***
	(4.4)	(5.9)
Average children per ADC family	−15.16***	−13.01***
	(−6.5)	(−6.1)
TPO	1.54***	—
	(3.5)	
(TPO − 1) × black population percentage	—	0.20***
		(4.6)
N	131	182
Adjusted R^2	0.79	0.68

Note: t-statistics in parentheses.
***$p \leq .01$.

Sources

Alabama Department of Public Welfare, *Annual Report for the Fiscal Year October 1, 1939–September 30, 1940,* table 1, pp. 48–50.

Alabama Department of Public Welfare, *Statistics,* 1950 (monthly), table 2.

Alabama Department of Pensions and Security, *Statistics,* 1960 (quarterly), table 4. Data reported for March, June, September, and December 1960.

Arizona Department of Public Welfare, *Annual Report, July 1, 1951–June 30, 1952,* table 11. Data are for 1951–1952, closest year available.

Arizona Department of Public Welfare, *Annual Report, 1959–1960,* table 2, p. 15.

Arkansas Department of Public Welfare, *Annual Report for the Fiscal Year Ending June 30, 1940,* 65–77. Number of children is for June 1940. (Note: This month had the highest number of cases for the fiscal year, so these figures are probably higher than average.)

California Department of Public Welfare, *Report to the Governor's Council,* 1940 (monthly). October missing.

California Department of Social Welfare, *Biennial Report, July 1, 1948 to June 30, 1950,* tables 19–20. Numbers of children and families are for June 1950.

California Department of Social Welfare, *Public Welfare in California, Annual Summary of Statistical and Fiscal Data,* 1959–1960, table 29.

Colorado Department of Public Welfare, *Annual Report,* 1940, 20–21. Data are for December 1940.

Colorado Department of Public Welfare, *Annual Report,* 1950, 18.

Colorado Department of Public Welfare, *Annual Report,* 1960, table 2, p. 27; table 3, pp. 28–29.

District of Columbia Board of Public Welfare, Public Assistance Division, *Sixth Annual Report, July 1, 1939 to June 30, 1940,* 2–4, 2T, 14T.

District of Columbia Department of Public Welfare, *Annual Report,* Fiscal Year 1961. Data are for FY 1960; data are for families only.

Florida Welfare Board, *Public Assistance Statistics,* 1940 (monthly).

Florida Welfare Board, *Public Assistance Statistics,* 1950 (monthly). October missing.

Florida Department of Public Welfare, *Florida Public Welfare News,* 1960 (monthly).

Georgia Department of Public Welfare, *Public Welfare Statistics,* 1940 (quarterly).

Georgia Department of Public Welfare, *Public Welfare Statistics in Georgia,* 1950 (quarterly).

Georgia Department of Public Welfare, *Public Welfare Statistics in Georgia,* 1960 (quarterly), table 12/13.

Idaho Public Assistance Department, *Public Assistance Statistics,* 1940 (monthly). January and February missing.

Idaho Department of Public Assistance, *Biennial Report,* 1959–1960, tables 6, 13. Data are for families only.

Idaho Public Assistance Department, *Public Assistance Statistics,* 1950 (monthly).

Indiana Department of Public Welfare, *Annual Report for the Fiscal Year Ended June 30, 1940,* table 11, pp. 36–37. Data are for June 1940.

Iowa Department of Social Welfare, *Public Welfare in Iowa,* 1950 (quarterly), tables 3–4.

Louisiana Department of Public Welfare, *Thirteenth Annual Report, July 1, 1949–June 30, 1950,* tables 6, 9. Number of children as of June 30, 1950; $/child = total FY outlays/12/# children on June 30.

Louisiana Department of Public Welfare, *Louisiana Public Welfare Statistics,* 1960 (monthly). Monthly outlays and number of cases (i.e., families).

Maryland Department of Public Welfare, *Twentieth Biennial Report,* 1939–1940, table A-8, p. 41. Data are for September 1940.

Michigan Social Welfare Commission, *Biennial Report, July 1938–June 1940,* table 19, p. 37; table 10-B, pp. 92–93; table 12-B, pp. 102–105. Data are for FY 1939–1940.

Michigan Social Welfare Commission, *Sixth Biennial Report,* 1948–1950, table 6, pp. 114–115; table 8, pp. 118–119; table 10, pp. 122–123. Data are for FY 1949–1950; cases administered directly by state office (70 families, 167 children, $67,947.80) excluded.

Michigan Social Welfare Commission, *Sixth Biennial Report,* 1958–1960, table 6, pp. 134–135; table 8, pp. 138–139; table 10, pp. 142–143. Data are for FY 1959–1960; cases administered directly by state office (120 families, 292 children, $158,010) excluded.

Minnesota Division of Social Welfare, *Annual Report for the Fiscal Year July 1, 1939 through June 30, 1940,* 28–29. Data are for FY 1939–1940.

Minnesota Division of Social Welfare, *Annual Report,* 1950, table 2, pp. 46–47. Data are for FY 1949–1950.

Mississippi Department of Public Welfare, *Third Biennial Report, July 1, 1939–June 30, 1941,* table 14, pp. 60–61. Data are for June 1941.

Mississippi Department of Public Welfare, *Eighth Biennial Report, July 1, 1949–June 30, 1951,* table 19, pp. 62–63. Data are for June 1951.

Mississippi Department of Public Welfare, *Thirteenth Biennial Report, July 1, 1959–June 30, 1961,* table R-12, pp. 88–89. Data are for June 1961.

Missouri State Social Security Commission, *Public Assistance in Missouri, 1939–1940,* tables 4–6.

Missouri Division of Welfare, *Fourth Annual Report, Fiscal Year 1949–1950,* table 1, pp. 74–77. Data are for FY 1949–1950.

Missouri Division of Welfare, *Fourteenth Annual Report, Fiscal Year 1959–1960,* table 1, pp. 82–85. Data are for FY 1949–1950.

Montana Department of Public Welfare, *Report for the Period Beginning March 2, 1938 and Terminating June 30, 1940,* table 47, p. 104. Data are for June 1940.

Montana Department of Public Welfare, *Report for the Period Beginning July 1, 1948 and Terminating June 30, 1950,* table 11, p. 31. Data are for June 1950.

Nebraska Department of Assistance and Child Welfare, *Fourth Annual Report, Year Ending June 30, 1940,* 52–61.

Nebraska Division of Public Welfare, *Twenty-Fourth Annual Report, Year Ending June 30, 1960,* table 9, pp. 44–45; table 10, pp. 46–47; table 11, pp. 48–49. Data are for FY 1959–1960.

Nevada Department of Public Welfare, *Report for the Biennium Ending June 30, 1960,* table 11, p. 26. Number of children estimated by subtracting number of families from number of persons (as indicated in footnote).

New Hampshire Department of Public Welfare, *Twenty-Third Biennial Report, for the Biennial Period Ending June 30, 1940,* table 2, pp. 44–46. Data are for FY 1939–1940.

New Jersey Division of Welfare, Bureau of Assistance Statistics, 1960 (monthly), table 3.

New York State Department of Social Welfare, *Social Statistics* (quarterly), vol. 3, nos. 3–4; vol 4, nos. 1–2, 1940, table 9. Data for New York City (which comprises five counties) not reported by county.

New York State Department of Social Welfare, *Social Statistics* (monthly), vol. 12, 1950, table 8/7. Data for New York City not reported by county.

New York State Department of Social Welfare, *Social Statistics Annual Supplement for 1960,* tables 9, 12. Data for New York City not reported by county.

North Carolina Board of Charities and Public Welfare, *Biennial Report, July 1, 1938 to June 30, 1940,* pp. 76–79. Data are for FY 1939–1940.

North Carolina Board of Public Welfare, *Biennial Report, July 1, 1948 to June 30, 1950,* table 12, pp. 112–117. Data are for FY 1949–1950.

North Carolina Board of Public Welfare, *Biennial Report, July 1, 1958 to June 30, 1960,* table 20, pp. 102–107. Data are for FY 1949–1950.

Public Welfare Board of North Dakota, *Public Welfare Bulletin,* 1940 (monthly). October and December missing.

Public Welfare Board of North Dakota, *North Dakota Welfare News and Views,* 1950 (monthly). August–December missing; Data are for families only.

Ohio Department of Public Welfare, *Nineteenth Annual Report, Year Ended December 31, 1940,* pp. 174–182.

Ohio Department of Public Welfare, *Public Welfare Statistics,* December 1950, table 14, pp. 39–40.

Ohio Department of Public Welfare, *Thirty-Ninth Annual Report, Fiscal Year Ended June 30, 1960,* 19–22. Data are for families only.

Oklahoma Department of Public Welfare, *Fourth Annual Report, for the Fiscal Year July 1, 1939–June 30, 1940,* table 25, pp. 54–55. Data are for June 1940.

Oklahoma Department of Public Welfare, *Report for the Fiscal Year July 1, 1949–June 30, 1950,* tables 20–21, pp. 47–50. Number of families and total expenditures for June 1950; number of children estimated by calculating average children per family by county for fiscal year (from table 21) and multiplying by number of families (from table 20).

Oklahoma Department of Public Welfare, *Annual Report, Fiscal Year Ending June 30, 1960,* tables 2, 30.

Oregon Public Welfare Commission, *Report of Public Welfare in Oregon for the*

Calendar Year 1940, 21–23, 43–47. Number of families for December 1940; $/family estimated from total year expenditure.

Oregon Public Welfare Commission, *Report of Public Welfare in Oregon for the Fiscal Year July 1, 1949–June 30, 1950,* table 14, p. 44. Data are for FY 1949–1950; data are for families only.

Oregon Public Welfare Commission, *Public Welfare in Oregon,* 1960 (monthly), table 6.

Pennsylvania Department of Public Assistance, Bureau of Research and Statistics, *Pennsylvania Public Assistance Statistics,* 1940 (monthly). Number of children calculated by subtracting number of cases from number of persons (as directed in table footnotes).

Pennsylvania Department of Public Assistance, *Public Assistance Review,* December 1950, table 10, p. 6. Number of children estimated by subtracting number of cases from number of persons (assuming only one parent per family—1940 Pennsylvania report makes this explicit).

South Carolina Department of Public Welfare, *South Carolina Public Welfare Statistics,* 1940 (monthly), table 8. July–December missing.

South Carolina Department of Public Welfare, *Public Welfare Statistics,* 1950 (monthly), table 10.

South Carolina Department of Public Welfare, *Twenty-third Annual Report, for the Year Ended June 30, 1960,* 29, 37–39. Data are for families only.

South Dakota Department of Public Welfare, *Annual Report for the Period July 1, 1949 to June 30, 1950,* 28–29, 34–35. Number of families = "average recipients per month," table 1; number of children estimated by averaging number of children on July 1, 1949, and June 30, 1950, table 3; Meade County—there is an apparent mistake in table 1, which reports 50 families per month, whereas table 3 reports 18–23 families, 43–60 children. I use 50 children and 18 + 32/2 = 21 families.

South Dakota Department of Public Welfare, *Annual Report for the Period July 1, 1959 to June 30, 1960,* 58–59.

Tennessee Department of Public Welfare, *Statistics,* 1950 (monthly), table 10. Data are for July 1950.

Tennessee Department of Public Welfare, *Annual Report, Fiscal Year July 1, 1959 to June 30, 1960,* table 7. Number of children estimated in report based on average of 2.79 children per family, hence $/child estimated by dividing $/family by 2.79; Data are for June 1960.

Texas Department of Public Welfare, *Annual Report,* 1950, tables 45–46. Data are for August 1950.

Texas Department of Public Welfare, *Annual Report,* 1960, tables 48–49. Number of children and families for August 1960.

Utah Department of Public Welfare, *Public Assistance in Utah,* 1950 (monthly), table 5c.

Utah Department of Public Welfare, *Public Assistance Statistics and Services for Children,* 1960 (monthly), table 5c.

Virginia Department of Public Welfare, *Public Welfare Statistics,* 1940 (monthly), table 5.

Virginia Department of Public Welfare and Institutions, *Public Welfare Statistics,* 1950 (quarterly). Data are for March, June, and September; December reports only families, not children.

Virginia Department of Public Welfare and Institutions, *Public Welfare Statistics,* 1960 (quarterly). Data are for December only; others report families, not children.

Washington Department of Social Security, *Public Assistance in the State of Washington,* 1950 (monthly), table 9.

Washington Department of Social Security, *Public Assistance in the State of Washington,* 1960 (monthly), table 6.

West Virginia Department of Public Assistance, *Report, July 1, 1938 to June 30, 1940,* 75. Data are for families only.

West Virginia Department of Public Assistance, *Annual Report, July 1, 1949 to June 30, 1950,* 33. Data are for families only.

West Virginia Department of Public Assistance, *Annual Report, July 1, 1959 to June 30, 1960,* table 1. Data are for families only.

Wisconsin Department of Public Welfare, *Public Assistance in Wisconsin,* 1940 (monthly). January–July missing.

Wisconsin Department of Public Welfare, *Public Assistance in Wisconsin,* 1950 (monthly), table 3. Money payments only (excluding medical, hospital, and burial); families and children in own or relative's home (excluding foster homes).

Wisconsin Department of Public Welfare, *Public Assistance in Wisconsin,* 1960 (monthly), table 3. Money payments only (excluding medical, hospital, and burial); families and children in own or relative's home (excluding foster homes).

Wyoming Department of Public Welfare, *Biennial Report, October 1, 1938–September 30, 1940,* tables 2, 4. Data are averages for two-year period.

Notes

1. Race, Institutions, and Welfare in American Political Development

1. Martin Luther King Jr., "Letter from Birmingham Jail," in *Why We Can't Wait* (New York: Mentor, 1964), 92–93.
2. Benjamin I. Page and Robert Y. Shapiro, *The Rational Public: Fifty Years of Americans' Policy Preferences* (Chicago: University of Chicago Press, 1992), 62–63, 68–81; William G. Mayer, *The Changing American Mind: How and Why American Public Opinion Changed Between 1960 and 1988* (Ann Arbor: University of Michigan Press, 1992), 22–27, 365–374.
3. Carol M. Swain, *Black Faces, Black Interests: The Representation of African American Interests in Congress* (Cambridge: Harvard University Press, 1993).
4. See the essays in Toni Morrison, ed., *Race-ing Justice, En-gendering Power: Essays on Anita Hill, Clarence Thomas, and the Construction of Social Reality* (New York: Pantheon, 1992).
5. Dona Cooper Hamilton and Charles V. Hamilton, *The Dual Agenda: Race and Social Welfare Policies of Civil Rights Organizations* (New York: Columbia University Press, 1997); Edward G. Carmines and James A. Stimson, *Issue Evolution: Race and the Transformation of American Politics* (Princeton: Princeton University Press, 1989); Eileen L. McDonagh, "The 'Welfare Rights State' and the 'Civil Rights State': Policy Paradox and State Building in the Progressive Era," *Studies in American Political Development* 7 (1993): 225–274.
6. Page and Shapiro, *The Rational Public*, 123–129; Fay Lomax Cook and Edith J. Barrett, *Support for the American Welfare State: The Views of Congress and the Public* (New York: Columbia University Press, 1992); Robert Y. Shapiro and John T. Young, "Public Opinion and the Welfare State: The United States in Comparative Perspective," *Political Science Quarterly* 104 (1989): 59–89.
7. Paul Pierson, *Dismantling the Welfare State?: Reagan, Thatcher, and the Politics of Retrenchment* (Cambridge: Cambridge University Press, 1994).

8. Theda Skocpol, "African Americans in U.S. Social Policy," in *Classifying by Race,* ed. Paul E. Peterson (Princeton: Princeton University Press, 1995).

9. David T. Ellwood, *Poor Support: Poverty in the American Family* (New York: Basic Books, 1988).

10. Martin Isaac Gilens, "Racial Attitudes and Opposition to the American Welfare State" (Ph.D. diss., University of California, Berkeley, 1991); Charles Murray, *Losing Ground: American Social Policy, 1950–1980* (New York: Basic Books, 1984).

11. William Julius Wilson, *The Truly Disadvantaged: The Inner City, the Underclass, and Public Policy* (Chicago: University of Chicago Press, 1987); Thomas J. Sugrue, *The Origins of the Urban Crisis: Race and Inequality in Postwar Detroit* (Princeton: Princeton University Press, 1996).

12. Stanley B. Greenberg, *Middle Class Dreams: The Politics and Power of the New American Majority* (New York: Times Books, 1995), 39.

13. Paul E. Peterson, *The Price of Federalism* (Washington: Brookings Institution, 1995); Margaret Weir, "The Politics of Racial Isolation in Europe and America," in *Classifying by Race,* ed. Peterson.

14. William Julius Wilson, *When Work Disappears: The World of the New Urban Poor* (New York: Alfred A. Knopf, 1996); Jennifer L. Hochschild, *Facing Up to the American Dream: Race, Class, and the Soul of the Nation* (Princeton: Princeton University Press, 1995).

15. The names of Old-Age Insurance and Aid to Dependent Children have changed several times since 1935. OAI is now OASDHI (Old-Age, Survivors, Disability, and Health Insurance). ADC became AFDC (Aid to Families with Dependent Children) before being replaced in 1996 by a very different program called Temporary Assistance to Needy Families. For convenience, I will refer to them by their original names and acronyms throughout. On the method of comparison, see Arend Lijphart, "Comparative Politics and the Comparative Method," *American Political Science Review* 65 (1971): 682–698; Theda Skocpol and Margaret Somers, "The Uses of Comparative History in Macrosocial Inquiry," *Comparative Studies in Society and History* 22 (1980): 174–197; Gary King, Robert O. Keohane, and Sidney Verba, *Designing Social Inquiry: Scientific Inference in Qualitative Research* (Princeton: Princeton University Press, 1994).

16. Charles Tilly, "Reflections on the History of European State-Making," in *The Formation of National States in Western Europe,* ed. Charles Tilly (Princeton: Princeton University Press, 1975), 14–15; Douglass C. North, *Institutions, Institutional Change and Economic Performance* (Cambridge: Cambridge University Press, 1990).

17. Gunnar Myrdal, *An American Dilemma: The Negro Problem and Modern Democracy* (New York: Harper & Brothers, 1944).

18. Myrdal, *An American Dilemma,* 1021–1022. Emphasis in original.

19. Herbert Blumer, "The Future of the Color Line," in *The South in Continuity and Change,* ed. John C. McKinney and Edgar T. Thompson (Durham,

N.C.: Duke University Press, 1965), 322–336; Earl Black and Merle Black, *Politics and Society in the South* (Cambridge: Harvard University Press, 1987); T. H. Marshall, "Citizenship and Social Class," in *Class, Citizenship, and Social Development* (Garden City, N.Y.: Doubleday, 1964).

20. Jennifer L. Hochschild, *The New American Dilemma: Liberal Democracy and School Desegregation* (New Haven: Yale University Press, 1984). See also Anthony W. Marx, *Making Race and Nation: A Comparison of the United States, South Africa, and Brazil* (Cambridge: Cambridge University Press, 1998); C. Vann Woodward, *The Strange Career of Jim Crow,* 3d rev. ed. (New York: Oxford University Press, 1974); Edmund S. Morgan, *American Slavery, American Freedom: The Ordeal of Colonial Virginia* (New York: W. W. Norton, 1975).

21. Robert C. Lieberman, "Social Construction," *American Political Science Review* 89 (1995): 437–441.

22. Paul E. Peterson, "A Politically Correct Solution to Racial Classification," in *Classifying by Race,* ed. Peterson.

23. Marx, *Making Race and Nation.*

24. Ira Katznelson, *Liberalism's Crooked Circle: Letters to Adam Michnik* (Princeton: Princeton University Press, 1996), 178–179.

25. Grant McConnell, *Private Power and American Democracy* (New York: Alfred A. Knopf, 1966).

26. Max Weber, "Class, Status, Party," in *From Max Weber: Essays in Sociology,* trans. and ed. H. H. Gerth and C. Wright Mills (New York: Oxford University Press, 1946), 180–195; Ira Katznelson, "Power in the Reformulation of Race Research," in *Race, Change, and Urban Society,* ed. Peter Orleans and William Russell Ellis Jr. (Beverly Hills, Calif.: Sage Publications, 1971); Ira Katznelson, "Comparative Studies of Race and Ethnicity: Plural Analysis and Beyond," *Comparative Politics* 5 (1972): 136–137.

27. Stokely Carmichael and Charles V. Hamilton, *Black Power: The Politics of Liberation in America* (New York: Random House, 1967); Louis L. Knowles and Kenneth Prewitt, eds., *Institutional Racism in America* (Englewood Cliffs, N.J.: Prentice-Hall, 1969); Edward S. Greenberg, Neal Milner, and David J. Olson, eds., *Black Politics: The Inevitability of Conflict* (New York: Holt, Rinehart and Winston, 1971).

28. See Jonathan Chait, "Backfire on Campus," *The American Prospect* 22 (summer 1995): 44–45.

29. Marguerite Ross Barnett, "A Theoretical Perspective on American Racial Public Policy," in *Public Policy for the Black Community: Strategies and Perspectives,* ed. Marguerite Ross Barnett and James A. Hefner (Port Washington, N.Y.: Alfred Publishing Co., 1976), 7–8.

30. Theda Skocpol, *Protecting Soldiers and Mothers: The Political Origins of Social Policy in the United States* (Cambridge: Harvard University Press, 1992); Theda Skocpol, *Social Policy in the United States: Future Possibilities in Historical Perspective* (Princeton: Princeton University Press, 1995).

31. Stephen Skowronek, *Building a New American State: The Expansion of National Administrative Capacities, 1877–1920* (Cambridge: Cambridge University Press, 1982); Martin Shefter, "Party and Patronage: England, Germany, and Italy," *Politics and Society* 7 (1977): 403–451; Martin Shefter, "Party, Bureaucracy, and Political Change in the United States," in *Political Parties: Development and Decay,* ed. Louis Maisel and Joseph Cooper (Beverly Hills, Calif.: Sage Publications, 1978), 211–266; Richard Franklin Bensel, *Sectionalism and American Political Development: 1880–1980* (Madison: University of Wisconsin Press, 1984).

32. V. O. Key Jr., *Southern Politics in State and Nation* (New York: Alfred A. Knopf, 1949); Ira Katznelson, Kim Geiger, and Daniel Kryder, "Limiting Liberalism: The Southern Veto in Congress, 1933–1950," *Political Science Quarterly* 108 (1993): 283–306.

33. E. E. Schattschneider, *Politics, Pressures and the Tariff* (New York: Prentice-Hall, 1935), 288. See also Theodore J. Lowi, "American Business, Public Policy, Case-Studies, and Political Theory," *World Politics* 16 (1964): 677–715.

34. Pierson, *Dismantling the Welfare State?*

35. McConnell, *Private Power and American Democracy;* Theodore J. Lowi, *The End of Liberalism: The Second Republic of the United States,* 2d ed. (New York: W. W. Norton, 1979). Russell L. Hanson makes a useful distinction between federal and national state building in "Federal Statebuilding During the New Deal: The Transition from Mothers' Aid to Aid to Dependent Children," in *Changes in the State: Causes and Consequences,* ed. Edward S. Greenberg and Thomas F. Mayer (Newbury Park, Calif.: Sage Publications, 1990).

36. Lowi, *End of Liberalism;* Bill Scheuerman, "The Rule of Law and the Welfare State: Toward a New Synthesis," *Politics and Society* 22 (1994): 195–213.

37. By labeling such policies egalitarian, I am simply making a procedural claim about the treatment of individuals subject to them. I suggest neither that policies of this procedural character serve the ends of justice nor that they entail equality in the fuller deontological sense that, for example, Ronald Dworkin evokes in his argument for "equal concern and respect." Ronald Dworkin, *Taking Rights Seriously* (Cambridge: Harvard University Press, 1977). See also Douglas Rae et al., *Equalities* (Cambridge: Harvard University Press, 1981).

38. On the concept of the deserving and undeserving poor in American history, see Michael B. Katz, *In the Shadow of the Poorhouse: A Social History of Welfare in America* (New York: Basic Books, 1986).

39. On state capacity, see Theda Skocpol, "Bringing the State Back In: Strategies of Analysis in Current Research," in *Bringing the State Back In,* ed. Peter B. Evans, Dietrich Rueschemeyer, and Theda Skocpol (Cambridge: Cambridge University Press, 1985).

40. James Q. Wilson, *Bureaucracy: What Government Agencies Do and Why They Do It* (New York: Basic Books, 1989).

41. This argument obviously has its roots in James Madison's *Federalist* No. 10. See also McConnell, *Private Power and American Democracy.*

42. Paul E. Peterson, *City Limits* (Chicago: University of Chicago Press, 1981); Martha Derthick, "Up-to-Date in Kansas City: Reflections on American Federalism," *PS: Political Science and Politics* 25 (1992): 675. See also Martha Derthick, "Crossing Thresholds: Federalism in the 1960s," *Journal of Policy History* 8 (1996): 64–80.

43. Terry M. Moe, "The Politics of Bureaucratic Structure," in *Can the Government Govern?,* ed. John E. Chubb and Paul E. Peterson (Washington, D.C.: Brookings Institution, 1989); Terry M. Moe, "The Politics of Structural Choice: Toward a Theory of Public Bureaucracy," in *Organization Theory: From Chester Barnard to the Present and Beyond,* ed. Oliver E. Williamson (New York: Oxford University Press, 1990).

44. Hochschild, *The New American Dilemma.*

45. Wilson, *Bureaucracy,* 157–175.

46. I have adapted this concept from Martha Derthick, *Agency Under Stress: The Social Security Administration in American Government* (Washington, D.C.: Brookings Institution, 1990), 175–181.

47. This aspect of administrative structure is similar to one of Wilson's central questions in his "worms-eye-view" of bureaucracy: What is it that an agency's operators, the people who actually carry out its function, do? Wilson, *Bureaucracy,* 27–28.

48. See Grant McConnell, *The Decline of Agrarian Democracy* (Berkeley: University of California Press, 1953).

49. On the colonization of administrative capacity, see Kenneth Finegold and Theda Skocpol, "Economic Intervention and the Early New Deal," *Political Science Quarterly* 97 (1982): 255–278; and Robert C. Lieberman, "The Freedmen's Bureau and the Politics of Institutional Structure," *Social Science History* 18 (1994): 405–437. On the organizational evolution of the American welfare state more generally, see Edward D. Berkowitz and Kim McQuaid, *Creating the Welfare State: The Political Economy of 20th-Century Reform,* rev. ed. (Lawrence: University Press of Kansas, 1992).

50. Alan Brinkley, *The End of Reform: New Deal Liberalism in Recession and War* (New York: Alfred A. Knopf, 1995).

51. Joel Williamson, *The Crucible of Race: Black-White Relations in the American South Since Emancipation* (New York: Oxford University Press, 1984); see also Woodward, *The Strange Career of Jim Crow.*

2. Race, Class, and the Organization of Social Policy: The Social Security Act

1. Franklin D. Roosevelt, "Campaign Address on Progressive Government at the Commonwealth Club, San Francisco, Calif., September 23, 1932," in *The Public Papers and Addresses of Franklin D. Roosevelt,* ed. Samuel I. Rosenman (New York: Random House, 1938), 1: 742–756; Robert Eden,

"On the Origins of the Regime of Pragmatic Liberalism: John Dewey, Adolf A. Berle, and FDR's Commonwealth Club Address of 1932," *Studies in American Political Development* 7 (1993): 74–150; Sidney M. Milkis, *The President and the Parties: The Transformation of the American Party System Since the New Deal* (New York: Oxford University Press, 1993).

2. Richard Sterner, *The Negro's Share: A Study of Income, Consumption, Housing, and Public Assistance* (New York: Harper & Brothers, 1943), 214–223; Gunnar Myrdal, *An American Dilemma: The Negro Problem and Modern Democracy* (New York: Harper & Brothers, 1944), 357–358; Nancy J. Weiss, *Farewell to the Party of Lincoln: Black Politics in the Age of FDR* (Princeton: Princeton University Press, 1983), 166–167; Michael B. Katz, *In the Shadow of the Poorhouse: A Social History of Welfare in America* (New York: Basic Books, 1986), 244–245; Ann Shola Orloff, "The Political Origins of America's Belated Welfare State," and Kenneth Finegold, "Agriculture and the Politics of U.S. Social Provision," in *The Politics of Social Policy in the United States*, ed. Margaret Weir, Ann Shola Orloff, and Theda Skocpol (Princeton: Princeton University Press, 1988).

3. Jill Quadagno, *The Transformation of Old Age Security: Class and Politics in the American Welfare State* (Chicago: University of Chicago Press, 1988); Richard Franklin Bensel, *Sectionalism and American Political Development, 1880–1980* (Madison: University of Wisconsin Press, 1984), 147–174; Lee J. Alston and Joseph P. Ferrie, "Labor Costs, Paternalism, and Loyalty in Southern Agriculture: A Constraint on the Growth of the Welfare State," *Journal of Economic History* 45 (1985): 95–117; Lee J. Alston and Joseph P. Ferrie, "Resisting the Welfare State: Southern Opposition to the Farm Security Administration," in *The Emergence of the Modern Political Economy*, ed. Robert Higgs (Greenwich, Conn.: JAI Press, 1985), 91–114; Gareth Davies and Martha Derthick, "Race and Social Welfare Policy: The Social Security Act of 1935," *Political Science Quarterly* 112 (1997): 217–235.

4. David R. James, "The Transformation of the Southern Racial State: Class and Race Determinants of Local-State Structures," *American Sociological Review* 53 (1988): 191–208. The quotation is on p. 206.

5. Ira Katznelson, "Was the Great Society a Lost Opportunity?," in *The Rise and Fall of the New Deal Order, 1930–1980*, ed. Steve Fraser and Gary Gerstle (Princeton: Princeton University Press, 1989).

6. Ira Katznelson, *The Long 1940s* (manuscript, Columbia University).

7. The bill prepared by the administration was called the Economic Security Act. But when the House Ways and Means Committee changed the name of what was originally to be called the Social Insurance Board to the Social Security Board, the bill was renamed the Social Security Act. Thomas H. Eliot, *Recollections of the New Deal: When the People Mattered* (Boston: Northeastern University Press, 1992), 110.

8. T. H. Marshall, "Citizenship and Social Class," in *Class, Citizenship, and Social Development* (Garden City, N.Y.: Doubleday, 1964).

9. Franklin D. Roosevelt, "Message to the Congress Reviewing the Broad Objectives and Accomplishments of the Administration, June 8, 1934," in *Public Papers and Addresses,* ed. Rosenman, 3: 291; Frances Perkins, *The Roosevelt I Knew* (New York: Viking, 1946), 282–283. According to Perkins, Roosevelt was rather irritated when, in 1942, the idea of "cradle-to-grave" social insurance was attributed to Sir William Beveridge.

10. Jill Quadagno, *The Color of Welfare: How Racism Undermined the War on Poverty* (New York: Oxford University Press, 1994); Marshall, "Citizenship and Social Class."

11. U.S. Social Security Board, *Social Security in America: The Factual Background of the Social Security Act as Summarized from Staff Reports to the Committee on Economic Security,* Social Security Board Publication No. 20 (Washington, D.C.: Government Printing Office, 1937), 247–248.

12. The narrative and analysis that follow rely heavily, of course, on the indispensable work on Social Security: Martha Derthick, *Policymaking for Social Security* (Washington, D.C.: Brookings Institution, 1979).

13. Roosevelt, "Message to the Congress, June 8, 1934," in *Public Papers and Addresses,* ed. Rosenman, 3: 291–292.

14. See Edwin E. Witte, *The Development of the Social Security Act* (Madison: University of Wisconsin Press, 1962).

15. V. O. Key Jr., *Southern Politics in State and Nation* (New York: Alfred A. Knopf, 1949), 345–382. For a more nuanced view, see Ira Katznelson, Kim Geiger, and Daniel Kryder, "Limiting Liberalism: The Southern Veto in Congress, 1933–1950," *Political Science Quarterly* 108 (1993): 283–306.

16. Roosevelt cited Southern leadership in Congress when he told Walter White, secretary of the NAACP, that he could not support anti-lynching legislation in 1934. "I did not choose the tools with which I must work," he told White. "Had I been permitted to choose them I would have selected quite different ones. But I've got to get legislation passed by Congress to save America. The Southerners by reason of the seniority rule are chairmen or occupy strategic positions on most of the Senate and House committees. If I come out for the anti-lynching bill now, they will block every bill I ask Congress to pass to keep America from collapsing. I just can't take that risk." Walter White, *A Man Called White: The Autobiography of Walter White* (New York: Viking, 1948), 169–170; Weiss, *Farewell to the Party of Lincoln,* 105–106; Alan Brinkley, "The New Deal and Southern Politics," in *The New Deal and the South,* ed. James C. Cobb and Michael V. Namorato (Jackson: University of Mississippi Press, 1984), 98–99.

17. Geoffrey C. Ward, *A First-Class Temperament: The Emergence of Franklin D. Roosevelt* (New York: Harper & Row, 1989). On Roosevelt's relationship with the South more generally, see Frank Freidel, *F.D.R. and the South* (Baton Rouge: Louisiana State University Press, 1965).

18. James T. Patterson, *The New Deal and the States: Federalism in Transition* (Princeton: Princeton University Press, 1969).

19. V. O. Key Jr., *The Administration of Federal Grants to States* (Chicago: Public Administration Service, 1937).

20. Theda Skocpol, *Protecting Soldiers and Mothers: The Political Origins of Social Policy in the United States* (Cambridge: Harvard University Press, 1992); Social Security Board, *Social Security in America,* 156–167, 233–245.

21. The NRA was declared unconstitutional in *Schechter Poultry Corporation* v. *United States* (the "sick chicken case"), 295 U.S. 495, on 27 May 1935, one week after the Social Security Act was reported out of the Senate Finance Committee. Arthur M. Schlesinger Jr., *The Age of Roosevelt: The Politics of Upheaval* (Boston: Houghton Mifflin, 1960), 252–255, 275–280. On the administration's anxiety over the Social Security Act's constitutionality, see Perkins, *The Roosevelt I Knew,* 286.

22. See Schlesinger, *The Politics of Upheaval,* 385–408; Ellis W. Hawley, *The New Deal and the Problem of Monopoly: A Study in Economic Ambivalence* (Princeton: Princeton University Press, 1966); Colin Gordon, *New Deals: Business, Labor, and Politics in America, 1920–1935* (Cambridge: Cambridge University Press, 1994).

23. U.S. Committee on Economic Security, *Report to the President* (Washington, D.C.: Government Printing Office, 1935), 3–4, 8–9; Witte, *Development of the Social Security Act,* 21, 27, 31, 128; Philip Harvey, *Securing the Right to Employment: Social Welfare Policy and the Unemployed in the United States* (Princeton: Princeton University Press, 1989).

24. Roosevelt, "Campaign Address on Progressive Government,"; Franklin D. Roosevelt, "The Annual Message to Congress, January 6, 1941" [the "four freedoms" speech], in *Public Papers and Addresses,* ed. Rosenman (New York: Harper & Brothers, 1950), 10: 670–672; Franklin D. Roosevelt, "'Unless There Is Security Here at Home, There Cannot Be Lasting Peace in the World'—Message to the Congress on the State of the Union, January 11, 1944" [the "economic bill of rights" speech], in *Public Papers and Addresses,* ed. Rosenman, 13: 32–42.

25. Kevin R. Cox, "The Social Security Act of 1935 and the Geography of the American Welfare State" (Paper presented to the Association of American Geographers, Atlanta, 1993).

26. Merrill G. Murray, "The Case for Payroll Recording as Against the Stamp System," 16 October 1934, Files of the Social Security Administration, Record Group 47, National Archives, Washington, D.C., Box 20. Hereafter these files will be cited as RG 47. Bryce Stewart, "Unemployment Insurance," RG 47, Box 21, p. 3.

27. Witte, *Development of the Social Security Act,* 131, 152.

28. Committee on Economic Security, *Report,* 18, 49. Emphasis added. See also Witte, *Development of the Social Security Act,* 32.

29. Senate Committee on Finance, *Economic Security Act,* 74th Cong., 1st sess., 1935, 199.

30. Arthur J. Altmeyer, *The Formative Years of Social Security* (Madison: Univer-

sity of Wisconsin Press, 1966), 14–15; Perkins, *The Roosevelt I Knew*, 291–292.

31. For an account, see Eliot, *Recollections of the New Deal.*

32. Bryce Stewart, "Unemployment Insurance," RG 47, Box 21; Merrill G. Murray, "Fundamental Principles to be Incorporated in Federal Bill for Unemployment Insurance," RG 47, Box 20.

33. Altmeyer, *Formative Years*, 17–18, 22–23; Witte, *Development of the Social Security Act*, 3–4, 111–118.

34. Altmeyer, *Formative Years*, 19–24; Witte, *Development of the Social Security Act*, 118–121.

35. See Joseph P. Harris, "Memorandum Concerning the Additional Standards Which Might Be Provided in a National Act for State Unemployment Insurance," RG 47, Box 18.

36. Interview with Thomas H. Eliot, Oral History Collection, Columbia University, 29–30.

37. Altmeyer, *Formative Years*, 25–26; Witte, *Development of the Social Security Act*, 146–147. The committee here undoubtedly took as a cue Justice Harlan Fiske Stone's remark to Perkins, in response to her fears about the constitutionality of the economic security program, that the taxing power of the federal government "is sufficient for everything you want and need." Perkins, *The Roosevelt I Knew*, 286.

38. Altmeyer, *Formative Years*, 16.

39. Jane Perry Clark, "Analysis of Types of Federal-State Relationships in Relation to a Program of Economic Security," RG 47, Box 17.

40. See Dona Cooper Hamilton and Charles V. Hamilton, *The Dual Agenda: Race and Social Welfare Policies of Civil Rights Organizations* (New York: Columbia University Press, 1997); Nancy J. Weiss, *The National Urban League, 1910–1940* (New York: Oxford University Press, 1974), 275–276; "Urban League Confab Here of Emphatic Importance," *Pittsburgh Courier*, 23 February 1935, 6.

41. "Interest in Negro Lacking, Says Wile," *New York Times*, 20 February 1935.

42. On the persistence of feudal forms of master-servant relations in American labor law, see Karen Orren, *Belated Feudalism: Labor, the Law, and Liberal Development in the United States* (Cambridge: Cambridge University Press, 1991).

43. House Committee on Ways and Means, *Economic Security Act*, 74th Cong., 1st sess., 1935, 796–798; Senate Committee on Finance, *Economic Security Act*, 74th Cong., 1st sess., 1935, 640–647; Robert C. Lieberman, "Race and the Organization of Welfare Policy," in *Classifying by Race*, ed. Paul E. Peterson (Princeton: Princeton University Press, 1995).

44. Senate Committee on Finance, *Economic Security Act*, 641–642, 645.

45. Alan Brinkley, *Voices of Protest: Huey Long, Father Coughlin, and the Great Depression* (New York: Alfred A. Knopf, 1982); Ann Shola Orloff, *The Politics of Pensions: A Comparative Analysis of Britain, Canada, and the United*

States, 1880–1940 (Madison: University of Wisconsin Press, 1993), 284–287.

46. See Abraham Holtzman, *The Townsend Movement: A Political Study* (New York: Bookman Associates, 1963); Edwin Amenta and Yvonne Zylan, "It Happened Here: Political Opportunity, the New Institutionalism, and the Townsend Movement," *American Sociological Review* 56 (1991): 250–265; Edwin Amenta, Bruce G. Carruthers, and Yvonne Zylan, "A Hero for the Aged? The Townsend Movement, the Political Mediation Model, and U.S. Old-Age Policy, 1934–1950," *American Journal of Sociology* 98 (1992): 308–339.

47. Brinkley, *Voices of Protest.*

48. Eliot, *Recollections of the New Deal,* 98.

49. *Congressional Record,* 74th Cong., 1st sess., 1935, 79, pt. 6: 6069–6070; pt. 9: 9650.

50. Key, *Southern Politics;* Alexander Heard, *A Two-Party South?* (Chapel Hill: University of North Carolina Press, 1952), 3–19; Dewey W. Grantham Jr., *The Democratic South* (Athens: University of Georgia Press, 1963); David M. Potter, *The South and the Concurrent Majority,* ed. Don E. Fehrenbacher and Carl N. Degler (Baton Rouge: Louisiana State University Press, 1972); Quadagno, *Transformation of Old Age Security.*

51. In the 74th Congress, which passed the Social Security Act, all 22 senators and 100 of 102 representatives from the South (the eleven former Confederate states) were Democrats. The two exceptions were representatives from eastern Tennessee, a traditional Republican stronghold since the Civil War. Data compiled from U.S. Congress, *Congressional Directory,* 74th Cong., 1st sess., 2d ed. (Washington, D.C.: Government Printing Office, 1935).

52. Bensel, *Sectionalism and American Political Development,* 155–174, 317–367. In the 74th Congress, 9 of the 20 most senior senators and 38 of the 86 most senior representatives were Southerners. The speaker of the House and both majority leaders were Southerners. Southerners chaired 12 of 33 committees in the Senate and 21 of 47 in the House. These included the tax, appropriations, military and naval affairs, agriculture, and banking committees of both houses as well as the House judiciary and commerce committees. Compiled from *Congressional Directory,* 74th Cong., 1st sess., 2d ed.

53. Key, *Southern Politics;* Katznelson, Geiger, and Kryder, "Limiting Liberalism."

54. In fact, administration strategists, who had considered seeking the creation of a special committee to consider the economic security program, were somewhat surprised when Doughton expressed interest in sponsoring the bill. Witte, *Development of the Social Security Act,* 79–80; Perkins, *The Roosevelt I Knew,* 296.

55. Thomas H. Eliot, "The Social Security Bill: 25 Years After," *Atlantic Monthly* 206 (August 1960): 74.

56. See James T. Patterson, *Congressional Conservatism and the New Deal: The*

Growth of the Conservative Coalition in Congress, 1933–1939 (Lexington: University of Kentucky Press, 1967); John Egerton, *Speak Now Against the Day: The Generation Before the Civil Rights Movement in the South* (New York: Alfred A. Knopf, 1994), 85–91.

57. George Brown Tindall, *The Emergence of the New South, 1913–1945* (Baton Rouge: Louisiana State University Press, 1967), 111–113, 359–369; Paul E. Mertz, *New Deal Policy and Southern Rural Poverty* (Baton Rouge: Louisiana State University Press, 1978), 1–19; Patterson, *The New Deal and the States.*

58. Social Security Board, *Social Security in America*, 156–167, 233–246; Theda Skocpol, Christopher Howard, Susan Goodrich Lehmann, and Marjorie Abend-Wein, "Women's Associations and the Enactment of Mothers' Pensions in the United States," *American Political Science Review* 87 (1993): 686–701; Christopher Howard, "Sowing the Seeds of 'Welfare': The Transformation of Mothers' Pensions, 1900–1940," *Journal of Policy History* 4 (1992): 188–227.

59. See Barry D. Karl, *The Uneasy State: The United States From 1915 to 1945* (Chicago: University of Chicago Press, 1983), 173; Katznelson, Geiger, and Kryder, "Limiting Liberalism." In fact, Richard Bensel identifies the New Deal as a moment of relatively low sectional stress in American history. Bensel, *Sectionalism and American Political Development*, 53, 58, 155–174.

60. "'Solid' South Seen Splitting on New Deal," *New York Herald Tribune*, 17 June 1935, 1; Weiss, *Farewell to the Party of Lincoln.*

61. Social Security Board, *Social Security in America*, 156–167, 233–246; Patterson, *The New Deal and the States*; Howard, "Sowing the Seeds of 'Welfare'."

62. William E. Leuchtenberg, *Franklin D. Roosevelt and the New Deal, 1932–1940* (New York: Harper & Row, 1963), 114–117, 143–166; Schlesinger, *The Politics of Upheaval.*

63. Eliot Interview, 30; Altmeyer, *Formative Years*, 25–26; Witte, *Development of the Social Security Act*, 146–147; Perkins, *The Roosevelt I Knew*, 286.

64. Robert C. Lieberman, "The Freedmen's Bureau and the Politics of Institutional Structure," *Social Science History* 18 (1994): 405–437; Skocpol, *Protecting Soldiers and Mothers*; Orloff, *The Politics of Pensions.*

65. Theda Skocpol, "African Americans in U.S. Social Policy," in *Classifying by Race*, ed. Peterson.

66. The only exception was the amendment introduced by Senator Bennett Champ Clark of Missouri that would have allowed employers to substitute private pension plans for OAI. The Senate adopted the amendment, but the House-Senate conference committee dropped it. See Witte, *Development of the Social Security Act*, 105–108.

67. Senate Committee on Finance, *Economic Security Act*, 199.

68. "House Group Drops Farm Job Insurance," *New York Times*, 22 February 1935; "Security Fight Costs Aid of 20 Legislatures," *New York Herald Trib-*

une, 26 February 1935; Lieberman, "Race and the Organization of Welfare Policy."

69. "Exempted," editorial, *Pittsburgh Courier,* 9 March 1935.

70. Arthur M. Schlesinger Jr., *The Age of Roosevelt: The Coming of the New Deal* (Boston: Houghton Mifflin, 1958), 308–309; Derthick, *Policymaking for Social Security,* 229–232.

71. White, *A Man Called White,* 169–170; Freidel, *F.D.R. and the South.*

72. *Congressional Record* 79, pt. 6: 6068–6069.

73. House Committee on Ways and Means, *Economic Security Act,* 74th Cong., 1st sess., 1935, 902.

74. The real bombshell of Morgenthau's testimony was his sudden skepticism about the CES's proposed financing scheme for Old-Age Insurance, which called for the buildup of a large reserve fund in the Treasury and contemplated the eventual use of general revenues to fund benefits. Witte, *Development of the Social Security Act,* 152–153; Perkins, *The Roosevelt I Knew,* 297–298; Eliot, *Recollections of the New Deal,* 102; Eliot Interview, 19, 49.

75. House Committee on Ways and Means, *Economic Security Act,* 902, 911.

76. House Committee on Ways and Means, *Economic Security Act,* 559; Senate Committee on Finance, *Economic Security Act,* 514–515. Epstein had icy relations with the Committee on Economic Security, whose staff he felt had not paid him due consideration during the writing of the bill. This may explain why, although he was ostensibly an administration witness, his testimony differed substantially from the CES position on this and several other matters. Witte sketches the deterioration of Epstein's relations with the committee in a scathing footnote in *Development of the Social Security Act,* 82–84.

77. Senate Committee on Finance, *Economic Security Act,* 1935, 576. The only advisory council member (out of twenty-three) representing the farm sector was Louis J. Taber, master of the National Grange, who never attended a meeting. Roosevelt chose a Southerner, President Frank P. Graham of the University of North Carolina, as chairman of the council primarily to improve the bill's status in the eyes of Southern members of Congress. Witte, *Development of the Social Security Act,* 30, 50.

78. J. Douglas Brown, *An American Philosophy of Social Security: Evolution and Issues* (Princeton: Princeton University Press, 1972), 19–20; Charles McKinley and Robert W. Frase, *Launching Social Security: A Capture-and-Record Account* (Madison: University of Wisconsin Press, 1970), 313–314; Davies and Derthick, "Race and Social Welfare Policy."

79. House Committee on Ways and Means, *Economic Security Act,* 244–247, 112.

80. Social Security Board, *Social Security in America,* 183.

81. Detlev Zöllner, "Germany," in *The Evolution of Social Insurance, 1881–1981,* ed. Peter A. Köhler and Hans F. Zacher (London: Frances Pinter, 1982), 32.

82. Gerhard A. Ritter, *Social Welfare in Germany and Britain*, trans. Kim Traynor (Leamington Spa, Warwickshire: Berg, 1983); Zöllner, "Germany."

83. Ritter, *Social Welfare in Germany and Britain*, 11–12; Herbert Hofmeister, "Austria," in *The Evolution of Social Insurance*, ed. Köhler and Zacher.

84. Barrington Moore Jr., *Social Origins of Dictatorship and Democracy: Lord and Peasant in the Making of the Modern World* (Boston: Beacon Press, 1966); Dietrich Rueschemeyer, Evelyne Huber Stephens, and John D. Stephens, *Capitalist Development and Democracy* (Chicago: University of Chicago Press, 1992); Gaston V. Rimlinger, *Welfare Policy and Industrialization in Europe, America, and Russia* (New York: John Wiley & Sons, 1971); Shearer Davis Bowman, *Masters and Lords: Mid-19th Century U.S. Planters and Prussian Junkers* (New York: Oxford University Press, 1993).

85. Senate Committee on Finance, *Economic Security Act*, 1935, 219–220.

86. *Congressional Record*, 74th Cong., 1st sess., 1935, 79, pt. 6: 5991.

87. More than two-fifths of the Southern labor force worked in agriculture in 1930. U.S. Census Bureau, *Fifteenth Census of the United States: 1930, Population* (Washington, D.C.: Government Printing Office, 1931), U.S. Summary, table 5, p. 18; state volumes, table 4. Unlike voting restrictions in Southern states, this provision offered no loopholes such as grandfather clauses or literacy tests to limit its impact on whites. Alston and Ferrie, "Labor Costs, Paternalism, and Loyalty," 98.

88. Were it possible to include these workers in the data, the findings would not differ appreciably. Ewan Clague, a Social Security Board statistician, used 1930 census data for a similar analysis in 1937. "Were data available for 1937," he argued, "it is likely that the proportions would vary somewhat but not enough to alter the picture in any appreciable degree." He estimated that there were approximately 2.1 million workers in domestic service in 1937. My estimate totals 2.0 million. Ewan Clague, "The Problem of Extending Old Age-Insurance to Cover Classes Now Excluded," presentation to the Advisory Council on Social Security, 5 November 1937, RG 47, Box 9.

89. For the data, see Lieberman, "Race and the Organization of Welfare Policy."

90. Senate Committee on Finance, *Economic Security Act*, 66, 509.

91. Howard, "Sowing the Seeds of 'Welfare'."

92. Sterner, *The Negro's Share*, 83–88.

93. U.S. Bureau of the Census, *Poverty in the United States, 1990*, Current Population Reports, Series P-60, No. 175 (Washington, D.C.: Government Printing Office, 1991).

94. See Skocpol, *Protecting Soldiers and Mothers;* Howard, "Sowing the Seeds of 'Welfare'."

95. Sterner, *The Negro's Share*, 48–58, 280–281. As Herbert Gutman and others have pointed out, poverty and family structure may not be entirely independent of each other. Herbert G. Gutman, *The Black Family in Slavery and Freedom, 1750–1925* (New York: Pantheon, 1976), 462–463.

96. Wilbur J. Cohen, "The Social Security Act of 1935: Reflections Fifty Years Later," in *The Report of the Committee on Economic Security of 1935* (Washington, D.C.: National Conference on Social Welfare, 1985), 9.

97. Senate Committee on Finance, *Economic Security Act*, 70–71.

98. Clark, "Analysis of Types of Federal-State Relationships." Grant-in-aid programs already in place in 1935 employed a wide variety of mechanisms for federal direction of state activity, some more overtly coercive than others. Key, *Administration of Federal Grants*.

99. Gilbert Y. Steiner, *Social Insecurity: The Politics of Welfare* (Chicago: Rand McNally, 1966), 4.

100. Senate Committee on Finance, *Economic Security Act*, 220–222, 338–339, 344, 578–579, 122, 12; House Committee on Ways and Means, *Economic Security Act*, 125–126; *Congressional Record* 79, pt. 9: 9419.

101. House Committee on Ways and Means, *Economic Security Act*, 974–977.

102. Rogers M. Smith, "Beyond Tocqueville, Myrdal, and Hartz: The Multiple Traditions in America," *American Political Science Review* 87 (1993): 561.

103. Senate Committee on Finance, *Economic Security Act*, 641–643. See also Weiss, *Farewell to the Party of Lincoln*, 166–167.

104. *Congressional Record* 79, pt. 5: 5692–5693; "House Counts Votes to Pass Security Bill," *New York Herald Tribune*, 16 April 1935, 4; "Word of Warning," editorial, *Amsterdam News*, 28 January 1935, 8; "Security Choice Faces President," *New York Times*, 1 March 1935, 3.

105. "Security Measure Pressed in Senate," *New York Times*, 15 June 1935, 2.

106. See Allen Francis Kifer, "The Negro Under the New Deal, 1933–1941" (Ph.D. diss., University of Wisconsin, 1961), 217; Weiss, *Farewell to the Party of Lincoln*, 50; Ralph J. Bunche, *The Political Status of the Negro in the Age of FDR*, ed. Dewey W. Grantham (Chicago: University of Chicago Press, 1973), 106; Raymond Wolters, *Negroes and the Great Depression: The Problem of Economic Recovery* (Westport, Conn.: Greenwood Publishing Co., 1970); John B. Kirby, *Black Americans in the Roosevelt Era: Liberalism and Race* (Knoxville: University of Tennessee Press, 1980), 34, 126; Egerton, *Speak Now Against the Day*, 91–104; Desmond King, *Separate and Unequal: Black Americans in the Federal Government* (Oxford: Oxford University Press, 1995); Philip Selznick, *TVA and the Grass Roots: A Study of Politics and Organization* (Berkeley: University of California Press, 1949).

107. Andrew J. Polsky, *The Rise of the Therapeutic State* (Princeton: Princeton University Press, 1991), 153.

108. Witte, *Development of the Social Security Act*, 144–145. Witte's personal assistant, Wilbur Cohen, was present at all the executive sessions of both congressional committees.

109. *Congressional Record* 79, pt. 5: 5780.

110. *Congressional Record* 79, pt. 9: 9268, 9285.

111. *Congressional Record* 79, pt. 5: 5796; pt. 6: 5976–5983.

112. Daniel Nelson, *Unemployment Insurance: The American Experience, 1915–*

1935 (Madison: University of Wisconsin Press, 1969); Roy Lubove, *The Struggle for Social Security, 1900–1935* (Pittsburgh: University of Pittsburgh Press, 1986), 144–178; Edwin Amenta, Elisabeth S. Clemens, Jefren Olsen, Sunita Parikh, and Theda Skocpol, "The Political Origins of Unemployment Insurance in Five American States," *Studies in American Political Development* 2 (1987): 137–182.

113. Orloff, *The Politics of Pensions,* 286–287; Perkins, *The Roosevelt I Knew,* 284, 294–296; Mark H. Leff, "Taxing the 'Forgotten Man': The Politics of Social Security Finance in the New Deal," *Journal of American History* 70 (1983): 359–381.

114. Social Security Board, *Social Security in America,* 91–92. See also Gordon, *New Deals,* 261–279.

115. William Haber and Merrill G. Murray, *Unemployment Insurance in the American Economy: An Historical Review and Analysis* (Homewood, Ill.: Richard D. Irwin, 1966), 106.

116. Edwin E. Witte, "Unemployment Insurance," in *Social Security Perspectives: Essays by Edwin E. Witte,* ed. Robert J. Lampman (Madison: University of Wisconsin Press, 1962), 221–223; Witte, *Development of the Social Security Act,* 127–128, 133–135, 141–142; Altmeyer, *Formative Years,* 22–24, 35, 40.

117. Witte, *Development of the Social Security Act,* 128.

118. Senate Committee on Finance, *Economic Security Act,* 504–505.

119. The former came from Senator Bennett Champ Clark of Missouri and the latter from Representative Bart Lord of New York. Senate Committee on Finance, *Economic Security Act,* 166–167; *Congressional Record* 79, pt. 6: 5890.

120. *Congressional Record* 79, pt. 6: 5967.

121. See, for example, Perkins's statement to the Finance Committee. Senate Committee on Finance, *Economic Security Act,* 123. On the competing types of unemployment insurance proposals, see Lubove, *Struggle For Social Security,* 168–173. On the Lundeen bill, see Richard M. Valelly, *Radicalism in the States: The Minnesota Farmer-Labor Party and the American Political Economy* (Chicago: University of Chicago Press, 1989), 168–169.

122. House Committee on Ways and Means, *Economic Security Act,* 797–798; Senate Committee on Finance, *Economic Security Act,* 646; House Committee on Labor, *Unemployment, Old Age, and Social Insurance,* 74th Cong., 1st sess., 1935, 326–328, 145–154, 610–613, 635–637; T. Arnold Hill, "The Negro's Need for Unemployment Insurance," in *The H.R. 2827 Handbook for Speakers, Writers, and Organizers* (National Congress for Unemployment and Social Insurance, 1935), Industrial Relations Collection, Firestone Library, Princeton University. [H.R. 2827 was the Lundeen bill.] George E. Haynes of the Federal Council of Churches documented discrimination in federal programs, including public works, in his testimony. See Senate Committee on Finance, *Economic Security Act,* 487–489. See also

Kifer, "The Negro Under the New Deal"; Hamilton and Hamilton, *The Dual Agenda.*

123. Christopher Jencks has pointed out that the unemployment rate is an inadequate indicator of joblessness because it does not consider "discouraged workers," unemployed people who are not even looking for work. It is, however, the best indicator available for the 1930s. Moreover, typically only those looking for work were eligible for unemployment insurance. Christopher Jencks, *Rethinking Social Policy: Race, Poverty, and the Underclass* (Cambridge: Harvard University Press, 1992), 122. For the data, see Robert C. Lieberman, "Race and the Development of the American Welfare State from the New Deal to the Great Society" (Ph.D. diss., Harvard University, 1994).

124. By the 1930s there were very few children aged ten to thirteen in the labor force, so the difference here is quite small.

125. On the comparability of unemployment statistics over time, see Alba M. Edwards, *Sixteenth Census of the United States: 1940, Population, Comparative Occupation Statistics for the United States, 1870–1940* (Washington, D.C.: Government Printing Office, 1943). When recalculated with the 1930 base, the percentages were not substantially different.

126. Robert C. Weaver, *Negro Labor: A National Problem* (New York: Harcourt, Brace, 1946); A. Philip Randolph, "The Trade Union Movement and the Negro," *Journal of Negro Education* 5 (1936): 54–58.

127. National Resources Planning Board, *Security, Work, and Relief Policies* (Washington, D.C.: Government Printing Office, 1942); Haber and Murray, *Unemployment Insurance,* 439–440; Altmeyer, *Formative Years,* 18.

128. House Committee on Ways and Means, *Economic Security Act,* 797–798; Senate Committee on Finance, *Economic Security Act,* 645–646, 1225; Bernard K. Johnpoll and Harvey Klehr, eds., *Biographical Dictionary of the American Left* (New York: Greenwood Press, 1986), 6–7.

129. Amenta et al., "The Political Origins of Unemployment Insurance."

130. Witte, *Development of the Social Security Act,* 117–118.

131. Theron F. Schlabach, *Edwin E. Witte: Cautious Reformer* (Madison: State Historical Society of Wisconsin, 1969), 116–126.

132. Witte, *Development of the Social Security Act,* 116, 121.

133. House Committee on Ways and Means, *Economic Security Act,* 387–389.

134. House Committee on Ways and Means, *Economic Security Act,* 373.

135. Eliot, *Recollections of the New Deal,* 110–111.

136. Senate Committee on Finance, *Economic Security Act,* 738.

137. Skocpol, *Protecting Soldiers and Mothers,* 138; Skocpol, "African Americans in U.S. Social Policy."

3. Old-Age Insurance: From Exclusion to Inclusion

1. See Theda Skocpol, "The Limits of the New Deal System and the Roots of Contemporary Welfare Dilemmas," in *The Politics of Social Policy in the*

United States, ed. Margaret Weir, Ann Shola Orloff, and Theda Skocpol (Princeton: Princeton University Press, 1988); John Myles, *Old Age in the Welfare State: The Political Economy of Public Pensions*, rev. ed. (Lawrence: University Press of Kansas, 1989).

2. Martha Derthick, *Policymaking for Social Security* (Washington, D.C.: Brookings Institution), 213–216; W. Andrew Achenbaum, *Social Security: Visions and Revisions* (Cambridge: Cambridge University Press, 1986), 35.

3. Jerry R. Cates, *Insuring Inequality: Administrative Leadership in Social Security, 1935–54* (Ann Arbor: University of Michigan Press, 1983).

4. Arthur J. Altmeyer, *The Formative Years of Social Security* (Madison: University of Wisconsin Press, 1966), 228. See Robert M. Cover, "Social Security and Constitutional Entitlement," in *Social Security: Beyond the Rhetoric of Crisis*, ed. Theodore R. Marmor and Jerry L. Mashaw (Princeton: Princeton University Press, 1988).

5. See Paul E. Peterson, "The Rise and Fall of Special Interest Politics," *Political Science Quarterly* 105 (1990–1991): 545–546.

6. Paul Pierson, *Dismantling the Welfare State?: Reagan, Thatcher, and the Politics of Retrenchment* (Cambridge: Cambridge University Press, 1994).

7. Arthur M. Schlesinger Jr., *The Age of Roosevelt: The Coming of the New Deal* (Boston: Houghton Mifflin, 1958), 308–309. See also Derthick, *Policymaking for Social Security*, 229–232.

8. Christine L. Day, *What Older Americans Think: Interest Groups and Aging Policy* (Princeton: Princeton University Press, 1990); Henry J. Pratt, *Gray Agendas: Interest Groups and Public Pensions in Canada, Britain, and the United States* (Ann Arbor: University of Michigan Press, 1993).

9. Cates, *Insuring Inequality*.

10. James Madison, *Federalist No. 10*; Grant McConnell, *Private Power and American Democracy* (New York: Alfred A. Knopf, 1966).

11. William H. Riker, *Federalism: Origin, Operation, Significance* (Boston: Little, Brown, 1964), 152.

12. See Allen Francis Kifer, "The Negroes Under the New Deal, 1933–1941" (Ph.D. diss., University of Wisconsin, 1961); Raymond Wolters, *Negroes and the Great Depression: The Problem of Economic Recovery* (Westport, Conn.: Greenwood Publishing Co., 1973); Nancy J. Weiss, *Farewell to the Party of Lincoln: Black Politics in the Age of FDR* (Princeton: Princeton University Press, 1983).

13. Jennifer L. Hochschild, *The New American Dilemma: Liberal Democracy and School Desegregation* (New Haven: Yale University Press, 1984).

14. Charles McKinley and Robert W. Frase, *Launching Social Security: A Capture-and-Record Account, 1935–1937* (Madison: University of Wisconsin Press, 1970), 417.

15. James Q. Wilson, *Bureaucracy: What Government Agencies Do and Why They Do It* (New York: Basic Books, 1989), 158–171. Wilson's description of the Social Security Administration as a "production" agency, whose outcome

and outputs are both observable, derives principally from the agency's OAI benefit-paying function, which did not begin until 1941.

16. Derthick, *Policymaking for Social Security;* Theodore R. Marmor, "Entrepreneurship in Public Management: Wilbur Cohen and Robert Ball," in *Leadership and Innovation: A Biographical Perspective on Entrepreneurs in Government,* ed. Jameson W. Doig and Erwin C. Hargrove (Baltimore: Johns Hopkins University Press, 1987).

17. Birchard E. Wyatt and William H. Wandel, *The Social Security Act in Operation: A Practical Guide to the Federal-State Social Security Program* (Washington, D.C.: Graphic Arts Press, 1937), 37.

18. Interview with Ewan Clague, Oral History Collection, Columbia University, 72.

19. Walter White to Social Security Board, 6 November 1936; Louis Resnick, Director of Informational Services, Social Security Board, to White, 18 November 1936; White to Resnick, 25 November 1936; "Further Protest on Social Security Blank," Press Release, 27 November 1936, NAACP Papers, part 10, reel 19.

20. McKinley and Frase, *Launching Social Security,* 85–88.

21. McKinley and Frase, *Launching Social Security,* 407–432; Altmeyer, *Formative Years,* 47–52; Interview with Thomas H. Eliot, Oral History Collection, Columbia University, 63–68.

22. Edwin Amenta, Bruce G. Carruthers, and Yvonne Zylan, "A Hero for the Aged? The Townsend Movement, the Political Mediation Model, and U.S. Old-Age Policy, 1934–1950," *American Journal of Sociology* 98 (1992): 308–339.

23. Edward D. Berkowitz, "The First Advisory Council and the 1939 Amendments," in *Social Security After Fifty: Successes and Failures,* ed. Edward D. Berkowitz (Westport, Conn.: Greenwood Press, 1987), 58–61.

24. Cates, *Insuring Inequality.*

25. Derthick, *Policymaking for Social Security;* Marmor, "Entrepreneurship in Public Management"; Gary P. Freeman, "Voters, Bureaucrats, and the State: On the Autonomy of Social Security Policymaking," in *Social Security: The First Half-Century,* ed. Gerald D. Nash, Noel H. Pugach, and Richard F. Tomasson (Albuquerque: University of New Mexico Press, 1988); Brian Balogh, "Securing Support: The Emergence of the Social Security Board as a Political Actor," in *Federal Social Policy: The Historical Dimension,* ed. Donald T. Critchlow and Ellis W. Hawley (University Park: Pennsylvania State University Press, 1988).

26. Alan Brinkley, *The End of Reform: New Deal Liberalism in Recession and War* (New York: Alfred A. Knopf, 1995).

27. On planning vs. budgeting in American political development, see Ira Katznelson and Bruce Pietrykowski, "Rebuilding the American State: Evidence From the 1940s," *Studies in American Political Development* 5 (1991): 301–339; and Patrick J. Wolf, "Reorganization, Competition, and

Crises: Fundamental Explanations for the Bureau of the Budget's 'Golden Era,'" Occasional Paper 93–114, Center for American Political Studies, Harvard University, 1993. On planning in the Social Security Administration, see Derthick, *Policymaking for Social Security;* and Cates, *Insuring Inequality.* On government planning in general, see John Friedmann, *Planning in the Public Domain: From Knowledge to Action* (Princeton: Princeton University Press, 1987).

28. Altmeyer, *Formative Years,* 68–71; McKinley and Frase, *Launching Social Security,* 364.

29. Robert C. Lieberman, "The Freedmen's Bureau and the Politics of Institutional Structure," *Social Science History* 18 (1994): 405–437; William H. Glasson, *Federal Military Pensions in the United States* (New York: Oxford University Press, 1918), 273.

30. McKinley and Frase, *Launching Social Security,* 311–313.

31. McKinley and Frase, *Launching Social Security,* 342–356.

32. McKinley and Frase, *Launching Social Security,* 368.

33. Altmeyer, *Formative Years,* 70.

34. McKinley and Frase, *Launching Social Security,* 311–312.

35. Frances Perkins, *The Roosevelt I Knew* (New York: Viking, 1946), 282–283.

36. Sidney M. Milkis, *The President and the Parties: The Transformation of the American Party System Since the New Deal* (New York: Oxford University Press, 1993).

37. James A Hagerty, "Landon Condemns the Security Law; Would Amend It," *New York Times,* 27 September 1936, 1. The text of Landon's speech appears on p. 31.

38. Arthur M. Schlesinger Jr., *The Age of Roosevelt: The Politics of Upheaval* (Boston: Houghton Mifflin, 1960), 635–638; Wilbur J. Cohen, "The Evolution and Growth of Social Security," in *Federal Policies and Worker Status Since the Thirties,* ed. Joseph P. Goldberg, Eileen Ahern, William Haber, and Rudolph A. Oswald (Madison, Wis.: Industrial Relations Research Association, 1976), 56–58. On Hearst and Landon, see Rodney P. Carlisle, *Hearst and the New Deal: The Progressive as Reactionary* (New York: Garland Publishing, 1979), 166–179.

39. Edward D. Berkowitz, *Mr. Social Security: The Life of Wilbur J. Cohen* (Lawrence: University Press of Kansas, 1995), 40–41.

40. McKinley and Frase, *Launching Social Security,* 358–359, 447–459.

41. Marmor, "Entrepreneurship in Public Management."

42. Frances Fox Piven and Richard A. Cloward, *Regulating the Poor: The Functions of Public Welfare* (New York: Pantheon, 1971). The quotation is on p. 147.

43. Australia, New Zealand, and South Africa, for example, excluded persons of non-European extraction from noncontributory old-age assistance. U.S. Social Security Board, *Social Security in America: The Factual Background of the Social Security Act as Summarized from Staff Reports to the Committee on*

Economic Security, Social Security Board Publication No. 20 (Washington, D.C.: Government Printing Office, 1937), 184.

44. See, for example, the testimony of George E. Haynes, executive secretary of the National Council of Churches, House Committee on Ways and Means, *Economic Security Act,* 74th Cong., 1st sess., 1935, 597–609.

45. Frank G. Davis, "Burden-Benefit Under Social Security: The Case of Poor Blacks," Occasional Paper, vol. 3., no. 3 (Washington, D.C.: Institute for Urban Affairs and Research, Howard University, 1977); Frank G. Davis, *The Black Community's Social Security* (Washington, D.C.: University Press of America, 1978); "Social Security and Race," Policy Report No. 128 (Dallas: National Center for Policy Analysis, 1987).

46. Walter White to Social Security Board, 6 November 1936, NAACP Papers, part 10, Library of Congress, Manuscripts Division (microfilm, reel 19).

47. Desmond King, *Separate and Unequal: Black Americans in the Federal Government* (Oxford: Oxford University Press, 1995); John David Skrentny, *The Ironies of Affirmative Action: Politics, Culture, and Justice in America* (Chicago: University of Chicago Press, 1996).

48. The source for all data is U.S. Bureau of the Census, *Fifteenth Census of the United States: 1930, Population* (Washington, D.C.: Government Printing Office, 1933), vol. 4, table 13, pp. 25–34.

49. In the pre-Keynesian world of the 1920s and 1930s, there was no concept of a "labor force" that included the involuntarily unemployed. Those who were not working were presumed to be unwilling to work at the going market wage.

50. On employment patterns in the South, see Jacqueline Jones, *The Dispossessed: America's Underclasses From the Civil War to the Present* (New York: Basic Books, 1992).

51. U.S. Treasury Department, Division of Tax Research, "The Extension of Old-Age and Survivors Insurance to Agricultural and Domestic Service Workers and to the Self-Employed," 1 December 1947; Senate Committee on Finance, *Social Security Revision,* 81st Cong., 2d sess., 1950, 101.

52. These data count as noncovered those categories brought in by the 1950 amendments to the Social Security Act.

53. Altmeyer, *Formative Years,* 205–208, 211–216; Cates, *Insuring Inequality,* 70–85.

54. Figure 3.3, it should be noted, compares data that are not precisely comparable. The benefits ratio (top line) uses all beneficiaries as the denominator, whereas the income ratio (bottom line) uses white income as the denominator. If parallel data were available, the lines would be closer together, but the fundamental relationship that the figure reveals—that nonwhite benefits at least outstripped nonwhite wages—would remain.

55. "Memorandum on Discriminations Under the Federal Social Security Act," 22 October 1937, NAACP Papers, part 10, reel 19; House Committee on Ways and Means, *Social Security Act Amendments of 1949,* 81st Cong., 1st sess., 1949, 570.

56. Amenta, Carruthers, and Zylan, "A Hero for the Aged?"; Mark H. Leff, "Speculating in Social Security Futures: The Perils of Payroll Tax Financing, 1939–1950," in *Social Security,* ed. Nash, Pugach, and Tomasson; Derthick, *Policymaking for Social Security,* 132–157.

57. Pierson, *Dismantling the Welfare State?;* Paul Pierson, "When Effect Becomes Cause: Policy Feedback and Political Change," *World Politics* 45 (1993): 595–628.

58. Murray R. Benedict, *A Retirement System for Farmers,* Planning Pamphlet No. 49 (Washington, D.C.: National Planning Association, 1946).

59. Derthick, *Policymaking for Social Security.*

60. See Theodore J. Lowi, *The End of Liberalism: The Second Republic of the United States,* 2d ed. (New York: W. W. Norton, 1979).

61. See Gavin Wright, *Old South, New South: Revolutions in the Southern Economy Since the Civil War* (New York: Basic Books, 1986), 241–246; Jones, *Dispossessed.*

62. Nicholas Lemann, *The Promised Land: The Great Black Migration and How It Changed America* (New York: Alfred A. Knopf, 1991), 6. Lemann provides a vivid account of the "Second Great Migration."

63. John Morton Blum, *V Was For Victory: Politics and American Culture During World War II* (New York: Harcourt Brace Jovanovich, 1976), 185–188, 196–197, 212–215.

64. Blum, *V Was For Victory,* 199–207.

65. Peter J. Kellogg, "Northern Liberals and Black America: A History of White Attitudes, 1936–1952" (Ph.D. diss., Northwestern University, 1971).

66. Everett Carll Ladd Jr. with Charles D. Hadley, *Transformations of the American Party System,* 2d ed. (New York: W. W. Norton, 1978), 31–87; James L. Sundquist, *Dynamics of the Party System: Alignment and Realignment of Political Parties in the United States,* rev. ed. (Washington, D.C.: Brookings Institution, 1983), 198–239, 269–297; Samuel Lubell, *The Future of American Politics,* 3d ed. (New York: Harper & Row, 1965); Earl Black and Merle Black, *Politics and Society in the South* (Cambridge: Harvard University Press, 1987); John H. Aldrich, *Why Parties?: The Origin and Transformation of Party Politics in America* (Chicago: University of Chicago Press, 1995), 131–135.

67. Edward G. Carmines and James A. Stimson, *Issue Evolution: Race and the Transformation of American Politics* (Princeton: Princeton University Press, 1989); Ira Katznelson, Kim Geiger, and Daniel Kryder, "Limiting Liberalism: The Southern Veto in Congress, 1933–1950," *Political Science Quarterly* 108 (1993): 283–306.

68. Achenbaum, *Social Security,* 30.

69. Altmeyer, *Formative Years,* 88–91. Altmeyer's memorandum to Roosevelt appears on pp. 295–297.

70. Hugh Heclo, *Modern Social Politics in Britain and Sweden: From Relief to Income Maintenance* (New Haven: Yale University Press, 1975); Peter A. Hall, "Policy Paradigms, Social Learning, and the State: The Case of Eco-

nomic Policymaking in Britain," *Comparative Politics* 25 (1993): 275–296; John W. Kingdon, *Agendas, Alternatives, and Public Policies* (Boston: Little, Brown, 1984).

71. Berkowitz, *Mr. Social Security,* 47–48.

72. Derthick, *Policymaking for Social Security,* 89–109; Berkowitz, "The First Advisory Council."

73. "Final Report of the Advisory Council on Social Security," 10 December 1938, in House Committee on Ways and Means, *Social Security,* 76th Cong., 1st sess., 1939, 37–38.

74. M. A. Linton, "Observations on the Old Age Security Program Embodied in the Social Security Act," 5 November 1937, RG 47, Box 9.

75. Jay Iglauer, "Tentative Conclusions Growing Out of the First Meeting of the Advisory Council," RG 47, Box 9.

76. See, for example, Edwin E. Witte, "Thoughts Relating to the Old-Age Insurance Titles of the Social Security Act and Proposed Changes Therein," presented to the Social Security Advisory Council, 18–19 February 1939, RG 47, Box 138, p. 43.

77. Ewan Clague, "Problem of Extending Old Age-Insurance to Cover Classes Now Excluded," presentation to the Advisory Council on Social Security, 5 November 1937, RG 47, Box 9.

78. Wilbur Cohen, memorandum to George E. Bigge, 17 October 1938, RG 47, Box 138; Clague, "Problem of Extending," 9.

79. House Committee on Ways and Means, *Social Security,* 1219–1220, 1230–1231, 1240–1241, 1262–1264. The quotation is on p. 1262.

80. Clague, "Problem of Extending," 17.

81. W. S. Woytinksy, *Labor in the United States: Basic Statistics for Social Security* (Washington, D.C.: Social Science Research Council, Committee on Social Security, 1938), 86.

82. Advisory Council Minutes, quoted in Edward D. Berkowitz, "The First Social Security Crisis," *Prologue* 15 (1983): 138.

83. "Tentative Considerations Concerning the Tax and Reserve Program For Old Age Insurance For Discussion at Next Meeting of Advisory Council on Social Security," confidential memorandum, 7 April 1938, RG 47, Box 10; "Revised Considerations Concerning Benefits and Coverage Under the Old-Age Insurance Program," confidential memorandum, 22 October 1938, RG 47, Box 10.

84. Minutes, Advisory Council on Social Security, 22 October 1938, RG 47, Box 138, 32–44.

85. *New York Times,* 4 January 1939, 10.

86. Altmeyer, *Formative Years,* 103; "Doughton Assails Farm Security Aid," *New York Times,* 4 March 1949.

87. Dona Cooper Hamilton and Charles V. Hamilton, *The Dual Agenda: Race and Social Welfare Policies of Civil Rights Organizations* (New York: Columbia University Press, 1997).

88. On the National Negro Congress, see Wolters, *Negroes and the Great Depression*, 353–382.

89. House Committee on Ways and Means, *Social Security*, 1542–1545.

90. House Committee on Ways and Means, *Social Security*, 1442–1475, 1349–1351.

91. J. David Greenstone, *Labor in American Politics* (New York: Alfred A. Knopf, 1969), 327–330; Katznelson, Geiger, and Kryder, "Limiting Liberalism."

92. "Job Aid Revision Bars New Groups," *New York Times*, 18 March 1939, 8.

93. "Memorandum on Discriminations," NAACP Papers, 3.

94. House Committee on Ways and Means, *Social Security*, 1349–1350. Buck mentions that on his farm the packers are mostly women. See also the testimony of Samuel Fraser of the National Apple Association, representing a wide range of fruit and vegetable producers, and Ivan McDaniel, representing a consortium of California farmers. House Committee on Ways and Means, *Social Security*, 1679–1700, 2028–2055.

95. Altmeyer estimated the number of newly excluded workers to be 270,000 in his testimony to the Finance Committee. Following the passage of the amendments, the Social Security Board estimated the number to be between 300,000 and 400,000. Senate Committee on Finance, *Social Security Act Amendments*, 76th Cong., 1st sess., 1939, 6; "Tentative Statement on Extension of Old-Age and Survivors Insurance Coverage to Agricultural Workers," 14 November 1939, RG 47, Box 10, p. 2.

96. House Committee on Ways and Means, *Social Security Act Amendments of 1939*, 76th Cong., 1st sess., H. Rept. 728, 52; U.S. Bureau of the Census, *Negroes in the United States, 1920–1932* (Washington, D.C.: Government Printing Office, 1935), chap. 14, table 6, p. 289; "Memorandum on Discriminations," NAACP Papers, 3.

97. See Julian E. Zelizer, "Learning the Ways and Means: Wilbur Mills and a Fiscal Community, 1954–1964," in *Funding the Modern American State: The Rise and Fall of the Era of Easy Finance*, ed. W. Elliot Brownlee (Cambridge: Cambridge University Press, 1996).

98. For a more formal analysis of Southern committee power, see Robert C. Lieberman, "Race and the Development of the American Welfare State from the New Deal to the Great Society" (Ph.D. diss., Harvard University, 1994), 169–171.

99. McKinley and Frase, *Launching Social Security*, 377–381; Altmeyer, *Formative Years*, 119.

100. Altmeyer, *Formative Years*, 127–128, 135, 148–151.

101. Altmeyer, *Formative Years*, 152–155.

102. House Committee on Ways and Means, *Issues in Social Security*, 79th Cong., 1st sess., 1946, Committee Print, 33–38.

103. See Grant McConnell, *The Decline of Agrarian Democracy* (Berkeley: University of California Press, 1953).

104. House Committee on Ways and Means, *Amendments to Social Security Act,* 79th Cong., 2d sess., 1946, 361, 390–391, 393–394, 447–448, 454–455, 507. A. Willis Robertson was the father of Pat Robertson, the evangelist and politician.

105. Treasury Department, "Extension of Old-Age and Survivors Insurance."

106. On the financing provisions of the amendments, see Leff, "Speculating in Social Security Futures," 265–270.

107. Berkowitz, *Mr. Social Security,* 65–70.

108. Derthick, *Policymaking for Social Security,* 183–205.

109. Jill Quadagno, *The Transformation of Old Age Security: Class and Politics in the American Welfare State* (Chicago: University of Chicago Press, 1988), 104–110.

110. House Committee on Ways and Means, *Social Security Act Amendments of 1949,* 1896.

111. House Committee on Ways and Means, *Social Security Act Amendments of 1949,* 1857–1860, 1872–1878; Senate Committee on Finance, *Social Security Revision,* 771–773.

112. *Congressional Record,* 81st Cong., 2d sess., 14 June 1950, 96: 8587.

113. Testimony of Lloyd C. Halvorson, Economist, National Grange, House Committee on Ways and Means, *Social Security Act Amendments of 1949,* 1860.

114. Testimony of Hugh F. Hall, Assistant Legislative Director, American Farm Bureau Federation, Senate Committee on Finance, *Social Security Revision,* 773.

115. House Committee on Ways and Means, *Social Security Act Amendments of 1949,* 2081–2083, 2342; Senate Committee on Finance, *Social Security Revision,* 2365–2367.

116. "Farm Union Plans Organizing Drive," *New York Times,* 14 January 1950, 2.

117. Quadagno, *Transformation of Old Age Security,* 147.

118. House Committee on Ways and Means, *Social Security Act Amendments of 1949,* 281–282.

119. House Committee on Ways and Means, *Social Security Act Amendments of 1949,* 56; see Cates, *Insuring Inequality,* 134–135.

120. House Committee on Ways and Means, *Social Security Act Amendments of 1949,* 1052, 1590, 2184, 2226–2227, 2529; Senate Committee on Finance, *Social Security Revision,* 1306–1307.

121. House Committee on Ways and Means, *Social Security Act Amendments of 1949,* 2144–2148; Senate Committee on Finance, *Social Security Revision,* 1928–1932.

122. House Committee on Ways and Means, *Social Security Act Amendments of 1949,* 568–571, 1878–1879; Senate Committee on Finance, *Social Security Revision,* 1505–1506.

123. Michael E. Schiltz, *Public Attitudes Toward Social Security, 1935–1965*

(Washington, D.C.: Government Printing Office, 1970); Benjamin I. Page and Robert Y. Shapiro, *The Rational Public: Fifty Years of Trends in Americans' Policy Preferences* (Chicago: University of Chicago Press, 1992).

124. T. H. Marshall, "Citizenship and Social Class," in *Class, Citizenship, and Social Development* (Garden City, N.Y.: Doubleday, 1964).

125. House Committee on Ways and Means, *Social Security Act Amendments of 1949,* 1345–1375.

126. House Committee on Ways and Means, *Social Security Act Amendments of 1949,* 2193–2194, 2225.

127. House Committee on Ways and Means, *Social Security Act Amendments of 1949,* 1967, 2147, 2180–2182.

128. House Committee on Ways and Means, *Social Security Act Amendments of 1949,* 376, 1925–1935.

129. House Committee on Ways and Means, *Social Security Act Amendments of 1949,* 81st Cong., 1st sess., 1949, H. Rept. 1300, 5–6, 9.

130. *Congressional Record,* 81st Cong., 1st sess., 1949, 95, pt. 10: 13813.

131. *Congressional Record,* 81st Cong., 2d sess., 1950, 96, pt. 6: 8491.

132. Leff, "Speculating in Social Security Futures," 265–270; Amenta, Carruthers, and Zylan, "A Hero for the Aged?".

133. *Congressional Record* 96, pt. 7: 8788–8815.

134. House of Representatives, *Social Security Act Amendments of 1950,* 81st Cong., 2d sess., 1950, Conference Report, H. Rept. 2771, 94–95.

135. Lester B. Granger, "Domestic Workers 'Forgotten People'," *Amsterdam News,* 19 August 1950, Tuskegee Institute News Clippings File (microfilm), reel 114; "Good News for Maids, Domestics!," *Pittsburgh Courier,* 30 January 1954, Tuskegee File, reel 136. Granger was executive director of the National Urban League.

136. Berkowitz, *Mr. Social Security,* 91–93.

137. Calculated from *Social Security Bulletin* 13 (1950): 38–39; 17 (1954): 49–53.

138. Donald Bruce Johnson, ed., *National Party Platforms* (Urbana: University of Illinois Press, 1978), 1: 452, 484.

139. Donald R. McCoy, *Landon of Kansas* (Lincoln: University of Nebraska Press, 1966), 427.

140. Stephen Skowronek, *The Politics Presidents Make: Leadership from John Adams to George Bush* (Cambridge: Harvard University Press, 1993), 46; Mark H. Leff, "Historical Perspectives on Old-Age Insurance: The State of the Art on the Art of the State," in *Social Security After Fifty,* ed. Berkowitz, 33–34.

141. Quoted in Fred I. Greenstein, *The Hidden-Hand Presidency: Eisenhower as Leader* (New York: Basic Books, 1982), 50.

142. Altmeyer, *Formative Years,* 209–217; Derthick, *Policymaking for Social Security,* 144–157; Berkowitz, *Mr. Social Security,* 79–90.

143. Altmeyer, *Formative Years,* 221–235.

144. "Extending Social Security," *New York Times,* 2 June 1954, 30.

145. Quadagno, *Transformation of Old Age Security,* 148. See also Senator Albert Gore Sr.'s speech on the legislative accomplishments of the 83rd Congress, *New York Times,* 2 September 1954, 14.

146. *Congressional Record,* 83d Cong., 2d sess., 1954, 100, pt. 6: 7423, 7468.

147. *Congressional Record* 100, pt. 11: 14433–14434.

148. Holland's former colleague from Florida, Claude Pepper, had also supported inclusion of farmers and farm workers in 1950. After returning to Washington as a representative in 1962, Pepper became one of Congress's great champions of Old-Age Insurance.

4. Aid to Dependent Children and the Political Construction of the "Underclass"

1. Richard Sterner, *The Negro's Share: A Study of Income, Consumption, Housing, and Public Assistance* (New York: Harper & Brothers, 1943), 285.

2. Senate Committee on Finance, *Economic Security Act,* 74th Cong., 1st sess., 7 February 1935, 479–491.

3. Jill Quadagno provides more systematic evidence for the existence of discrimination in the administration of Old-Age Assistance. Jill Quadagno, *The Transformation of Old Age Security: Class and Politics in the American Welfare State* (Chicago: University of Chicago Press, 1988), 132–142.

4. *Chicago Defender,* 22 April 1939, 1.

5. Winifred Bell, *Aid to Dependent Children* (New York: Columbia University Press, 1965), 60–75. As with the political logic of OAI (see Chapter 3), this argument contradicts Jerry Cates's administrative leadership view. Jerry R. Cates, *Insuring Inequality: Administrative Leadership in Social Security, 1935–1954* (Ann Arbor: University of Michigan Press, 1983).

6. Bell, *Aid to Dependent Children,* 40–56.

7. See Allen Frances Kifer, "The Negro Under the New Deal, 1933–1941" (Ph.D. diss., University of Wisconsin, 1961); Raymond Wolters, *Negroes and the Great Depression: The Problem of Economic Recovery* (Westport, Conn.: Greenwood Publishing Co., 1973); Nancy J. Weiss, *Farewell to the Party of Lincoln: Black Politics in the Age of FDR* (Princeton: Princeton University Press, 1983).

8. U.S. Federal Security Agency, Social Security Board, *Characteristics of State Plans for Aid to Dependent Children,* Publication No. 18 (Washington, D.C.: Government Printing Office, 1940); Samuel M. Meyers and Jennie McIntyre, *Welfare Policy and Its Consequences for the Recipient Population: A Study of the AFDC Program* (Washington, D.C.: U.S. Department of Health, Education, and Welfare, 1969), 11–16.

9. Theodore J. Lowi, "American Business, Public Policy, Case-Studies, and Political Theory," *World Politics* 16 (1964): 677–715; Paul E. Peterson, *City Limits* (Chicago: University of Chicago Press, 1981), 43–44.

10. James Q. Wilson, *Bureaucracy: What Government Agencies Do and Why They Do It* (New York: Basic Books, 1989).

11. Bell, *Aid to Dependent Children*, 37–38; Walter I. Trattner, *From Poor Law to Welfare State: A History of Social Welfare in America*, 4th ed. (New York: Free Press, 1989), 279.

12. Wilson, *Bureaucracy*, 161; Tana Pesso, "Local Welfare Offices: Managing the Intake Process," *Public Policy* 26 (1978): 305–330.

13. Wilson, *Bureaucracy*, 245.

14. On budget processes, see Aaron Wildavsky, *The Politics of the Budgetary Process*, 4th ed. (Boston: Little, Brown, 1984); Aaron Wildavsky, *Budgeting: A Comparative Theory of Budgetary Processes*, 2d, rev. ed. (New Brunswick, N.J.: Transaction Books, 1986), esp. 219–244 on budgeting in the states. Allen Schick charts the increasing complexity and fragmentation of state budget processes in *Budget Innovation in the States* (Washington, D.C.: Brookings Institution, 1971).

15. Michael B. Katz, *The Undeserving Poor: From the War on Poverty to the War on Welfare* (New York: Pantheon, 1989); Fred Block, Richard A. Cloward, Barbara Ehrenreich, and Frances Fox Piven, *The Mean Season: The Attack on the Welfare State* (New York: Pantheon, 1987).

16. U.S. Social Security Board, *Social Security in America: The Factual Background of the Social Security Act as Summarized from Staff Reports to the Committee on Economic Security*, Social Security Board Publication No. 20 (Washington, D.C.: Government Printing Office, 1937), 233–239, 269–273.

17. Senate Committee on Appropriations, *District of Columbia Appropriations for 1963*, 87th Cong., 2d sess., 1420–1421. Officials reported that in the D.C. investigation they found some men hiding in bathrooms. See also Nicholas Lemann's depiction of agency "visits" in Chicago in *The Promised Land: The Great Black Migration and How It Changed America* (New York: Alfred A. Knopf, 1991). On the social control functions of welfare, see Frances Fox Piven and Richard A. Cloward, *Regulating the Poor: The Functions of Public Welfare* (New York: Pantheon, 1971).

18. This hypothesis assumes that the standard for determining ADC payments is based on a race-neutral standard for benefit levels. It is also plausible that there were different standards for determining benefit levels for black and white families, based on replacing some amount of "normal" income. This sort of standard would produce lower benefits for African-Americans but is in itself systematically discriminatory. See Arthur F. Raper, *Preface to Peasantry: A Tale of Two Black Belt Counties* (Chapel Hill: University of North Carolina Press, 1936), 258–259.

19. Sterner, *The Negro's Share*, 281–284.

20. Bell, *Aid to Dependent Children*.

21. Piven and Cloward, *Regulating the Poor*, 133–135.

22. Sterner, *The Negro's Share*, 277. See also Raper, *Preface to Peasantry*, 258.

23. Jacob Fisher, "The Comparability of Public Assistance Payments and Social Insurance Benefits," *Social Security Bulletin* 7 (December 1944): 9.

24. "Expose 'Tricks' in Old Age Pension Law," *Chicago Defender,* 22 April 1939, 1, 28; "Tell of Old Age Pension Abuses," *Chicago Defender,* 29 April 1939, 3; "Probe Administration of Old Age Assistance Act," *Chicago Defender,* 29 May 1939.

25. Gunnar Myrdal, *An American Dilemma: The Negro Problem and Modern Democracy* (New York: Harper & Brothers, 1944), 353–356; Sterner, *The Negro's Share,* 63–66.

26. Elizabeth Alling and Agnes Leisy, "Aid to Dependent Children in a Postwar Year," *Social Security Bulletin* 13 (August 1950): 5. The states were Arizona, Arkansas, Illinois, Kansas, Louisiana, Massachusetts, Missouri, Montana, Nebraska, North Carolina, Oklahoma, South Dakota, Utah, West Virginia, Wisconsin, and the District of Columbia. See "Characteristics and Incomes of Families Assisted by Aid to Dependent Children," *Social Security Bulletin* 9 (July 1946): 14–21.

27. Dorothy K. Newman, Nancy J. Amidei, Barbara L. Carter, Dawn Day, William J. Kruvant, and Jack S. Russell, *Protest, Politics, and Prosperity: Black Americans and White Institutions, 1940–1975* (New York: Pantheon, 1978), 260.

28. Newman et al., *Protest, Politics, and Prosperity,* 268.

29. Piven and Cloward, *Regulating the Poor,* 135–137, 364–365.

30. Meyers and McIntyre, *Welfare Policy and Its Consequences,* 31–34.

31. See V. O. Key Jr., *Southern Politics in State and Nation* (New York: Alfred A. Knopf, 1949).

32. Paul E. Peterson and Mark Rom, "American Federalism, Welfare Policy, and Residential Choice," *American Political Science Review* 83 (1989): 711–728.

33. Michael Harrington, *The Other America: Poverty in the United States* (New York: Macmillan, 1963), 110.

34. Social Security Board, *Characteristics of State Plans for Aid to Dependent Children.*

35. Martha Derthick, *The Influence of Federal Grants: Public Assistance in Massachusetts* (Cambridge: Harvard University Press, 1970); Martha Derthick, "Intercity Differences in Administration of the Public Assistance Programs: The Case of Massachusetts," in *City Politics and Public Policy,* ed. James Q. Wilson (New York: John Wiley & Sons, 1968), 244–245. For an alternative view of the use of units smaller than states for studying welfare policy, see Kirsten A. Grønbjerg, *Mass Society and the Extension of Welfare, 1960–1970* (Chicago: University of Chicago Press, 1977), 38–39. Grønbjerg correctly states that federal law restricts formal variation among sub-state units, but she underestimates the potential impact of the differential application of uniform laws and administrative procedures. See Bill Scheuerman, "The Rule

of Law and the Welfare State: Toward a New Synthesis," *Politics and Society* 22 (1994): 195–213.

36. The classic discussion is W. S. Robinson, "Ecological Correlation and the Behavior of Individuals," *American Sociological Review* 15 (1950): 351–357. See also Hubert M. Blalock Jr., *Causal Inferences in Nonexperimental Design* (Chapel Hill: University of North Carolina Press, 1964); and J. Morgan Kousser, "A Generation of Ecological Regression: A Survey and Synthesis" (Paper presented to the annual meeting of the Social Science History Association, Baltimore, 1993).

37. Key, *Southern Politics.*

38. Piven and Cloward, *Regulating the Poor;* Derthick, "Intercity Differences," 248. Derthick identifies a third type of administrative activity that might differ from county to county, intangible treatment of clients in ways that express certain attitudes. Though this kind of activity does not have a direct effect on levels of coverage or benefits, it might indirectly alter coverage levels by discouraging or encouraging certain groups of potential applicants.

39. Evelyn Z. Brodkin, *The False Promise of Administrative Reform: Implementing Quality Control in Welfare* (Philadelphia: Temple University Press, 1986); Michael Lipsky, *Street-Level Bureaucracy: Dilemmas of the Individual in Public Services* (New York: Russell Sage Foundation, 1980).

40. Other studies of state policymaking have used the same variable. See, for example, Ira Sharkansky and Richard I. Hofferbert, "Dimensions of State Politics, Economics, and Public Policy," *American Political Science Review* 63 (1969): 867–879. The poverty thresholds in this analysis are $2000 in 1950 and $3000 in 1960. These are not quite equivalent in real dollars. The 1950 figure corresponds approximately to the federal poverty level for a family of three, whereas the 1960 figure corresponds to the poverty level for a family of four. Income distribution data at the county level are not available for 1940.

41. Myrdal, *American Dilemma,* 355; Christopher Howard, "Sowing the Seeds of 'Welfare': The Transformation of Mothers' Pensions, 1900–1940," *Journal of Policy History* 4 (1992): 201. Theda Skocpol makes this point with regard to mothers' pensions in "African Americans in U.S. Social Policy," in *Classifying by Race,* ed. Paul E. Peterson (Princeton: Princeton University Press, 1995).

42. Derthick treats black population as a "socioeconomic" variable rather than treating race as a distinct causal factor, presumably on the assumption that towns with high black populations have a higher level of "need" for public assistance. But this strategy does not consider the possibility that racial groups with the same level of "need" receive different treatment at the hands of welfare administrators. If Derthick is right, race should not be significant in a model that controls for other socioeconomic factors. Derthick, "Intercity Differences," 248.

43. Black population and median family income are, not surprisingly, negatively correlated, but weakly enough so that there is no multicollinearity problem. The correlation coefficients are -0.56 in 1950 and -0.46 in 1960.

44. U.S. Bureau of the Census, *1960 Census of Population* (Washington, D.C.: Government Printing Office, 1964), vol. 1., pt. 1, 463.

45. Alling and Leisy, "Aid to Dependent Children in a Postwar Year," 8–9.

46. Paul E. Peterson and Mark C. Rom, *Welfare Magnets: A New Case for a National Standard* (Washington, D.C.: Brookings Institution, 1990).

47. The data are from state documents available in Littauer Library, Harvard University; Firestone Library, Princeton University; and Lehman Library, Columbia University. There are also some states for which documents were available that did not report the appropriate data at the county level. The Appendix summarizes the states and years that appear in the sample and provides detailed bibliographic information and explanatory notes on the data. For a statistical test that shows that there is no selection bias in the data, see Robert C. Lieberman and John S. Lapinski, "American Federalism, Race, and the Administration of Welfare" (manuscript, Columbia University, 1997).

48. The Appendix contains the details of the analysis for this and all other figures in this section.

49. Martin Isaac Gilens, "Racial Attitudes and Opposition to the American Welfare State" (Ph.D. diss., University of California, Berkeley, 1991).

50. Myrdal, *American Dilemma,* 353.

51. Elijah Anderson, *Streetwise: Race, Class, and Change in an Urban Community* (Chicago: University of Chicago Press, 1990), 59; Greenleigh Associates, "ADC Facts, Fallacies, Figures," in Senate Committee on Finance, *Public Assistance Act of 1962,* 87th Cong., 2d sess., 1962, 296. See also Linda Gordon, "Black and White Visions of Welfare: Women's Welfare Activism, 1890–1945," *Journal of American History* 78 (1991): 559–590.

52. Robert Moffitt, "An Economic Model of Welfare Stigma," *American Economic Review* 73 (1983): 1023–1035.

53. Steven P. Erie, *Rainbow's End: Irish-Americans and the Dilemmas of Machine Politics, 1840–1985* (Berkeley: University of California Press, 1988), 165–170. See also Ira Katznelson, *Black Men, White Cities: Race, Politics, and Migration in the United States, 1900–30, and Britain, 1948–68* (Chicago: University of Chicago Press, 1976); and Ralph J. Bunche, *The Political Status of the Negro in the Age of FDR,* ed. Dewey W. Grantham (Chicago: University of Chicago Press, 1973).

54. In the same campaign, Daley appealed to the white vote by spreading false, race-baiting rumors about his Democratic primary opponent, Robert E. Merriam. Merriam's second wife, one rumor had it, was part black. Fraudulent leaflets were distributed in white neighborhoods suggesting that Merriam would end red-lining and other practices that kept neighborhoods racially segregated. Daley's appeal to the black vote was clearly not the result of advanced notions of racial liberalism. Richard J. Daley for Mayor cam-

paign leaflet, Robert E. Merriam Papers, Special Collections, Regenstein Library, University of Chicago, Box 44, Folder 4; Mike Royko, *Boss: Richard J. Daley of Chicago* (New York: E. P. Dutton, 1971), 56–57, 89–91. I am grateful to Frank Valadez for bringing the Daley campaign cartoon to my attention.

55. On welfare and the white middle class, see Peterson and Rom, "American Federalism"; and Thomas Byrne Edsall with Mary D. Edsall, *Chain Reaction: The Impact of Race, Rights, and Taxes on American Politics* (New York: W. W. Norton, 1991).

56. The ADC data are from Senate Committee on Appropriations, *District of Columbia Appropriations For 1963*, 2484. The cities are: Atlanta, Baltimore, Boston, Chicago, Cleveland, Dallas, Denver, Houston, Los Angeles, Milwaukee, Minneapolis, New Orleans, New York, Philadelphia, Pittsburgh, St. Louis, San Antonio, San Francisco, Seattle, and Washington, D.C. In most cases, ADC administration was at the county level, so all data are for the appropriate county except for Baltimore, New York, St. Louis, and Washington, D.C.

57. David R. Mayhew, *Placing Parties in American Politics: Organization, Electoral Settings, and Government Activity in the Twentieth Century* (Princeton: Princeton University Press, 1986). Mayhew assigns each state a TPO score on a scale of one (little organization) to five (dense and influential organization).

58. Mayhew, *Placing Parties*, 23.

59. See Paul E. Peterson, *The Politics of School Reform, 1870–1940* (Chicago: University of Chicago Press, 1985), 44–51.

60. For an excellent account of the great postwar migration and the experiences of black migrants to Northern cities see Lemann, *The Promised Land*.

61. Erie, *Rainbow's End*, 254–258; Peterson, *City Limits*, 156–162; Peterson, *Politics of School Reform*, 44–51.

62. Key, *Southern Politics*.

63. Derthick, *Influence of Federal Grants*; Cates, *Insuring Inequality*.

64. R. Shep Melnick, *Between the Lines: Interpreting Welfare Rights* (Washington, D.C.: Brookings Institution, 1994).

65. Michael Lipsky, "Protest as a Resource," *American Political Science Review* 62 (1968): 1144–1158; Frances Fox Piven and Richard A. Cloward, *Poor People's Movements: Why They Succeed, How They Fail* (New York: Pantheon, 1977).

66. Skocpol, "African Americans in U.S. Social Policy"; Theda Skocpol, *Protecting Soldiers and Mothers: The Political Origins of Social Policy in the United States* (Cambridge: Harvard University Press, 1992).

67. Skocpol, "African Americans in U.S. Social Policy."

68. Arthur J. Altmeyer, *The Formative Years of Social Security* (Madison: University of Wisconsin Press, 1966), 111–113.

69. *Congressional Record*, 79th Cong., 2d sess., 1946, 92, pt. 8: 10758; Alt-

meyer, *Formative Years*, 155–157; *Congressional Quarterly Almanac* 2 (1946): 460–464.

70. See Bell, *Aid to Dependent Children*, 53–54.

71. Cates, *Insuring Inequality*, 104–135; Gilbert Y. Steiner, *The State of Welfare* (Washington, D.C.: Brookings Institution, 1971), 77–80; Blanche D. Coll, *Safety Net: Welfare and Social Security, 1929–1979* (New Brunswick, N.J.: Rutgers University Press, 1995), 91–92, 98–99, 157.

72. Quoted in Gilbert Y. Steiner, *Social Insecurity: The Politics of Welfare* (Chicago: Rand McNally, 1966), 116.

73. Maurine McKeany, *The Absent Father and Public Policy in the Program of Aid to Dependent Children* (Berkeley: University of California Press, 1960), 5.

74. Joel F. Handler and Ellen Jane Hollingsworth, *The "Deserving Poor": A Study of Welfare Administration* (Chicago: Markham Publishing Co., 1971), 80–82.

75. John Kenneth Galbraith, *The Affluent Society* (Boston: Houghton Mifflin, 1958); Trattner, *Poor Law to Welfare State*, 280–281.

76. Fred I. Greenstein, *The Hidden-Hand Presidency: Eisenhower as Leader* (New York: Basic Books, 1982), 49–51, 115.

77. Edward G. Carmines and James A. Stimson, *Issue Evolution: Race and the Transformation of American Politics* (Princeton: Princeton University Press, 1988), 35–37, 46–47.

78. Edward D. Berkowitz and Kim McQuaid, *Creating the Welfare State: The Political Economy of Twentieth-Century Reform*, rev. ed. (Lawrence: University Press of Kansas, 1992), 179–182; Steiner, *State of Welfare*, 78–79.

79. Steiner, *Social Insecurity*, 28.

80. Bell, *Aid to Dependent Children*. Many states simply carried "suitable home" clauses over from their mothers' pensions laws.

81. Bell, *Aid to Dependent Children*; Piven and Cloward, *Regulating the Poor*, 139–140.

82. Bell, *Aid to Dependent Children*, 137–151; "Suffer Little Children," *Nation* 191 (24 September 1960): 171.

83. "Louisiana Children Aided," *New York Times*, 27 October 1960, 37.

84. Quoted in Bell, *Aid to Dependent Children*, 147.

85. Quoted in Coll, *Safety Net*, 209.

86. Harrington, *The Other America*; Dwight Macdonald, "The Invisible Poor," *The New Yorker*, 19 January 1963, 82–132; Trattner, *Poor Law to Welfare State*, 288–289; James T. Patterson, *America's Struggle Against Poverty, 1900–1980* (Cambridge: Harvard University Press, 1981), 94–95, 99–100.

87. Thomas J. Sugrue, "Crabgrass-Roots Politics: Race, Rights, and the Reaction Against Liberalism in the Urban North, 1940–1964," *Journal of American History* 82 (1995): 568.

88. On the Northern white "backlash," see Doug McAdam, *Political Process and the Development of Black Insurgency, 1930–1970* (Chicago: University of Chicago Press, 1982), 181–229; Gary Orfield, "Race and the Liberal Agenda:

The Loss of the Integrationist Dream, 1965–1974," in *The Politics of Social Policy in the United States,* ed. Margaret Weir, Ann Shola Orloff, and Theda Skocpol (Princeton: Princeton University Press, 1988); and Edsall and Edsall, *Chain Reaction.*

89. Joseph P. Ritz, *The Despised Poor: Newburgh's War on Welfare* (Boston: Beacon Press, 1966).

90. Jacqueline Jones, *The Dispossessed: America's Underclasses From the Civil War to the Present* (New York: Basic Books, 1992).

91. Ritz, *Despised Poor,* 94.

92. Ritz, *Despised Poor.* On the paranoid style, see Richard Hofstadter, *The Paranoid Style in American Politics and Other Essays* (New York: Alfred A. Knopf, 1965).

93. Compare, for example, articles in the *New York Times Magazine,* which took the former view, and the *Saturday Evening Post,* the tribune of middlebrow conservatism, which declared that "surely a community should have some defense against Bankruptcy by Bastardy." A. H. Raskin, "Newburgh's Lessons for the Nation," *New York Times Magazine,* 17 December 1961; "Now It's Illegal to Curb Welfare Abuses," editorial, *Saturday Evening Post,* 5 August 1961, 8.

94. New Jersey Legislature, Welfare Investigating Committee, *Legislative Report on the Aid to Dependent Children Program in New Jersey* (Trenton, 1963), 1–2.

95. Until the late 1950s, merely owning a television was sufficient reason to render a family ineligible for ADC. As for telephones, the investigators explained that certain models and colors cost more to install and rent (remember, the phone company owned all the phones). Finally, although the investigators recognized that a liquor store was often the only place in the neighborhood that would cash a recipient's check and that many liquor stores often sold other items as well, they still followed up by going to the liquor stores that the survey subjects named to inquire about their purchasing habits. Senate Committee on Appropriations, *District of Columbia Appropriations For 1963,* 1423–1435.

96. Senate Committee on Appropriations, *District of Columbia Appropriations For 1963,* 1026–1050, 1457–1458.

97. Secretary of HEW Abraham Ribicoff and Assistant Secretary of HEW for Legislation Wilbur Cohen told the Senate Finance Committee in 1962 that the D.C. study's findings were atypical. Senate Committee on Finance, *Public Assistance Act of 1962,* 154.

98. Skocpol, *Protecting Soldiers and Mothers.*

99. Piven and Cloward, *Regulating the Poor,* 192.

100. Greenleigh Associates, "ADC Facts, Fallacies, Future," in Senate Committee on Finance, *Public Assistance Act,* 292.

101. House Committee on Ways and Means, *Public Welfare Amendments of 1962,* 87th Cong., 2d sess., 1962, 272, 133; Steiner, *State of Welfare,* 37–39.

102. David Ward Howe, column, Chicago *Defender,* 1 July 1939.

103. House Committee on Ways and Means, *Public Welfare Amendments,* 289. A few Northern states had reciprocal agreements waiving residency requirements for migrants between specific states, but no state had such an agreement with any Southern state.

104. Greenleigh Associates, "ADC Facts, Fallacies, Future," 295. The study surveyed a random sample of 1010 ADC recipients in Cook County, Illinois (Chicago). Ninety percent of the sample was nonwhite.

105. The Supreme Court ruled in 1969 that residency requirements for public assistance were unconstitutional in *Shapiro* v. *Thompson,* 394 US 618 (1969). See Peterson and Rom, *Welfare Magnets;* Martha F. Davis, *Brutal Need: Lawyers and the Welfare Rights Movement* (New Haven: Yale University Press, 1993).

106. House Committee on Ways and Means, *Public Welfare Amendments of 1962,* 87th Cong., 2d sess., 1962, H. Rept. 1414, 85–86.

107. See Laura Kramer Gordon, "The Intake Process: Application and Decision in a Public Welfare Bureaucracy" (Ph.D. diss., State University of New York at Stony Brook, 1972), 9–10.

108. Senate Committee on Finance, *Public Assistance Act,* 424, 230–231.

109. Senate Committee on Finance, *Public Assistance Act,* 596, 267.

110. James L. Sundquist, *Politics and Policy: The Eisenhower, Kennedy, and Johnson Years* (Washington, D.C.: Brookings Institution, 1968), 125–134.

111. Steiner, *State of Welfare,* 38; Bell, *Aid to Dependent Children,* 170–173.

112. Charles Murray, *Losing Ground: American Social Policy, 1950–1980* (New York: Basic Books, 1984).

113. William Julius Wilson, *The Truly Disadvantaged: The Inner City, the Underclass, and Public Policy* (Chicago: University of Chicago Press, 1987); Edsall and Edsall, *Chain Reaction;* Jill Quadagno, *The Color of Welfare: How Racism Undermined the War on Poverty* (New York: Oxford University Press, 1994).

114. *Social Security Bulletin,* Annual Statistical Supplement, 1967, 124.

115. Piven and Cloward, *Regulating the Poor,* 354–365.

116. On the assembly and adoption of the Economic Opportunity Act, see Sundquist, *Politics and Policy,* 134–149; Daniel P. Moynihan, *Maximum Feasible Misunderstanding: Community Action in the War on Poverty* (New York: Free Press, 1969).

117. James A. Morone, *The Democratic Wish: Popular Participation and the Limits of American Government* (New York: Basic Books, 1990), 218–252; J. David Greenstone and Paul E. Peterson, *Race and Authority in Urban Politics: Community Participation and the War on Poverty* (New York: Russell Sage Foundation, 1973).

118. Economic historians Lee Alston and Joseph Ferrie argue that Southerners retained the power to block welfare legislation in 1964 but no longer had the incentive to do so. But their analysis ignores several important facts. First, by

their own account, Southern Democrats were less powerful on the House Education and Labor and Senate Labor Committees, which wrote the Economic Opportunity Act, than on the Ways and Means and Finance Committees, which controlled Social Security legislation. Second, as they also acknowledge, the act was amended in committee to increase the parochialism of its institutional structure. Third, they imply that the legislative pattern of 1964 differs from the pattern of 1935. But in both cases, a Democratic president initiated a social program with national aspirations, only to see it compromised by congressional committees before its overwhelming adoption. In fact, the vote for the Social Security Act was considerably more lopsided, both among Southerners and Congress at large, than the vote for the Economic Opportunity Act. "If paternalism was still valuable to the South," Alston and Ferrie write, "Southern legislators would not have *allowed* welfare programs aimed at alleviating poverty in Northern urban areas" (emphasis added). But Southerners "allowed" the Social Security Act to pass. They also "allowed" the Civil Rights Acts of 1957 and 1964 to pass. Alston and Ferrie vastly overstate Southern power in Congress and misread the legislative process. The question is not what legislation Southerners will "allow." If they had had unlimited blocking power, the American welfare state would look quite different than it does. As Democratic leaders, Southerners could not regularly block major legislative initiatives of presidents of their own party. Rather, they used their strategic position in Congress and the Democratic Party to amend legislation, in 1964 as in 1935, to protect the racial structure of Southern society as far as possible. But in 1964, millions of African-Americans had moved North, where they formed an essential part of the Democratic coalition. Not surprisingly, the Northern wing of the party was more able and more inclined to challenge Southerners and restrict their power. Lee J. Alston and Joseph P. Ferrie, "Paternalism in Agricultural Labor Contracts in the U.S. South: Implications for the Growth of the Welfare State," *American Economic Review* 83 (1993): 852–876. The quotation is on p. 869.

119. *Congressional Record,* 88th Cong., 2d sess., 1964, 110, pt. 14: 18198–18199. When Smith's office announced in August of 1957 that a barn on his Virginia farm had burned down and that he had gone there to see to the matter, Speaker Sam Rayburn is reported to have said, "I knew Howard Smith would do most anything to block a civil rights bill, but I never suspected he would resort to arson." *New York Times,* 21 August 1957, 16. See also Bruce J. Dierenfield, *Keeper of the Rules: Congressman Howard W. Smith of Virginia* (Charlottesville: University Press of Virginia, 1987), 158–159.

120. Carmines and Stimson, *Issue Evolution;* House Committee on Education and Labor, Subcommittee on the War on Poverty Program, *Economic Opportunity Act of 1964,* 88th Cong., 2d sess., 1964, 322; Sundquist, *Politics and Policy,* 147.

121. *Congressional Quarterly Almanac* 21 (1965), 406.

122. Morone, *The Democratic Wish,* 233–242.
123. Greenstone and Peterson, *Race and Authority in Urban Politics.*
124. Steiner, *State of Welfare,* 44–46.
125. *Congressional Record,* 90th Cong., 2d sess., 1967, 113, pt. 17: 22783, 23058–23059.
126. Senate Committee on Finance, *Social Security Amendments of 1967,* 90th Cong., 1st sess., 1967, 1132.
127. Senate Committee on Finance, *Social Security Amendments,* 1260–1261, 1263.
128. On the NWRO, see Piven and Cloward, *Poor People's Movements;* Guida West, *The National Welfare Rights Movement: The Social Protest of Poor Women* (New York: Praeger, 1981).
129. Eve Edstrom, "Irate Welfare Mothers Hold 'Wait-In'," *Washington Post,* 20 September 1967, 1; Eve Edstrom, "Protesting Welfare Mothers Rebuked," *Washington Post,* 21 September 1967, 2; Senate Committee on Finance, *Social Security Amendments,* 1537; *Congressional Quarterly Almanac* 23 (1967), 907; Robert Mann, *Legacy to Power: Senator Russell Long of Louisiana* (New York: Paragon House, 1992), 269.
130. *Congressional Record,* 90th Cong., 1st sess., 1967, 113, pt. 24: 33542.
131. Ironically, Joseph Tydings was the son of Senator Millard Tydings, one of the original group of conservative anti–New Deal Democratic senators in the 1930s. See Mann, *Legacy to Power,* 267–272.
132. Yarborough was defeated for reelection (by Lloyd Bentsen) in 1970 partly because of his racial liberalism. He was the only Southern senator to vote for the Civil Rights Act of 1964 and one of a handful to support the Civil Rights Act of 1957, the Voting Rights Act of 1965, and the open housing bill of 1968. Chandler Davidson, *Race and Class in Texas Politics* (Princeton: Princeton University Press, 1990), 27–29, 224, 237.
133. Kirsten Grønbjerg, David Street, and Gerald D. Suttles, *Poverty and Social Change* (Chicago: University of Chicago Press, 1978); David Street, George T. Martin Jr., and Laura Kramer Gordon, *The Welfare Industry: Functionaries and Recipients in Public Aid* (Beverly Hills, Calif.: Sage Publications, 1979).
134. Grønbjerg, *Mass Society,* 141–143; Gordon, "The Intake Process."
135. Derthick, *Influence of Federal Grants,* 22–23; Gordon, "The Intake Process," 56–57.
136. Street, Suttles, and Gordon, *The Welfare Industry,* 72–75.
137. Handler and Hollingsworth, *The "Deserving Poor,"* 80–82, 119, 143, 149.
138. Moynihan, *Maximum Feasible Misunderstanding;* Ira Katznelson, "Was the Great Society a Lost Opportunity?," in *The Rise and Fall of the New Deal Order, 1930–1980,* ed. Steve Fraser and Gary Gerstle (Princeton: Princeton University Press, 1989); Margaret Weir, *Politics and Jobs: The Boundaries of Employment Policy in the United States* (Princeton: Princeton University Press, 1992).

139. Thomas J. Sugrue, *The Origins of the Urban Crisis: Race and Inequality in Postwar Detroit* (Princeton: Princeton University Press, 1996).

5. Unemployment Insurance: Inclusion, Exclusion, and Stagnation

1. Margaret Weir, *Politics and Jobs: The Boundaries of Employment Policy in the United States* (Princeton: Princeton University Press, 1992).
2. Desmond King, *Actively Seeking Work?: The Politics of Unemployment and Welfare Policy in the United States and Great Britain* (Chicago: University of Chicago Press, 1995).
3. See Michael B. Katz, ed., *The "Underclass" Debate: Views from History* (Princeton: Princeton University Press, 1993); Margaret Weir, "The Politics of Racial Isolation in Europe and America," in *Classifying by Race,* ed. Paul E. Peterson (Princeton: Princeton University Press, 1995).
4. Forty percent were white and twenty-six percent were Latino. G. Joachim Elterich and Linda Graham, *Impact of Extension of Coverage to Agricultural Workers Under PL 94–566, Their Characteristics and Economic Welfare* (Washington, D.C.: Department of Labor, Employment and Training Administration, 1977), 22–23.
5. This paragraph describes the essential structure of UI benefit determination under all state laws. With relatively wide variation on the particulars, the basic structure is the same in all states. William Haber and Merrill G. Murray, *Unemployment Insurance in the American Economy: An Historical Review and Analysis* (Homewood, Ill.: Richard D. Irwin, 1966), 106–123. On the relationship between law and administration in the welfare state, see Bill Scheuerman, "The Rule of Law and the Welfare State: Toward a New Synthesis," *Politics and Society* 22 (1994): 195–213.
6. Harry Silverstone, "The Administration of Unemployment Compensation," *Yale Law Journal* 55 (1945): 207–208.
7. Walter Matscheck and Raymond C. Atkinson, *Problems and Procedures of Unemployment Compensation in the States,* Publication No. 65 (Chicago: Public Administration Service, 1939), 44.
8. Haber and Murray, *Unemployment Insurance,* 114–119.
9. Haber and Murray, *Unemployment Insurance,* 430.
10. Joseph M. Becker, *The Problem of Abuse in Unemployment Benefits: A Study in Limits* (New York: Columbia University Press, 1953), 95.
11. On the function of administrative rules and regulations in setting parameters for caseworker discretion, see David Street, George T. Martin Jr., and Laura Kramer Gordon, *The Welfare Industry: Functionaries and Recipients in Public Aid* (Beverly Hills, Calif.: Sage Publications, 1979), 71–74; and Martha Derthick, "Intercity Differences in Administration of the Public Assistance Program: The Case of Massachusetts," in *City Politics and Public Policy,* ed. James Q. Wilson (New York: John Wiley & Sons, 1968).

12. A. Kent MacDougall, "Unemployment Insurance: Give Away or Deserved Help?," reprinted from Passaic-Clifton (N.J.) *Herald News,* 1957, Industrial Relations Collection, Firestone Library, Princeton University.

13. T. H. Marshall, "Citizenship and Social Class," in *Class, Citizenship, and Social Development* (Garden City, N.Y.: Doubleday, 1964); Judith N. Shklar, *American Citizenship: The Quest for Inclusion* (Cambridge: Harvard University Press, 1991).

14. These were Alabama, Alaska, and New Jersey. Haber and Murray, *Unemployment Insurance,* 119; U.S. Department of Labor, Manpower Administration, Unemployment Insurance Service, *Comparison of State Unemployment Insurance Laws,* BES No. U-141 (Washington, D.C.: Government Printing Office, 1965).

15. Leonard P. Adams, *Public Attitudes Toward Unemployment Insurance: A Historical Account With Special Reference to Alleged Abuses* (Kalamazoo, Mich.: W. E. Upjohn Institute for Employment Research, 1971).

16. All but eleven state UI laws originally included experience rating, and by 1947 all states had adopted it in some form. Joseph M. Becker, *Experience Rating in Unemployment Insurance: An Experiment in Competitive Socialism* (Baltimore: Johns Hopkins University Press, 1972), 11–16.

17. Raymond Munts, "Policy Development in Unemployment Insurance," in *Federal Policies and Worker Status Since the Thirties,* ed. Joseph P. Goldberg, Eileen Ahern, William Haber, and Rudolph A. Oswald (Madison, Wis.: Industrial Relations Research Association, 1976), 78–80.

18. For a description of the "charge-back" method of merit rating, see Matscheck and Atkinson, *Problems and Procedures,* 62–66.

19. One early study in Wisconsin found that nearly three-fourths of disputed UI claims were decided in favor of employees, suggesting that employers were overzealous in challenging benefits, at least initially. Walter Matscheck and R. C. Atkinson, *The Administration of Unemployment Compensation Benefits in Wisconsin, July 1, 1936 to June 30, 1937,* Publication No. 58 (Chicago: Public Administration Service, 1937), 49, 80–81.

20. Becker, *Problem of Abuse,* 99–100, 171, 315; Matscheck and Atkinson, *Administration of Unemployment Compensation Benefits,* 15, 28–29; Richard A. Lester, "The Uses of Unemployment Insurance," in *The Princeton Symposium on the American System of Social Insurance: Its Philosophy, Impact, and Future Development,* ed. William G. Bowen, Frederick H. Harbison, Richard A. Lester, and Herman M. Somers (New York: McGraw-Hill, 1968), 165–171; R. Clyde White, *Administering Unemployment Compensation: A Comparison and Critique* (Chicago: University of Chicago Press, 1939), 266–310.

21. On the common law and American labor, see Karen Orren, *Belated Feudalism: Labor, the Law, and Liberal Development in the United States* (Cambridge: Cambridge University Press, 1991).

22. This was the Unemployment Compensation Interpretation Service. White, *Administering Unemployment Compensation*, 166.

23. Matscheck and Atkinson, *Problems and Procedures*, 5.

24. Haber and Murray, *Unemployment Insurance*, 106–23; Saul J. Blaustein, *Unemployment Insurance in the United States: The First Half Century* (Kalamazoo, Mich.: W. E. Upjohn Institute for Employment Research, 1993), 265–327.

25. Raymond C. Atkinson, *The Federal Role in Unemployment Compensation Administration* (Washington, D.C.: Social Science Research Council, Committee on Social Security, 1941), 42–53.

26. V. O. Key Jr., *The Administration of Federal Grants to States* (Chicago: Public Administration Service, 1937), 69–71.

27. Atkinson, *Federal Role*, 45–47; Haber and Murray, *Unemployment Insurance*, 402–403. See Terry M. Moe, "The New Economics of Organization," *American Journal of Political Science* 28 (1984): 739–777.

28. Francis E. Rourke, *Intergovernmental Relations in Employment Security* (Minneapolis: University of Minnesota Press, 1952), 2–14, 55–60; New Jersey Unemployment Insurance Task Force, *Final Report* (Trenton, 1975), 63–64; Murray Rubin, *Federal-State Relations in Unemployment Insurance: A Balance of Power* (Kalamazoo, Mich.: W. E. Upjohn Institute for Employment Research, 1983), 27–30. Robert P. Stoker nicely contrasts authority and exchange paradigms for the implementation of federal policy in *Reluctant Partners: Implementing Federal Policy* (Pittsburgh: University of Pittsburgh Press, 1991).

29. David G. Williams, *Cooperative Federalism in Employment Security: The Interstate Conference* (Ann Arbor, Mich.: Institute of Labor and Industrial Relations, 1974); Haber and Murray, *Unemployment Insurance*, 456–460.

30. An amusing tongue-in-cheek exchange at a hearing of the Senate Finance Committee in 1954 revealed the tension in the ICESA's role. The committee's chairman, Senator Eugene Millikin, questioned Bernard Teets, executive director of the Colorado Employment Security Commission:

> The Chairman. Would [the ICESA] be a lobbying organization by any stretch of the imagination?
> Mr. Teets By no stretch of the imagination. It is a working committee representing the States in those matters of interest coming before it.
> The Chairman. You wouldn't dream of telling Congress the conclusions you reached, would you?
> Mr. Teets Only upon request of the Senators representing the States.
> The Chairman. I am requesting that you tell us what you know about that.

> Senate Committee on Finance, *Employment Security Administrative Financing Act*, 83d Cong., 2d sess., 1954, 39.

31. Matscheck and Atkinson, *Administration of Unemployment Compensation Benefits,* 70; Atkinson, *Federal Role,* 83–84; Matscheck and Atkinson, *Problems and Procedures,* 5–6; White, *Administering Unemployment Compensation,* 61, 246–248.

32. Atkinson, *Federal Role,* 54–60; Raymond C. Atkinson, Louise C. Odencrantz, and Ben Deming, *Public Employment Service in the United States* (Chicago: Public Administration Service, 1938), 216–218.

33. Merrill G. Murray, "Unemployment Insurance: Risks Covered and Their Financing," in *In Aid of the Unemployed,* ed. Joseph M. Becker (Baltimore: Johns Hopkins University Press, 1965), 63–78.

34. Seasonal and cyclical variation posed particularly acute administrative problems in the early years of Unemployment Insurance. Matscheck and Atkinson, *Administration of Unemployment Compensation Benefits,* 29–31, 62–63.

35. Williams, *Cooperative Federalism,* 87, 101.

36. See Jerry R. Cates, *Insuring Inequality: Administrative Leadership in Social Security, 1935–54* (Ann Arbor: University of Michigan Press, 1983).

37. Matscheck and Atkinson, *Unemployment Compensation Administration,* 28–30, 53, 55–58.

38. King, *Actively Seeking Work?;* Atkinson, Odencrantz, and Deming, *Public Employment Service,* 115–116; Haber and Murray, *Unemployment Insurance,* 427–429.

39. Atkinson, Odencrantz, and Deming, *Public Employment Service,* 257; Leonard P. Adams, "The Public Employment Service," in *In Aid of the Unemployed,* ed. Becker, 203; Becker, *Problem of Abuse,* 284. See also Weir, *Politics and Jobs,* 10.

40. New York State Advisory Council on Employment and Unemployment Insurance, *Supplementary Report, 1960* (New York: New York State Department of Labor, 1960). Motley's long minority report follows a terse official statement.

41. Matscheck, *Administration of Unemployment Compensation Benefits,* 15; Matscheck, *Unemployment Compensation Administration,* 28–30, 53.

42. Recognizing this potential source of goodwill, employers in Wisconsin advocated unemployment insurance schemes that would permit them to pay benefits themselves. White, *Administering Unemployment Compensation,* 164–165; Roger Sherman Hoar, *Unemployment Insurance in Wisconsin* (South Milwaukee, Wis.: The Stuart Press, 1932), 63–84. Old-Age Insurance checks are, of course, also mailed from a remote office, depriving Social Security workers of the same kind of face-to-face opportunity to build goodwill. There is less tension in OAI's client relations, however, so OAI might suffer less from this missed opportunity. OAI benefits, moreover, are paid from a single source, the federal treasury, rather than from state funds.

43. Matscheck, *Unemployment Compensation Administration,* 32, 54.

44. Becker, *Problem of Abuse,* 181–182, 193.

45. Adams, *Public Attitudes Toward Unemployment Insurance*. The Gallup poll data appear on pp. 21–22.

46. See Robert S. Lynd, *Knowledge for What? The Place of Social Science in American Culture* (Princeton: Princeton University Press, 1939); Samuel P. Hays, *Conservation and the Gospel of Efficiency: The Progressive Conservation Movement, 1890–1920* (Cambridge: Harvard University Press, 1959); Brian Balogh, "Reorganizing the Organizational Synthesis: Federal-Professional Relations in Modern America," *Studies in American Political Development* 5 (1991): 119–172; Guy Alchon, *The Invisible Hand of Planning: Capitalism, Social Science, and the State in the 1920s* (Princeton: Princeton University Press, 1985).

47. Karl Pribram and Philip Booth, *Merit Rating and Unemployment Compensation* (Washington, D.C.: U.S. Social Security Board, Bureau of Research and Statistics, 1937), 40–54; Matscheck and Atkinson, *Problems and Procedures*, 67.

48. Weir, *Politics and Jobs*, 87. See also Figure 2.3. Official unemployment rate statistics are a conservative estimate of minority labor-market disadvantages because they do not count "discouraged workers," those who are not looking for a job and have left the labor market entirely. African-Americans and other minorities have historically been more likely to fall into this category.

49. Haber and Murray, *Unemployment Insurance*, 229.

50. Henry E. Felder, *A Statistical Evaluation of the Impact of Disqualification Provisions of State Unemployment Insurance Laws*, Unemployment Insurance Occasional Paper 79–81 (Washington, D.C.: U.S. Department of Labor, Employment and Training Administration, 1979), 70–72. The five states in the study are Arizona, Georgia, Kansas, Louisiana, and New York.

51. Haber and Murray, *Unemployment Insurance*, 111–113, 202–207.

52. Becker, *Problem of Abuse*, 366.

53. Henry E. Felder, *Characteristics of Unemployment Insurance Benefit Exhaustees: An Agenda for Research*, Prepared for the National Commission on Unemployment Compensation, April 1978, Industrial Relations Collection, Firestone Library, Princeton University.

54. William Haber, *How Much Does It Cost?*, A Report to the Michigan Employment Security Commission on Long-Range Unemployment Insurance Benefit Financing and Fund Solvency in Michigan (1951), 362.

55. U.S. Bureau of Labor Statistics, *Monthly Report on the Characteristics of the Insured Unemployed;* Christopher G. Gellner, "Regional Differences in Employment and Unemployment, 1957–1972," *Monthly Labor Review* 97 (March 1974): 20.

56. Truly comparable ecological analysis, based on small geographical units, would require similar county-level data. Because county governments did not play a comparable role in UI administration, very few data are available at the county level. Very rudimentary tests of a geographically based ecological

approach, based on scraps of data, provide little useful evidence, although they show no sign of egregious discrimination. Robert C. Lieberman, "Race and the Development of the American Welfare State from the New Deal to the Great Society" (Ph.D. diss., Harvard University, 1994), 382–386.

57. The presentation of these states in these years simply reflects the availability of data. However, it also allows for some rudimentary comparisons—between North and South and between industrial and agricultural states, for example—and for a sweep, however sketchy, across time. For more detailed analysis, see Lieberman, "Race and the Development of the American Welfare State," 392–400.

58. The American textile industry in 1940 was entering a long period of decline. Between 1940 and 1960, textile employment fell by nearly twenty percent. In the South, textile employment grew by fifteen percent, less than half the overall rate of growth of Southern employment. In the South, there was a strong color line in textile mills; black workers generally held only the lowest status and lowest paying jobs, and textile mills often hired white women over black workers. James G. Maddox with E. E. Liebhafsky, Vivian W. Henderson, and Herbert M. Hamlin, *The Advancing South: Manpower Prospects and Problems* (New York: Twentieth Century Fund, 1967), 56–57, 67–68; Donald Dewey, *Four Studies of Negro Employment in the Upper South* (Washington, D.C.: National Planning Association, 1953), 179–212.

59. V. O. Key Jr., *Southern Politics in State and Nation* (New York: Alfred A. Knopf, 1949).

60. West Virginia Department of Employment Security, Research and Statistics Division, *A Five-Year History of Covered Workers and Claimants, 1968–1972* (Charleston, 1974).

61. It is possible to focus on African-Americans here rather than the less precise category "nonwhite" not only because of the excellent West Virginia data but also because the 1970 Census provides data for the more finely detailed racial categories.

62. Racial breakdowns were quietly added to the Department of Labor's monthly published report of UI statistics beginning in December 1969. Presumably this addition reflects the generally increased concern in the federal government with racial matters, although the reports themselves say nothing about the change.

63. U.S. Department of Labor, Manpower Administration, *Unemployment Statistics* (Washington, D.C.: Government Printing Office, 1970–71, monthly), table 1.

64. U.S. Bureau of the Census, *1970 Census of Population* (Washington, D.C.: Government Printing Office, 1973), vol. 1, tables 172–173.

65. The 1970 Census reports employment data only for the category "Negro," making some estimation necessary to produce figures comparable to the Labor Department's "nonwhite" UI data. In order to estimate the nonwhite

percentage of the insured unemployed, I made the simple assumption that the unemployment rate for all nonwhites was the same as for African-Americans. For most states, almost all nonwhites were African-American, and so the assumption does little violence to the data. This estimating procedure, however, resulted in the elimination of Hawaii from the analysis. A majority of Hawaii's population was native Hawaiian, generating the nonsensical result that Hawaii's insured unemployed population was over 100 percent nonwhite.

66. For the data used to generate Figures 5.2 and 5.3, see Lieberman, "Race and the Development of the American Welfare State," tables 6.7 and 6.8.

67. Felder, *Statistical Evaluation,* 52–53; South Carolina Employment Security Commission, Research and Statistics Section, *A Study of the Characteristics of Unemployment Insurance Claimants in the Charleston, Columbia, and Greenville Local Office Areas* (Columbia, 1970).

68. Felder, *Statistical Evaluation,* 107–108.

69. Unsigned letter to NAACP, 18 August 1946, NAACP Papers, part 9, series C, Library of Congress, Manuscripts Division (microfilm, reel 8).

70. "Memorandum on Discriminations Under the Federal Social Security Act," 22 October 1937, NAACP Papers, part 10, reel 19.

71. Burton R. Morley, *Characteristics of the Labor Market in Alabama Related to the Administration of Unemployment Compensation* (Tuscaloosa: Bureau of Business Research, University of Alabama, 1937), 4; California Department of Employment, *A Sourcebook on Unemployment Insurance in California* (Sacramento, 1953), 48–49.

72. Walter H. Franke, "The Long-Term Unemployed," in *In Aid of the Unemployed,* ed. Becker, 48–51.

73. The general finding of benefit adequacy studies has been that UI benefits are sufficient to sustain single earners but not families. However, a recent econometric study argues that UI benefits are high enough that recipients are indifferent between their unemployed and pre-unemployment situations. Edward J. Harpham, "Federalism, Keynesianism, and the Transformation of the Unemployment Insurance System in the United States," in *Nationalizing Social Security in Europe and America,* ed. Douglas E. Ashford and E. W. Kelley (Greenwich, Conn.: JAI Press, 1986), 160–161; David Kuechun Shim, "The Impact of Interstate Economic Competition and Internal Politics on Unemployment Insurance Benefits: A Quantitative Analysis" (Senior Honors Thesis, Harvard College, 1991), 2–10; Blaustein, *Unemployment Insurance in the United States,* 291–299; Joseph M. Becker, *The Adequacy of the Benefit Amount in Unemployment Insurance* (Kalamazoo, Mich.: W. E. Upjohn Institute for Employment Research, 1961); U.S. Department of Labor, Bureau of Employment Security, *Unemployment Insurance and the Family Finance of the Unemployed: An Analysis of Six Benefit Adequacy Studies, 1954–1958,* BES No. U-203 (Washington, D.C.: Government Printing

Office, 1961); Christopher O'Leary, *An Econometric Analysis of Unemployment Benefit Adequacy* (Kalamazoo, Mich.: W. E. Upjohn Institute for Employment Research, 1990).

74. Arthur J. Altmeyer, *The Formative Years of Social Security* (Madison: University of Wisconsin Press, 1966), 132–136, 152–155, 61–62, 79, 93.

75. Orren, *Belated Feudalism.*

76. This was the Gearhart resolution (after its sponsor, Representative Bertrand W. Gearhart of California), which was adopted by a Republican-controlled Congress to overturn a series of court decisions that had expanded the definition of "employee" to include salesmen, independent contractors, and other commission-based workers in both UI and OAI coverage. The amendment eliminated 625,000 workers from coverage under these two programs. *Congressional Quarterly Almanac* 4 (1948): 143–144.

77. Joseph H. Ball, "The Implementation of Federal Manpower Policy, 1961–1971: A Study in Bureaucratic Competition and Intergovernmental Relations" (Ph.D. diss., Columbia University, 1972).

78. See Paul E. Peterson, *City Limits* (Chicago: University of Chicago Press, 1981); Albert O. Hirschman, *Exit, Voice, and Loyalty: Responses to Decline in Firms, Organizations, and States* (Cambridge: Harvard University Press, 1970).

79. Hawaii and Puerto Rico covered workers in sugar cultivation; Minnesota and the District of Columbia (which has no agriculture) covered some farm workers. In California, coverage of farm workers was to begin in 1976, just before the federal extension of coverage. Domestic workers were covered only in Arkansas, New York, and Hawaii, which is an anomaly in many policy areas because its geographical isolation all but eliminates the pressure of interstate competition. Approximately 350,000 farm workers out of 1.1 million and 26,000 domestic workers out of 1.4 million were covered under state laws before federal coverage was adopted in 1976. House Committee on Ways and Means, *Unemployment Compensation Amendments of 1975,* 94th Cong., 1st sess., 1975, H. Rept. 755, 2; Blaustein, *Unemployment Insurance,* 275–277; *Congressional Quarterly Weekly Report* 34 (1976): 2948–2949; White, *Administering Unemployment Compensation,* 84.

80. U.S. Bureau of Employment Security, *Comparison of State Unemployment Laws,* various years; U.S. Bureau of Employment Security, *State Unemployment Insurance Statutory Provisions, 1960;* and U.S. Bureau of Employment Security, *Unemployment Insurance: State Laws and Experience* (Washington, D.C.: Department of Labor, 1968); Blaustein, *Unemployment Insurance in the United States,* 278–282, 302–306.

81. U.S. Bureau of Employment Security, *Comparison of State Unemployment Laws,* various years; U.S. Bureau of Employment Security, *State Unemployment Insurance Statutory Provisions, 1960;* and U.S. Bureau of Employment Security, *Unemployment Insurance: State Laws and Experience* (Washington,

D.C.: Department of Labor, 1968; Blaustein, *Unemployment Insurance in the United States*, 282–291.

82. See King, *Actively Seeking Work?*.

83. U.S. Bureau of Employment Security, *Comparison of State Unemployment Insurance Laws*, various years. For African-American migration statistics, see William Edward Vickery, "The Economics of Negro Migration, 1900–1960" (Ph.D. diss., University of Chicago, 1969).

84. See Thomas J. Sugrue, *The Origins of the Urban Crisis: Race and Inequality in Postwar Detroit* (Princeton: Princeton University Press, 1996).

85. *Congressional Quarterly Weekly Report* 17 (1959): 527, 626, 678, 701.

86. Munts, "Policy Development," 96–98; Shim, "The Impact of Interstate Economic Competition," 3; Paul E. Peterson and Mark C. Rom, *Welfare Magnets: A New Case for a National Standard* (Washington, D.C.: Brookings Institution, 1990), 8.

87. Haber and Murray, *Unemployment Insurance*.

88. Dona Cooper Hamilton and Charles V. Hamilton, *The Dual Agenda: Race and Social Welfare Policies of Civil Rights Organizations* (New York: Columbia University Press, 1997).

89. Robert G. McCloskey, *The American Supreme Court* (Chicago: University of Chicago Press, 1960).

90. House Committee on Ways and Means, *Unemployment Insurance*, 83d Cong., 2d sess., 1954, 124–127.

91. U.S. National Resources Planning Board, Committee on Long-Range Work and Relief Policies, *Security, Work, and Relief Policies* (Washington, D.C.: Government Printing Office, 1942), 536–537; Ira Katznelson and Bruce Pietrykowski, "Rebuilding the American State: Evidence From the 1940s," *Studies in American Political Development* 5 (1991): 301–339; Edwin Amenta and Theda Skocpol, "Redefining the New Deal: World War II and the Development of Social Provision in the United States," in *The Politics of Social Policy in the United States*, ed. Margaret Weir, Ann Shola Orloff, and Theda Skocpol (Princeton: Princeton University Press, 1988); Edwin E. Witte, *The Development of the Social Security Act* (Madison: University of Wisconsin Press, 1962), 115–126.

92. Haber and Murray, *Unemployment Insurance*, 439–443; Altmeyer, *Formative Years*, 131–136, 152–153, 161–162.

93. Munts, "Policy Development." On organized labor's pro–welfare state orientation after the New Deal, see J. David Greenstone, *Labor in American Politics* (New York: Alfred A. Knopf, 1969).

94. St. Clair Drake and Horace R. Cayton, *Black Metropolis: A Study of Negro Life in a Northern City* (New York: Harcourt, Brace and World, 1970; Chicago: University of Chicago Press, 1993); F. Ray Marshall, *The Negro and Organized Labor* (New York: John Wiley & Sons, 1965); Sumner M. Rosen, "The CIO Era, 1935–1955," in *The Negro and the American Labor*

Movement, ed. Julius Jacobson (New York: Anchor, 1968); Philip S. Foner, *Organized Labor and the Black Worker, 1619–1973* (New York: Praeger, 1974). On the political relationship between African-Americans and organized labor see Greenstone, *Labor in American Politics,* 248–261.

95. Altmeyer, *Formative Years,* 175–177; Rourke, *Intergovernmental Relations,* 33–40. Edward D. Berkowitz and Kim McQuaid, *Creating the Welfare State: The Political Economy of Twentieth-Century Reform,* rev. ed. (Lawrence: University Press of Kansas, 1992), 138–141. On the Department of Labor as exemplar of interest-group liberalism, see Theodore J. Lowi, *The End of Liberalism: The Second Republic of the United States,* 2d ed. (New York: W. W. Norton, 1979), 77–91; Gary Mucciaroni, *The Political Failure of Employment Policy, 1945–1982* (Pittsburgh: University of Pittsburgh Press, 1990), 126–131. For an example of the powerful impact of institutional norms balancing labor and business interests in the Labor Department, see Terry M. Moe, "Interests, Institutions, and Positive Theory: The Politics of the NLRB," *Studies in American Political Development* 2 (1987): 236–299.

96. Adams, *Public Attitudes Toward Unemployment Insurance;* Benjamin I. Page and Robert Y. Shapiro, *The Rational Public: Fifty Years of Trends in Americans' Policy Preferences* (Chicago: University of Chicago Press, 1992), 123.

97. Chandler Davidson, *Race and Class in Texas Politics* (Princeton: Princeton University Press, 1990), 117–118.

98. Letter from Executive Director, New York Employment Security Agency, 15 December 1944, cited in California State Senate, *Report of the Senate Interim Committee on Unemployment Insurance* (1945), 51; White, *Administering Unemployment Compensation,* 85; U.S. Social Security Board, *Social Security in America: The Factual Background of the Social Security Act as Summarized from Staff Reports to the Committee on Economic Security,* Social Security Board Publication No. 20 (Washington, D.C.: Government Printing Office, 1937), 21.

99. The [Pitney-Bowes] Postage Meter Co., *The Collection of State Unemployment Insurance Taxes and Contributions by Means of Stamps—Adhesive and Meter Impressed* (Stamford, Conn., 1945), Industrial Relations Collection, Firestone Library, Princeton University. The memorandum includes sample stamp books and examples of various kinds of stamps and meter imprints.

100. *Labor Looks at Unemployment Insurance,* Report of the Conference Workshop of Organized Labor on Employment Security (Chicago: University of Chicago Press, 1931), 31.

101. House Committee on Ways and Means, *Temporary Unemployment Compensation Act of 1958,* 85th Cong., 2d sess., 1958, H. Rept. 1656, 37–38.

102. California State Senate, *Report of the Senate Interim Committee,* 52; Clare C. Cooper, *Unemployment and Minority Groups in California* (Berkeley: Center for Planning and Development Research, Institute of Urban and Regional Development, University of California, 1965), 348–351.

103. *Congressional Quarterly Weekly Report* 16 (1958): 561–563; Key, *Southern*

Politics; Ira Katznelson, Kim Geiger, and Daniel Kryder, "Limiting Liberalism: The Southern Veto in Congress, 1933–1950," *Political Science Quarterly* 108 (1993): 283–306.

104. Quoted by Marion Williamson, the commissioner of the Georgia Employment Security Agency, in Senate Committee on Finance, *Unemployment Compensation,* 160.

105. Testimony of J. Eldred Hill, attorney general of Virginia, Senate Committee on Finance, *Unemployment Compensation,* 85th Cong., 2d sess., 1958, 135–136.

106. Senate Committee on Finance, *Unemployment Compensation,* 171.

107. Roger Waldinger and Thomas Bailey, "The Continuing Significance of Race: Racial Conflict and Racial Discrimination in Construction," *Politics and Society* 19 (1991): 291–323.

108. Weir, *Politics and Jobs,* 80–81.

109. Elliot Liebow, *Tally's Corner: A Study of Negro Streetcorner Men* (Boston: Little, Brown, 1967), 29–71. The quotation is on p. 35.

110. Harpham, "Federalism," 162–163.

111. Weir, *Politics and Jobs,* 41–58; Margaret Weir, "Ideas and Politics: The Acceptance of Keynesianism in Britain and the United States," in *The Political Power of Economic Ideas: Keynesianism Across Nations,* ed. Peter A. Hall (Princeton: Princeton University Press, 1989); Alan Brinkley, *The End of Reform: New Deal Liberalism in Recession and War* (New York: Alfred A. Knopf, 1995).

112. Weir, *Politics and Jobs,* 141–142.

6. Race, Welfare, and the Future of American Politics

1. Richard M. Valelly, *Radicalism in the States: The Minnesota Farmer-Labor Party and the American Political Economy* (Chicago: University of Chicago Press, 1989).

2. T. H. Marshall, "Citizenship and Social Class," in *Class, Citizenship, and Social Development* (Garden City, N.Y.: Doubleday, 1964).

3. Douglas S. Massey and Nancy A. Denton, *American Apartheid: Segregation and the Making of the Underclass* (Cambridge: Harvard University Press, 1993); Thomas J. Sugrue, *The Origins of the Urban Crisis: Race and Inequality in Postwar Detroit* (Princeton: Princeton University Press, 1996).

4. William Julius Wilson, *The Declining Significance of Race: Blacks and Changing American Institutions,* 2d ed. (Chicago: University of Chicago Press, 1980).

5. As Dona and Charles Hamilton point out, the early 1960s was the beginning of a "complementary stage" of the two parts of the "dual agenda" of African-American political organization. These two parts of a common agenda had in fact been at odds since the Progressive Era. Dona Cooper Hamilton and Charles V. Hamilton, *The Dual Agenda: Race and Social Welfare Policies of*

Civil Rights Organizations (New York: Columbia University Press, 1997); Eileen L. McDonagh, "The 'Welfare Rights State' and the 'Civil Rights State': Policy Paradox and State Building in the Progressive Era," *Studies in American Political Development 7* (1993): 225–274.

6. Charles Murray, *Losing Ground: American Social Policy, 1950–1980* (New York: Basic Books, 1984). See also George Gilder, *Wealth and Poverty* (New York: Basic Books, 1981); Lawrence M. Mead, *Beyond Entitlement: The Social Obligations of Citizenship* (New York: Free Press, 1986); Lawrence M. Mead, *The New Politics of Poverty: The Nonworking Poor in America* (New York: Basic Books, 1992). Christopher Jencks takes a more moderate position, arguing that although welfare programs do reduce poverty, they also encourage destructive behavior among inner-city African-Americans. Christopher Jencks, *Rethinking Social Policy: Race, Poverty, and the Underclass* (Cambridge: Harvard University Press, 1992). David Ellwood similarly locates the nuances of this tension in a series of conundrums that lead social policy simultaneously to uphold and contradict deeply held American values. David T. Ellwood, *Poor Support: Poverty in the American Family* (New York: Basic Books, 1988).

7. U.S. Department of Labor, Office of Policy Planning and Research, *The Negro Family: The Case for National Action* [the "Moynihan Report"] (Washington, D.C., 1965).

8. Michael B. Katz, "The Urban 'Underclass' as a Metaphor of Social Transformation," in *The "Underclass" Debate: Views from History*, ed. Michael B. Katz (Princeton: Princeton University Press, 1993), 16. See Robert Greenstein, "Losing Faith in *Losing Ground*," *The New Republic*, 25 March 1985, 12–17.

9. Michael B. Katz, *The Undeserving Poor: From the War on Poverty to the War on Welfare* (New York: Pantheon, 1989), 143–165.

10. William Julius Wilson, *The Truly Disadvantaged: The Inner City, the Underclass, and Public Policy* (Chicago: University of Chicago Press, 1987).

11. See William Julius Wilson, "Studying Inner-City Social Dislocations: The Challenge of Public Agenda Research," *American Sociological Review* 56 (1991): 1–14.

12. Jennifer Hochschild, *Facing Up to the American Dream: Race, Class, and the Soul of the Nation* (Princeton: Princeton University Press, 1995); William Julius Wilson, *When Work Disappears: The World of the New Urban Poor* (New York: Alfred A. Knopf, 1996).

13. Wilson, *The Truly Disadvantaged*, 8.

14. Herbert J. Gans, *The War Against the Poor: The Underclass and Antipoverty Policy* (New York: Basic Books, 1995).

15. Katz, "The Urban 'Underclass' as a Metaphor"; Michael B. Katz, "The 'Underclass'," in *Improving Poor People: The Welfare State, the "Underclass," and Urban Schools as History* (Princeton: Princeton University Press, 1995).

16. Wilson, *Truly Disadvantaged*, 118. See also Theda Skocpol, "Targeting

Within Universalism: Politically Viable Policies to Combat Poverty in the United States," in *The Urban Underclass*, ed. Christopher Jencks and Paul E. Peterson (Washington, D.C.: Brookings Institution, 1991).

17. Wilson, *Truly Disadvantaged;* Wilson, *When Work Disappears;* Skocpol, "Targeting Within Universalism"; Theda Skocpol, "African Americans in U.S. Social Policy," in *Classifying by Race*, ed. Paul E. Peterson (Princeton: Princeton University Press, 1995).

18. Robert Greenstein, "Universal and Targeted Approaches to Relieving Poverty: An Alternative View," in *The Urban Underclass*, ed. Jencks and Peterson.

19. Theda Skocpol, *Boomerang: Clinton's Health Security Effort and the Turn Against Government in U.S. Politics* (New York: W. W. Norton, 1996).

20. Theda Skocpol, *Protecting Soldiers and Mothers: The Political Origins of Social Policy in the United States* (Cambridge: Harvard University Press, 1992).

21. See John David Skrentny, *The Ironies of Affirmative Action: Politics, Culture, and Justice in America* (Chicago: University of Chicago Press, 1996).

22. Paul E. Peterson, "A Politically Correct Solution to Racial Classification," in *Classifying by Race*, ed. Peterson.

23. At a fundraiser for New York Mayor David Dinkins, an African-American, Clinton said that "too many of us are still unwilling to vote for people who are different than we are . . . This is not as simple as overt racism. That is not anything I would charge to anybody who doesn't vote for Dàvid Dinkins or Bill Clinton or anybody else. It's not that simple. It's this deep-seated reluctance we have, against all our better judgment, to reach out across these lines." Todd S. Purdum, "Supporting Dinkins, Clinton Worries About Role of Race," *New York Times*, 27 September 1993, A1. Ultimately defeated, the "racial justice" clause would have allowed persons convicted of capital crimes to introduce data about the racial imbalance in executions as evidence in their defense against the death penalty. Whatever the clause's merits as public policy, the debate briefly focused public attention on the issue. On Clinton's public rhetoric of race, see Wilson, *When Work Disappears*, xx–xxi; on his affirmative action review, see Christopher Edley Jr., *Not All Black and White: Affirmative Action, Race, and American Values* (New York: Hill and Wang, 1996).

24. Paul E. Peterson and Mark C. Rom, *Welfare Magnets: A New Case for a National Standard* (Washington, D.C.: Brookings Institution, 1990); Paul E. Peterson, *The Price of Federalism* (Washington, D.C.: Brookings Institution, 1995).

25. The return to a faith in progressive government is the theme of four stimulating recent books. E. J. Dionne Jr., *They Only Look Dead: Why Progressives Will Dominate the Next Political Era* (New York: Simon & Schuster, 1996); Michael Tomasky, *Left for Dead: The Life, Death, and Possible Resurrection of Progressive Politics in America* (New York: Free Press, 1996); Jacob Weisberg, *In Defense of Government: The Fall and Rise of Public Trust* (New York:

Scribner, 1996); Stanley B. Greenberg and Theda Skocpol, eds., *The New Majority: Toward a Popular Progressive Politics* (New Haven: Yale University Press, 1997).

26. Anthony W. Marx, *Making Race and Nation: A Comparison of the United States, South Africa, and Brazil* (Cambridge: Cambridge University Press, 1998).

27. Edward G. Carmines and James A. Stimson, *Issue Evolution: Race and the Transformation of American Politics* (Princeton: Princeton University Press, 1989); Ira Katznelson, *City Trenches: Urban Politics and the Patterning of Class in the United States* (New York: Pantheon, 1981).

28. Exod. 13:8.

29. Michael Walzer, *Exodus and Revolution* (New York: Basic Books, 1985).

30. E. E. Schattschneider, *Party Government* (New York: Rinehart & Company, 1942), 123; Edmund S. Morgan, *American Slavery, American Freedom: The Ordeal of Colonial Virginia* (New York: W. W. Norton, 1975).

31. Katznelson, *City Trenches.*

32. W. E. Burghardt Du Bois, "The Freedmen's Bureau," *Atlantic Monthly* 87 (March 1901): 354.

Appendix: Quantitative Study of ADC

1. On the definition of the South, see Ira Katznelson, Kim Geiger, and Daniel Kryder, "Limiting Liberalism: The Southern Veto in Congress, 1933–1950," *Political Science Quarterly* 108 (1993): 284.

Index

ADC. *See* Aid to Dependent Children (ADC)
ADC to Children of Unemployed Parents (ADC–UP), 162–163, 172
Administrative structure, 17–22. *See also individual programs*
Advisory Council on Employment and Unemployment Insurance, 189
Advisory Council on Social Security, 41, 95–97, 99, 101
AFDC. *See* Aid to Families with Dependent Children (AFDC)
Affirmative action, 3, 223, 228
African-Americans: Americans' beliefs about, 1–2; in American welfare state, 5–9; class bias and, 26; family structure of, 50–51, 133–134, 155–157, 160; unemployment among, 60–62, 192–193, 213–214; northern migration of, 93–94, 129, 147–148; poverty among, 157–158; political identity of, 219–226; middle–class, 220–221; slavery and, 231–232
Agricultural Extension Service, 108
Agricultural processing workers, 113, 209
Agricultural workers, 25–26, 30–31; and OAI, 39–48, 81–86, 92–93, 96–117; and UI, 58 59, 179, 194, 211–213
Aid to Dependent Children (ADC): inclusion in, 8; institutional structure of, 8–9, 15, 16, 51–56, 119–126, 174–176; administrative structure of, 20, 122–126; eligibility for, 48–51, 119, 131–134, 163; opposition to creation of, 51–53; as parochial program, 118–119, 150–166, 219; discretionary/noncontributory de-
sign of, 121–122; political patronage and, 123–124; policymaking environment, 124–125; discrimination in, 126–148; variables in, 132–133; regional differences in, 136–137; social stigma of, 137–138; and urban politics, 140–148; reform of, 148–149, 155–166; policy development, 148–166; funding of, 151–153; 1962 Amendments to, 161–166; welfare workers, 162–163, 173–174; federal vs. state control in, 163–164; and the War on Poverty, 166–174; quantitative study of, 235–245; data sources on, 246–250. *See also* Aid to Families with Dependent Children (AFDC)
Aid to Families with Dependent Children (AFDC), 3, 5, 162–163
Alger, Bruce, 163
Altmeyer, Arthur J., 33, 69–70, 76, 95, 97, 104, 106, 115–116, 152
American Association of Retired Persons, 70
American Association for Social Security, 41
American Communist Party, 62
American Council on Human Rights, 109
American Farm Bureau Federation (AFBF), 104, 107–108, 114, 164
American Federation of Labor, 63
American Public Welfare Association, 164
Amsterdam News, 54
Amter, Israel, 62
Anomaly thesis, 9–10
Austria, 42
Ayres, William H., 169